The Boss of Bethnal Green

ALSO PUBLISHED BY SPITALFIELDS LIFE BOOKS

Travellers' Children in London Fields
Colin O'Brien

The Gentle Author's London Album

Brick Lane
Phil Maxwell

Underground
Bob Mazzer

Spitalfields Nippers
Horace Warner

London Life
Colin O'Brien

Baddeley Brothers

The Gentle Author's Cries of London

East End
John Claridge

THE BOSS
OF
BETHNAL GREEN

*Joseph Merceron, the Godfather
of Regency London*

JULIAN
WOODFORD

**Spitalfields Life
Books**

First published in 2016 by Spitalfields Life Books Ltd

1

© Julian Woodford 2016

A CIP catalogue for this book is available from the
British Library

ISBN 978-0-9576569-6-3

A Spitalfields Life Book
Edited by The Gentle Author

Designed by David Pearson
Typeset in Adobe Caslon Pro

Printed by Legatoria Editoriale Giovanni Olivotto Spa
Viale Dell'Industria 2
36100 Vicenza
Italy

Published by
Spitalfields Life Books Ltd
16 Victoria Cottages
Spitalfields
London E1 5AJ

www.spitalfieldslife.com
@thegentleauthor

To my parents

CONTENTS

LIST OF ILLUSTRATIONS

INTRODUCTION

A few hundred yards to the east of the glass and steel of the City of London, Brick Lane is one of England's most celebrated thoroughfares. In spite of the growing number of office towers and the gentrification of nearby Spitalfields Market, the surrounding area has retained its identity as a melting-pot of cultures. This is Banglatown, where eastern music pulsates from shop doorways, street names are given dual billing in Bengali and English, and where delicatessens and design studios compete for customers' attention with the lane's famous curry houses. On Sundays, it hosts one of London's most popular street markets. These days Brick Lane is a fashionable place.

Yet Brick Lane's history is much deeper than Banglatown. Situated between the City and London's historic docklands, Spitalfields has been described as 'an urban fault line' and 'a bridge between the included and the excluded'. Brick Lane typifies these descriptions, with a history programmed to repeat two themes: the textile industry and the communities of migrants who have sustained it. For thousands of refugees from many countries, across a dozen generations and three centuries, Brick Lane has been a place to gather and consolidate, where skills, hard work and resilience can meld into success and a new life. Banglatown is simply its latest incarnation, evolving seamlessly from its predecessor 'Little Jerusalem' and, before that, 'Petty France'. The Bengalis arrived in the 1950s and 1960s to take over the rag trade previously dominated by the East End Jewish community, who moved to London's northern suburbs after the Second World War. The Jews had in turn replaced the silk-weaving Huguenots, Protestant refugees who made Spitalfields their home after escaping persecution in France upon Louis XIV's Revocation of the Edict of Nantes in 1685.[1]

The survival and adaptability of two of the street's most notable buildings perfectly express the idea of Brick Lane as a stage, on which successive migrant communities have played out their lives. To the south, on the corner of Fournier Street stands the Jamme Masjid, since 1976 one of London's largest mosques.

For much of the 20th century it was a synagogue, and before that it spent a decade as a Methodist chapel. Originally, before a brief occupation by the London Society for Promoting Christianity amongst the Jews, it was a Huguenot church. High on a wall is the date of its completion, 1743, and a sundial with its motto: *Umbra Sumus* ('we are shadows'). A couple of hundred yards to the north, the imposing former Black Eagle brewery of Truman, Hanbury & Buxton dominates the view up the lane.

These days the brewing business has moved on, and the buildings have been redeveloped into a complex of shops, restaurants and bars. In the mid-18th century, however, after the main building was erected, the Black Eagle was one of the largest breweries in the world. It was here that, in 1764, immediately across the street from the bustle of the brewery, Joseph Merceron was born. It was here that he grew up, and from here that he ran a business and political empire that spread from the neighbouring area of Bethnal Green to much of Regency London's East End.[2]

This book has been a decade in its gestation. I first came across Joseph Merceron's name late in 2005, when I happened upon a brief reference to him in Roy Porter's *London: A Social History*. It described Merceron as an early corrupt political 'Boss' who had dominated the East End some 150 years before it became the home of the Kray twins. By a strange coincidence, I had seen Merceron's name just the day before, listed as a defendant in a series of legal cases at the National Archives. I was intrigued: Merceron is not a common name in England. Was this the same man? The internet confirmed that it was, and revealed that Merceron had clearly been a larger-than-life character. His story seemed to anticipate the plot of the classic Marlon Brando movie *On the Waterfront*, where a corrupt gangster

Brick Lane Jamme Masjid

The Old Truman Brewery, Brick Lane

is taken on – and eventually toppled – by a brave and determined local priest. But Merceron seemed to have been indestructible: after serving his time in prison, he had simply returned home to the East End to begin his corrupt rule all over again.[3]

Over the next few days, I found that Merceron was name-checked by virtually every book about the history of the darker side of London, from academic classics like Dorothy George's *London Life in the 18th Century* to true-crime exposés like Fergus Linnane's *London's Underworld*. I soon learned that all these accounts had their origins in *The Rule of the Boss*, a chapter in Sidney and Beatrice Webb's seminal 1906 work on English local government, *The Parish and the County*. The Webbs, a husband-and-wife team of early socialists, were embarking on a nine-volume treatise still regarded as a classic by historians. They intended that the centuries of inefficiency and corruption they painstakingly described would be swept away by the statistical analysis and central planning espoused by the early Labour movement. The Webbs' impeccable research had somehow unearthed parts of Merceron's story, seeing him as the perfect illustration of corruption within English parochial self-government. Visiting New York, Beatrice was quick to note the parallel between Merceron's rule in Bethnal Green and that of 'Boss' William Tweed of Tammany Hall half a century later. Reviewing a later volume of the Webbs' masterwork, in which Merceron was again mentioned, the Marxist academic Harold Laski wrote that 'they have added new figures to our history; the school books of the next generation will make Merceron [and his like] illuminating examples of what a democracy must avoid.' As it turned out, Professor Laski was wrong: the Second World War intervened, and the subsequent prominence given to 20th century history in school curricula meant that the details of Merceron's story have been largely forgotten.[4]

The Rule of the Boss is an intriguing read, but the Webbs were not biographers, and had no interest in dissecting the personal life behind Merceron's rule. Their account leaves fundamental questions unanswered. Who exactly was Joseph Merceron? Where did he come from? What drove him? How did he become so wealthy? How did he gain power while so young, and retain it for so long? Frustratingly, all subsequent accounts I could find regurgitated parts of the Webbs' story but failed to provide the answers. In *An Acre of Barren Ground* (2005), Jeremy Gavron had drawn some interesting conclusions about Merceron's links to the brewer Sampson Hanbury but had struggled to make headway with the wider story. Even a brief reference to Merceron in the *Dictionary of National Biography* could shed no further light.[5]

Convinced that Merceron's story was worth telling, I delved deeper. Searching through the births, marriages and deaths columns of *The Times*, with the help of the electoral register and a dose of good luck, I tracked down Merceron's remarkable great-great-granddaughter, the late Susan Kendall – then aged 93 – who proved extraordinarily hospitable and informative, despite my intention of publicizing the career of her family's black sheep. Her nephew Daniel Merceron gave me access to Merceron's 200-year-old tin chest: full of deeds, letters and other papers which shed new light on his misdeeds, added colour to his personal life and provided crucial clues to the existence and location of other original records. An ancient painting of a distinguished ancestor, smuggled across the Channel in a sack by Merceron's Huguenot great-grandfather as he fled religious persecution in France, began to explain his determination to restore a lost family fortune. I discovered the depths of an obsession with money which led him to lock away his half-sister in a lunatic asylum and steal the inheritances of his nephews, as well as that of a mentally ill orphaned girl, all before he was 23 years old.

Equally fascinating was the discovery that Merceron had somehow acquired the pistol with which the madman James Hadfield tried to assassinate King George III at the Drury Lane theatre in 1800. Piecing together the story of how Hadfield's gun fell into Merceron's hands, I uncovered his links to a network of government spies, set up to monitor the activities of underground revolutionary societies during the Napoleonic wars. By keeping Merceron and his associates in power successive British governments, desperate to stamp out radical republicanism after the French Revolution, turned a blind eye to his criminal operations. In doing so, they abetted a social catastrophe. Merceron's story turns out to be more than a tale about a man and his money. It is also about the origins of London's East End, a world of riots, lynching, public executions and extreme poverty where whole families could easily starve or freeze to death. As Merceron became extraordinarily wealthy, his neighbourhood of Bethnal Green became the epitome of the East End Victorian slum. By 1838, when a young Charles Dickens chose it as the home of the murderer Bill Sikes in *Oliver Twist*, Bethnal Green was bankrupt, the home of cholera and typhus, with more than a thousand starving paupers crammed into its rotting workhouse.

The book is set out in four parts. 'Emergence' (1764–87) establishes the historical and geographical context for Merceron's life and demonstrates the ruthless greed and thirst for power which enabled him to take control of Bethnal Green at such a young age. 'Dominance' (1788–1810) follows Merceron's rise through London's local government to the peak of his domination of the East End at the age of 46, coinciding with a period of serious political and social unrest in London triggered by the French Revolution and Napoleonic Wars. During this period Merceron became a leading magistrate and part of the Pitt government's front line against radical republicanism. 'Belligerence' (1810–18) is the dramatic centrepiece of Merceron's story, depicting his legal battles with a group of opponents led by Bethnal Green's Rector, the Reverend Joshua King, and culminating in Merceron's imprisonment for fraud and corruption in 1818. 'Resurgence' (1818–39) deals with Merceron's brief imprisonment in the King's Bench prison, his triumphant return to Bethnal Green and the campaign of retaliation which resulted in the restoration of his absolute rule, the last 15 years of his life characterised by the increasing distress of the local populace as Bethnal Green sank into wretched poverty, a magnet for infectious disease.

A NOTE ABOUT MONEY

The nature of inflation and compound interest is such that the amounts of money involved in transactions in Regency England can seem misleadingly trifling today. Joseph Merceron's reported wealth on his death in 1839 of more than £300,000 was a very large sum indeed by the standards of the day.

There are websites which can be used to convert historical amounts into modern equivalent values. An example is at: www.measuring-worth.com/ppoweruk. As this site makes clear, there is no single agreed basis on which such conversion calculations should be made. Very different results would be obtained if amounts from 1800, for example, were inflated based on growth in prices, compared with the equivalent inflation based on the relative share of GDP then and now. Using the latter index, which is probably a more appropriate measure when comparing an individual's relative wealth in society, Merceron's assets would have made him almost a billionaire in today's terms.

When looking at values of everyday transactions, on the other hand, many historians agree that multiplying Regency amounts by a factor of 100 gives a reasonably good approximation of today's value. To provide context, comparative amounts based on this factor have been provided in the text. Even on this very prudent basis, Merceron's £300,000 would equate to approximately £30 million today.

PROLOGUE

The Boss of Bethnal Green

STRANGER
Whom are they ushering from the world, with all
This pageantry and long parade of death? …

TOWNSMAN
… I would ride the camel
Yea, leap him flying, through the needle's eye
As easily as such a pampered soul
Could pass the narrow gate.
Robert Southey, The Alderman's Funeral [6]

All the great and good of London's East End were there. Twenty thousand people, packed six deep in places along the Bethnal Green Road, had turned out to see the cortège on its way to St Matthew's church. Just before one o'clock the procession arrived, at a sedate walking pace. The jet-black horses, with their sable plumes, were blinkered to prevent anything from distracting the stately progress of the hearse.

It was a warm July day and many excited onlookers, keen to secure the best vantage points, had been there all morning swapping tales. The dead man had been a fixture in Bethnal Green for so long that hardly anyone could remember life without him. Some recalled the story of the orphan Mary Cheesman, a mentally ill girl he had robbed of all her property just before she died. Others remembered the time he drummed up a mob to trash old Mr Racine's silk warehouse in retaliation for Racine's opposition in a parish election. A few of the older spectators had lined that same street, 20 years before, on the day the deceased had returned triumphantly from prison to begin his reign over Bethnal Green all over again. But on this day, the 24th July 1839, the crowd had been drawn from their homes and workplaces by curiosity, lured by the irresistible show of a celebrity funeral and the chance of one last look at a local legend. It was the end of the reign of the tyrant, Joseph Merceron, who had dominated their lives for half a century.

Merceron was the original 'Boss' of Bethnal Green, the Godfather of Regency London, controlling its East End underworld long before celebrity mobsters such as the infamous Kray twins made it their territory. His funeral at the church of St Matthew, Bethnal Green – the very same church where the Krays' funerals would be held more than 150 years later – reflected his importance: it was by far the biggest event to take place at the church since it was established in the 1740s. It was impressive by any standards, with the cortège encompassing most of London's social spectrum.

Following close behind the Merceron family was George Byng, the 75-year-old Member of Parliament and one of the most influential politicians in the land. Byng had been elected to Parliament on more than a dozen occasions, always aided by votes procured through Merceron's influence on local voters. Behind Byng trooped a host of solemn local dignitaries and tradespeople. The portly directors of joint-stock companies, fattened by grand-sounding and often illusory schemes to improve London's docks, railways and water supplies, mingled with corrupt magistrates and commissioners of sewers, whose coffers had been enriched through the bribes of brewers and contractors. An army of pompous parish officers – churchwardens, overseers of the poor, pavement trustees and vestry clerks – all united under Merceron's leadership in using parish funds for their own purposes – preceded a parade of publicans, many the keepers of gin-shops and brothels. Behind this group came the local tradesmen – butchers, bakers, bricklayers and carpenters. All had crossed the Boss's palm at one time or another to

St Matthew's, Bethnal Green

gain lucrative contracts to supply or maintain schools, workhouses or prisons.[7]

Given the turnout, it might seem odd that Bethnal Green's Rector, Joshua King, was absent from the funeral. But King's arrival in Bethnal Green 30 years earlier had interrupted Merceron's domination of local affairs and they had remained bitter enemies ever since. Their battles over the ensuing decade had resulted in the national exposure of the Boss's misdeeds and his imprisonment for fraud and corruption in 1818. On his release, Merceron's relentless quest for vengeance drove the Rector to seek a quiet life 200 miles away in rural Cheshire, leaving Bethnal Green – and Merceron's funeral – in the hands of a mercenary curate.[8]

For Reverend King and most of the local populace, Merceron's rule had brought nothing but desperation. At the end of the procession, almost disregarded, came the ragged children from the Bethnal Green workhouse, scrubbed and ordered onto the streets to pay their respects to the man who had contributed more than anyone else to their misery. For years, they and their predecessors had slept three or four to a bed, cold and often starving, while Merceron plundered the funds intended for their relief. In 1839, on average, two children were buried every day in Bethnal Green. Life expectancy among the poorest classes was just 16 years. Bethnal Green's very name evoked visions of deprivation and evil deeds, a reputation which intensified in 1831 when the 'London Burkers' – a murdering gang who sold their victims' corpses for anatomical research – were found to live there. By 1837, cholera and typhus had left their mark and the first Victorian sanitary reformers had begun to expose the district as a national disgrace when the young novelist Charles Dickens selected it as an obvious and realistic home for Bill Sikes and Nancy, the murderer and the prostitute in *Oliver Twist*.[9]

Joseph Merceron's rule over Bethnal Green began at the age of 23 and lasted – despite a short spell in prison – for more than 50 years. During that time, as landlord, parish officer, magistrate or in a myriad of other positions of power, he controlled almost every aspect of local life. He owned or managed hundreds of houses but was also responsible for setting and collecting the rates and taxes. He controlled a quarter of Bethnal Green's public houses, turning many of them into brothels and gambling dens, but for many years he was also the man who licensed them. His stranglehold on local amenities was so absolute that every local shopkeeper and artisan needed his protection in order to work and survive. Opponents faced interminable lawsuits, were thrown arbitrarily in the workhouse or debtors' prison, or had their businesses wrecked by rampaging mobs.

From his base in Brick Lane, Merceron controlled a huge swathe of the infrastructure of London's East End. How did a man of humble beginnings, the son of a refugee pawnbroker, rise to such a level of importance? His domination coincided with a period in which the area became a hotbed of civil unrest, from the weavers' riots of the 1760s to the movements for electoral reform leading to the Reform Act of 1831. For decades, increasingly desperate and paranoid governments saw the corrupt elite of the East End as the front line in the fight to hold back the tides of revolution and reform. In doing so, successive ministries went out of their way to turn a blind eye to Merceron's activities, leaving him free to enrich himself at the expense of the local population. By his death he was extraordinarily wealthy – by some estimates almost a billionaire at today's values – while Bethnal Green had become the poorest of London slums. This is his story.

PART I

Emergence
1764–87

CHAPTER I

Blue Apron Men

*The Justices of Middlesex are generally the scum of the earth;
carpenters, brickmakers and shoemakers; some of whom are
notoriously men of such infamous characters that they are
unworthy of any employ whatever; and others so ignorant,
that they can scarcely write their own names.*

Edmund Burke[10]

London, January 1764: a new age was beginning. The era of the artist
William Hogarth, on whom we rely heavily for depictions of the
18th century metropolis, was about to end with his death that
October. The 25-year-old King George III (1738–1820) was just
three years into his long reign; his eldest son, the future Prince
Regent and King George IV was only 17 months old. The Seven
Years' War with France and Spain had ended in 1763. William Pitt,
the British minister seen as the man behind Britain's success in the
conflict, had stepped down from government in 1761 after falling
out with the new King, choosing instead to focus on educating his
precocious young son William Pitt the Younger (1759–1806), who
would dominate England's politics during the latter half of George
III's reign.

That month, the capital's coffee houses – the meeting places where
London's elite shared political, business and social gossip – buzzed
with the latest news of John Wilkes MP, the darling of radical
Londoners and one of the elder Pitt's leading supporters. The previous year, Wilkes' imprisonment for publishing criticism of the King
over the terms of the peace had led to widespread riots. Upon his

release, Wilkes had been seriously wounded in a duel and fled to France just before Christmas. When summoned back by Parliament he refused to attend, blaming his injuries. On 19th January the House of Commons expelled him, paving the way for his conviction for seditious libel a few weeks later.[11]

The English weather was as tempestuous as its politics. On 13th January an unusually violent storm raged across the south coast, leaving 'such a number of ships driven ashore and wrecked as never before seen in one season'. The River Thames burst its banks, preventing barges from the west of England from bringing essential food supplies to London. That week also saw the newspapers report sightings of 'a large ball of fire' in the skies over Kent.[12]

In London's poorer East End, conditions were dismal. The end of the war had resulted in a serious economic depression for the silk weavers who mostly lived and worked in Spitalfields, immediately to the east of the city boundary. In the previous October, several thousand desperate journeymen weavers – employed by the day and thus lacking any job security in difficult times – paraded through the streets, disguised as sailors and armed with cutlasses, burning an effigy of an unpopular master weaver and breaking the looms of those who refused to join them. Now, they were collecting signatures for a petition to the King to draw attention to their plight.[13]

In the midst of this tumult, on Sunday 29th January 1764 Joseph Merceron was born on Brick Lane, which formed the boundary between the parishes of Spitalfields and its eastward neighbour Bethnal Green. His parents were James Merceron, a Huguenot (French Protestant) pawnbroker and former silk weaver, and his second wife Ann. The Mercerons had three other children: Annie, Joseph's two-year-old sister, John, almost thirteen, and Catherine, eight, the latter two being the surviving offspring from James's first marriage.

Four weeks later, Joseph was christened at the local Huguenot church known as *La Patente*, in Brown's Lane (the building and lane still exist but are known as Hanbury Hall and Hanbury Street) just a short walk from his parents' house.

Hanbury Hall, Hanbury Street

The Mercerons, like other Huguenot families in the area, clung tightly to their nationality. Joseph's details in the register of baptisms – the first recorded at *La Patente* for 1764 – were entered in French, which many families still insisted on speaking out of respect for their ancestors. *La Patente* was one of several churches catering to the large Huguenot community in the area (so large, in fact, that the area was nicknamed 'Petty France') and providing an important cultural link to their homeland. Most of its congregation was made up of silk weavers, descendants of refugees who had fled France after Louis XIV's Revocation of the Edict of Nantes in 1685.[14]

The Revocation removed at a stroke the rights and physical protection previously guaranteed to the French Protestant community. The original Edict, passed by the French King Henri IV in 1598, had enabled the Huguenots to co-exist with the French Catholic majority and to contribute to society from within the safety of garrisoned towns. With their protection removed, up to 50,000 refugees fled to England over the next 35 years. About a third of them settled in London in two groups, in Soho (in the wealthier west end) and in Spitalfields to the east. While the Soho Huguenots encompassed a broad range of occupations, the Spitalfields community were more specialised, mostly engaged in silk weaving and its associated trades. The London silk industry had been based in the area for more than a century and its location, immediately outside the City walls, meant that the weavers enjoyed the benefits of geographical proximity while avoiding the City's restrictive trading rules.[15]

When the Huguenots first arrived, Spitalfields was just a part of the large and mostly rural parish of Stepney. Brick Lane marked the eastern edge of the metropolis; in 1729, as the increasing immigrant population led to the creation of the parish of Christ Church Spitalfields, it was the obvious line along which to fix the parish's eastern boundary. To the east lay a maze of well-tended gardens – the Huguenots were noted for their fondness for growing flowers and vegetables – stretching for half a mile, ending in a boggy and typhus-infested area of brickfields and stagnant marshland. Beyond this was the countryside, with a network of paths crossing the fields towards the villages of Bethnal Green and Mile End just visible in the distance.[16]

As the Spitalfields population grew, the poorer journeymen weavers were forced eastwards across the Brick Lane boundary into smaller cottages built on the marshy fields. By the 1740s, this transplanted population was sufficiently large to justify the creation of another semi-urban parish, that of St Matthew, Bethnal Green. The new parish had two population centres: the weavers' cottages lining the eastern side of Brick Lane and, a mile or so further still to the east, the larger houses situated around the pond and village green which gave Bethnal Green its name. As a compromise, the new church of St Matthew was built in the open fields, halfway between the two centres.[17]

This neighbourhood (which continued, rather confusingly, to be known as 'Spitalfields' although it comprised both Spitalfields and Bethnal Green parishes) is depicted beautifully in John Rocque's famous map of London of 1746, with its gardens, trees, fields, marshes and even the sites of the French chapels. A simple way of visualising the district is to imagine it as the facing pages of an open book, with the parishes of Spitalfields and Bethnal Green as the left and right-hand pages respectively and Brick Lane as the spine between them, holding the area together yet separating master from journeyman; rich from poor.

To the west of Brick Lane were the Spitalfields townhouses of the wealthier master weavers, today restored as the valuable homes of 'Neo-Georgian' artists, writers and architects; the lower windows covered with distinctive wooden shutters, the woodwork often painted in characteristically dark shades of red, green, brown or grey. Typically four stories high, the idiosyncratic design of these houses included garret windows running the entire breadth of the building to maximise the daylight reaching the looms inside. In contrast, the streets and alleys of Bethnal Green, to the east of Brick Lane, were occupied by tumbledown tenements crammed with poor families,

134 (formerly 77) Brick Lane, site of the Merceron pawnshop

all desperately trying to scratch out a living from piecework weaving, cutting and stitching.[18]

The Merceron pawnshop at 77 Brick Lane was at the epicentre of this district, among a row of ramshackle buildings directly opposite Sir Benjamin Truman's imposing and famous *Black Eagle* brewery. The *Black Eagle* was one of the largest breweries in the world. To those living opposite, the mingled odours of yeast, malt and spilt beer – not to mention the steaming output of the many dray horses – must have been overpowering, even by the pungent standards of the times. The noise, too, was tremendous, as the shouts of draymen punctuated the rumble of horse-drawn carriages and carts up and down the lane. Despite Brick Lane's importance as the only convenient route from the Thames to Spitalfields, Hackney and beyond, it would be another decade before it was paved. For the time being, it was 'much out of repair and incommodious'. The Mercerons had to negotiate potholes, mud and worse as they picked their way home from church in their best clothes.[19]

After Joseph's baptism, the family gathered in the parlour behind the shop with relatives and friends, warming themselves by the fire and raising a toast to the baby's health and happiness. Staring down at them from a nearby wall was the family's prized possession: an old portrait of a slim, distinguished and rather severe-looking man of about 50; with high cheekbones and a dark, pointed beard, in a black doublet and the tonsure of an Augustinian cleric. Its inscription read, simply: *Germanus Merceron, 1642*.[20]

Prior to their emigration to England, the Mercerons had been a wealthy and influential family in France, holding a number of important public positions in the towns along the Loire valley. Germanus had joined the Order of Augustinians in 1610 and two decades later was appointed assistant to the Bishop of Angers. At around the same time, his brother Robert was an adviser to Louis XIII (King of France 1610–43) and tax collector at the royal chateau of Chaumont.

Despite these impeccable Catholic credentials, at some point in the ensuing 50 years the family converted to Protestantism. The

Germanus Merceron, 1642

change of faith was sufficiently strong to lead Robert's grandson François, accompanied by his 10-year-old son, to escape to London after the Revocation. Emigration from France was strictly forbidden. Many refugees heading for England were forced to hide in the holds of ships transporting wine to London in order to dodge soldiers or customs officials. Like many refugee families, the Mercerons left behind virtually everything they owned but according to family folklore the portrait of Germanus accompanied them on the voyage, wrapped in a sack, an emblem of family pride and a constant reminder of past greatness.[21]

Virtually nothing is known of François other than his flight to London. His son, also named François, became a silk weaver and married another émigré, Marthe Dubocq; their son, James – Joseph's father – was born on 11th October 1723. James was 40 years old at the time of Joseph's birth and had lived and worked on or around Brick Lane all his life. He had followed his father into the weaving trade, completing his apprenticeship to become a master in 1746. Four years later he married his first wife Marie Simon, another Huguenot. In addition to John and Catherine, the couple had four other children, of which three failed to survive infancy and the fourth, another Marie, was buried at the age of seven within days of her mother in July 1759 as a result of a shared illness.[22]

Although all James's children were christened at *La Patente*, the French chapels did not have their own burial grounds; Marie Merceron and her daughter were buried in the pretty, tree-lined churchyard of St Matthew, Bethnal Green. This connection with the church may have nudged James further along the process of assimilation into English customs and religion: less than a year later, when he married his second wife Ann Masson, he did so at St Matthew's despite Ann being a Huguenot.

James was on the way to commercial success. Just weeks before Marie's death, he had purchased the lease on the row of 14 houses and shops on Brick Lane where his own shop stood. His second marriage may have triggered a further improvement in his fortunes:

around this time he decided to begin a new career as a pawnbroker. The move would prove an inspired, or fortuitous, response to the vicissitudes of the precarious silk-weaving trade, which within two years had entered a serious depression. It would also lead James into local politics.[23]

After Joseph's sister Annie was born in September 1761, James took an increasingly active interest in the Bethnal Green vestry. In April 1762 he was appointed a headborough (an assistant to the parish constable), an unpaid and unpopular job with responsibility for inspecting and reporting on the local public houses for keeping late hours or gambling. Many men baulked at the idea of informing on their neighbours, agreeing to pay a fine into the parish coffers instead of taking the job, but James completed his year of office and by the time his son Joseph was born he had become a regular and active participant at vestry meetings.[24]

By this time the family's hardest years were over. The switch to pawnbroking had proved a masterstroke and James was amassing a considerable fortune. He had begun to invest in the booming local property market and built dozens of houses, often four or five at a time, on the streets straddling the north end of Brick Lane on an 18-acre estate known as the *Red Cow*.[25]

The population of the metropolis was growing rapidly, increasing by about a third – from around 675,000 to 1,000,000 – between 1750 and 1801. The 1760s saw a huge increase in the demand for housing in London, the city's perimeter expanding as the surrounding fields were dug up and replaced by houses. In Spitalfields, already packed full of buildings, the only way to expand was eastwards, over the fields of Bethnal Green. The area was badly drained, but this disadvantage was outweighed by the presence of a rich seam of brick clay – bricks had been made nearby for centuries.[26]

The development of low-quality terraced housing required little capital or expertise and the building process was simple and collaborative. A small-time developer such as James would lease a small plot of land and put up the outer shell of a row of tiny cottages.

He would then sublet them, at a profit, to his associates – carpenters, bricklayers and plasterers, tradesmen colloquially known as 'blue apron men' – who would subcontract the remaining work among themselves. To boost profits, each house would be let as two or three separate tenements. In the absence of comprehensive building regulations, developers cut corners wherever they could. Pierre Grosley, a French lawyer visiting London in 1765, was horrified when he discovered that human waste was being incorporated into the local bricks:

> It is true, the outside appears to be built of brick, but the wall consists only of a single row of bricks; and those being made of the first earth that comes to hand, and only just warmed at the fire…in the new quarters of London, brick is often made upon the spot where the buildings themselves are erected; and the workmen make use of the earth they find in digging the foundations. With this earth they mix…the ashes gathered in London by the dustmen. I have even been assured that the excrements taken out of necessary-houses entered into the composition of bricks of this sort.[27]

James's entry into the building trade coincided with the rise to local prominence of David, or 'Davy', Wilmot, an ambitious builder who started out as a bricklayer but soon set up in business with his brother John, an architect and surveyor, as successful developers of cheap tenement housing. James and the Wilmots would become increasingly close allies. Over the next decade, they would dominate the local politics of Bethnal Green and their families would extend that dominance over much of the East End for another two generations.

Like James, the Wilmots were quick to realize the area's potential for development. From 1761 they began to lease large plots of land along the Bethnal Green Road and over the next few years erected dozens of houses. In a relentless but unimaginative drive for self-publicity, the brothers soon created Wilmot Grove and

Wilmot Square (both owned by John) and Wilmot Street (owned by David).

Here in the Bethnal Green marshes there was no drainage or refuse collection, and access to running water was sporadic. Such buildings inevitably became miserable slums, but the demand for houses was such that even the worst cottages would be rented and many survived even into Victorian times. Nearby Camden Gardens, built by David Wilmot, was described in 1838 as:

> ...a number of small ground-floor houses; each house contains only two rooms...the largest is about seven feet by nine, and the smallest barely large enough to admit a small bed...In winter the houses are exceedingly damp; the windows are very small; there is no drainage of any kind; it is close upon a marshy district...fever is very apt to break out...often all the members of a family are attacked by it, and die one after another...[28]

Their successful property speculation resulted in James Merceron and David Wilmot becoming increasingly influential voices within the Bethnal Green vestry. It was a source of real local power. In those days, Parliament had virtually no involvement in the daily lives of the people; across England, most day-to-day government was conducted by parish vestries (so called because they typically met within the Vestry, or robing room, of the parish church) under the supervision of local magistrates. But vestries varied widely from place to place. In rural areas, they had stability. The squire (typically both magistrate and a dominant figure in the vestry) had a personal interest in dealing fairly with the men of his parish: they were his workforce and the source of his continuing prosperity. There was also a large element of continuity, with the same families dominating vestry proceedings for generation after generation. The new urban parishes like Bethnal Green were quite different. Here, as Sidney and Beatrice Webb wrote in 1904, 'the economic and social relations by which...the component parts of the vestry organization were

Wilmot Street, Bethnal Green

held together, either had never existed or were in progress of rapid disintegration'.[29]

By the 1760s Bethnal Green had already become an enormous parish, even by the standards of a major city like London. By its establishment in 1743 its population was about 15,000, having doubled within 30 years, and it was continuing to grow rapidly. From the date of its creation, it was afflicted by acute poverty. Most of the master weavers lived across the parish boundary in Spitalfields or in the City of London and it was argued in 1743 that the people of Bethnal Green – typically journeymen weavers and the petty tradesmen who supplied them – were too poor to afford their own church and clergy. The parochial separation of masters from journeymen also meant that the parish lacked leadership. There was no 'squirearchy', and it was reported that those of the 'better sort' who had lived in Bethnal Green had moved out because 'dissoluteness of morals and a disregard for religion' were corrupting the young. The result was a power vacuum which sharp and ambitious men such as James Merceron and David Wilmot were quick to fill.[30]

Most positions of responsibility within the vestry, such as churchwardens and overseers, were filled by annual election each April or September. Not all aspects of local government were under immediate vestry control. Independent trusts were responsible for paving; street cleaning and lighting; the night watch (what passed for a local police force) and for overseeing the poor. In most cases, however, the vestry as a whole nominated these trustees and so control of the vestry ensured an absolute dominance over local government.[31]

The Bethnal Green vestry operated under what was known as the 'open' system, a form of early British democracy whereby all householders above a certain property threshold had the right to a vote. Crucially, in 1763, the vestry's voting threshold was lowered to include those renting at more than £15 per annum. This opened Bethnal Green's urban democracy to thousands of poor householders, mostly journeymen weavers, some living three or four families to a house. Most of this nascent electorate – newcomers to the parish, unknown to one another and with no interest in local affairs – would never set foot in the vestry room. But enough took an interest to ensure that men like James Merceron and David Wilmot could, by promising favours or by bribery, buy their way into power.[32]

James rose quickly through the vestry hierarchy. In April 1764, after completing his year as a headborough, he was rewarded with election as one of Bethnal Green's 20 Governors of the Poor. A year later he became parish constable, the 'eyes and ears' of the local magistrates – an onerous position, described by the writer Daniel Defoe as the 'parish drudge', taking up 'so much of a man's time that his own affairs are frequently totally neglected'.[33]

James's election as constable came as Spitalfields and Bethnal Green descended into a period of violent civil unrest. During the Seven Years' War, as the British captured export markets previously dominated by the French, the London silk weavers had experienced a period of relative prosperity. By 1765, with the war over, 1,500 looms were idle and 5,000 weavers unemployed. Over the next few years conditions continued to deteriorate, despite the introduction of a government ban on the import of French silks. The mood on the streets around Brick Lane became increasingly volatile, exacerbated by racial tensions between Irish and English journeymen and French masters, the air echoing with the sounds of gunfire and rioting. After repeated outbreaks of violence, the vandalizing or 'cutting' of looms was made a capital offence. But the threat of execution had little effect: on 26th July 1768 'a great number of evil-disposed persons, armed with pistols, cutlasses and other offensive weapons' broke into the houses of several Spitalfields masters and destroyed the silk in their looms. A month later, during another bout of vandalism, a young man was shot dead by the mob while trying to protect his master's work.[34]

By this time, David Wilmot had been made Bethnal Green's overseer of the poor and in September 1768, just a fortnight after the murder, James Merceron became a trustee of the nightly watch. The watch system was widely regarded as a joke: Pierre Grosley, the visiting French lawyer, noted that London 'is guarded during the nights only by old men chosen from the dregs of the people who have no arms but a lanthorn [lantern] and a pole…and whom it is customary for young rakes to beat and use ill, when they come reeling from the taverns where they have spent the night'.[35]

Despite the prospect of generous rewards, no one dared inform against the weavers and there were no prosecutions for the August 1768 shooting. The emboldened journeymen now began to organise themselves into unions or combinations. One such group, dominated by an Irish contingent and provocatively styling themselves the Bold Defiance, forged links with similarly disaffected weavers in Dublin and toured the inns around Brick Lane armed with pistols, swords and cutlasses to extort subscriptions to a strike fund.[36]

When the disturbances continued into 1769 and the authorities decided to strengthen the local magistracy, they chose David Wilmot. Despite his lack of education, Wilmot was by no means an atypical selection as a Middlesex magistrate. The absence of a 'squirearchy' in the urban parishes around London meant that the role of magistrate – as with the senior positions in the vestry – typically fell to a small trader or even to a member of the labouring classes. Such men, who lacked an independent income to subsidize their unpaid judicial work, became known as 'trading justices', basically dispensing verdicts in return for fees. Contemporary novelists had satirized them for years. Henry Fielding's Justice Thrasher, in *Amelia* (1751), had 'never read one syllable' of the law, and 'was never indifferent in a cause but when he could get nothing on either side'.[37]

Wilmot was under-qualified for his new role and over the next two decades the press would delight in highlighting his ignorance and humble origins. In 1788, an anonymous letter to *The Times* noted his beginnings as a bricklayer's labourer:

Being a pains-taking man, and industriously saving the greatest part of his earnings, he soon got above the world, and in process of time, when he had learned to read and write, became a Justice of the Peace…at the porter house or tavern, he is the soul of conviviality, telling with great humour several stories of that part of his life which was spent under the hod and upon the scaffold, where with an onion, a crust, an old jacket, and pale visage, he was as happy as he now is, with a tailed wig, a red face, and a full suit of superfine drab.[38]

For all his ignorance, it was now Wilmot upon whose shoulders rested the responsibility for keeping order in the increasingly turbulent Spitalfields streets. Thanks to James's foresight, or good luck, in changing careers, the Mercerons had grown steadily better off during the worst years of the Depression. The weaving trade was wildly volatile, with frequent interruptions to the supply of imported raw silk and demand fluctuating at the whim of fashion. In hard times, the journeymen – laid off by masters who lacked any reserves of capital – turned in desperation to their local pawnbroker for funds. The greater the weavers' misery, the more James prospered; he was soon one of the wealthiest men in the neighbourhood. In the formative years of Joseph's childhood, as Spitalfields descended almost to anarchy, the Mercerons would be especially dependent on Wilmot's ability to hold back the tide of popular revolt.[39]

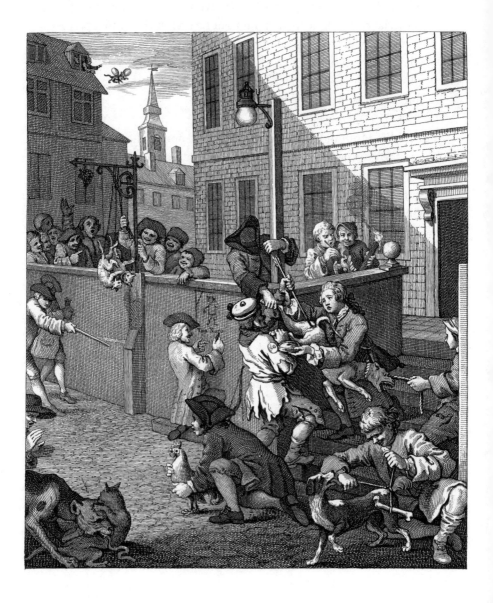

The First Stage of Cruelty

CHAPTER II

The Tyrant in the Boy

While various scenes of sportive woe
The infant race employ
And tortur'd victims bleeding show
The Tyrant in the Boy.
James Townley (Merceron's headmaster at Merchant Taylors'
School), lines accompanying *The First Stage of Cruelty*
by William Hogarth[40]

What sort of boy was Joseph Merceron? How began the relentless thirst for power and wealth that would characterise his adult life? From where sprang his energy and determination, his obsession with money, his capacity to bear a grudge against anyone, great or small, who wronged him – even from within his own family?

While we know little of Merceron's childhood, it is easy to surmise how these traits might have arisen: he was his parents' youngest child, his mother's only son; the centre of attention in a refugee family that had begun to recover prosperity and self-respect after generations of struggle and prejudice. This, together with the supreme self-confidence displayed in later life, hints at him being a spoilt and precocious child. We know he was bright, outgoing and an instinctive leader. We also know he was a loud, bad-tempered bully. I picture him at the head of a gang of boys, dominating them by sheer force of personality and by no means afraid to use physical force if necessary.

There was another influence: the menacing presence of violence on the streets of Spitalfields that pervaded Merceron's childhood.

Between the ages of six and nine, his life was punctuated by the sounds of gunfire, rioting and military deployments. The nature of his father's business and James' position in authority left the Mercerons in constant danger of looting – or worse, should a riot get out of control. In his formative years, the boy had every opportunity to see for himself the power of the mob.

Unusually for a Wednesday, on the morning of 6th December 1769, the Merceron pawnshop was closed. Its shutters were locked tight while a restless crowd gathered outside. Eventually a cry went up as a procession led by a series of handcarts turned into Brick Lane from the Whitechapel Road. In the first cart two condemned Irishmen, John Valline and John Doyle, their faces pale, perched uncomfortably on their coffins. In the second, sending a chill through the watching crowd, lay the temporary gallows that would be used to hang them.

The procession had set off from Newgate prison almost three hours earlier, passing through the City of London before heading east. From the top of Brick Lane it would turn east again along the Bethnal Green Road, passing the church and Justice Wilmot's house, before coming to a final halt outside *The Salmon & Ball* inn on the corner of the village green. In a move that had roused the local people to fury, the authorities had ordered the executions to take place in Bethnal Green – where Doyle and Valline lived – to terrorize the rioting weavers into submission, but the success of this plan was far from certain. There was every risk of violence and bloodshed, with whispers of a planned rescue.[41]

The events leading up to the execution had begun that summer. A wealthy master weaver, Louis Chauvet, had forbidden his 450 journeymen to join a campaign for better working conditions and had adopted a position of spirited defiance against the cutters. In response, on two separate incidents in August, an angry mob firing pistols into the air broke into Chauvet's premises and cut the silk in dozens of his looms, leaving the neighbourhood greatly alarmed and apprehensive of further riots.[42]

Undaunted, Chauvet recruited a band of mercenaries to act as a private guard and offered a huge reward for information leading to the arrest of the men who had wrecked his business. Despite this, the fear of reprisal was so great that for several weeks no one came forward. Eventually in late September a weaver named Thomas Poor and his wife presented themselves to Justice Wilmot. Claiming that their own looms had been cut in the August riots, the Poors named a number of those responsible, including Doyle and Valline, who were subsequently arrested.[43]

Many local people were outraged at the Poors' perceived treachery and the informers were forced into hiding. Days later, the magistrates authorized an armed raid by troops on *The Dolphin,* an alehouse just off the north end of Brick Lane, after a tip-off that the Bold Defiance were meeting there to collect subscriptions. Disaster followed. The protesters refused to surrender and opened fire, killing a soldier. In response, the troops fired indiscriminately. Two innocent customers were shot dead as four cutters were arrested and the rest escaped across the rooftops. A week later another skirmish resulted in the deaths of five more rioters, with many others wounded.[44]

Valline and Doyle were tried at the Old Bailey, London's Central Criminal Court, on 18th October 1769. Both men denied the charges against them and compelling evidence emerged that the Poors, nursing a grievance against them, had turned them in to get their hands on Chauvet's reward. But the authorities were determined to make an example of the Irishmen. The jury had been hand-picked to ensure a guilty verdict and the two men were sentenced to hang. Weeks of argument followed over the location of the execution. The judge had ordered it to take place several miles away at Tyburn, the usual site of such events in London, but the master weavers – keen to dispose of Valline and Doyle in front of their own community to discourage further loom cutting – lobbied successfully to change the location to 'the most convenient place near Bethnal Green church'. The City of London sheriffs petitioned the King against the change of venue but were overruled.[45]

Several thousand people assembled outside *The Salmon & Ball* to see Valline and Doyle hang. Bricks and stones were thrown during the assembly of the gallows. The Irishmen protested their innocence to the end, but to no effect. Doyle's last words, an angry tirade against the Poors' mercenary duplicity, were enough to ignite an already explosive situation. As soon as the hanging was over, the crowd tore down the gallows, surged back to Spitalfields and re-erected it outside Chauvet's warehouse, breaking his windows and burning his furniture. Only the arrival of troops forced them to disperse.[46]

The same day, a few miles away at the Old Bailey, three other loom cutters were convicted in a trial that would lead to further serious repercussions for the residents of Spitalfields. The three were accused of cutting the looms of a small-time master weaver named Daniel Clarke. As in the case of the Poors, there were strong hints that Clarke had fabricated parts of his evidence in order to claim a reward. As before, the jury ignored these hints and the three men were convicted and hanged.[47]

For a year, the authorities' harsh stance against the cutters seemed to have worked and an uneasy peace returned to the streets. During this period, James Merceron became an increasingly senior figure within the Bethnal Green vestry. At Easter 1770, he was appointed as a commissioner of the local Court of Requests, effectively making him a junior magistrate with the power to imprison people for up to 40 days for the non-payment of the tiniest of debts. This authority was widely abused: for a small bribe, some commissioners would lock a man away on the mere word of a neighbour. Such powers were to be feared and James's appointment made him one of the most powerful men in the neighbourhood. A year later, he obtained further power and influence by becoming Overseer of the Poor for Bethnal Green.[48]

James had also built up a large leasehold property portfolio, mostly situated within the *Red Cow* estate owned by a local gentleman named Henry Busby. In 1770, in partnership with his friend John Wolveridge, James leased from Busby several acres of prime building

The Salmon & Ball, Bethnal Green

land known as 'Hare Field' at the north end of Brick Lane with a view to developing it. Before they could begin work, however, Hare Field became the site of the worst mob violence Spitalfields had ever seen.[49]

The spark was lit around lunchtime on an unusually cold, snowy day in April 1771. Daniel Clarke, the informer whose evidence led to the hanging of three cutters the previous year, had begun to feel complacent. The magistrates had advised him to always carry his pistols in case of reprisal, but Clarke had left them at home and was walking the streets near Brick Lane when he was spotted, with a cry of 'there goes that blood-selling rascal!' A crowd gathered, stones were thrown and Clarke was knocked to the ground and repeatedly kicked. Missing his hat and wig and bleeding from a cut above the eye, he struggled free and took refuge in the house of a friend while a messenger ran to inform his wife.[50]

By the time Clarke's wife arrived at the scene with his pistols, the crowd had dispersed. With the weather worsening – it was now snowing hard – the Clarkes waited for an hour before setting off home. But as soon as they set foot outdoors the mob materialised again. Mrs Clarke was allowed to escape but Clarke was trapped. His pistol failed and he fought his way back inside the house. The crowd smashed the windows with stones and brick ends, screaming that they would hang, burn or drown the informer and anyone who sheltered him. In desperation Clarke ran for it over the back garden wall and the mob gave chase.

The snowstorm worsened. Clarke dodged his pursuers in the maze of narrow streets, blood pouring from the wound on his head. Reaching Brick Lane he headed north past the Merceron pawnshop towards the marshy fields, aiming for the sanctuary of the church or Justice Wilmot's house just beyond it. Exhausted, he made it as far as Hare Field where James's partner John Wolveridge was working his garden, but here the mob was too great for him and he was knocked over, beaten and stripped to his breeches and stockings. They dragged him to a pond among the old brick workings, forced him into the icy water and pelted him with earth and bricks, laying his skull entirely open.

By this time, news of the attack had spread and a great crowd was gathering. It was still snowing heavily. Clarke was stranded in the freezing pond for more than half an hour while a gang of children, cheered on by the adults, flung more stones at him. John Wolveridge attempted to intervene, asking the crowd to allow him to take Clarke to the nearby London Hospital, but the mob would have none of it and turned him away. Clarke was now out of the water, spread-eagled on a sand heap and pelted with handfuls of gravel. A cord was tied around his neck; he was dragged back into the water and repeatedly pushed under. Finally, freezing, terrified and at the point of death, he was hauled out. The *Gentleman's Magazine* reported that 'never did any poor mortal suffer more than he did; he begged of them several times to shoot him; but they kept stoning him'. At about four o'clock, more than three hours after he was first accosted, he died 'in the greatest agonies'.[51]

The authorities acted quickly. Davy Wilmot, aided by London's chief magistrate Sir John Fielding, offered generous rewards for the names of the ringleaders. Despite the obvious risk of further reprisals, the amounts offered were eventually enough to bring forward several informers willing to testify in court. In early July, two men were found guilty of Clarke's murder. The scenes after their trial at the Old Bailey came close to anarchy. A soldier giving evidence against them was attacked by an angry mob as he left court; Wilmot was forced to flee the crowd at a gallop. To deter any more disturbances, the authorities again decided to execute the guilty men in their own neighbourhood. The hangings took place in Hare Street, outside the entrance to Hare Field and just around the corner from the Mercerons' house. More than one hundred soldiers with fixed bayonets were placed around the gallows, with another troop stationed to guard Wilmot's house.[52]

After a further year of unrest, peace was finally achieved by the passing of the Spitalfields Act of 1773. This protectionist legislation gave the local magistrates the power to fix the prices of finished silks, ensuring that prices remained above a minimum level and thereby discouraging masters from slashing wages. In return, workers' combinations such as the Bold Defiance were outlawed. After a decade of violence and uncertainty, life for the Mercerons could return to some semblance of normality.

The family's history and circumstances were entirely conducive to the incubation of a child's urge for greatness. The Huguenots were intensely aware of their origins and proud of the extreme sacrifices made by their forebears. In their treasured portrait of Germanus, the Mercerons had a daily reminder of the ancestral power, influence and wealth stripped from them for the sake of their beliefs. The Huguenots were also renowned for their industry and thrift. James was no exception, combining his career as a pawnbroker and slum landlord with his onerous parish duties – a work ethic clearly inherited by his youngest son. Joseph Merceron must also have noticed the difference between his own family's increasing prosperity and the plight of most of his neighbours. But instead of sparking a philanthropic yearning, the stream of desperate, miserable and filthy creatures trudging in and out of his father's shop made him resolve never to sink to such a level. The legend, no doubt repeated endlessly, of Joseph's great-grandfather's flight from France, left him in no doubt of the ephemeral nature of fortune; his direct observation of local poverty must have made him determined never to experience it for himself.

Little is known of Joseph Merceron's early schooldays. He must have started school in about 1771, the year of Daniel Clarke's murder, and probably attended one of several nearby day schools. Such institutions would later be described by the Radical agitator Francis Place (who attended one around this time) as 'all alike' and offering basic teaching, usually limited to reading, writing and arithmetic. The discipline was brutal. Sir Samuel Romilly (another third generation Huguenot immigrant, later a lawyer and politician who would play a part in Merceron's downfall) also attended such a school, whose sole recommendation appeared to be that it had 'once been kept by a French refugee'. Romilly's schoolmaster would thrash the boys at the least excuse.[53]

When not at school, it seems likely that much of Joseph's childhood was spent helping his father in the pawnshop, an experience which may have contributed to his obsession with money. Exacerbated by the economic crisis impacting the weaving industry, the 1770s was a boom time for London's pawnbrokers. There were hundreds of them in London and the authorities exercised virtually no control over their activities, despite repeated complaints of extortion. The odds were stacked overwhelmingly in the pawnbroker's favour. *The Times* suggested drily that the instantly recognizable pawnbroker's street sign, comprising three golden balls, reflected the commercial reality that 'when a man carries anything to a pawn-broker, it is two to one against his ever seeing it again'.[54]

The pawnbroking business had changed little since William Hogarth satirized 'Mr Gripe', the pawnbroker in his famous 1751 engraving *Gin Lane*.

Gripe is the best-dressed man in the scene, peering cynically over his spectacles as a desperate carpenter and his wife pawn their tools, while society collapses around them from the effects of gin. Despite a clampdown on gin retailers, the drink had remained relentlessly popular with the poor. Twenty years after the 'gin-craze' had ended, *Gin Lane* was still an accurate caricature of London's meanest streets. The pawnbroker's shop remained – as Charles Dickens would write in *Sketches by Boz* (1835) – one of the most striking 'receptacles for misery and distress with which the streets of London unhappily abound'.[55]

James's own shop window was packed with pawned goods, their deadline for redemption long since passed – silk clothes, watches, rings and silverware such as buckles, buttons and thimbles. Inside the shop, the visitor's eye would be drawn to a brightly coloured array of silk cloaks and handkerchiefs hung, together with a variety of hats,

Gin Lane

from nails on the wall or doorposts. On or behind the counter, glass display cabinets showed goods to their maximum advantage, while the remaining space was taken up with the valuer's crucial equipment: pewter measuring jugs for vinegar and ale; scales of different sizes for weighing butter and tea or for testing money, each with their attendant set of weights in brass, iron or lead.[56]

Women were often engaged in the business and it is likely that Ann and all the children worked in the shop from time to time. The broker needed assistants to make out tickets and shuttle back and forth to the storeroom while he valued the pawn and kept a watchful eye on the customer. The valuation of pledges was a skilled business and not often delegated; James would have prided himself as a judge of the weight of gold. If the loan, and the invariably exorbitant interest, were not repaid by the specified deadline – typically three to four months – then the item was forfeited and the broker could sell it at a healthy profit.[57]

The profits from James's pawnshop added to an increasing flow of rental income from his property sideline. In 1774, the 'blue apron men' of the East End converted an ostensible threat to their profitability into yet another opportunity for corruption. In an attempt to improve the safety of slum dwellings, the government tightened building standards, requiring new houses to be certified by a surveyor appointed by the local magistrates. But in Bethnal Green, the new legislation added little apart from bureaucracy and nepotism. Through his brother's influence with his fellow magistrates, John Wilmot was appointed as the Middlesex county surveyor. A building certificate from the period shows the result: a house 'near Wilmot Square', built in 1777 by 'Mr [David] Wilmot, bricklayer' was approved by 'Mr John Wilmot, surveyor' and the certificate sworn before 'D Wilmot, JP'. Several of James's own houses were signed off by the Wilmots in similar fashion, and by 1775 his portfolio had increased to more than 50 properties.[58]

That Easter, James was ill and resigned as a Governor of the Poor. In October he updated his will, placing his whole estate in trust for his wife's lifetime, with half the income to her and the remainder shared equally between his four surviving children. His eldest son, John, by now 24, was living with his wife Gabrielle and their baby daughter in one of James's Brick Lane properties. Catherine was 20 and unmarried; Annie was 14 and Joseph 11.

It is clear from the drafting of his will that James was concerned at the possibility of a dispute over his estate; he left meticulous instructions as to how the properties should be apportioned between the children after his second wife's death. Surprisingly, he excluded John as an executor, instead appointing Ann, Catherine and his friend Peter Paumier. Perhaps John could not be trusted to look after the interests of his half-siblings. Paumier's role was almost certainly to oversee an equitable distribution of the estate in the event of a dispute but, as we shall see, this was to fail spectacularly.[59]

Having recovered by the following spring, James became a proud godfather to his first grandson, James Francis Merceron, born to John and Gabrielle in March. Around this time, his parish career reached its peak when he was elected a churchwarden of Bethnal Green, and for the next two years he dominated the vestry alongside his old ally Davy Wilmot, who had been appointed as parish treasurer. Their supremacy coincided with misery for the poor, as labouring wages in London fell to their lowest level for 50 years. The preacher and founder of Methodism John Wesley, visiting the parish in 1777, noted 'such poverty as few can conceive without seeing it'. For the Mercerons, however, life had never been so good. James was now sufficiently wealthy to invest in his youngest son's future, and the previous autumn had enrolled the 12-year-old Joseph as a day scholar at the prestigious Merchant Taylors' School in the City of London.[60]

The school was situated in Suffolk Lane, a tiny street on the north bank of the Thames and only about a mile's walk from Brick Lane. It was already more than 200 years old and one of the top public schools in England. The school had been suffering from a lack in popularity, but from 1760 its progressive headmaster, James Townley, had raised standards and by the time of Joseph's arrival the school had virtually a full complement of 250 boys.[61]

Townley was the author of *High Life Below Stairs*, one of the 18th century's most successful plays, and had tried to broaden the boys' education by introducing the study of mathematics. Nevertheless, the school day was still heavily focused on the classics, with recitations from the Bible and Greek and Latin translation forming regular parts of the daily routine. It was a Spartan regime. The school day ran from seven a.m. until five p.m. even in winter. The boys were all crowded into a single large hall. The crowding may at least have provided some warmth, as there was no other heating provided apart from candles.[62]

Joseph spent only a year at Merchant Taylors', but it was enough to add a polish to his education and to mark him out as significantly different within his own family and local peers. It also gave him added self-assurance and a network of contacts among the sons of City merchants, which would prove enormously helpful in his later career. To these attributes, a set of more practical skills were added through helping his father in the pawnshop. James drilled into him the importance of having the odds on his side in financial transactions. He knew how to drive a hard bargain and had few qualms about exploiting other people to get what he wanted. It was now time for Joseph to choose a career. His half-brother John had been apprenticed as a joiner; although he occasionally helped in the shop, he was primarily engaged in James's building enterprise. But Joseph's greatest strength lay in his brains, not his hands, and James would not have sent him to Merchant Taylors' only to have him become another 'blue apron man'. Instead, James secured him a clerkship to a local lottery office keeper. It would be the perfect finishing school for Joseph's financial education, an ideal complement to the pawnshop for grounding him in the darker arts of the world of finance.[63]

London had become lottery mad. Although state lotteries had existed for a century or more, they became spectacularly popular in the 1770s as a means of raising capital for major building ventures.

For the poor, however, they were yet another source of misery and ruin. In words that resonate today, one magistrate told a parliamentary Select Committee in 1816 that:

> Among the immediate causes of thefts and other offences against the public peace, lotteries hold an undoubted place. It is a scandal to the Government, thus to excite people to practise the vice of gaming, for the purpose of drawing a revenue from their ruin; it is an anomalous proceeding by law to declare gambling infamous…and by law also to set up the giant gambling of the State Lottery, and to encourage persons to resort to it by the most captivating devices which ingenuity…can invent.[64]

Although lottery tickets were expensive, they could be paid for in instalments and traded while partly paid. Such trading led to the establishment of more than 400 lottery offices in London alone. Some office keepers, keen to make extra money, set up as bookmakers offering a bewildering variety of secondary contracts. These were known as 'lottery insurances' but in reality were simply bets on whether a particular number would win a prize, regardless of the ownership of the ticket in question.[65]

The winning tickets were drawn at London's Guildhall over a 40-day period of feverish anticipation and wild publicity, during which ticket sales reached crazy levels. While the draw was on, the takings of local tradesmen fell dramatically; all except the pawnbrokers who, conversely, saw a vast increase in business as the gambling public pawned everything to fund their addiction. Each day, hundreds of people gathered outside the lottery offices to learn whether they had won. Towards the end of the draw, the less scrupulous office keepers would 'shut up shop and decamp, for fear of being brought to account for their cheats and roguery'.[66]

In the lottery shop, Joseph was kept at his ledgers for long hours, six days a week. On Sundays, however, he became a leading member of a gang of several hundred 'bullock runners' who gathered every week in his father's field next to St Matthew's church. Every Sunday morning, hundreds of cattle and sheep were driven along the Bethnal Green Road on their way to market at Smithfield. As the animals trotted by, the gang would purchase a bullock from one of the drovers. The runners (each armed with an ash sapling with its root smoothed into a knob at one end and a sharp nail tied to the other) would drive it mad by prodding it, pushing peas or stones into its ears and forcing the sharp end of their sticks up its backside, all while the church service went on next door. When the bullock could take no more, the gang would drive it through the busiest roads of the parish 'so as to endanger the lives of all persons passing along the street'. Years later, Joseph recalled with pride having often been 'first in the chase' in his youth. The damage to property, and the fright induced by the rampaging bullock and the baying mob, were considerable and made a powerful impression on him. Over the ensuing decades, calling out the bullock hunters to pay a visit to an opponent's premises became one of his favourite means of meting out retribution.[67]

After completing his term of office as churchwarden at Easter 1778, James Merceron began to reduce his involvement in parish affairs. He was reappointed to the Court of Requests at Easter 1779 but a year later his name was absent from minutes of the election of officers. He died on 6th April 1780, aged 56. In his last days, James could reflect that he had provided well for his family. The thriving pawnbroking business and the rent from dozens of tenements ensured a healthy income, enough for the comfort and security of his widow and all his children. By sending Joseph to one of the best schools in the country, even if only for a year, he had given his youngest son a good start in life. James had planned carefully for his own demise. He died confident that his assets would be allocated with scrupulous fairness between his children and that the distribution of his estate would be achieved without any bad feeling between them. He could not have been more wrong.[68]

CHAPTER III

Doing Davy

He who holds the purse strings holds the power.
Bertolt Brecht[69]

In June 1780, just weeks after James Merceron's death, the mob was back on the streets. What began as a series of ostensibly anti-Catholic protests rapidly evolved into the Gordon Riots, an indiscriminate and brutal rampage against authority in general. Breweries were pillaged; London's main prison at Newgate was set ablaze and its prisoners released. The slow reactions of a poorly defined and tangled web of authority – the government, Middlesex magistrates, City of London Corporation and the military – resulted in confusion, indecision and paralysis. The destruction continued for almost a week, until King George III himself – furious at the failure of the authorities – said 'that the magistrates had not done their duty, but that he would do his own' and ordered the soldiers to preserve the peace by force.[70]

Quiet returned, but not before Bethnal Green had experienced its share of violence. Gangs of Spitalfields weavers had been prominent among the rioters all week and, as the destruction reached its climax in the evening of Wednesday 7th June, the mob headed east along the Bethnal Green Road. Their target was Davy Wilmot, one of the magistrates with whom the King was so furious. This time, there was no armed guard to save Wilmot's house in Camden Row and a group of rioters destroyed it while, almost simultaneously, another mob demolished his office in Worship Street, Shoreditch. In Camden Row, a witness claimed to have seen a mob a thousand strong gathered around Wilmot's house, making a bonfire of whatever wood they could rip from it. Many were on the roof, throwing down the lead and tiles.[71] In *Barnaby Rudge* (1841), set against the backdrop of the Gordon Riots, Charles Dickens captured the mood of destruction perfectly:

> The tumbling down of nodding walls and heavy blocks of wood, the hooting and the execrations of the crowd, the distant firing of military detachments, the distracted looks and cries of those whose habitations were in danger, the hurrying to and fro of frightened people with their goods; the reflections in every quarter of the sky of deep, red, soaring flames, as though the last day had come and the whole universe were burning; the dust, and smoke, and drift of fiery particles, scorching and kindling all it fell upon: the hot unwholesome vapour, the blight on everything; the stars, and moon, and very sky, obliterated – made up such a sum of dreariness and ruin, that it seemed as if the face of Heaven were blotted out, and night, in its rest and quiet, and softened light, never could look upon the earth again.[72]

Perhaps unsurprisingly, but justifying the King's criticism, Wilmot had gone into hiding. In his absence, looters continued to strip his house bare. The next day, one of the rioters, John Gamble, was heard bragging in a public house that he had 'done Davy'. Gamble was soon informed against. A few weeks later he was convicted at the Old Bailey and sentenced to death along with 23 other rioters. To minimize the risk of further violence the authorities decided to spread the executions across the capital. On 20th July, in an echo of the weavers' riots a decade earlier, Gamble was hanged in Bethnal Green.[73]

Once the riots were over, life for the Mercerons returned to dealing with the aftermath of James's death and the management of his business interests. Joseph's older half-brother John took the lead. 29 years old, married for a second time with three children and expecting a fourth, John had tried his hand at several careers. Originally apprenticed as a joiner, he had also worked as an undertaker and had assisted his father as a pawnbroker and appraiser. Given his experience, it was natural that he should take over the pawnbroking business and his joinery skills made him well qualified to do any building work on the family properties. Either through lack of time or ability, John could not manage the finances of the property business as well. With Joseph's experience at the lottery office, it was a natural step for the younger brother to take on this aspect of the business. Joseph left his clerkship and took over the administration of James's property trust, which by this time generated most of the family's income. The job involved dealing with difficult tenants, ground landlords, lawyers and contractors, negotiating leases and collecting and paying rent and rates. Brash and assertive, Joseph seems to have been exceptionally good at it. A considerable and natural aptitude for money matters, refined and polished at the pawnshop and lottery office, gave him an instinctive grasp of a landlord's power. Everything that followed suggests that the 16-year-old quickly learned when and how to use this power. Above all, he understood that a favour extended, no matter how small, created a debt to be called in later.[74]

Joseph had a strong personal stake in his new job. His father's will had specified exactly how the family properties would be allocated between his four children after Ann's death, and the details became an obsession for the young man. Perhaps he dreamed that his own share of James's legacy would be the seed from which his fortune would grow, returning the Merceron family back to their rightful place in society. Soon after his father's death, Joseph purchased an exercise book of the type still used in schools today. On the cover he wrote his name and the date. Inside, neatly and with great care, he copied James's will. The book became a treasured possession and an important record of his first property rights. Its cover was decorated with a line engraving of a rural scene. In the foreground of the picture, two pigeons flutter away, scared off by a magpie that has muscled in on their lunch. As a metaphor for Joseph's subsequent handling of the family money, the picture was remarkably apposite.[75]

Joseph's new career brought him into contact with a number of influential local figures. Among these was James Grant, for many years the chief clerk at Truman's Brewery. Growing up across the road from the brewery gates, young Joseph must have seen Grant come and go hundreds of times and had somehow made his acquaintance, perhaps by offering to run errands or by looking after Grant's horse. In 1781, Sir Benjamin Truman died and leaving no son and heir appointed Grant the managing director of the brewery. Joseph began to court Grant assiduously. His knowledge of the local property market would have been most useful to Grant, who needed to keep a close eye on new developments to make sure that Truman's were quick off the mark in obtaining any new licensed premises. Soon, Grant would be referring to Joseph as 'my friend' and would eventually leave money to him in his will.[76]

Another acquaintance was the Mercerons' own landlord, Henry Busby, owner of the *Red Cow* estate that by this time comprised around 400 properties and included the Mercerons' building land at Hare Field. Early in 1784, Joseph pulled off an audacious coup, somehow persuading Busby to appoint him as agent for the entire estate. Soon afterwards, Busby's patronage won him a second major client, an elderly clergyman and important local landowner named Anthony Natt. In the back of his exercise book, Joseph wrote: '1st Dec 1784 was appointed Collector by Mr Natt & gave him two bonds for security. The one for £300 signed by myself and my mother and the other for £200 signed by myself and Mr J Grant.' It was an impressive start; clearly the friendship with Grant was paying off. By the end of 1784, still a month short of his 21st birthday, Joseph was responsible for collecting the rents on more than 500 houses.[77]

He was also trading in property on his own account. In 1775, his father had drawn up plans for the development of Hare Field into housing lots but had never got round to completing the project. Joseph stood to inherit the field on his mother's death and realizing the potential of the site he resurrected the plans shortly after his appointment as Busby's agent. The field was marked out into streets, a few houses erected at the corners and the land advertised for sale as 139 'advantageous building leases'. This was a well-tested formula for developers: with very little outlay, and without ever taking on the risk of erecting and having to sell all the houses, a plot such as this could be bought and sold on to a number of small builders. Joseph made a significant and immediate profit.[78]

It was during this period, as Merceron came of age and registered his first business successes, that he developed the striking signature that suggests so much about his personality. In 1780, when the 16-year-old signed the cover of his new exercise book, the signature was neat but unremarkable. By 1784, shortly after his appointment as Busby's agent, it was completely transformed. Even in a period where men's signatures were often extravagant, his flamboyant autograph took some beating: four inches long, underlined with a thick flourish and four curlicues, its initial capital more than two inches high. According to graphology manuals its exaggerated size, underlining and rightward slant indicate attention-seeking, recklessness and egocentricity, all consistent with what we know of Merceron's personality.

The dramatic change in the signature between 1780 and 1784 suggests a deliberate investment of time and effort. The sight of it dominating those of his colleagues year after year in the vestry minute book is reminiscent of John Hancock's enormous autograph

Joseph Merceron's signature

on the 1776 American Declaration of Independence; the timing suggests Merceron may have read or heard of Hancock's effort and attempted to replicate the effect.[79]

By June 1786, still only 22 and as a result of Henry Busby's influence, Merceron was appointed a Commissioner of the Land Tax for the Tower Division of Middlesex, one of a small number of men appointed to supervise the assessment and collection of an important source of government revenue. That year, he began to reveal the extent to which he was prepared to go for the sake of money and power. John Merceron, his wife heavily pregnant with a fifth child, fell suddenly and seriously ill. The local apothecary was called in to prescribe medicines but could do nothing for him. With hope fading, Merceron took control of the situation, but his mind was not on his half-brother so much as on the small print of their father's poorly drafted will. Merceron knew that if John should die before his stepmother, then his share of their father's estate would not pass to his own children but would be shared between Merceron and Catherine, the surviving half-siblings (Annie, Merceron's other sister, had died in 1782). However unfortunate, the wording of the will was clear: if John should die now, his children would get nothing.[80]

Merceron mentioned none of this to his dying brother. Instead, he assured John that he would look after the children and, on 30 March, helped him to draft a brief will, roping in three Brick Lane shopkeepers to witness it. The will makes it clear that John still believed his share of James's estate would pass to his own children. Crucially, he named Merceron as an executor. John died a week later, on 8th April 1786. He never saw his daughter Mary, who was born on 9 July. Meanwhile, alone in his office, Merceron copied John's will into his exercise book, immediately beneath that of his father.[81]

While plotting against his brother, Merceron was also engaged in an equally callous manoeuvre to get his hands on the property of a young woman named Mary Cheesman. Among the houses that Merceron managed for Anthony Natt was a portfolio of about 50 tenements near the north end of Brick Lane belonging to Miss

Cheesman, who was Natt's great niece and who had been severely mentally disabled from birth – what was termed, in those days, as 'an idiot'. Stories abounded of Mary relieving herself in public and exposing herself to passing workmen. She had inherited the property from her grandfather, and when her father died in 1783 (Mary greeted this news with fits of giggles) she was taken into Natt's care, the properties falling to him to administer as executor of the grandfather's will. The Cheesman properties were well known to Merceron, being situated close to his own house. They were old and dilapidated, but he would have known that the underlying freeholds were sound and potentially profitable. Before long, he approached Natt with a plan. On 6th May 1786, Mary turned 21 and became legally entitled to her inheritance. Four days later, Merceron and Natt took her into the City of London offices of Natt's attorney, where they bullied the frightened and confused young woman into signing away a significant portion of her property to Natt for just five shillings. Privately, Natt had agreed that Merceron would be given several of the properties in return for his involvement.[82]

This was just the first stage of the piecemeal theft of Mary Cheesman's property, a process that took several years to complete. For the remainder of 1786, however, Merceron's attention was elsewhere. On 26th October, his mother died. In her will (once again, copied methodically into Merceron's exercise book) she left him all her own small property. Of far greater significance to him, however, was the distribution of his father's estate that Ann's death triggered.[83]

The deaths of James, John and Ann Merceron left behind a tangle of wills, property and family relationships. The sole surviving executor under James's will was Merceron's half-sister, Catherine. Merceron was the only executor of his mother's will and was joint executor of his brother's with John's brother-in-law, Louis Godefroy. Over the next few weeks, he contrived to remove Godefroy and Catherine from the administration of the wills and distribution of assets, managing it all himself. It seems likely that he bribed Godefroy to keep him out, but the story with Catherine appears more sinister.

For much of the next 35 years, Merceron had his half-sister in-carcerated in a notorious lunatic asylum, Hoxton House, while he misappropriated her share of the family money. Catherine was cer-tainly sane at the time of her father's death, or James would surely have altered his will. Did she have a breakdown upon or shortly after James's death? According to a history of the London asylums around that time, money was the only requirement for the admission of a patient and many sane people were locked away for no other reason than 'the intrigues of relatives or friends, from ulterior motives'. If Merceron did have Catherine confined to get his own hands on the family money, he was not the first to try such a trick.[84]

Having precluded any interference, Merceron informed John's widow Mary that neither she nor her children had any right to a share in James's estate. As if this were not punishment enough, he advised the widow that her husband's own estate, comprising a small amount of cash and a few miserable sticks of broken furniture, had amounted to just £40. After paying for the funeral and the apothe-cary's bill, there was precious little left and it was soon spent on food, clothes and schooling for the children. While Mary and her children were left penniless, the income from Merceron's inflated share of the family properties, when added to his commissions as agent for Busby and Natt, meant he was earning in the region of £600 per annum.[85]

Merceron's inheritance entitled him to a vote at the Bethnal Green vestry. He is first recorded at a vestry meeting on 18th September 1786, shortly before his mother's death and presumably in his ca-pacity as agent to Busby and Natt. He soon became a regular and prominent contributor to the proceedings. As luck would have it, his initiation into local government coincided with a period of almost complete apathy by his fellow vestrymen. At his first meeting, only eight other men were present, out of a total of perhaps a thousand entitled to be there. A few months later, another meeting was post-poned as 'not one vestryman came'.[86]

To the mostly old and ignorant men running Bethnal Green, led by the unpopular and increasingly frail Wilmot, Merceron's outspoken energy must have seemed overwhelming. His practical and commercial grasp of business, developed during six years as a rent collector, polished by his appointment as a Tax Commissioner and backed by the influential patronage of Busby, Natt and Grant, immediately led the other vestrymen to recognize him as a leader. He soon formed allegiances. Senior vestryman John Bampton, a Brick Lane tallow chandler, was an old friend of Merceron's father. Bampton's business was in difficulties; Merceron astutely offered to assist, probably by way of a loan. There was, as always, a payback: the compromised Bampton would use his influence to support Merceron's advance within the vestry. In the weeks around Easter 1787, with Bampton's assistance, Merceron manoeuvred himself onto a number of vestry committees dealing with almost every aspect of the parish finances. He used this opportunity to probe more deeply into the activities of a number of the vestry officers, including Wilmot, who remained the parish treasurer. What Merceron found would give him just the ammunition he needed to begin his advance up the local political ladder.[87]

One of the Bethnal Green churchwardens that year was Robert Wrightson, the 40 year-old owner of a successful gun-carriage manufactory. After investigating the vestry accounts for some weeks, Merceron began to whisper allegations of fraud against Wrightson and Wilmot. No proof was presented, but Wilmot's position was left increasingly precarious and an enmity was forged between Merceron and Wrightson that would last half a century.[88]

When the vestry met on 19th July, there were two main items of business. The first was to consider a proclamation by King George III against the profanation of the Sabbath and ordering the local magistrates and parish officers to take action. Given Merceron's passion for leading the Sunday bullock hunting, this must have caused him much amusement. But the other agenda item most captivated his attention. The accusations of fraud had proved too much for Wilmot, who tabled his resignation as the parish treasurer. Davy had been 'done' again.[89]

The vestry resolved to meet again a week later to elect a successor. Merceron, seizing his opportunity, quickly secured the support of Busby and Natt and announced his intention to serve in Wilmot's place. There was little or no opposition. Few, if any, of the vestrymen had any financial or business background. Those that did, such as Wrightson, had already been discredited. Busby and Natt agreed to stand as guarantors of a £1,000 bond as security. Merceron readily acceded to a resolution to produce his accounts for audit by the vestry. It was enough. The following week, by a unanimous vote, he was appointed treasurer of Bethnal Green. He immediately set up a committee, packed with his own supporters, to conduct a root and branch review of the parish poor's rate administration.[90]

Three years earlier, aged 20, Merceron was a fairly typical product of the East End: loud, cheeky and street-smart as he collected the rents on his father's tenement houses. Now he found himself in complete control of the finances of one of London's largest parishes. Its entire annual income passed directly through his hands, and he had complete discretion over its disbursement. Concerns were expressed in the vestry about the appropriateness of handing over such a huge fiduciary responsibility to a 23-year-old, but these were easily dealt with. After all, William Pitt the Younger had been made Prime Minister just three years previously at almost the same age. Merceron's appointment was, nevertheless, a remarkable achievement. As he might have said to himself, it was just the beginning.[91]

PART II

Dominance
1788–1810

CHAPTER IV

Cerberus

Churchwarden I've been, let me see, very often;
You know it's a place of much trust;
And its monstrous fatigues and hardships to soften
We eat, aye and drink till we burst.

Anon.[92]

Bethnal Green was experiencing the rapid creation of a political machine. Small-time corruption at the heart of local government was nothing new, especially in the parishes run by 'blue apron men' around the edges of the City of London. Nevertheless, within a few years of his appointment as parish treasurer, Merceron's nefarious activities had eclipsed those of his predecessors and other local rivals.

More than half a century earlier, the writer Daniel Defoe had complained bitterly of parish 'blood-suckers': officials who feasted at the public expense and even dumped pauper women over the parish boundary just before childbirth to avoid responsibility for maintaining their offspring. According to Defoe, vestries were often rotten to the core or dominated by powerful cliques. Such accusations had been applicable to Bethnal Green for decades. As a leading vestryman James Merceron would have been no stranger to small-scale corruption or bribery; on his death, his family probably lost a significant source of income from these sources. Once in power, Joseph Merceron rapidly increased both the number and scale of Wilmot's petty scams. Within two years of joining the vestry, and still aged only 24, he was chairing Bethnal Green's vestry meetings and in complete control of the parish.[93]

57

Even allowing for Merceron's extrovert personality, there were several other factors behind his domination over Bethnal Green's politics. First, his power (as landlord, landlord's agent and parish treasurer) to raise or lower the rents and rates of hundreds of tenant families gave him enormous influence, backed by the support of local worthies such as Grant, Busby and Natt. Second, as treasurer, he became solely responsible for negotiating and awarding contracts to supply the parish with goods or services. Butcher, baker, collier, carpenter, bricklayer – all were desperate to be awarded a lucrative poorhouse contract and more than willing to bribe the treasurer to get it. Third, the power and influence thereby gained enabled him to pack the vestry with trusted supporters whose integrity had been compromised by financial incentives.[94]

Many of these supporters were themselves 'blue apron men'. As a witness to a later parliamentary inquiry put it, Merceron brought his influence to bear on the vestry 'to elect the most ignorant and the lowest characters, on whom he can depend, to fill all parish offices'. Typical of these were Stephen Witherden, a carpenter, and Charles Masterman, a bricklayer, whom over the years Merceron enriched through a steady supply of lucrative building contracts. Both repaid him by years of loyalty, Witherden going so far as perjury in an attempt to keep his master from prison, although Masterman eventually turned traitor and gave crucial evidence against Merceron.[95]

Such men were perfectly suited both to bully reluctant vestrymen into voting for Merceron and to frighten off potential opponents. Nevertheless, Merceron also needed men of a different stamp to help him navigate the legal minefield of vestry business. Parish law was enormously complex: the standard handbook, Richard Burn's 1755 text *The Justice of the Peace and Parish Officer*, comprised 5 hefty volumes and would eventually run to more than 30 editions. A key role was that of vestry clerk, whose job was to act as secretary and legal adviser to the vestry. When Merceron became Bethnal Green's treasurer, its vestry clerk was an aged lawyer named Philip May, who according to one account was 'as wet a dog as ever you smoked a pipe with'. Merceron soon replaced the elderly clerk with May's son, James, a diligent but timid young solicitor with a rapidly growing family (he would have 21 children). These attributes made James May highly susceptible to Merceron's pecuniary influence as the treasurer spread his tentacles into every aspect of the parish administration. Over the next quarter-century, by awarding May generous salary increases, lucrative private and parochial legal work and by excusing him from paying the poor's rates, Merceron ensured that the vestry clerk was firmly in his power.[96]

At Easter 1788 Merceron was unanimously re-elected as Bethnal Green's treasurer. He was again backed by Henry Busby, who by this time had come to trust him completely. After the death of his wife the previous autumn, Busby had made a new will appointing Merceron as his executor and trustee and made him the legal guardian over his four teenage daughters. The renewed mandate from the vestry, together with Busby's backing, gave Merceron a platform to expand the scale of his activities. The parish began to borrow money, with the innovative young treasurer placing adverts in the press to raise funds by the sale of life assurance annuities. Merceron had already developed a number of the traits that would characterise his years in power. Vestry meetings became sparsely attended and the seat of local government in effect moved to Merceron's Brick Lane office. The various committees he had instigated to review the financial administration of the parish were packed with the same handful of submissive colleagues and became little more than a mechanism for identifying existing scams, turning them to his own account.[97]

Perhaps the biggest potential source of bounty for a corrupt parish official was the rating system. David Wilmot had been known to run a common fraud of a type exposed as far back as 1744 by the *Gentleman's Magazine*. It was ridiculously simple: corrupt vestrymen would appraise their own properties (as well as those of friends, supporters or those who bribed them) at considerably less than the true annual value, while increasing the assessments on opponents or those who refused to pay. There was no independent scrutiny of the rating process, and vestrymen would often refuse to make the detailed records available for inspection. Any appeal against a rate assessment was to the local magistrates, who were typically – as in Wilmot's case – themselves vestrymen and complicit in the scam.[98]

After taking over as treasurer, Merceron had expanded this scheme considerably. Under the pretext of a survey to ensure that all properties in the parish were 'properly rated', a small committee chaired by Merceron systematically altered the assessments, reducing them on their own properties and raising them on anyone who dared to oppose them. Years later, a witness to a parliamentary Select Committee would recall the Saturday morning ritual at the old Merceron pawnshop on Brick Lane. Parishioners, desperate for money or food, would queue up for an audience with the Boss to plead for a reduction in their rates or taxes – requests that Merceron would often grant on condition that the favour would be called in later. His aggressive personality quickly dissuaded potential opponents: any challenge to his authority would be met with the threat of litigation. No one was immune: even old family friends found themselves facing a lawsuit. But it was not long before a group of vestrymen decided to fight back. Soon, for the first time but certainly not the last, Merceron found himself at the centre of a dispute that would bring Bethnal Green to national attention as the epitome of local government corruption.[99]

The dispute started innocuously as a petty squabble over five cottages situated just outside Bethnal Green's boundary with the neighbouring parish of Hackney. As part of Merceron's rating scam, someone had moved the parish boundary marker a few yards so that the cottages now appeared to be in Bethnal Green. The poor cottagers were understandably incensed when officials from both parishes tried to charge them for rates and taxes, refusing to pay either parish until the dispute was settled. Eventually the matter reached the attention of *The Times*, which saw it as a perfect illustration of abuses by parish officials against which it was campaigning.[100]

The newspaper had been launched only three years previously, as the *Daily Universal Register,* and had only been renamed *The Times* at the beginning of 1788. In an attempt to grab the public's attention, its editor and owner John Walter had begun a campaign to reform the Poor Laws. By May 1788, it being clear that Parliament had no intention of any such reform, Walter announced that in consequence '...the overseers and parish officers are preparing their several summer excursions, to look for the begetters of bastards in a very comfortable style; and most of the quarterly feasts are ordered by the stewards for that purpose... The parish must either generously or ungenerously contribute to all these disbursements.'[101]

The dispute in Bethnal Green fitted this story perfectly. The parishes of Hackney and Bethnal Green, Walter explained, were at loggerheads over the issue, and 'the official demagogues of each, are continually in council over a bottle of wine, or a bowl of punch on this important affair. Sober parishioners plainly perceive, that what with guzzling and eating, and the fees to counsel, this dispute will cost at least twenty times more than the value of the five little huts to be litigated.'

The matter was allowed to rest during the summer parliamentary vacation but in September 1788 Walter returned to the fray with a caustic editorial. He had, he said, been tipped off that 'the feasting junto of the Green' were due to hold a vestry dinner, and suggested sarcastically that it was to be paid for by the taxes levied on the disputed cottages. 'In the whole county of Middlesex' he thundered, 'there is not a parish that expends less on, and exacts more from, its inhabitants'. This was about to change. Walter's informants intended to overturn Merceron and his friends and by eradicating corruption promised to reduce the rates by at least 50 percent within a year. All property would be fairly rated, and there would be 'such overhauling and investigating of accounts, as shall make Bethnal Green a model, for every other parish in London'. Walter pledged the full support of *The Times* in the battle to follow.[102]

If Walter was looking for publicity for his story, his editorial did the trick. Letters – typically anonymous – poured in from both factions in the dispute and from the public at large, and he was able to keep the story going for the next three weeks. 'An Old Inhabitant of Bethnal Green' wrote in support of Walter's assertions, saying that there was 'not such another junto to be found in any parish in or about London'. This was followed by a mock defence of the vestry by a 'A Parish Officer', pointing out that the unequal rating of houses was standard practice, and threatening retribution for the complainants 'to deter them from stirring in affairs which do not belong to them'.[103]

The campaign came to a head on Saturday 27th September, when Walter recounted the details of a recent parish meeting held to hear parishioners' appeals against Merceron's rate demands. The vestry was accused of curtailing the meeting after an hour, with two-thirds of the parishioners unheard. The ageing David Wilmot – still the local magistrate – was in the chair, according to Walter, 'in all the magistratical dignity of a trading justice, to hear and determine complaints. His very wig struck the poor weavers with awe, whilst his eye, aiming at a dignity it could not assume, attempted to command respect from all.' Walter provided his readers with a cameo of the proceedings:

Parishioner. I am rated 4s. 6d. in the pound for the poor, at the full rate I pay, whilst one of your houses, to my knowledge, Mr. Justice, does not pay for more than half the rent it lets for, and whilst another house I can point out, on the Green, is let at £30 per annum, and only rated at £15.

Justice. Pay your rate.

Par. I desire to know why one house should pay more in proportion than another, and why I should be full rated, when other parishioners are only half rated.

Justice. Pay your rate.

Par. I suppose because I wear a good coat, your parish blood-suckers think they may exact what they please, and that I will pay sooner than dispute.

Justice. Pay your rate, I say.

Clerk (sticking the pen behind his ear). Don't trouble his worship so much, you may make him angry.[104]

The parishioners' complaints were in vain, even though several of them declared that the amounts levied would result in them being beneficiaries, rather than payers, of the poor's rate. Walter reported that after the meeting Wilmot 'took a gentle airing to create an appetite' after which he was 'most sumptuously entertained by the vestrymen, as is the custom, at the parish expense'. In the absence of parliamentary intervention to curtail the powers of 'a set of wretches who so grossly and so apparently abuse the trust reposed in them', railed Walter, the poor parishioners must continue to 'groan under a weight of the most bare-faced injustice'. The only way out, he concluded, was 'to soften the hearts of their oppressors' by bribery, 'perhaps in the manner that the mouth of Cerberus[105] is gratified, by a sop'.

Walter's account of this meeting triggered a further series of letters. In one, we find the first public reference to the 24-year-old Merceron:

Our young Treasurer, it seems, could not escape the malignant pen of this literary assassin, although he is as harmless a lad as ever broke bread in a parish – nor did I ever hear any thing to his disadvantage, except a few witticisms on the *wideness of his mouth*, which the malicious now say, made your paper hint at him as the Cerberus that receives the sop – but that is a cursed lie; for all the profit he has, is only that which arises from keeping the parish money as other Treasurers did, until it is paid away by order of Vestry.

By this point, the correspondence in *The Times* had run its course. Walter, in common with other newspaper owners, was being paid secretly by the Treasury to ensure that his coverage was favourable to the government. In February 1789, the arrangement backfired when *The Times* printed articles accusing the Duke of York (the King's second son) of insincerity in celebrating George III's recovery from illness. The Duke sued successfully for libel; Walter refused to disclose the author of the articles and was fined and imprisoned in Newgate. By the time he was released, more than two years later in March 1791, the impact of the French Revolution on British politics meant that parish reform was no longer a priority. Indeed, the fear of a similar revolution fermenting among the lower orders in London's poorer neighbourhoods would lead the government to actively support the existing corrupt regimes. In Bethnal Green, Merceron and his 'junto' would continue to feast on the Poor Law for decades to come.[106]

In the summer of 1789, as the ruling elite of England turned its attention to unfolding events in France, came the deaths of two influential East End figures. Each had played an important part in Merceron's early life and their deaths would lead to opportunities to consolidate his power. In June, Justice David Wilmot passed away, removing Merceron's only real local opposition and leaving his actions largely devoid of scrutiny. Then in early July, the week of the storming of the Bastille, James Grant died unexpectedly. He left a legacy to Merceron in his will and, more importantly, a gaping hole in the management of the Truman's brewery.[107]

For reasons that have never been fully explained, Grant's stake in the business was purchased by the 20-year-old Sampson Hanbury, grandson of a wealthy tobacco merchant and related to a number of highly influential Norfolk Quaker families, including the Barclay and Gurney banking dynasties. Hanbury immediately took up residence in Sir Benjamin Truman's fine old house across the road from Merceron's home on Brick Lane and took control of the adjoining brewery.

Tall, blond, arrogant, handsome and a fine huntsman (despite his 17 stones in weight), Hanbury was, in every sense, a larger-than-life

Sampson Hanbury

character. Almost immediately, he and Merceron, five years his senior, became good friends. They soon realised they had overlapping business interests. Merceron's growing property empire included a number of alehouses and naturally it suited Hanbury that the trade of as many of these as possible should be tied to his brewery. The result was a corrupt collaboration that would enrich both men and help Truman's to more than double its output over the ensuing 30 years.[108]

At Easter 1790 Merceron was appointed in David Wilmot's place in a number of parish offices, appointments accompanied by the first of many annual votes of thanks by his vestry colleagues for his 'steady integrity' and attention to Bethnal Green's interests. An example of the sort of attention and integrity he was truly displaying came just a few weeks later. One of the lesser parish offices was that of 'searcher', usually an old woman whose job was to report on the cause of each death in the parish in order to facilitate the completion of monthly statistical returns for London as a whole, known as the 'Bills of Mortality'. The local magistrates had taken issue with the vestry's nomination for the role and swore in an alternative candidate of their own choosing. A furious Merceron went to law, obtained a favourable (and presumably expensive) counsel's opinion and forced the magistrates to back down. He then persuaded the vestry to charge the legal costs (which would have exceeded the annual salary of the searcher several times over) to be met out of the poor's rate funds.[109]

Such flexing of the vestry's muscle over even minor matters rapidly became a habit. The non-resident Rector was forced to defer to the vestry over the appointment of a new curate. A former churchwarden was threatened with legal action over his expenses. The fines for being excused from parish office (by which the unwilling could buy their way out of vestry duties, and which found their way into Merceron's private bank account) were increased significantly. When the vestry elected to purchase a number of stoves to heat the church, Merceron moved that they be paid for – illegally – from the poor's rate account. A vote was demanded. In a move that would be re-peated countless times over the next three decades, favours were called in. Merceron packed the vestry room with supporters, oppo-nents were intimidated and the motion was won. Soon, confident that his placemen in the vestry would back him, it became habitual for Merceron to use the poor's rate fund for any purpose he chose.[110]

Merceron had also continued to execute his plan to part the un-fortunate Mary Cheesman from her property. After helping the corrupt clergyman Anthony Natt to seize the management of Mary's assets two years earlier, Merceron had been rewarded with a share of the property via a series of deceptions in which the builder Charles Masterman played an important role. The Cheesman estate included a row of houses, including an inn known as *The Queen's Head*, just around the corner from Merceron's house on Brick Lane. First, Merceron commissioned an unscrupulous surveyor to pronounce the properties in terrible repair. In the summer of 1790, he conspired with Natt to force Mary to lease the properties very cheaply to Masterman.

A week later, Merceron paid a call on the landlord of *The Queen's Head*. He announced that Masterman was now the inn's owner and threatened the landlord with eviction unless he paid Masterman £150 and renewed his lease at extortionate terms. Unknown to the landlord and to Mary Cheesman, Masterman's involvement in these dealings was simply as a front for Merceron. After a complex and secret sequence of transactions, Merceron became the owner of the eight properties, including the lucrative public house. In doing so he made a profit – and Mary Cheesman a loss – over the lease term of about £1,800, equivalent to about £180,000 in today's terms. He paid Masterman just two shillings and sixpence for his trouble.[111]

That November, Mary Cheesman became gravely ill. Merceron and Natt wasted no time in enacting the final stage of their fraud, drafting a will on Mary's behalf and forcing her to sign it. She died on 19th March 1791. The will made Natt her executor and be-queathed her remaining properties (worth around £2,000) to Natt's sons. It would be a decade before Mary's relatives discovered what had happened.

Soon after Mary Cheesman's death, Merceron was married. His bride, Ann, was the 22 year-old daughter of Henry Cothery, master of *The Green Man* livery stables in Coleman Street, near the City of London's Guildhall. The wedding took place on 21st May 1791 in the Cothery's local church, St Stephen's. In a break with family tradition, it was the first time a Merceron had married a non-Huguenot: Ann was of English extraction, with a respectable middle-class ancestry. On her mother's side a great-grandfather was a Northamptonshire clergyman, a distant cousin was a vicar in Surrey and her uncle, the poetically named Sainsbury Sibley, was a Cheapside haberdasher. Ann's mother owned two farms near St Albans in Hertfordshire and settled both on Ann upon her marriage.[112]

A tiny newspaper clipping found among Merceron's private papers suggests that he saw his marriage to Ann, like almost everything else in his life, as a business transaction:

MATRIMONIAL – A young man, 25 years of age, of business habits, and possessed of an independency (arising from property) of upwards of £100 per annum, is desirous of being ALLIED to a LADY whose age and pecuniary circumstances do not materially differ with those of himself. It will be necessary that the character of the lady is unblemished: that she is of a free and open disposition, and that her education has not been entirely neglected: but, at the same time, it is important that she should be so far domesticated as to be able to take the management of the advertiser's home – All communications will receive the most polite attention, and the greatest secrecy may be depended upon on the part of the advertiser, to whom all letters (post-paid) may be addressed.[113]

Everything about the clipping is consistent with Merceron's style and circumstances. Was this how he found Ann? Fanciful speculation perhaps, but it does seem to fit and there must have been some reason for either Merceron or Ann to keep the clipping. Of course, their romance may have had a more prosaic beginning: *The Green Man* livery stables, where Ann grew up, were located just a stone's throw from the offices of Anthony Natt's lawyer, where Merceron and Natt had relieved Mary Cheesman of her property and where Merceron was a frequent visitor. He might well have hired horses from Ann's father and in doing so met his future wife.

By the autumn of 1791 Ann was pregnant and on 16th June 1792 gave birth to a son, Henry, named after his maternal grandfather and presumably as a mark of respect to Henry Busby. A daughter, Ann, followed 16 months later. A few days after Henry's birth, Merceron gave his tiny son a first lesson in life's priorities, presenting him with a five-shilling piece that Ann wrapped in a screw of paper with a note explaining 'this crown being the first piece of money belonging to Henry was given to him by his Father in the month of June 1792'.[114]

Around this time, another opportunity arose for Merceron to boost the value of his property portfolio: by paving the local streets. In doing so he was following a trend, begun by the Westminster Paving Act of 1762, which was driving an immense improvement in London's appearance and sanitation, while enriching the investors and contractors fortunate enough to be involved. In 1787, the paving of Westminster had been praised as introducing 'a degree of elegance and symmetry into the streets of the metropolis, that is the admiration of all Europe and far exceeds anything of the kind in the modern world'. At Easter 1791, Merceron had set up a vestry committee to explore the possibility of paving the main streets of Bethnal Green 'with the best nine-inch Aberdeen Granite'. The committee consisted of Merceron and Henry Busby – the men with most to gain from the enterprise – together with a few compliant acolytes. Unsurprisingly, almost half of the streets recommended by the committee to be paved were on the Busby estate.[115]

Busby's death in the winter of 1791–2 gave Merceron, as executor and trustee, full responsibility over the *Red Cow* estate. He pushed rapidly ahead with the local Act of Parliament to pave the streets, shamelessly funding its progress from the poor's rate fund. As with the purchase of stoves to keep the vestrymen warm, such improper transactions had become routine without the smallest murmur of dissent by the other vestrymen. The use of the poor's rate funds for their intended purposes was another matter. In each of his first four years as Bethnal Green's treasurer, Merceron disbursed promptly the rates collected during the year. Yet after his marriage he simply held on to the substantial sums collected from the parish and pocketed the interest. At the end of 1792 he retained more than £400 of the funds collected. A year later the balance in his hands had risen to almost £1,000, a quarter of the total assessed rate for the year. Allowing for the fact that a further quarter was never collected, and that a significant proportion of expenditure was on improper items such as the paving Bill or the vestry stoves, it seems that very little money actually reached the poorhouse. In May 1793 an overseer complained at being forced to relieve the poor from his own pocket and then having to reclaim the money from Merceron quarterly in arrears. The vestry unanimously dismissed the complaint.[116]

A quarter-century later, Merceron's abuse of the Bethnal Green poor's rate funds would bring about his temporary downfall. But in the 1790s, in the aftermath of the French Revolution and during the long war that followed, the political climate would shift significantly towards a harsh conservatism and an untrusting fear of any reform empowering the lower orders. *The Times* ceased to print letters complaining of abuses by 'parish blood-suckers'. The publication of Thomas Paine's *Rights of Man* in 1791 had fuelled the growth across England of reformist, and sometimes republican, societies. Vestry reform had disappeared from government agendas, to be replaced by genuine fears of French invasion or a home-grown revolution. These fears would lead Prime Minister William Pitt the Younger, himself hitherto a reformer, to institute his own 'reign of terror' with authoritarian counter-measures threatening civil liberties across the land. Joseph Merceron would play an enthusiastic and significant part in the events of the next decade, as London's ruling elites clamped down on anyone exhibiting disloyalty to King or Crown. He would do so as a Justice of the Peace with the full support of central government. Since David Wilmot's death in 1789, Bethnal Green had no resident magistrate, an unsatisfactory state of affairs for a populous parish at such a turbulent time. In 1793, as war broke out with France, Merceron was nominated to take Wilmot's place. Two years later, at the age of 31, he was sworn in as a magistrate of the County of Middlesex.[117]

CHAPTER V

The English Bastille

As he went through Coldbath Fields he saw
A solitary cell
And the Devil was pleased, for it gave him a hint
For improving his prisons in Hell.
                            Samuel Taylor Coleridge[118]

Henry Mayhew and John Binny's 1862 text *Criminal Prisons of London* describes Coldbath Fields Prison as follows:

The huge prison doorway itself has a curious George the Third air about it, with its inscription of black letters cut into the painted stone, telling one that it is

THE HOUSE OF
CORRECTION
FOR THE
COUNTY OF MIDDLESEX
1794

A pair of gigantic knockers, large as pantomime masks, hang low down on the dark green panels of the folding gates...whilst, arranged in tassels at the top of each side pillar, are enormous black fetters, big enough to frighten any sinful passer-by back into the paths of rectitude.[119]

Coldbath Fields, as it was colloquially known, was built in 1794 near modern-day King's Cross (today the site is occupied by the huge

Royal Mail sorting office at Mount Pleasant). A short walk away was the Sessions House on Clerkenwell Green, the courthouse of the Middlesex magistrates responsible for its supervision. A contemporary print shows the prison bathed in summer sunlight, surrounded by a tall brick wall, outside which sheep graze contentedly in the fields. But this pastoral scene betrays nothing of the brutal regime within. As a 'house of correction' the prison was designed for short-term felons: 'men and women, boys and girls...indiscriminately herded together...while smoking, gaming, singing, and every species of brutalising conversation and demeanour, tended to the unlimited advancement of crime'. Meanwhile, prison governor Thomas Aris, a former baker, 'walked about bearing in his hand a knotted rope, and ever and anon, he would seize some unlikely wight by the collar or arm, and rope's-end him severely'.[120]

It appears that for several years the supervising justices were blissfully unaware of Aris's conduct. Having spent the enormous sum of £70,000 on their showcase, their only concern seems to have been to ensure that favourable public comparisons were drawn with the nearby rival prison at Newgate, which was under the control of the City of London. The magistrates – and the public – remained in a state of ignorance until 1797, when the government ordered that Coldbath Fields be used to house a group of political prisoners and naval mutineers held without trial under Prime Minister William Pitt's 'reign of terror' against potential revolutionaries. The callous treatment of these prisoners was no different than that meted out to regular felons, but their notoriety and contacts enabled them to spread word of Aris's tyranny, leading to a national scandal. The resulting spotlight would fall not just on Aris, but also on the small group of supervising magistrates which by this time included Joseph Merceron.[121]

Merceron's appointment as a magistrate and his consequent involvement in the Coldbath Fields scandal came as several factors combined to create a period of major political and social upheaval. First and foremost, Britain had been at war with France since

Coldbath Fields Prison, Clerkenwell

February 1793; by the beginning of the following year there were serious fears of a French invasion. Second, the French Revolution had given further impetus to the campaign for greater democracy and representation in England, especially among the educated but disenfranchised middle classes. Less than a decade earlier, this campaign had attracted wide support among the governing elite, with Pitt himself at the head of a failed attempt in 1785 to reallocate parliamentary seats from the 'rotten boroughs' to the larger counties and cities. But as heads rolled in France, and as the more extreme elements within the democratic societies in England demanded a revolution of their own, a deep conservatism took root within the Pitt administration. Genuine fears of a populist uprising, in all probability opening the door to an invasion by France, were coupled in ministers' minds with the knowledge that, since the Gordon Riots of 1780, the capital's authorities were wholly incapable of dealing with major civil unrest.

Outside the City, the fragmented system of parish watch trusts – each accountable to a different controlling body – was made even less effective by the inability of vestries to co-ordinate policing with each other and with the City of London Corporation. The model of 'Bow Street Runners' adopted by the novelist and magistrate Henry Fielding in Westminster was increasingly seen as the way forward for the metropolis, leading to the creation of a number of police offices around the edges of the City from 1763. All attempts to impose co-ordination, however, were met with hostility by a public fearful of what it saw as French-style centralism. The resulting mess was exploited by criminal gangs who, by basing themselves near the boundaries of the various jurisdictions (notably those around the eastern edges of the City such as Spitalfields and Bethnal Green) were able to escape across parish borders with little fear of capture. This situation had existed for years – in 1773, Davy Wilmot had been forced to call on the Lord Mayor to deal with a band of rioting weavers taking refuge in Moorfields, just out of his jurisdiction – but had been getting worse, and the Gordon Riots in 1780 demonstrated the cost of continued inaction. Nevertheless, the strength of vested interests made for slow progress.[122]

A Bill put forward by William Pitt in 1785 to expand and formalise the system of police offices was defeated, with the chairman of the Middlesex magistrates William Mainwaring (the impact on his career as a 'trading justice' outweighing his supposed loyalty to Pitt) particularly vociferous in his opposition. Seven years later, Pitt pushed through a watered-down version of his Bill that became the Middlesex Justices Act of 1792. In order to get the Act through Parliament (the leader of the opposition, Charles James Fox, called it 'a power pregnant with abuse') the City of London was excluded from its impact, and so the issue of co-ordination across boundaries was never fully addressed. However, a number of important breakthroughs were made. By establishing a network of paid magistrates under direct Home Office control, the 1792 Act significantly weakened the power of the Middlesex Bench in judicial matters and took away the main source of income for the 'trading justices'. It also provided a small force of constables operating under government control along the lines of Fielding's Bow Street Runners and, crucially, gave Pitt the basis of a new Secret Service that would be of fundamental importance to the government in the two decades of war that followed.[123]

In the aftermath of the French Revolution, a number of reformist clubs and associations had sprung up across England. The most significant of these was the London Corresponding Society ('LCS'), formed by the shoemaker Thomas Hardy in January 1792, with the principal aim of achieving universal adult suffrage. Similar societies flourished in the larger provincial cities. Feeding on the ideas put forward by Thomas Paine in his *Rights of Man*, the first part of which was published in the same month, the LCS grew rapidly, attracting over 2,000 members within six months. It was particularly strong in London's eastern suburbs, with perhaps 50 percent of its membership living in an area spreading roughly from Moorgate to Spitalfields and Bethnal Green. Alarmed at the expansionist foreign policy of the new French government, and at signs of convergence between the LCS reformists and the French, Pitt's government issued a proclamation against seditious writings. With the onset of war in February 1793, Pitt began to clamp down firmly on potential revolutionary activity and the Home Office began to establish a network of spies.[124]

Given the magnitude of the perceived threat, this was a natural step. The Home Office had only a couple of dozen staff of its own. But, thanks to the Middlesex Justices Act, it had a ready-made network of about one hundred stipendiary magistrates and constables, mostly based in the very area – the East End – where the revolutionary fervour seemed to be at its worst. Early in 1794, provincial magistrates were asked by the Home Office to report on 'Jacobin activity' in their neighbourhoods, while in the East End a number of carefully selected stipendiary magistrates and officials began to employ spies under the co-ordination of Richard Ford, a former MP and himself one of the first stipendiaries, at the Home Office. In May 1794, principally as a result of information received from a spy who had infiltrated the LCS in Whitechapel, *habeas corpus* was suspended and several leaders of the society were arrested and charged with high treason. But weaknesses in the government's case led to the men being acquitted in a series of high profile trials.[125]

The government's problems were not helped by the exceptionally severe winter of 1794–5 that, compounded by successive poor harvests and the disruption in trade caused by the war, led to increasing food prices and political and civil unrest. May 1795 saw the advent of the 'Speenhamland system', named after the Berkshire parish that initiated it, whereby workers' wages were topped up by weekly allowances from the parish, funded out of the poor's rate and calculated by reference to the price of bread (this system, which implicitly removed the responsibility from employers to maintain a reasonable minimum wage, was eventually copied across southern England). By the late summer, a spate of food riots had swept the country. Conditions in Spitalfields and Bethnal Green were desperate: John Thelwall, one of the LCS leaders acquitted of treason, wrote of 'poor

weavers and their families crowded together in vile, filthy and un-
wholesome chambers, destitute of the most common comforts, and
even of the common necessaries of life.' It was no wonder that the
LCS found it a fertile recruiting ground.[126]

Such was the political and economic situation when, on 26th
October 1795, Joseph Merceron donned his magistrate's wig and
robes and climbed the steps of the imposing Sessions House on
Clerkenwell Green for his first Middlesex Sessions meeting. This
was a world away from Brick Lane. The Sessions House, built in the
aftermath of the Gordon Riots, was awe-inspiring and was said to
rival any courthouse in England. In their series of prints the *Microcosm of London* (1809), the artists Thomas Rowlandson and Augustus
Pugin captured the magnificent entrance hall, crowned with a circu-
lar dome. Inside, a crowd gathers in small groups, some in earnest
conversation with the magistrates in their wigs and black gowns.
Behind them a double staircase leads up to the court and committee
rooms, situated behind Corinthian pillars and a huge glass screen
that produced 'a light and very beautiful effect'.[127]

Merceron's new companions were a peculiar set: an odd mix of
doddering country squires and old-style 'trading justices', to which
had been added the new and professional – if only in the sense that
they were paid – stipendiaries from the police offices established
three years earlier. Among them were several well-known London
figures. Their chairman was the 60 year-old William Mainwaring,
one of the two MPs for Middlesex since 1784.

A staunch Tory and supporter of the Establishment, Mainwaring
had embarked on a successful legal career that led him to become
a magistrate and then, after the Gordon Riots, chairman of the
Middlesex Bench. This had hitherto been an unpaid position but on
his appointment Mainwaring became the recipient of a secret annual
government salary of £350 (later increased to £750), officially unknown to his fellow magistrates. In 1799 he went into banking,
establishing with his son George and a friend the small firm of
Mainwaring, Son, Chatteris & Co.[128]

Middlesex Sessions House, Clerkenwell

William Mainwaring

Mainwaring's fellow justices included the Whig MP George Byng: 'neither learned, eloquent nor profound' but sufficiently wealthy that the lack of these attributes did not matter. Richard Ford (as previously described, in charge of the government's embryonic spy network at the Home Office) was well known as the jilted lover of the actress Dora Jordan, who had left him for George III's son the Duke of Clarence, the future King William IV. Patrick Colquhoun, a stipendiary magistrate at David Wilmot's former office in Worship Street, would achieve lasting fame as the author of a voluminous analysis of London's policing. Energetic in the pursuit of justice, Ford and Colquhoun were somewhat exceptional. Most of their colleagues were elderly, lazy or otherwise hopelessly ineffective at their jobs, and Merceron had no difficulty in becoming rapidly influential among them.[129]

By chance, the agenda for Merceron's first meeting as a Middlesex magistrate was topped by a list of charges preferred against Thomas Aris, the governor of Coldbath Fields prison, for fraud, misconduct and abuse of his authority. But events conspired to prevent the magistrates from discussing the matter. A mile away, an enormous and restless crowd had assembled at a rally organised by the LCS in Copenhagen Fields, Islington. As news of it reached the magistrates, the Sessions was abruptly adjourned as a riot was feared, but the leaders of the demonstration managed to retain order and the crowd contented themselves with addressing a remonstrance to the King about their condition.[130]

Three days later, as George III travelled to the opening of Parliament, he was met by an even larger crowd chanting 'No War! No King! No Pitt!' and the window of the King's carriage window was shattered with a stone. The crowd's actions gave Pitt the excuse to launch a series of repressive laws which became known as the 'Gagging Acts': the Seditious Meetings Act – by which it became unlawful for more than 50 people to meet without obtaining the prior approval of the magistrates – and the Treasonable Practices Act, which prohibited the incitement to hatred or contempt of the King or government. The Gagging Acts led to public outrage, especially in London, where the Middlesex electors summoned Mainwaring and Byng to a meeting with the aim of voting an address to the King to repeal them.[131]

Merceron's appointment as a magistrate elevated him into the elite group of men governing the East End. The Tower Hamlets (the group of parishes, including Bethnal Green, sited outside the City walls immediately to the north and east of the Tower of London) formed a separate division of the County of Middlesex for administrative purposes. Its small group of magistrates met regularly at their own courthouse on Osborn Street, Whitechapel, the southward continuation of Brick Lane. Merceron soon ingratiated himself with the clique that dominated proceedings, led by Daniel Williams, surgeon and apothecary, the senior magistrate at the Whitechapel police office. The receipt of a government salary had not prevented Williams from adopting the style of the old trading justices, and he had established himself in a number of lucrative positions of responsibility, including chairing the annual meeting at which the hundreds of public houses in the Tower Hamlets were licensed.

Williams was assisted in his various duties by two local solicitors who acted as Clerks of the Peace, Charles Lush and Major Wright. These men had created an incestuous network of business and family relationships that permeated every aspect of business and government in the East End. Lush had married David Wilmot's daughter, using this connection to get himself appointed as clerk to the Worship Street police office. His son, James Wilmot Lush, was articled to Major Wright's legal practice and would later marry Wright's daughter. Charles Lush was also a paid agent of Sampson Hanbury's brewery, an obvious conflict of interest given his role as clerk to the licensing sessions. This enabled him to provide Hanbury with information and influence in the licensing process. Both he and Wright were clerks to the local Commission of Land and Assessed Taxes, of which Merceron would soon become the chairman. Williams, Wright and Lush had something else in common: their employment

George Byng and William Mainwaring

in the police offices in Whitechapel and Worship Street led to their involvement in Richard Ford's espionage activity and, as the decade continued, they would be increasingly active in employing spies.

In January 1796, as a result of the complaints against Aris, the magistrates voted to formalise their supervision of Coldbath Fields and established a Prisons Committee under the chairmanship of Dr Samuel Glasse, a classical scholar and prominent evangelical. The real driving force, however, was Daniel Williams, who was appointed Glasse's deputy, and Merceron – an increasingly close friend of Williams – soon became a regular and prominent attendee of the committee. His eagerness to participate was probably triggered by his consequential ability to influence lucrative contracts to supply and maintain the prison, rather than by any desire to engage in the governance of the penal system. Whatever his motivation, he would soon find himself embroiled in a political scandal.[132]

The committee initially brushed aside any concerns about Aris's conduct. In June, it reported to the Middlesex Sessions that 'the system adopted…by the judicious conduct of Mr Aris the Governor seemed likely to be attended with the best consequences'. The prisoners may not have agreed: three months later there was a riot at the gaol.[133]

In February 1797, continuing fears of a French invasion together with the strain created by military spending led to a run on the banks and triggered a financial crisis. The Bank of England's reserves of bullion and coin fell alarmingly, forcing a temporary suspension of cash payments. Merceron was one of 2,000 merchants and bankers who signed a formal agreement to trade with paper money, in an attempt to boost public confidence in the banking system. Two months later, the crisis reached the Royal Navy when the sailors of the Channel fleet lying at Spithead, off Portsmouth, mutinied over pay and conditions. Despite government suspicions that the mutiny was linked to revolutionary activity elsewhere, it soon became clear that the sailors' revolt, though firm, was peaceful and within a few weeks the government agreed to their demands.[134]

Worse was to come. In May, the men of the navy's North Sea fleet at the Nore, in the Thames estuary, also mutinied. This time, the action was more overtly political. With the mutineers threatening to block the Thames shipping lanes, the government intervened aggressively and the revolt was put down. The Duke of Portland, the Home Secretary, was convinced that an LCS conspiracy was at work and sent Daniel Williams to Portsmouth to investigate. Williams, however, was unequivocal in dismissing any LCS connections, assuring Portland:

> ...that no such connexion or correspondence...ever did exist... By stopping up the mouth of the Thames they were suspected of designs for which [we] can by no means give them credit... the want of beer and fresh beef prompted them to revenge, and that and nothing else induced them to interrupt the trade of the river. It was done on the spur of the occasion...with the assistance of the newspapers only...[135]

This was not the conclusion the Home Secretary had sought. Disregarding it, Portland wrote to the admiral leading the court martial for the mutineers' leader, Richard Parker, stating 'you may prove almost anything you like against him, for he has been guilty of everything that's bad.' Parker was duly found guilty and hanged from the yardarm of his ship, sending a clear indication of the government's firmness to all would-be revolutionaries. Dozens of other sailors had been arrested. Portland, keen to house the mutineers in conditions discouraging further revolt, wrote directly to Thomas Aris, instructing him that 24 of the mutineers were to be delivered to Coldbath Fields, kept separately within the gaol but otherwise treated in the same manner as other prisoners.[136]

This was a remarkable development. In giving his instructions directly to Aris, Portland was circumventing the normal chain of command of the prison. Aris was employed by the County of Middlesex, not the Home Office, and as such took his orders from the magistrates. But as well as being Home Secretary, Portland also happened to be the father of the Lord Lieutenant of Middlesex – the officer appointing the county's magistrates on behalf of the Crown. When Aris reported Portland's intervention to the Middlesex Prisons Committee at their meeting on 13th September, the magistrates were angry but took no further action. But the seeds had been sown for a situation in which neither the Home Office nor the magistrates publicly accepted accountability for the treatment of the political prisoners.

Regardless, Portland and the supervising magistrates must have clearly understood how Aris treated those confined to his care. Even before the mutineers arrived, a group of political prisoners already held at the gaol embarked upon what seems to have been a well-planned campaign to publicise their plight. A letter had appeared in the *Morning Chronicle* in which John Smith, an LCS member held without trial on charges of sedition under the Gagging Acts, made various allegations of improper treatment and called the prison 'a Bastille'. Another prisoner, Joseph Burke, sent a letter – intercepted by the magistrates – to his lawyer in which he 'desired it to be made as public as possible that if he dies here it may be seen by what means he has been murdered.'[137]

The magistrates, unused to dealing with prisoners capable of articulating their complaints in the press, were embarrassed and furious. It seems never to have crossed their minds that there might have been any substance to the complaints. Merceron was a member of a small committee that summoned both Smith and Burke to explain themselves. The accounts of these interrogations reveal only too clearly the prisoners' fears of Aris and their lack of confidence in the magistrates to uphold their complaints.[138]

The year 1798 brought a further escalation of revolutionary fervour and with it a corresponding ratcheting up of Pitt's counter-measures. An LCS splinter group of determined revolutionaries had teamed up with the United Irishmen, a like-minded group in Ireland where poverty and the repression of the Catholic population had created a violent hatred of English rule, even to the point of welcoming a French invasion. In the early months of the year, three United Irishmen, including the Irish politician Arthur O'Connor, were captured with papers discussing connivance with the French. Around the same time, Home Office spies began to report the existence of an English offshoot, the United Englishmen, whose membership included several prominent LCS men and who were most active in the streets between Shoreditch and Spitalfields, particularly the tangle of alleys and courts around Brick Lane. Merceron, as the local magistrate, major landlord and owner of several public houses where these men congregated, found himself on the front line of the government's response.[139]

The authorities' monitoring operation was centred in the Worship Street police office in Shoreditch. At its heart was the chief clerk Charles Lush, Merceron's friend and solicitor. Chief among the spies was John Tunbridge, a Shoreditch hairdresser who had infiltrated the LCS, the United Englishmen and a sister organisation called the Sons of Liberty. Tunbridge told the authorities that the United Englishmen and Sons of Liberty were regularly practising military-style drill at night in the garden of *The Seven Stars* – one of Merceron's alehouses – near Brick Lane, where they made it 'a rule to begin singing as soon as they had done business, that people might have less suspicion of them and might think it a club'. Another public house kept under close watch was *The Turkish Slave* (also owned by Merceron and situated just two doors from his Brick Lane office), which was raided in 1799, the magistrates confiscating a portrait of Robespierre from over the fireplace.[140]

It seems highly likely that Merceron's ownership of these republican lairs facilitated the intelligence gathering process. Together with Daniel Williams and Sampson Hanbury, he already had a stranglehold over the local alehouse trade. Charles Lush was not only a spymaster but was also clerk to the licensing magistrates and a paid agent of Hanbury's. Between them, these men decided where new pubs were built, who would keep them and whether they would be licensed. The innkeepers were invariably employees either of Merceron or Hanbury. From a Home Office standpoint it was a perfect arrangement, keeping revolutionary societies above ground where they could be watched and infiltrated.

The mounting intelligence let Pitt to the conviction that a further clampdown on the LCS was necessary. The escape of seven Nore mutineers from Coldbath Fields in April 1798 provoked him to decisive action. On 18th April, 19 members of the United Englishmen were arrested at a public house in Clerkenwell. The next day, 16 members of the LCS central committee were arrested as they met in nearby Drury Lane. On 20th April Pitt renewed the suspension of *habeas corpus,* enabling him to detain those arrested indefinitely without trial. Once again, the magistrates' concerns were overridden and the majority of the detainees were delivered into the care of Governor Aris at Coldbath Fields.[141]

The Nore mutineers' escape exacerbated the tensions between the Home Office and the magistrates over exactly who was responsible for the political prisoners. An increasingly embarrassed Portland wrote angrily to William Mainwaring, blaming the magistrates for the escape. On 23rd April Merceron and his colleagues gathered at the prison to consider their response to Portland's letter. They were in a defensive mood. Quite naturally, the magistrates were insistent that the problem stemmed from the use of the prison for a purpose for which it was never designed. They claimed that the mutineers were 'desperate and refractory in the extreme', and that the practice of holding state prisoners in the gaol was 'very detrimental' to the management system in place.[142]

Soon afterwards, the magistrates' case was strengthened when Aris discovered evidence of a plot among the remaining mutineers to storm the prison. The justices used this as an opportunity to attempt to pass responsibility back to the Home Office. They wrote again to Portland, demanding to be relieved and stating that the mutineers required 'a degree of vigilance and coercion incompatible with the system of this prison'. But Portland had nowhere else to keep the men. He stood his ground, the magistrates' pleas came to nothing and the prisoners remained at Coldbath Fields.[143]

The best known and most controversial of the political prisoners held at Coldbath Fields was Colonel Edward Marcus Despard. Born into a well-off Anglo-Irish family, Despard was a former army hero, colonial administrator and brother-in-arms of Lord Nelson. His talents, however, had been spurned by the government. Seduced by the works of Thomas Paine, he had become a leading light of the LCS and now, at least according to the Home Office spies, had turned into a dangerous revolutionary. The authorities were convinced that Despard was at the centre of revolutionary plotting among the United Englishmen and United Irishmen. Spies had warned of an armed uprising in London that would form the cue for a French invasion. It was rumoured that George III was to be assassinated, and that Despard was among the leaders of the plot.[144]

Much of the government's evidence against Despard was hearsay. Nevertheless, the colonel had been arrested and was held, without trial or any right of appeal, in a cell just a few feet square, without a fire and which flooded when it rained. Unlike his fellow prisoners, Despard was a gentleman with friends in high places, including several Members of Parliament. His wife, Catherine, had agitated constantly on his behalf since his arrest and protested in writing to the Duke of Portland about the conditions in which Despard was held. When Portland failed to respond, Catherine tried another angle, contacting two of her husband's MP friends: John Courtenay, an erudite Irish wit and consistent opponent of Pitt's administration, and the 28-year-old Radical Sir Francis Burdett. It was a move that would rapidly lead to Coldbath Fields becoming a source of serious embarrassment for the government.[145]

Burdett, who would many years later be described by Benjamin Disraeli as 'the Greatest Gentleman I ever knew', was a fifth generation baronet and scion of an ancient Midlands political family, just setting out on the journey that would make him the fashionable favourite of Westminster. Strikingly handsome, his tall and spare

Sir Francis Burdett

frame – capped with an unruly mop of curly black hair and usually shown to great effect by white velvet breeches, turned down boots, blue frock coat and white cravat – made him a popular subject for the political caricaturists of the day.

Wealthy in his own right, Burdett became spectacularly rich in 1793 by marrying Sophia Coutts, heiress to the banking empire. In 1796 Sophia's father, Thomas Coutts, had purchased a seat in Parliament for his son-in-law and by 1798 Burdett had developed a reputation as a persistent opponent of the war with France and the government's campaign of domestic repression, stating that 'the best part of my character is a strong feeling of indignation at injustice.' Catherine Despard's appeal to him coincided with a dinner party at which Burdett was shown letters from the political prisoners written with wooden splinters dipped in their own blood. Burdett's indignation duly blazed, and he and Courtenay readily agreed to intervene on Despard's behalf. Towards the end of 1798, Burdett visited Coldbath Fields three times to see for himself the conditions in which prisoners were being kept. His intervention had an immediate effect: after his first visit, the idea of unwelcome publicity stirring up public agitation led the Duke of Portland to instruct Aris to remove Despard and five other prisoners to better accommodation.[146]

On 21st December, the House of Commons debated Pitt's Bill to renew the suspension of *habeas corpus* and the conditions at Coldbath Fields became public knowledge. Opposing the renewal, Courtenay and Burdett disclosed what they had seen when visiting the prison: tiny, narrow cells with no means of heating or lighting and no furniture apart from poor beds. Courtenay blamed the supervising magistrates. In a pointed reference to Dr Glasse, he said 'he understood that some reverend gentlemen were among the magistrates who managed it; and who, no doubt, kindly subjected their prisoners to so much pain in this world, that the less punishment might be inflicted on them in the next'.[147]

Courtenay took great delight in recounting to the House his journey with Burdett to Coldbath Fields. They had taken a cab,

Sir Francis Burdett visiting Coldbath Fields

and as an experiment he had asked the driver merely to take him 'to the Bastille'. The driver, he told MPs, had set them down at the prison gates without needing any further explanation. The story was ridiculed by the pro-government press, most notably in a caricature, *Citizens Visiting the Bastille*, by James Gillray. In the print, Burdett seeks admittance at the prison gates, saying 'I want only to see if my Brother Citizens have Candles, and Fires and good Beds, and clean Girls, for their accommodation…'. In his pocket can be seen 'secret correspondence' with Despard and other United Irishmen. Aris, jangling a huge set of keys, refuses to let him in, while Courtenay drives up in a cab, telling the driver 'To the Bastille, you dog!'[148]

Courtenay's attack provoked an immediate reaction from William Mainwaring in defence of his fellow magistrates and Governor Aris. He denied Burdett's and Courtenay's accusations. Governor Aris, he insisted, was 'remarkable for his humanity', and Mainwaring knew of 'no severity being used…every care was exerted for preserving the health and comfort of the persons confined.' He concluded, with some force, that 'there was not a more comfortable place of the kind in the whole country'.[149]

Mainwaring received strong support from William Wilberforce MP, an ally of Pitt who had had significant input into the drafting of the Gagging Acts. His information on Coldbath Fields came directly from Glasse, who was a close friend. Wilberforce concurred with Mainwaring's statement, reading out a letter from Glasse that alleged that Courtenay's and Burdett's claims were gross misrepresentations. According to Glasse, the prisoners 'enjoyed good health, and were allowed as good food as ever [he] had at his own table'.

The conviction with which Mainwaring and Wilberforce made their statements had satisfied most MPs. Pitt concluded the debate by claiming that the security situation in the country had recently improved, precisely because of the firm measures he was now proposing to renew. In the poorly attended vote that followed, almost the last parliamentary business before Christmas, Burdett and Courtenay were hopelessly outnumbered and the government won by 96 votes to just 6. It appeared that Merceron and his fellow magistrates were off the hook.[150]

CHAPTER VI

Infamy, Oppression, Cruelty and Extortion

*Pride and obstinacy are the predominant parts of
Mr Pitt's character, right or wrong he never yields,
and he now chose to show his power by protecting
the gaoler in defiance of public opinion.*

Robert Southey[151]

Immediately after the Christmas of 1798, hostilities were renewed. A letter from Catherine Despard had been published in the *Courier* and the *Morning Post* outlining her husband's callous treatment, outraging the government with its outspoken criticism of the Duke of Portland. In the Commons, tempers flared. Courtenay gave a passionate defence of Mrs Despard. The attackers were quick to suggest foul play: Pitt's young protégé (and future Prime Minister) George Canning claimed that Mrs Despard was 'an illiterate woman', who could not possibly have been the true author of the letter. *The Times* stooped even lower:

> Mrs Despard, who writes so elegantly in one of the Morning papers, is by birth a Negress; whom Colonel Despard picked up while serving in America. As we have never yet heard of her receiving a polished education, some people are inclined to doubt whether she is the authoress of the letters that have appeared in print, and of those which have been addressed to the Secretary of State in her name.[152]

Reassured by the magnitude of their victory in the recent vote, Pitt and Portland pressed their advantage. Richard Ford coached Aris in swearing a deposition, which was printed in *The Times* and detailed Burdett's latest visit to the prison. In it, the governor firmly rebutted the accusations of cruelty levelled against him, alleged that Burdett was friendly with some of the LCS prisoners and, more disturbingly, some of the Nore mutineers. Aris also insinuated that Burdett was the real author of Catherine Despard's letter to the *Morning Post.*[153]

Burdett described Aris's deposition as an atrocious libel and categorically denied knowing any of the prisoners, other than Despard, prior to his visit. The damage, however, had been done. Portland immediately used the accusations to justify banning Burdett from setting foot in any prison in the kingdom. But in order to prevent a further outcry from Burdett's supporters he also instructed the Middlesex magistrates to 'make due enquiry into all the circumstances of this case'.[154]

On 10th January 1799, Merceron joined his fellow magistrates at Clerkenwell Green to begin their enquiries. Aris read out his deposition to them and repeated his claims that Burdett's conduct was destabilising the prison, insisting that the baronet's visits 'had excited so turbulent a spirit among the mutineers and others' that he feared great danger.[155]

The magistrates' investigation lasted for several days and, from the beginning, had all the hallmarks of a fix. The day after it began, a Grand Jury – supposedly comprising disinterested members of the public but in reality a hand-picked list of government supporters – visited Coldbath Fields, reported 'their perfect satisfaction of the cleanliness of the prison, the wholesomeness of the provision [and] the treatment of the prisoners' and expressed their opinion that 'it does honour to the magistrates and others who have the direction and management of the same'. The magistrates steadfastly refused to hear directly from any of the prisoners, although certain written evidence was admitted, including a paper found in the possession of an LCS prisoner that corroborated many of Burdett's and Courtenay's accusations. According to this paper, the LCS prisoners had been locked in dark, damp, solitary cells for 23 hours a day, for six weeks at a time, with just a bag of straw, a blanket and thin rug, a tin can and a chamber pot for company. Food rations were limited to bread and water. Aris was accused of routinely threatening violence and the use of iron fetters should any prisoner complain of his treatment to anyone outside the prison. But when Aris was cross-examined about these allegations he denied them, admitting only that he had beaten one of the mutineers with a stick and with his fists for his own defence.[156]

The pattern was repeated over the ensuing days. The magistrates would hear second-hand allegations of abuse, never deeming it necessary to examine the prisoners making the allegations, but accepting without hesitation the denials of the prison officials concerned. An example concerned a letter sent by a group of LCS prisoners to the coroner conducting an inquest on a prisoner who had died in custody. According to the letter, the dead man had been committed merely as a vagrant, 'barely clothed' and 'put in a cold, damp cell in the midst of a severe frost without fire'. 'Since we have been here', the prisoners concluded, 'we have witnessed a sum of misery concealed from public view by arts which secure its authors from deception and which if known would not be suffered in a civilised country.' But the coroner was unmoved and announced that he was 'perfectly satisfied' that the man had died a natural death 'by visitation of God'.[157]

When the inquiry came to the case of Colonel Despard, Merceron and his fellow magistrates interviewed several prison officers, who all denied ill-treating the colonel. Remarkably, Aris claimed that Despard had told him that he would never have allowed his wife to write to the *Morning Post,* had he known of it. Days earlier, the magistrates had heard Aris swear under oath that he had overheard Burdett discussing the proposed publication of Mrs Despard's letter with both Colonel and Mrs Despard. Now, he was insisting that Despard had not known of the letter until after it was published, yet still the magistrates took no action.[158]

Courtenay and Burdett had not given up. With Burdett banned from the prison, Courtenay helped Despard draw up a petition and presented it to Parliament on 20th February. In it, Despard affirmed that his wife's letter to the papers had been correct in all material respects. He listed further examples of his ill treatment and requested to be examined directly by MPs. A ruffled Pitt resorted to his mastery of parliamentary procedure to scupper the idea. Whilst acknowledging that Despard's 'extremely material' allegations warranted a full investigation, he pointed out that the form of the colonel's petition was incorrect and a breach of parliamentary privilege, meaning it could not be received by the House.[159]

Frustrated, Burdett now gave notice of his intention that, despite the fact that his own investigations had been circumvented by Portland's banning order, he intended to bring forward a motion regarding the scandal at the prison.[160]

This news stung Pitt and Portland into action. On 5th March, two days before Burdett's motion was due, the House was presented with the result of the magistrates' inquiry, fully exonerating Aris's conduct. The following day, in a move that could only have been initiated with the approval of Pitt, a Tory MP proposed a Select Committee to enquire into the state of the prison. It was a masterstroke. Burdett could not possibly argue against the proposal and was forced to withdraw his own motion, only to find himself and Courtenay excluded from the Committee.[161]

The Select Committee met over the next few weeks. Its terms of reference, strongly influenced by Portland, simply followed the path already trodden by Merceron and his colleagues: Aris and his staff were interviewed in detail, but it was not thought necessary or appropriate to interview Despard or the other prisoners. The MPs did interview some of the magistrates – when asked about Despard's living conditions, one old Etonian could not see any cause for complaint and likened the colonel's bed to his own at school. Some new information did emerge – a heavily indebted Aris had borrowed money from several of his prisoners – but on 19th April the Committee duly delivered the whitewash that Pitt desired. The magistrates could not be faulted: the Committee felt their conduct had been 'exemplary and meritorious'; it was 'extremely improbable, that any impropriety of conduct, or unnecessary severity in the gaoler, could long have escaped their notice'. The Committee saved its only criticism for Burdett and Courtenay, stating its 'full and direct refutation of the unfounded statements, and absurd and wicked reports, which have been industriously circulated with respect to the prison.'[162]

Burdett was furious at this further cover-up and determined to oppose the report vehemently when it came before the Commons. On 21st May he proposed a motion to reject the report, describing it as an attempt to hide a 'foul, premeditated system of torture and iniquity'. He described Aris as a monster who turned every article in the prison to his own profit, and described the cells as 'fitter for beasts than men'. Pitt's supporters responded with a succession of lame defences. One reminded Burdett that Aris's 'humane character' had been sworn to by several 'distinguished persons' – by which he meant the prison surgeon, chaplain and turnkeys, all reliant on Aris for their employment. William Mainwaring acknowledged that Aris had behaved improperly in borrowing money from prisoners, but saw no evidence of extortion. Burdett's only real support came from Richard Brinsley Sheridan who insisted that Aris, the magistrates and the Committee had failed to do their duty. It was ultimately to no avail, and the House rejected Burdett's motion by 147 votes to just 6.[163]

A week later Merceron was back at Coldbath Fields where Colonel Despard was at last brought in front of the magistrates at his own request to refute Aris's evidence. It was too late to make any difference. The government decided to disperse the political prisoners around the country in order to defuse the situation and, in August, Despard was moved to Shrewsbury prison. For the time being, his departure removed the spotlight from Coldbath Fields, Aris and from a relieved Merceron and his colleagues.[164]

The following spring, the nation's attention was diverted by the sensational news of what appeared to be a plot by revolutionaries to assassinate George III, a development that seemed to justify everything the government had been saying about the threats posed to life and liberty by Despard and his friends. The government's response to the crisis over the ensuing weeks shows signs of having been finely orchestrated. Four men who played key parts in the resulting investigation and trial (including the jury foreman, another juror and a key prosecution witness) were Merceron's close associates, men who were in the habit of working under his immediate direction. The resulting trial would lead to Merceron acquiring his most treasured possession.

On the morning of Thursday 15th May, the King was carrying out an inspection of army field exercises in Hyde Park when a member of his entourage, standing just a few yards away, was shot in the thigh by a musket ball. Unsurprisingly, none of the soldiers present admitted to being the culprit and in the confusion of the exercise it was impossible to identify who had fired the shot. Efforts were made to play down the episode and pass it off, at least publicly, as an accident, but over the course of the day rumours spread around the capital, becoming twisted and exaggerated to the point where no-one could be quite sure what had happened.[165]

That evening, the royal family travelled to Sheridan's Drury Lane theatre for a command performance starring the celebrated Mrs Jordan. Thousands had gathered to satisfy themselves of the King's well-being, with the theatre unusually crowded. As the King moved to the front of the royal box to acknowledge the applause, a man in the pit fired at him with a horse pistol. The shot narrowly missed (the ball was later found embedded in the cornice of the royal box, about two feet from where the King had been standing) and the would-be assassin was rapidly overpowered by his neighbours. As it happened, chief among them was Merceron's friend Major Wright, East End solicitor, clerk of the peace and probable spymaster, who was sitting immediately in front of the man. It was Wright who first collared the assassin and picked up the weapon, still smelling of gunpowder, from the floor. Somewhat surprisingly, he was allowed to retain it.[166]

To the public, it seemed at first as though the feared revolution had begun. Yet, despite the obvious appearance that the King was under attack from Jacobin or republican elements, the government almost immediately announced that this was not the case. It was soon understood that the Hyde Park shooting had been caused by the inadvertent mixing of live and blank ammunition: 'plainly and out of all question an accident', as the Foreign Secretary Lord Grenville wrote next day to his brother. Over the next 36 hours, as senior ministers interrogated the Drury Lane gunman and interviewed witnesses to the incident, it began to emerge that while a genuine attempt on the King's life, it had not been the organised launch of a revolution but rather an insane attempt to trigger the second coming of Christ. The culprit was a former soldier, James Hadfield, who had lost his mind after being wounded in action, captured and tortured in France in 1794. On Hadfield's return to England, the army had simply discharged him onto the streets of London. He had subsequently fallen under the influence of Bannister Truelock, an equally mad itinerant cobbler and preacher, who persuaded Hadfield he could trigger the apocalypse by killing the King and dying in the attempt. [167]

It seemed clear that Hadfield was at least partially mad; and when Truelock was hauled in for questioning he too muttered darkly to ministers that 'Gog and Magog were about to appear very soon, that all kings are to be put down and their power taken away'. Within 24 hours of the shooting, Lord Grenville was confidently telling his brother that Hadfield: 'is a soldier...discharged from the 15th Light Dragoons in 1796 for lunacy. There seems little doubt that he will on his trial establish that plea'. The government was quick to promulgate this explanation: the next morning, *The Times* gave a detailed account of Hadfield's madness. Privately, though, there remained serious fears that Hadfield, mad or otherwise, was the dupe of determined revolutionaries.[168]

James Hadfield attempts to assassinate King George III

That weekend, as the government continued publicly to reassure people that the shooting was the work of a lone madman, Richard Ford's spy network went into overdrive to discover the truth. Perhaps unsurprisingly, the results were conflicting, as several paid informers attempted to cash in on the crisis by exaggerating their reports to make them more interesting. At Worship Street, Charles Lush met with the spy 'T' (presumably the hairdresser, Tunbridge), but his subsequent report to Ford was generally dismissive of T's suggestions linking Hadfield to the LCS. Next day, the Worship Street magistrates wrote to Portland with intelligence of disaffection in the armed forces stationed around Shoreditch. William Hamilton Reid, a regular informer, sent in three letters claiming Hadfield's and Truelock's madness was affected and linking both men to 'infidel societies'. The following Tuesday, 20th May, Ford received a further letter (on which he scribbled 'from a very confidential person who can be depended on') that listed Hadfield, Truelock and the pawnbroker who had provided Hadfield with the pistol as LCS delegates. More worryingly, the same source stated that the LCS had infiltrated several army regiments with the intention of corrupting soldiers; the three regiments cited included Hadfield's, the 15th light dragoons.[169]

Over the next few weeks, preparations for Hadfield's trial for high treason polarised the political classes. Radical politicians subscribed a fund for his defence and hired the future Lord Chancellor, Thomas Erskine, to act as defence counsel.[170]

By this time, the government had accepted that, based on the opinion of several leading doctors, Hadfield was suffering from at least sporadic insanity. Despite the claims of several informers, and tempting as it may have been to blame the assassination attempt on the LCS and its supporters, ministers also seem to have rejected the possibility that Hadfield was merely the tool of revolutionary agents. As the law stood, sporadic insanity was insufficient to justify a 'not guilty' verdict. But the government took no chances, rigging the jury. The 'long list' from which the jury was selected included five of Merceron's fellow East End magistrates including Daniel Williams, who as head of the Whitechapel police office could hardly be supposed to be neutral. Unsurprisingly, he was objected to by the defence. The final 12 jurors nevertheless included two magistrates, Luke Flood (the foreman) and Thomas Windle, who would both be revealed a decade later as having direct links to Merceron's corrupt licensing of the very same alehouses used by the radical societies in the 1790s. Windle, in particular, would be accused of acting under Merceron's immediate direction and of being indemnified by him 'for everything he did'.[171]

Hadfield's trial took place on 26th June 1800 at the Court of King's Bench in Westminster Hall. There being no doubt that Hadfield had tried to shoot the King, the case turned simply on whether he had been insane at the time and the prosecution made no attempt to insinuate a wider plot. A number of witnesses testified to the events in the theatre. Among them was Major Wright, who explained how he had found the pistol on the floor in capturing Hadfield after the shooting. Thomas Erskine, leading the defence, made a brilliant speech, supported by the testimony of a stream of witnesses, that made it clear beyond doubt that Hadfield's crime was driven by insanity brought on by the wounds he had sustained in fighting for king and country. Eventually, the Lord Chief Justice halted the trial, with half of Erskine's witnesses still unheard. Announcing that he was convinced by Erskine's case, and setting an important new legal precedent, he instructed the jury to find Hadfield 'not guilty, he being under the influence of insanity at the time the act was committed'. Hadfield was taken off to Bethlem, where he spent 41 long years before dying of tuberculosis aged 69.[172]

No-one at the time seemed to take any interest in the fate of Hadfield's pistol. After finding it on the floor of the theatre where Hadfield had dropped it, Major Wright was allowed to take it home with him. The next day, he took it to the Home Office and identified it as evidence in the presence of the Prince Regent. He produced it again at the trial and, remarkably, was then allowed to keep it, at which point it disappeared from public view. Back home in the East

James Hadfield's pistol

End, however, Wright showed off his trophy to his friends. He would dine off the story of his involvement for the rest of his life, and on his death his effects included a print of the attempted assassination. The gun, however, is not mentioned in his will. Before he died, Wright had given it to his old friend Joseph Merceron. The weapon has remained in the quiet possession of the Merceron family ever since.[173]

Although neither of the shootings of 15th May 1800 were proved to be genuine revolutionary acts, they proved useful to the government in justifying its increasingly authoritarian tactics. In particular, the publicity over Hadfield's trial meant that the threat of revolution was still in the public mind when, in July, Sir Francis Burdett renewed his attack on the Middlesex magistrates over a further scandal at Coldbath Fields.[174]

That May, just a fortnight after the events at Drury Lane, a Middlesex jury attending a trial for attempted rape expressed alarm at the condition of Mary Rich, the 13-year-old victim in the case. Investigating further, they were horrified to discover that Mary, homeless and unemployed, had been confined to Coldbath Fields as a vagabond pending her testimony and held on bread and water for more than a month. The jurors resolved to inspect the prison themselves. After several visits they reported their findings to the magistrates at Clerkenwell Green. The jury confirmed that prisoners awaiting trial were treated 'most improperly', held on bread and water and without adequate bedding. Mary Rich, it seemed, was just one of many examples of such treatment.[175]

Displaying a bias that had become routine, Merceron and his colleagues went through the motions of conducting their own investigations. The Prisons Committee interviewed the prison nurse – herself a prisoner given special privileges by Aris in return for sexual favours – who described Rich as 'a bad little girl' and told the magistrates 'that she had been with several boys on the stairs in a way not proper to mention.' Taking the nurse's story on trust, the justices dismissed the jury's concerns. Their report, signed by Daniel Williams, concluded that 'Mary Rich was properly treated during her confinement and that every necessary care and attention had been paid to her by the Governor and the Doctor and that she had lived better since she had been in the prison than in her usual mode of living with her father and mother'.[176]

This time, however, the magistrates' attempt to hush up what was going on under their noses was doomed to fail. Jury foreman William Dickie, disgusted with the magistrates' response, sent Burdett a copy of the notes he had taken during his visits to the prison. Crucially, one of the jury's visits had been unannounced and, catching Aris by surprise, had exposed the appalling conditions of vagrants, debtors and pauper prisoners carefully concealed from the jury's previous official inspections. Dickie's notes gave further evidence of abuse, citing the prisoners' hesitancy in giving evidence for fear of reprisals, the insufficiency of food and warmth and claims that Aris would frequently beat prisoners with a stick.[177]

Dickie's evidence enabled Burdett to reignite his campaign against the magistrates. After the cover-up of the previous year and the opprobrium heaped upon him by Pitt and Portland, here was evidence suggesting he had been right all along. Burdett tabled the papers in the Commons on 11th July and called for an immediate investigation.[178]

Sheridan, in seconding Burdett's motion, made an impassioned speech claiming that 'never was so complicated a scene of infamy, oppression, cruelty and extortion exhibited before Parliament.' It was clear, he continued, that the magistrates had been fooled by Aris into giving a favourable account of the state of the prison, 'for when any persons went to visit the prison, it was the practice of the Governor only to show them those places which would best bear inspection, and everything that would tend to criminate him in the least, was studiously kept out of sight'. But he 'could not but implicate' Williams, Merceron and their colleagues who, by their own negligence, had made things easy for Aris. The Prisons Committee 'did nothing more than meet in the committee room and examine – whom? – the very persons from whom they could least expect any impartial accounts whether or not the prisoners were properly taken care of – the gaoler, the doctor and the parson.' As for the magistrates' contemptuous dismissal of the case of Mary Rich:

> ...it was a strange mode of arguing, that because her parents were poor, the wretched meagre diet of the gaol was excellent food; yet it was offered as an apology by the magistrates that the poor girl came from the school of wretchedness and poverty to that abominable gaol. But how came she there?...The poor child charged some person with committing a rape on her...but she was committed to be detained as a witness. Where in the law of England, do the magistrates read that a person complaining of an injury, a prosecutor, is to be detailed in his own cause; and kept on bread and water?'[179]

Furious, his credibility on the line, William Mainwaring rose to defend his fellow magistrates. Dickie's papers, he pointed out, were not the official jury report presented to the magistrates but instead 'unauthentic, inflammatory and false,' prepared solely for Burdett's use. Mainwaring's point struck home: Dickie's notes had no official status and it was improper parliamentary procedure for Burdett to table them in support of his motion. For all Sheridan's eloquence, Mainwaring had won the magistrates, and the government, a crucial breathing space.[180]

The next few days were difficult for the Middlesex magistrates. Having put his reputation on the line, Mainwaring desperately needed to establish the facts and called a Prisons Committee meeting for Friday, 18th July. By this time, a further jury had inspected the prison. The committee, dominated by Mainwaring, Merceron and Williams, summoned the foreman for a debriefing. The foreman confirmed that the jury's inspection had revealed no issues, but that while drinking in a nearby pub afterwards they had been approached by William Dickie. On hearing their findings, Dickie exclaimed: 'Ha! There Mr Aris has gammoned you, for you have not seen that place which you ought to have seen, nor have you seen the man who was obliged to drink his own urine for want of being supplied with water.' As a result, the jury had returned to the prison for a further inspection that morning. Worried at what would emerge from the jury's report, the magistrates resorted to intimidation. Each member of the jury was hauled individually in front of the magistrates and interrogated. Not one was willing to state that he had seen anything to corroborate Dickie's story.[181]

The following Monday, 21st July, Burdett announced in the Commons that he was expecting to receive further damning evidence of abuse on which he would move for an inquiry on 30th July, just before the end of the parliamentary session. This time the Prime Minister was noticeably shaken. Pitt was deeply unwell: 17 years at the head of government had worn him out and triggered a collapse in his health. He tried hard to put Burdett off, saying that an inquiry 'would irritate and goad the public mind', with the risk that 'passion was likely to prevail over reason', and suggested that given the volume of other parliamentary business still to be transacted, Burdett should defer the motion altogether until the next session. Burdett stood firm.[182]

The next day Burdett made a powerful speech in support of an immediate inquiry by the whole House. He had obtained further evidence of Aris's abuses, outlining the case of a prisoner who had died of starvation in the prison but whose condition had been concealed from the visiting jury just five days earlier. Burdett hinted that further sensational disclosures would follow. Sheridan listed the mounting evidence against Aris and reminded the House that Burdett had been 'indecently and unjustly' banned from visiting the prison, solely on the basis of the governor's evidence. Then came a critical intervention. George Tierney, a prominent opponent of Pitt, suggested a compromise: Burdett should withdraw his motion for an immediate investigation by the whole House and propose instead an address to the king, requesting a Royal Commission of Enquiry. Because of the impending summer recess, this would give Pitt an opportunity to get back on the front foot but would give Burdett the inquiry he wanted. Pitt had nowhere left to turn. Accepting defeat, he dropped Mainwaring, stating that if a motion for a Royal Commission were pressed, he would not oppose it.[183]

Burdett and Sheridan were overjoyed. The next day, Sheridan wrote to his wife: 'Yesterday's debate turned out more to my satisfaction than almost anything I ever took a part in since I have been in the House of Commons...I really think I smote Pitt's conscience. In short we carried our point.' The philosopher and penal reformer Jeremy Bentham, writing the same day, agreed: 'What a debate yesterday about prisons in the House! ...Mainwaring seems given up by Pitt and his reputation ruined...'[184]

In September 1800 the Royal Commission commenced its inquiry. It was chaired by William Huskisson, an up-and-coming MP who would later find a lasting fame as the world's first railway fatality when he was knocked down and killed by Stephenson's *Rocket* in 1830. Burdett and his friends excitedly awaited the outcome, but it turned out that Pitt had outmanoeuvred them yet again. The intervening summer vacation had given the Prime Minister time to ensure that the Commission's terms of reference were tightly framed, limiting the scope of enquiry to documentary evidence and excluding any examination of witnesses under oath. The inquiry was not even held at the prison: the commissioners were forced to assemble instead at the nearby Clerkenwell Sessions House because of an outbreak of food poisoning at the prison.[185]

As so often with political scandals, delaying tactics and the careful restriction of an enquiry's scope had allowed the public's anger to subside. Although Burdett's claims were vindicated (and despite Pitt pinning the blame squarely on the magistrates), no one was held accountable, no serious corrective action was taken and Aris remained in place. Burdett continued vainly to complain of further abuses, but little notice was taken in Parliament. In May 1801, the Lord Chief Justice threw out a prosecution against Aris for cruelty to a prisoner, refusing to accept that the supervising magistrates could possibly be at fault. He had known some of them for many years, he said, and speaking of the magistrates in general he asserted that 'men more honourable…more inclined beneficially to assist…those who called on them for protection, did not exist among the community of this kingdom.'[186]

The magistrates could relax. Indeed Williams, who as chairman of the Prisons Committee was probably most responsible for the scandal, was knighted the following year. Aris, meanwhile, obtained damages of £700 against William Dickie for defamation. Unable to pay, Dickie was confined to the Fleet prison and died there almost five years later.[187]

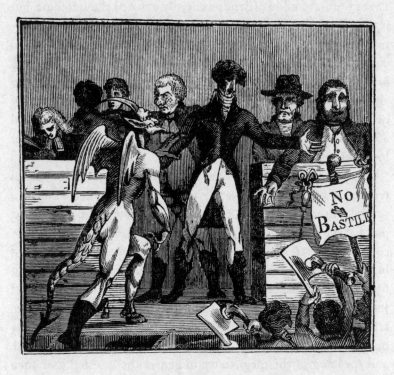

THE

SCUM UPPERMOST

WHEN THE

Middlesex Porridge-Pot Boils Over!!

———

Entered at Stationer's-Hall.

Middlesex Election Ballad, 1802

CHAPTER VII

Democracy in Action

'Ho! Ho!' – cries the Devil, 'Come bring me my boots!
Here's a kettle of fish that my appetite suits
To Brentford an airing
I'll take – 'tis past bearing
That my friends should be fetter'd by Justice Mainwaring:
But young Burdett I like, and we'll form a connection
To abolish gaol, gibbet and House of Correction.'

Election Ballad[188]

Their conduct voted 'exemplary and meritorious' by the House of Commons, their honour and benevolence acclaimed in open court by the Lord Chief Justice; the Middlesex magistrates responded by neglecting their responsibilities even further.

Merceron had joined the Prisons Committee enthusiastically in 1797, driven more by the remuneration he might extract from jobbery than by any high-minded interest in the penal system. Since then, as the remit of Coldbath Fields was expanded to include an increasing number of political prisoners, he had been a regular and prominent attendee. He had interviewed Colonel Despard regarding his treatment by Governor Aris and had inspected the prison many times. But now, with Pitt forced into abandoning his support for William Mainwaring, Merceron's response was to distance himself as far as he could from the Prisons Committee. After the furore over the Mary Rich case in the summer of 1800, he did not attend the Committee again that year and his attendance became sporadic for years afterwards. He was not alone in this: almost half of the

Middlesex Prisons Committee meetings in 1801 and 1802 had to be cancelled because fewer than the quorum of three magistrates turned up.[189]

He had, in any event, domestic matters to attend to. In March 1799 he moved his family out of the old pawnshop in Brick Lane to a much larger house a mile eastwards, on Bethnal Green itself. A third child, Elizabeth, had arrived two years earlier. With Merceron's rising status and the steady stream of income from both legal and illegal sources making servants a social necessity, the family needed more room.

Despite the rapid growth of the urban sprawl, the parish of Bethnal Green was still aptly named. In 1796, two thirds of the parish's 750 acres consisted of pasture, arable land or market gardens. The village green was lined with large houses: 'respectable', as a contemporary writer put it, 'but not of a very inviting character'. In 1761, the anti-quary Ebenezer Mussell, a founding father of the parish, had pains-takingly incorporated the ruins of the ancient City of London gate of Aldgate into his house on the corner of Old Ford Road. Across the road lived Merceron's patron, the Reverend Anthony Natt. Daniel Mendoza, the famous bare-knuckle prize-fighter, lived nearby. The Mercerons' new house, at 21 Bethnal Green East, was spacious and included a large garden, a coach house and stables. Merceron bought it at an auction for £1,100 in March 1799. A neighbouring house, 'desirably situated on the East-side of Bethnal Green' was auctioned two years later and gives an idea of the layout: '4 garrets, 3 bed-chambers, dining and drawing-rooms, breakfast parlour, large hall, staircase and offices, two stall stable, front court, large walled garden, &c'. For Merceron, keen to stay close to his business interests and known never to spend more money than he needed to, it was the perfect situation.[190]

Merceron's move eastwards was influenced by the fact that, for a family with three small children, Brick Lane was not a particularly healthy place to live. The turn of the 19th century coincided with the worst poverty in living memory for the weavers of Spitalfields and

Bethnal Green, as a sharp increase in food prices, caused by the war and by two successive poor harvests, took its toll. The workhouses of the two parishes were unable to cope, with almost 1,000 inmates between them, sleeping three or four to a bed. In the year to October 1800 more than 100 children and 40 adults died of starvation. Spitalfields was caught in a vicious cycle of deprivation. For decades the wealthy had moved out, leaving their houses to be subdivided and taken over by the poor. Deep in debt, the parish was four quarters in arrears with tradesmen. Consequently unable to pay their own poor's rates, many of these tradesmen had their goods seized and became paupers themselves. Here, on the outskirts of the City of London, the centuries-old premise that each parish should be self-supporting had been exposed as unworkable. It was a situation that would show parish officials at their best and – in Merceron's case – their worst.[191]

Merceron's opposite number as treasurer in the adjacent parish of Spitalfields was William Hale, a successful master weaver employing several hundred journeymen. Hale was everything that Merceron was not. Years later, a magazine wrote of him:

> There is perhaps no individual in the kingdom, to whom the poorer classes are under so substantial obligations, as they are to this intelligent philanthropist; no one who has displayed more practical knowledge and experience on all parochial and charitable concerns.[192]

As the winter of 1800 approached and the crisis deepened, Hale wrote to his friend Patrick Colquhoun, a Westminster magistrate, describing 'scenes of the most awful distress' throughout Spitalfields, Bethnal Green and Mile End. He told Colquhoun of whole families, 'almost expiring amidst the awful horrors of starvation' with 'scarcely a rag to cover their nakedness'. Unless external relief was granted, concluded Hale, 'I tremble for the consequences'. Colquhoun, who knew conditions in the East End well from his days as a police magistrate at Worship Street a decade earlier, took up the issue with a parliamentary Select Committee looking into food prices. Just before Christmas, a motion was carried in Parliament for the immediate provision of £20,000 from government funds to be recouped by a local tax on the adjoining parishes (notably those in the City of London, which could afford it). The funds were paid over to the parish officers of Spitalfields, Bethnal Green and Mile End for the immediate relief of the poor. As Hale later wrote: 'thus…the aged and infirm had their pledged beds redeemed, and innumerable articles of apparel were rescued from the pawnbroker's shop, and restored to the naked poor.'[193]

Except, it seems, in Bethnal Green. A decade of supremacy over the vestry had enabled Merceron to fill all its positions of responsibility with loyal supporters. His closest ally and childhood friend, Peter Renvoize, was repeatedly elected as churchwarden for much of this period, from which position he helped Merceron pull off his most audacious financial coup yet. Bethnal Green's share of the government relief grant was £12,200, equivalent to almost three times the annual poor's rates raised by the parish. Having obtained the money, Merceron appointed himself chairman of a vestry committee, with four of his closest associates, including Renvoize, to manage its distribution.[194]

What happened next is difficult to determine. But it is clear that, five months after the government had advanced the funds, there were still several thousand pounds sitting in Merceron's own account. In May 1801 Renvoize proposed that some of the money be used to build an extension to the workhouse for the use of the sick. It was a typical Merceron tactic – rather than using the funds to relieve the poor directly, he diverted them instead into the pockets of his contractor cronies. Renvoize's proposal was agreed and £700 was spent in adding four capacious wards to the workhouse. Next, Merceron hit on the idea of using the government grant to subsidise the poor's rates of his supporters. £3,500 was transferred to the poor's rate account, giving Merceron a pot of money to buy local support by waiving individual rate payments at his own discretion.[195]

By Easter 1802 Merceron was still in possession of almost £2,000 of the government grant. On being reappointed as treasurer – for the 15th successive year – he gave a progress report. He brazenly acknowledged the transfer to the poor's rate account and the workhouse extension, and admitted to the amounts remaining in his own hands. He also informed the vestry that, of the £12,200 received from government, more than £7,500 had been disbursed in the form of weekly doles to the poor, tradesmen's bills and 'incidental expenses'. Even here there was something underhand going on. According to its constitution, the vestry should have conducted an audit of these accounts with Merceron required to produce the vouchers to support each payment. But no such paperwork was produced. Instead the vestry voted thanks to Merceron's committee 'for their unwearied attention, good management, and prudent application of the said money, the good effect of which is experienced and felt by the whole parish'.[196]

Merceron's reputation for dishonest financial dealings was growing. In 1800, the twin half-sisters of Mary Cheesman came of age and, expecting to inherit Mary's property, were outraged to discover that they had been defrauded. They launched legal proceedings against Anthony Natt, but before the suit could be heard the 86-year-old Natt died, leaving Merceron £50 in his will 'for his long and faithful service'. With the Cheesman case pending it would have been awkward, to say the least, for Natt's family to lose Merceron's support, and Natt's will exhorted them to retain him as their agent and advisor. Rumours were circulating, though, of Merceron's lack of probity; it is striking that Natt felt the need in his will to stress that he had 'the highest persuasion' of Merceron's 'uprightness and integrity'.[197]

While Merceron was raiding the coffers in Bethnal Green, William Mainwaring was paying the price for the unquestioning support he had rashly given to his fellow Middlesex magistrates. After losing William Pitt's support over Coldbath Fields he found the autumn of 1800 a difficult time. That September, society hostess

Caroline Fox wrote that Mainwaring 'even supported as he is…will find it difficult to stem the torrent of popular clamour so justly excited by his conduct as a magistrate'.

Mainwaring had been re-elected unopposed to Parliament in both 1790 and 1796 but the prison scandal had generated significant opposition. In the summer of 1802 he found himself facing an electoral challenge from none other than Sir Francis Burdett. The previous year, the exhausted Pitt had been forced to give way as Prime Minister to Henry Addington, who had subsequently made a temporary peace with France and called a general election. Disillusioned by Pitt's successful manoeuvring over the Coldbath Fields inquiry, Burdett had been ready to abandon his parliamentary career. Nevertheless, he could not resist when friends called on him to stand against Mainwaring and Byng for election as MP for Middlesex and to make magisterial corruption and the prison scandal an election issue. An astute manipulator of popular opinion, he immediately announced his candidacy.

Parliamentary elections before the 19th century Reform Acts were very different from those of today. Of approximately 500 English MPs, about 400 were elected by cities and boroughs, most of them under the control of local landowners. 80 of the remaining seats were allotted, two each, to the 40 counties. These had a wider franchise, typically allowing a vote to all adult males with property worth more than 40 shillings (£2) per year. Despite rules around bribery and 'treating', candidates were expected to spend enormous sums on entertainment to encourage electors out to vote; as a result they would rarely risk such an expense unless confident of winning. The majority of seats were therefore rarely contested. On the rare occasions when a contest did take place, voting would begin with a hustings at which each candidate would speak, followed by a show of hands. Only if this were inconclusive would a poll take place, with electors casting their votes in public – there were no secret ballots – over the course of the day. If a clear winner emerged when votes were counted, his opponent was expected to concede. Occasionally, if the result was close, the poll could continue for several days. Such drawn-out contests were extremely unusual and generated a frenzy of public and press interest. Because of its large, unpredictable, shifting and partly radicalised electorate, the county of Middlesex had given rise to some of the most fiercely contested elections. In 1768, a famous contest had lasted a week, to shouts of 'Wilkes and Liberty!' Now, 34 years later, in an election that would take twice as long to resolve, the cry was 'Burdett and No Bastille!'[198]

The election opened on 13th July. Byng, the popular Whig candidate, was sure to be re-elected, and that morning *The Times* came out strongly in support of Mainwaring in what it correctly foresaw would become a contest with Burdett for the second seat. The newspaper portrayed Byng and Mainwaring as the tireless servants of their constituents and bemoaned Burdett's interference, highlighting his alleged LCS connections and deep pockets, born of his marriage into the wealthy Coutts family.[199]

Burdett's campaign began loudly. As he left his Piccadilly home for the hustings at Brentford, the street was full of hackney coaches bearing his name and decked with his purple campaign ribbons. *The Times* had 'seldom witnessed such a busy scene of bustle and preparation'. Throughout the journey he was accompanied by a band, preceded by three horsemen bearing a huge banner proclaiming 'No Bastille!' in gold letters. A gang of butcher's boys banging marrowbones and meat cleavers, the traditional instruments of street processions, followed behind.[200]

At Burdett's turn to be nominated at the hustings the focus of the speeches turned to 'the accursed Bastille', Coldbath Fields. By a happily timed coincidence the next day was July 14th, the anniversary of the storming of the Paris Bastille during the French Revolution. Burdett made the most of it. From the beginning, he based his campaign on the 'well authenticated cruelties' of the prison, which he described as 'the most horrible wickedness'. It was not a question, he shouted, of whether the voters supported him or Mainwaring but of whether they would support cruelty, torture and murder. His sup-

'Tis so hot! I'll return to the place whence I came

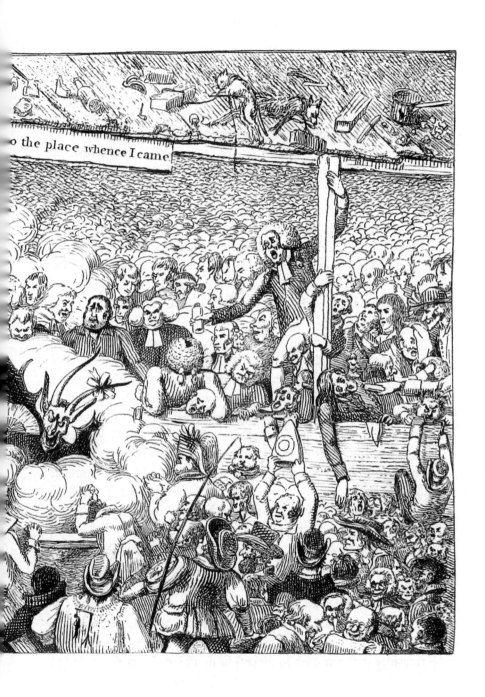

o the place whence I came

porters handed out printed accounts of the Mary Rich case together with Burdett's purple rosettes, and Burdett brought forward the girl's father for the crowd to see. As he spoke, supporters acted out a drama where a man in irons, dressed as one of the Nore mutineers, was repeatedly lashed until 'he sank under the weight and severity of his tortures'. The crowd was roused to fever pitch; when it came to Mainwaring's turn to speak, he could hardly be heard among the tumult.

The sheriffs ordered a show of hands, which suggested a majority of support for Byng and Burdett, but Mainwaring appealed for a poll. At the end of the day, the count was 1303 votes for Byng, 1097 for Mainwaring and only 699 for Burdett. Burdett, however, refused to concede and it was agreed to keep the poll open for a further day.[201]

The next day, Bastille Day, followed a similar pattern. At the close, Burdett still trailed Mainwaring by almost 500 votes yet again refused to admit defeat. What he lacked in hard votes, he made up in vocal support, and the crowds pulled his coach through Brentford to cheers of 'Burdett for Ever – and no Bastille!' while Mainwaring's was pelted with dirt as he crossed Kew Bridge on his way back to London. As each subsequent day passed, similar events were repeated: Burdett, refusing to concede, acclaimed by the crowds; Mainwaring's speeches drowned out, stones thrown at him on the hustings, and on one occasion his footman pulled from behind his carriage and assaulted.[202]

Where was Merceron as the 1802 election went on? George Byng would later write that Merceron had constantly attended him in his canvasses since 1796, so we can assume that he made the journey to Brentford each day and used his considerable influence over contractors and publicans to divert votes away from Burdett. Yet to Merceron, politics was simply a means to an end. Questions of personal power and influence were of far greater importance than party allegiance. Throughout his career, he forged strong and lasting relationships with national politicians from both main parties, although Radicals such as Burdett were certainly beyond the pale to him. The

1802 polling records reveal that Merceron, together with all his main associates, cast his votes for Byng and Mainwaring. He had strong working relationships with both men, for example he lobbied both in 1797 to seek a reduction in the scope of Pitt's new income tax. His name is notable for its absence, however, from the list of subscribers to Mainwaring's campaign fund. It would not have helped Mainwaring's case, however, to be publicly supported by the very magistrates responsible for supervising Aris's regime. Other prominent members of the Prisons Committee, such as Williams, were equally conspicuous by their absence from the list of Mainwaring's financial backers.[203]

The contest continued for a fortnight during which, despite Burdett's superior popular support, Mainwaring maintained a steady lead of several hundred votes. Burdett refused to back down, insisting throughout that Mainwaring's superiority was down to coercion by the corrupt magistrates. Eventually, on 28th July, the penultimate day of the poll, Burdett received a block of 375 votes from the shareholders in a factory. 280 of these voters also polled for Byng, and not a single one for Mainwaring. Despite concerns of impropriety, the sheriffs allowed the votes to stand. Burdett was now just 14 votes behind Mainwaring and the next day he narrowly edged into second place behind Byng.[204]

Burdett celebrated in style. The crowd carried him through Brentford on a sedan chair decorated with laurels. His procession back to London included 300 carriages accompanied by hundreds of people on foot, as householders waved purple handkerchiefs and ribbons from their windows. *The Times*, which had never wavered in its support for Mainwaring, had 'never witnessed so large an assemblage of persons on any similar occasion, nor such a motley scene of disgusting folly'. When the procession stopped for a few minutes outside St James's Palace on its way to Burdett's Piccadilly home, the paper's editor was apoplectic: 'Misguided fanatical patriot! Was it a necessary display of your victory, obtained by chicanery, to insult your Monarch?'

Over the next few days, Burdett crowed, claiming that his victory reflected the voters' rejection of Mainwaring, 'his humane friend The Steeled Gaoler' and the 'system of torture in the dungeons of Coldbath Fields'. The journalist William Cobbett reported that the contest 'has been regarded by the lower orders of people, as a struggle between the magistrates and the thieves', and a scene 'such as never was beheld, except in the environs of Paris, during the most dreadful times of the revolution.' The government response was petulant: the management of the Foreign Office accounts was taken out of the hands of Coutts' bank because of the family connection with Burdett. Eventually, months later, Mainwaring's supporters challenged the result on a petition, charging Burdett with bribery and corruption, but the parliamentary inquiry would not take place for a further 15 months.[205]

In Bethnal Green, Merceron's misappropriation of the government poor relief grant in 1800 had been the final straw for a group of vestrymen sickened by his corrupt practices. At the annual Easter elections in 1802 and 1803, two vestrymen named Manypenny and Pullen were elected as churchwardens on an anti-Merceron ticket and began to challenge him openly as to the destination of the government funds.[206]

Merceron resisted, refusing all calls for a detailed examination of his accounts. As Manypenny and Pullen became increasingly vociferous, Merceron announced that the vouchers supporting the disbursement of the money had been stolen during a burglary at his counting house. This provoked outrage: the idea that anyone would dare rob a man as powerful as Merceron was ludicrous, never mind the absurdity of stealing a pile of old receipts. The churchwardens requested assistance from the government; an official was sent to investigate the matter but without success.[207]

Matters came to a head at the annual vestry meeting to approve Merceron's poor's rate accounts on 31st March 1804. Furious that anyone should dare to challenge him, Merceron refused to grace the meeting with his presence and, for once, his supporters found themselves outnumbered. The audit revealed that, once again, a quarter of the annual poor's rate – more than £1,000 – remained unspent in Merceron's hands, and that he was still holding more than £300 of the government subsidy, more than three years after the money had been received.[208]

Two days later, Merceron was re-elected treasurer but Manypenny managed to persuade the vestry to pass a resolution requiring a formal annual audit of his accounts prior to his next re-election. When the meeting reconvened the next day Merceron again stayed away. In a heated debate, Manypenny argued that Merceron's corrupt rating practices had significantly reduced the amount available for the poor while simultaneously inflating the average rate charged on honest parishioners. The vestry agreed to a wholesale review of the rating system and went on to expel Merceron, Peter Renvoize and three of his other associates as commissioners of the Court of Requests. It was more than Merceron could stand and days later he resigned as treasurer.[209]

On 12th April, hundreds of vestrymen packed into St Matthew's church for the election of Merceron's replacement as treasurer. Merceron himself was absent, away at the Middlesex Sessions, but his associates had leaned heavily on their dependents to attend; the vestry room was so crowded that the meeting had to adjourn to the body of the church. The opposing parties each chose a candidate, and in a show of hands Merceron's man was narrowly declared the victor. The opposing party protested intimidation and, a few days later, Manypenny obtained enough support to rescind the previous election and convene a secret ballot. Knowing he was beaten, Merceron withdrew his candidate and Manypenny's man was elected unopposed. When Merceron's accounts were eventually audited he was found to be in possession of £650 of unspent poor's rate funds and was ordered to hand it over.[210]

Manypenny's victory was short-lived. Merceron's self-imposed exile from his Bethnal Green honeypot lasted just a year. Throughout it he ran a sustained campaign of criticism against his replacements, whom he accused of running the parish into debt. The following year, his successor as treasurer was intimidated into stepping down and Merceron was once again appointed. Manypenny and Pullen were banished from the vestry for good and Merceron's associates were returned to all their previous positions of power.[211]

Ironically, as his own corruption was being challenged in Bethnal Green, Merceron was himself involved in making similar claims about the handling of the Middlesex county finances. The previous summer, Merceron was a member of an audit committee that reported irregularities in the County Treasurer's accounts. On 12th April 1804, the day the Bethnal Green vestry was debating the election of Merceron's replacement as its treasurer, Merceron was at Clerkenwell helping to secure the dismissal of the County Treasurer and the appointment of William Mainwaring's son and business partner, George Boulton Mainwaring, in his place.[212]

George Mainwaring's appointment took effect from 5th July 1804. Four days later, the House of Commons Committee looking into his father's petition against his 1802 general election defeat by Sir Francis Burdett finally reached its conclusions. Both men were criticised. Burdett's suspicious block of late votes was deemed inadmissible and he was found to have been unduly elected, but William Mainwaring was found guilty of treating and declared ineligible to stand as an MP. Accordingly, the election was declared void and a by-election called. Burdett immediately announced he would stand again, 'to rescue the County from the hands of a set of contractors, jobbers, magistrates and pensioners, the tools of the ministerial party'.

With William Mainwaring disqualified, a group of City merchants persuaded his son to stand in his place. A list of George Mainwaring's backers indicates that Burdett's accusations of jobbery and ministerial 'tools' were accurate. Among them were several men inextricably tied both to Merceron and the Mainwarings' later corruption, and to government espionage activity: the Reverend Thomas Thirlwall, Daniel Hinley, Charles Lush and Major Wright. Thirlwall was a prominent East End magistrate and long-standing friend both of William Mainwaring and of Merceron. His support for Merceron bordered on the fanatical, to the extent that he would later jeopardise his entire career for him, with only a grovelling apology before the House of Commons saving Thirlwall from severe punishment. Lush and Wright, both lawyers, were shadowy figures whose official positions, as clerks to various governmental and administrative bodies in the East End, provided cover for their involvement in espionage activity. Daniel Hinley was another magistrates' clerk who would later be accused of collaborating with George Mainwaring in serious fraud.[213]

When William Mainwaring fought Burdett in 1802 he did so as a pillar of the Establishment: chairman of the Middlesex magistrates for over 20 years and a sitting MP for 18. His son had no such reputation, nor any real experience to speak of.[214] At the time of the election, George Boulton Mainwaring was 31 years old. After a solid public school and Oxbridge education, he had followed in his father's footsteps to Lincoln's Inn where he trained as a barrister, before joining the family banking partnership with his father in 1799. There were awkward rumours about his origins: George III once confided that 'young Mainwaring is not a son of Mainwaring... but a natural son of Mrs Mainwaring to whom she had given the name of Mainwaring to disguise this circumstance, and that she is said to use him particularly ill lest she should be suspected to be more partial to him than to her real children by Mainwaring'.[215]

The election was almost an exact re-run of the 1802 campaign. Each evening for a fortnight, as the polls closed, Burdett would re-mind the crowd, to loud cheering, of Mainwaring's links to Coldbath Fields and, in return, Mainwaring would be drowned out as he tried to denounce Burdett's relationship with the LCS and his friendship with Colonel Despard, executed as a traitor the previous year.[216]

At the end of the first day's voting, Burdett was ahead by a few dozen votes. But by the third day Mainwaring had edged ahead, and despite the abuse heaped daily at him by the mob he maintained a slender but consistent lead for the next 11 days.

With a day to go, Mainwaring led by just 86 votes. At the close there was mayhem, as the three different sets of poll books each gave a different result. In one, Burdett was ahead by 10 votes, in another Mainwaring led by five and a third had Burdett winning by a single vote. In a typical show of confidence Burdett declared himself victorious and set off on a triumphant procession back to town, where almost every building displayed Burdett's 'imperial purple' in flags or ribbons. As his coach reached Pall Mall, a band struck up 'Rule Britannia' and the streets were a blaze of light as the mob called for all houses to show illuminations.[217]

Burdett's celebrations were embarrassingly premature. Two days later, the Middlesex sheriffs announced that Mainwaring was in fact the winner, by five votes, and it was he who took his seat in the Commons while this time Burdett petitioned against the result. The arguments continued for 18 months before Mainwaring was finally confirmed victorious in February 1806, just as the Parliament was drawing to a close. It proved a hollow victory. Having followed the contest with interest, King George III noted that the cost of Mainwaring's victory had been such that, as 'a man of no fortune or consequence, he would probably find it necessary on a future occasion to substitute to his place some man of family and importance'. The King was right; at the next election, in 1806, Mainwaring stood down. By that time however, working ever more closely with Merceron, he and his father had found plenty of other ways to make their fortune.[218]

CHAPTER VIII

Absolute Power Corrupts Absolutely

*This is the state of human nature; whether men are
magistrates of Middlesex, or monks of St Dominick,
let them but have power uncontrolled, and they will
become cruel, wicked, tyrannical and oppressive.*
                                        The Universal Magazine[219]

Joseph Merceron's re-election as Bethnal Green's treasurer in 1805
marked the beginning of a ten-year period in which the group
of corrupt Middlesex magistrates reigned over a great swathe of
London's rapidly growing infrastructure. Docks, water companies,
commissions of sewers, prisons; even the finances of the militia fell
under their sway as Merceron, Sir Daniel Williams and William
and George Mainwaring obtained control of enormous sums of
public and private money, most of which were deposited in the
Mainwarings' private bank.

In the East End, Merceron was effectively a dictator. His first act
upon returning to power in Bethnal Green was to rescind the vestry
resolution subjecting his accounts to independent scrutiny. Thereafter,
the vestry ceased to meet with any regularity and any important
decisions were made in the secrecy of Merceron's Brick Lane office.
Parish funds poured into his bank account but seldom found their
way out again, as he expanded upon his old habit of holding back
or diverting the money intended for the relief of the poor. His
control over the various statutory authorities which governed the
local amenities was absolute. He chaired the Bethnal Green pavement commission and watch trust, and was the licensing magistrate

for all public houses in the parish, many of which he owned. He was promoted to chairman of the Tower Hamlets commissions for both property and assessed taxes, giving him the power to assess local residents for tax but also to judge any complaints against such assessments. Since the deaths of Henry Busby and Anthony Natt, Merceron had run their estates as if they were his own property. This made him landlord over hundreds of poor tenants, able to double their rent or rates at will and evict them if they failed to pay. Directorships of private companies soon followed, including a seat on the board of the Hand-in-Hand Fire Office, the oldest insurance company in England.

With the funds from all these positions passing through his hands, and with no independent scrutiny of his actions, he was becoming a very wealthy man. The only cloud on the horizon was the ongoing dispute over Mary Cheesman's will. In April 1805, the courts upheld Mary's half-sisters' complaint and ordered Merceron to hand over the proceeds of her estate. But still Merceron continued to resist, claiming he had spent all the money on repairs to the properties.[220]

While Merceron accumulated power in the East End, the Mainwarings were enjoying similar success from their bases at the Middlesex Sessions House in Clerkenwell and their bank on Cornhill in the City of London. With William Mainwaring as the chairman of the county magistrates and his son as the County Treasurer (and an MP until 1806), the scope for corruption was enormous; the previously little-known bank of Mainwaring, Son, Chatteris & Co found itself awash with funds. Between 1806 and 1812, the large current account balances held by the Commissions of Sewers for Westminster, Holborn & Finsbury and the Tower Hamlets were all transferred to the Mainwarings' bank. At the dates the accounts were transferred, William Mainwaring, Williams and Merceron respectively were chairmen of the Commissions concerned.[221]

George Boulton Mainwaring was involved in widespread corruption from the beginning of his tenure as County Treasurer in 1804. The treasurer's job was to collect a rate levied upon each parish in the county ('the county rate') and to use the funds to maintain those aspects of the county infrastructure (notably prisons, courthouses and bridges) that were not administered by individual parishes. Soon after his appointment, Mainwaring embarked on a fraud on the county funds that remained undiscovered for almost two decades. In fact, he and his accomplices covered their tracks so well that the full extent of the fraud was never entirely understood. It is clear, though, that it included thefts from the fund by which the building of Coldbath Fields prison had been financed. It is probably no co-incidence that in March 1807 Merceron forced a resolution through the Bethnal Green vestry exempting his transactions with George Mainwaring from any scrutiny or approval.[222]

The opportunities for corruption open to the magistrates in the first decade of the 19th century were expanded greatly by a series of large-scale projects which transformed London's infrastructure. First was the multi-million pounds development of the docks, beginning with the West India Docks in 1802, followed by the London Dock in 1805 and the East India Dock a year later.[223]

The building of the docks was an enormous undertaking. The West India Docks, on the Isle of Dogs, involved the digging of 54 acres of basin within a vast walled site, at a cost of £1 million. The London Dock in Wapping was only half this size but took more than twice as long to build, costing three times as much, partly because it re-quired the demolition of hundreds of local properties. A contributing factor to the spiralling cost may have been Merceron's appointment to the Board responsible for distributing the compensation fund.[224]

The docks were private ventures, whose shareholders had been at-tracted by the prospect of handsome returns from trade monopolies for their respective regions of the globe. The success of the docks helped lead to the next major speculation: the great water com-panies created between 1805 and 1810 with the promise of providing Londoners with clean drinking water piped directly to their homes. Before this London's water supply was controlled by five local companies, each of which generated huge profits from an effective monopoly in its respective area. These profits, and technological developments in the form of improved steam pumps and large-bore iron water pipes, meant that from 1805 the provision of water suddenly became an investment opportunity, as new companies were formed to compete with the existing monopolies.

The Middlesex magistrates were quick to involve themselves in these speculations. When the East London Water Works was incorporated in 1807, George Boulton Mainwaring became its initial chairman and his father was appointed treasurer. The company's share capital of £380,000 quickly found its way to the Mainwarings' bank. But before the East London works could open, both Mainwarings were forced to resign in November 1808 after George was accused of a fraud to artificially inflate the company's share price. He was replaced as chairman by Sir Daniel Williams, with Merceron also appointed a director around this time. Incredibly, despite compelling evidence of his guilt, Mainwaring was allowed to remain as the Middlesex County Treasurer.[225]

A similar speculation by a group of Manchester businessmen, the Manchester and Salford Water Works, also appointed William Mainwaring as its treasurer and banker. When in 1810 this same group established the Grand Junction Water Works, this time raising £225,000, George Boulton Mainwaring was named among its directors. The younger Mainwaring would also be implicated in an illusory enterprise known as 'the Bayswater Spring Company' which seems to have been a further failed attempt to extort money from the public.[226]

The East London Water Works' funds were spent in digging out 11 acres of reservoirs alongside the River Lea at Old Ford, to the east of Bethnal Green, and in building a fine pair of steam pumps. The opening of the new works in 1809 was a splendid affair watched by a crowd of several thousand, including a grandstand 'filled with beauty and fashion', with Sir Daniel Williams and the Lord Mayor joining hands to open the sluice gates accompanied by military bands and a 21-gun salute.[227]

The new works enjoyed great initial popularity. *The Times* later reported that 'no company of adventurers ever had more of the public favour, or enjoyed greater success'. But in reality the rapacious magistrates and their friends had little thought for their customers or for the quality of the water they provided. Within a few years they reached agreements not to compete with the neighbouring companies; prices and shareholder dividends rocketed, the water supply became intermittent and its quality fell sharply. The tidal flow of the Thames meant that the East London works' source water was frequently polluted by sewage, and the company's 'criminal indifference to the public safety' would ultimately lead to the deaths of more than 4,000 Londoners in the cholera epidemic of 1866. The Grand Junction works was even worse, raising its capital on the promise of 'an unintermittent supply' of 'pure and excellent soft water...excellent for all culinary and domestic purposes' from 'a reservoir...in the Vale of Ruislip'. This prospectus would turn out to have been scandalously misleading when it was revealed that the true source of the water was in the Thames at Chelsea, just yards from a sewage inlet.[228]

A further substantial source of profit to the East End magistrates was the Tower Hamlets militia. In 1797, Daniel Williams was appointed lieutenant colonel and Merceron a captain of the 2nd Regiment. Over the next 15 years, they developed a corrupt system that spread through the entire organisation.[229]

Due to a long-standing public mistrust of the idea of a large standing army, the system of local militias remained the bulwark of Britain's home defence. An Act of 1802 attempted to conscript more than 50,000 new militiamen. However, the system in place allowed a man to buy his way out of conscription and provide a substitute at a cost of about 20 guineas. In theory, the substitute would be from the same parish, or another within the same county; in the latter case, the parish of the conscripted man would compensate that of the substitute for the cost of supporting his family.[230]

The complexity of this system, combined with the enormous power vested in the senior officers of the militia regiments and the absence of independent scrutiny of their actions, created a perfect set of conditions for corruption on a wide scale. With substitutions authorised by Williams and Merceron as magistrates, helped by the ever-loyal Major Wright as their clerk, George Mainwaring at the county treasury responsible for processing the inter-parish payments and Williams's nephew David Stable as a regimental paymaster, there were fortunes to be made.[231]

Instead of recruiting from the Home Counties, as laid down by Parliament, recruiting sergeants of the Tower Hamlets militia would be sent on leave to the Midlands with instructions to entrap young men into enlisting. The innocent recruits would be marched the hundred or so miles to London, where they would find their promised ten-guinea bounty eaten away by the forced purchase of unnecessary and shoddy kit. Recruits were charged ludicrous amounts for uniforms and other essential items, generating huge profits for the quartermaster. Wages were paid late or not at all. None dared complain for fear of a spell in the guardhouse. Conditions were made so terrible that many recruits were driven to borrow the price of their discharge or desert in desperation. The real cost of a substitute was typically less than half the price paid by the leaver, the profit accruing to the senior officer responsible. The regimental finances were deliberately muddled by Stable, who was known to draw militia cheques against the Holborn & Finsbury Sewers Commission of which he was also clerk. His private wines and spirits dealership, a clear conflict of interest, also benefited from illegal sales to the militia. Eventually in 1813 Colonel Mark Beaufoy, Williams's opposite number in the 1st Regiment, was court-martialled for ruling over this system. Williams himself, whose close personal involvement was clear from the evidence of several witnesses, was never charged.[232]

By 1808, Merceron – absent from the management of Coldbath Fields prison for several years since the scandal raised by Sir Francis Burdett – had again become active alongside Williams on the Middlesex Prisons Committee. By this time, some semblance of order had been restored to the regime; despite Thomas Aris's continuing presence as governor, the prison had by and large managed to stay out of the newspapers. Williams had introduced a system of inspection and in June that year Merceron was among the visiting magistrates who reported that they had 'at all time found the prison perfectly clean and the prisoners healthy and without complaint...'[233]

Unsurprisingly, the reality was somewhat different. Less than a year later, it transpired that Aris had got into financial difficulties and had not paid the prison staff for some time. In April 1809, Merceron was present to hear the Governor's pitiful explanation. 'I have at this time 13 children alive', began Aris:

...my character in the eyes of the world has been ruined by Sir Francis Burdett and his adherents, prisoners have been encouraged to bring actions...against me, and although...I have upon every occasion had verdicts in my favour...the costs of defence amounted to many hundreds of pounds.[234]

Other complaints soon emerged. A female prisoner accused Aris's son (one of the turnkeys) of rape and making her pregnant. There were accusations of insufficient rations. The government, fearing a further scandal, set up yet another commission of inquiry; predictably, it found nothing wrong. Eventually, however, Aris's luck ran out. In September 1810 his son was implicated in the escape of two prisoners. Aris's spirited and somewhat impertinent defence of his son gave the investigating magistrates the excuse they needed to abandon their support for him. Summarily dismissed and at last disgraced, he spent the rest of his life in poverty.[235]

Aris's dismissal enabled the magistrates to claim that they had cleaned up their act. When Burdett forced yet another Commons inquiry into the prison in 1811, accusing the magistrates of 'whitewashing and purifying the character of their prison', the pro-government press responded with a robust defence, insisting the prison was 'regulated with great wisdom and no less humanity'.

This time, when the inquiry again found no significant grounds for complaint, even Burdett was forced to accept its conclusions.[236]

Merceron's domination of his own territory, meanwhile, had become so arbitrary and pervasive that it was impossible to challenge. Thanks to his position as a tax commissioner and magistrate, his empire had expanded beyond Bethnal Green to include most of the East End. In 1809, it was the turn of the people of the riverside parish of Shadwell to feel the extent of his power.

Shadwell was a rough district to the south of Bethnal Green, bordering the docks. Its residents were associated with shipping and its related trades, being, as a contemporary magistrate gratuitously put it: 'foreign sailors, Lascars, Chinese, Greeks and other dirty filthy people of that description'. For some years the Shadwell vestry had been dominated by two Merceron underlings, George Fox and William Homan, who between them had carved up most of the lucrative positions of responsibility, including the collection of taxes handed over to Merceron as the local commissioner. Fox and Homan were opposed by a group of 'respectable' vestrymen led by a ship-owner named Joseph Fletcher, who early in 1809 reported certain irregularities in Homan's conduct as a tax collector. Believing he had uncovered a fraud, Fletcher informed Merceron. Merceron proved unsympathetic, telling Fletcher abruptly that he was not interested in any complaint 'arising out of parish business' and warning him not to say anything further upon the subject.[237]

Undeterred, Fletcher pressed for an inquiry. That September, at the annual audit of the tax commission's accounts, he once more attempted to lodge a complaint. Amid great clamour, Merceron again defended the local tax collectors, declaring that the commissioners would not interfere in what he insisted was 'parish business'. When Fletcher persisted, Merceron resorted to an old trick that had served him well in the Bethnal Green vestry. Surrounded by pliant supporters, he called a show of hands, won the vote resoundingly and immediately adjourned the meeting before heading off with his friends for dinner.[238]

The lack of opposition had led Merceron to become increasingly audacious in his manipulation of the Bethnal Green rating system. With no independent inspection of the rate books, he resorted to brazen fraud. After allocating the rates with a semblance of equity, he would sign the books as magistrate and obtain the counter-signature of a compliant ally such as Williams. With the all-important magistrates' signatures in place, he then altered the underlying entries by hand to 'serve his friends and punish his enemies'. In 1808, for example, he more than doubled the rates on a portfolio of 73 houses on the Busby estate immediately after selling them. Any appeals were heard by Merceron himself, with predictable results. Those who complained were publicly humiliated or financially ruined. Those who might have intervened, such as James May, the vestry clerk, were looked after financially or otherwise. When complaints about May were made to the vestry in 1809, Merceron described them as 'frivolous and vexatious', ensuring they were rejected.[239]

Eventually, one man took it upon himself to challenge the system. In 1809, Robert Wrightson, the long-suffering gun-carriage manufacturer whom Merceron had bullied out of parish office at the very beginning of his career, lodged a formal complaint at a meeting of the local property tax commissioners with Merceron in the chair. Soon after, Wrightson found a furious Merceron waiting for him at his factory gate, making thinly veiled threats that reprisals would follow. Sure enough, Wrightson's rate was increased to three times the amount at which Merceron's own similar house was rated. Wrightson's complaints to the vestry were curtly rejected.

Refusing to be cowed, Wrightson undertook his own survey of the parish and formally petitioned the Middlesex Sessions about Merceron's valuation. The magistrates, however, simply referred Wrightson's complaint back to the Tower division justices – a group of a half-dozen or so magistrates dominated by Sir Daniel Williams and Merceron himself. Closing this farcical circle, Williams told Wrightson to take up the matter with Merceron. When Wrightson threatened legal action to force the justices to do their duty, the magistrates repeatedly adjourned the meeting and then announced that his case was time-barred, leaving him with a huge bill for the costs.[240]

Merceron now turned his attention to Wrightson's nephew, James Weston, serving him with an entirely malicious tax surcharge that was enough to ruin him completely. Weston appealed to the tax commissioners – chaired of course by Merceron – and unsurprisingly lost the case. Weston left the courtroom with Merceron's laughter ringing in his ears.[241]

Anyone who upset the tyrant, no matter how lowly, risked total ruin. Charlotte Cowdry was the mistress of a small girls' school to which Merceron had sent his youngest daughter, Elizabeth. Given the Mercerons' standing in the community this would have been quite an honour, but Miss Cowdry lived to regret the connection. After some dispute over Elizabeth's education, Merceron arbitrarily increased Miss Cowdry's rates from £40 to £60, triple the amount he himself paid. Simultaneously, despite having enjoyed the patronage of the most powerful family in the parish, Miss Cowdry's establishment mysteriously lost its popularity. As Merceron later explained it to a parliamentary Select Committee, 'her school fell off; she was in low circumstances.' The poor schoolmistress was forced to quit the parish, 'almost in the situation of a pauper'.[242]

To the inhabitants of Bethnal Green, Merceron's dominance seemed unassailable. But a new force was about to disturb the cosy compliance of the Bethnal Green vestry. On the death of the absentee Rector, his replacement, Joshua King, was 30 years old. The son of a Cheshire clergyman, King had followed his father into the church, becoming a Fellow of Brasenose College, Oxford, in whose gift the living of Bethnal Green lay. Unlike his predecessor, King was not a man to be bullied out of his parish or responsibilities and he immediately took up residence at the Bethnal Green rectory. An intelligent if self-interested man, it would not take him long to learn what he was up against.[243]

PART III

Belligerence
1810–18

CHAPTER IX

The Reverend King

…a fine portly man, fond of sport and a very good shot…[244]

Joshua King was born on 20th November 1778, the second of six children, in the village of Bidston in Cheshire. Bidston lay on the Wirral peninsula, across the River Mersey from the port city of Liverpool and almost two hundred miles north-west of London. He was probably destined to be a clergyman: his father, the Reverend Bryan King – 'a strikingly handsome man' – was Bidston's vicar and his ancestors had been incumbents of one Wirral parish or another for generations, dating back to the English Civil War (1642–51). His mother Ellen, 'a pretty, sensible and rather stately woman', was the daughter of a wealthy farmer and related to several of Cheshire's leading families.[245]

In 1792, when Joshua was 13, his father inherited the more lucrative living at the nearby village of Woodchurch and the family moved to the rectory there. Compared with Merceron's childhood in Spitalfields, life in Woodchurch was idyllic. Years later, Joshua's niece Ellen (by then married to the Bishop of Carlisle) wrote of childhood days at Bryan King's rectory, recalling 'a simple dignity about the people and place…the furniture was homely yet handsome, the china old and beautiful'. Every day, a stream of 'pedlars, beggars and tramps' would arrive at the scullery door to be given bread, cheese and milk; 'all were sure of a welcome and a hearty meal at the rectory'. It was a comfortable upbringing and Joshua and his brothers and sisters enjoyed playing in the large rectory garden. Sea bathing was no more than a brisk walk away and the young King learned to shoot on nearby farmland, becoming an accomplished marksman. With so much of the good life around him from early childhood, it is no surprise to find him described as a 'fine, portly man' as an adult.[246]

At the age of 18, on leaving Shrewsbury School, King followed in the family tradition and took his degree at Brasenose College, Oxford. On graduating in 1800 he remained in Oxford as a Fellow for several years. A brief spell followed as a curate in Liverpool until November 1809 when Brasenose College (whose right of appointment it was) selected King as the new Rector of the parish of St Matthew, Bethnal Green. It would not have appeared a particularly attractive proposition: the Bethnal Green vestry's hostility had forced his predecessor from the parish after six months and he had never set foot there again. The remuneration offered was also disappointing: it had 'always been difficult to dispose of the living, due to the smallness of the income'. The 1743 Act that established Bethnal Green as a parish gave the majority of tithe income to Brasenose College and the remainder to the vestry, from which the Rector was allowed a fixed salary of £130 per annum. While this would have been a comfortable salary in 1743, since then the population of the parish – and, in consequence, the extent of the Rector's duties – had doubled to more than 30,000 by the date of King's appointment. King's ready acceptance of the living suggests that, after waiting for so many years, he was desperate for the money. The option of absenting himself and paying a curate to take over the parish duties, as his predecessor had done, was not something he could afford. And so King moved in to the Bethnal Green rectory.[247]

Compared with the sea air, leafy surroundings and pheasant shooting of the Wirral, or the scholarly cloisters of Oxford, the noise, smoke and poverty of Bethnal Green must have made King feel as if he had arrived in hell. The poor's rate had almost doubled in the previous four years as the war continued to drive up food prices, making silk weaving uncompetitive. There had been between 500 and 700 people in the workhouse for most of the past decade. Bethnal Green's population was three times that of the whole of the

Wirral, yet King's was the only Anglican place of worship. Worst of all, the parish was controlled by a despot, Merceron, with no time for the niceties of the church.[248]

The new Rector soon discovered that his congregation were very different to the meek and polite folk that had accepted his father's hospitality in Woodchurch. Shortly after his arrival in Bethnal Green, King's Sunday morning service was disturbed by shouts outside the church. Hundreds of men and boys were gathered in an adjacent field, gambling on dogfights and duck hunts, soon followed by the fearsome ritual of the bullock hunt. Every week was the same. Sometimes the bull-baiting would continue into the Monday, encouraging weavers to abandon their looms and cause mayhem in the streets. Serious injuries were frequent and King learned that at least one person had been trampled to death.[249]

King approached Merceron, asking why such behaviour was tolerated and expressing his wish to be made a magistrate so that he might be able to prevent such profanities on the Sabbath. But any doubts as to where Merceron's sympathies lay were rapidly dispelled. 'There is no kind of amusement I am so fond of as bullock-hunting', he told King, '…in my younger days I was generally the first in the chase'. As for becoming a magistrate, Merceron told King to forget the idea; there were no vacancies and, even if one should arise he would see to it that a local builder friend would get the job.[250]

For the next couple of years King returned to his duties, clear that any opposition to Merceron was likely to make his life difficult. During this period he learned that, with no other source of income, a Rector's life was impossible to sustain on £130 per year. On discussing the matter with a number of vestrymen, however, he found some were sympathetic to his cause. Most were smarting from having been cheated or punished by Merceron, typically through the assessment of their poor's rates. Some, like Robert Wrightson, had harboured grudges against Merceron for years. Others had supported the brief parish coup of 1804 and had been persecuted by him ever since.

Among this small group, one man stood out. John Liptrap was the proprietor of a Whitechapel gin distillery, who lived in a fine house on Bethnal Green, a few doors along from Merceron's own. He was also a former sheriff of the City of London, a magistrate and a Fellow of the Royal Society. Liptrap and Wrightson had already agreed that it was time to challenge Merceron's rule; they considered King, with his energy and Oxford connections, just the man to head their campaign. A plan soon emerged. King's salary, fixed under the Act of Parliament by which Bethnal Green was governed, could only be increased by amending that Act, a move that would enable other changes to be made including altering the biased rules by which Merceron assessed and manipulated the poor's rates.

Encouraged by Liptrap and Wrightson, in 1812 King initiated a chain of events which resulted in a decade of bitter conflict in Bethnal Green. He called a vestry meeting to discuss the inadequacy of his salary and wrote to the parishioners setting out his case: 'My time is so fully occupied…in searching the registers, in baptising infants, in visiting the sick, and in burying the parish poor…I only receive, in the shape of a salary, one hundred and thirty pounds a year…for the numerous and incessant labours of my station…Permit me, then, to ask, whether I am adequately repaid?'[251]

King's letter might have gone down well among the respectful inhabitants of his father's rural parish. As an appeal to the hearts and minds of Bethnal Green's urban poor, however, it was wide of the mark. £130 was a salary so far beyond the wildest dreams of most vestrymen that King's complaints attracted little sympathy. Nevertheless, the vestry assembled as requested on 27th February to consider a series of resolutions proposed by Liptrap. They complimented King on the performance of his duties and proposed an application to Parliament to increase his salary. But there was more: the final resolution was a carefully worded allegation that Merceron had misappropriated a significant part of the 1800 government subsidy of £12,200. Merceron allowed the initial resolution complementing King to pass without argument, but when the vestry came to debate the proposed salary increase, he insisted he would not 'be saddled with anything that would alleviate the wants of the Rector', and won the resulting vote by 65 to 51. Before anyone could debate the final resolution about the alleged fraud, he abruptly announced the meeting adjourned and hurried his followers from the room.[252]

John Liptrap was not a man to be pushed aside. In fact, he had earned a reputation as a fearless upholder of his rights in the face of an opponent even more powerful than Merceron. In 1796, during his tenure as sheriff of the City of London, Liptrap had invited the Prince of Wales (the future Prince Regent and George IV) to dine at his house in Whitechapel. The Prince was in the process of disentangling himself from his disastrous marriage to Princess Caroline and during dinner developed an attraction for Liptrap's wife, a celebrated beauty. According to Robert Huish, the Prince's early biographer, Mrs Liptrap was flattered: 'her eye beamed with desire and passion, and her *LIP* was not the first *TRAP* which, by its lovely pouting, had ensnared the affection of the enamoured Prince'. When the ladies left the table, the Prince – unable to resist temptation – excused himself and followed them. When his guest of honour failed to return, Liptrap became concerned and went to investigate. Huish continues:

There were several places in the house to which it was possible that the Prince had retired, but there was one, in particular, in which it was highly improbable that he be found, and that was the bed-chamber of his lady. It was, therefore, the last which the worthy Sheriff visited – but, had he visited it first, it would have saved him a great deal of trouble, and calmed at once his anxiety for the safety of his Royal guest.[253]

Notwithstanding the interloper's identity, Liptrap responded in the only way open to a gentleman of the time: he drew his sword and chased the Prince out of the house. The heir to the throne found himself pursued around Liptrap's garden in pitch darkness, with no sign of an escape route. His only option was to vault the garden wall: 'and he now found the adage to be true, that a man should always look before he leaps. The Prince did not look; and therefore he leapt into as vile a compound of dirt and filth as ever received the body of a human being, much more that of a Prince.'[254]

Faced with Merceron's refusal to debate the allegations against him, Liptrap decided that the people of Bethnal Green needed to be told the truth about what their leader was up to, and called for a full independent investigation into the parish finances. The usually cursory annual audit of Merceron's accounts was due to take place about this time, prior to his expected reappointment as treasurer on Easter Monday. This gave Liptrap just a few weeks to intervene. By threatening legal action he obtained the vestry accounts and conducted his own investigation. He published his findings in an open letter to the parishioners on 17th March.[255]

Liptrap's report began by remarking upon the peculiar unanimity with which vestry decisions were routinely made:

> ...There appears to have been, for many years, but one eye and one hand in the parish...The principle of self-interest pervades the minds of some men to such an astonishing degree, as to make them feel justified in converting every thing to their own advantage, that their influence over weak minds may enable them to do. To withhold relief from destitute widows and children in the most inclement season of the year, under the specious pretext of economy, with ample funds in the Treasurer's pocket...were maxims sufficient to arouse the dullest feelings of humanity...

Next, Liptrap revealed Merceron's misapplication of the £12,200 government grant in 1800, including the use of approximately £4,000 to relieve his supporters from paying their share of the rates. Labelling the vestry 'gross and disgusting' for allowing such a transaction, Liptrap explained that Merceron had received a total of

£53,000 (approximately £5 million in today's terms) in poor's rates since 1800. Liptrap challenged the extent to which such funds had reached the distressed inmates of the workhouse. After suggesting that vestrymen use their votes to turn Merceron out, Liptrap ended with a startling claim. In his inspection of the rate-books, he had discovered more than 200 alterations of the rates, subsequent to their approval by the magistrates, 'at the caprice and mercy of an individual, of whose hand-writing there may be sufficient legal evidence to be submitted to a jury'.[256]

The accusations created an immediate stir, but Merceron reacted calmly. His initial response, a concise and formal open letter to the parish four days later, was understated, carefully avoiding the passionate language of his accuser. It reaffirmed Merceron's opposition to any increase of the Rector's salary and asserted that his own conduct had been transparent throughout 25 years as the parish treasurer and as a magistrate. He claimed that his accounts had always been publicly available for examination. Interestingly, he made no response to Liptrap's accusations about altering the rate books.[257]

The following week, Liptrap and his followers were prevented by force from attending a vestry meeting held to audit Merceron's accounts. Unsurprisingly, the audit proceeded without comment and was followed by an especially effusive vote of thanks to Merceron, who arranged for thousands of copies of the minutes to be distributed throughout Bethnal Green. Five days later, at the annual Easter Monday elections, Merceron's candidacy as treasurer was opposed for the first time in several years. But only 20 vestrymen dared to vote against him and he was re-elected by an overwhelming majority. The next day, his supporters' loyalty was rewarded, as those who were paid parish officials were voted substantial salary increases by the vestry.[258]

It was clear to Joshua King that, even with the clearest evidence of corruption, unseating Merceron through the fragile democracy of the vestry would be impossible. His own position was vulnerable: having made an enemy of Merceron, he would be lucky not to be hounded out of Bethnal Green altogether, let alone get the increased salary he was seeking. But King was resilient, and in any event had no obvious alternative employment prospects. With Liptrap's help he spent the rest of 1812 planning a two-pronged attack against Merceron. First, they prepared for a series of private legal actions based on the evidence uncovered by Liptrap's investigation. They also met secretly with lawyers to draw up proposals to amend the legislation governing Bethnal Green, with the aim of preventing Merceron from manipulating the poor's rates in return for votes.

That November, their campaign was boosted when the Court of Chancery found against Merceron in the long-running dispute over Mary Cheesman's estate. It had been 26 years since Merceron obtained Mary's properties by deception and he had repeatedly insisted under oath that he no longer retained any of her assets. The court compelled him to return the property to Mary's half-sisters.[259]

Weeks later, King and Liptrap launched legal proceedings against Merceron and two of his poor's rate collectors, charging them all with fraudulent alteration of the rates and Merceron with perjury over the Cheesman case. Simultaneously, announcements were placed in the press that an application would be made to Parliament to amend the Bethnal Green legislation. Such was the extent of the secrecy maintained in the preceding months that Merceron only learned of the latter development from the newspapers. Furious, he called a vestry meeting to oppose it. As usual, opponents were forcibly excluded and the vestry resolved unanimously that any alteration of the Bethnal Green Act would be 'absurd, impolitic and unwise'. A committee was formed, chaired by Merceron and given full authority to oppose King's proposed Bill.[260]

Almost immediately, a disaster struck the campaign against Merceron – John Liptrap was bankrupt. Despite his considerable success in public life, Liptrap had a record of financial troubles. He had been the subject of a previous bankruptcy in 1804 and according to the official records his latest problems were precipitated by his distillery company being held liable for debts amounting to more than £100,000. A crisis had been reached towards the end of the previous year and early in 1813 the government issued proceedings against him. Soon afterwards, Liptrap's fine house and furniture and the assets of his distillery were auctioned off and he departed from the politics of Bethnal Green as abruptly as he had arrived.[261]

Did Merceron engineer Liptrap's downfall? The magnitude of the distiller's debts and the fact of his previous bankruptcy suggest he may have been able to get into difficulty without assistance. But Merceron's nefarious influence with the licensing and supply of liquor in the East End meant that, once Liptrap's business was in trouble, it would have been easy for Merceron to force bankruptcy by applying pressure on his suppliers or distributors. Merceron's many acts of revenge for which direct evidence is available – and the fact that Liptrap's failure coincided so immediately with his public exposure of Merceron's corruption – suggest that this is all too probably the case.

Merceron's trial for fraud and perjury was scheduled for February 1813 in the Court of King's Bench, the supreme common law court in England, at Westminster Hall. The case against him looked strong, backed by detailed evidence in his own handwriting. The prognosis of his attorneys was ominous; the consequences of being found guilty would be catastrophic. Characteristically, Merceron decided to try to buy his way out of trouble, reasoning that if the price was right King might sacrifice his principles and drop the charges.

Merceron knew that, as things stood, King stood little chance of getting his salary increase. Any changes to the existing Bethnal Green Act would need parliamentary approval. This would be impossible without support from the Bethnal Green vestry, safely under Merceron's control, and from the two Middlesex MPs, George Byng and William Mellish, who could both be relied upon to back Merceron. Accordingly, Merceron decided to offer King the salary rise he wanted in return for dropping the charges against him.

To test this strategy, Merceron despatched a negotiating party to King in January 1813, led by the Reverend William Platt, an unscrupulous Methodist minister who had married John Wilmot's widowed daughter in 1806, in so doing becoming owner of considerable property in the parish. On 28th January, however, Platt reported back that he was unable to reach a deal. With his trial less than a month away, Merceron was running out of time.[262]

Merceron's political machine went into overdrive. Emissaries hurried to and fro between Bethnal Green and the City on secretive errands. The vestry, with opponents as usual forcibly prevented from attending, became the source of a slick public relations offensive. Resolutions that King's proceedings flowed from malice and revenge were passed and were distributed throughout Bethnal Green and copied to the Middlesex MPs.

On 23rd February Merceron took his place in the dock at the Court of King's Bench. Was he worried? The evidence suggests not, as it appears that he may have bribed court officials to bungle the arrangements. As the trial began, it was announced that the wrong jurors had been called; Merceron's lawyers duly protested and the case was postponed for several months, buying him valuable negotiating time.[263]

A fortnight later, the Bethnal Green Bill received its first reading in Parliament. The second reading was scheduled for the following week, and with his trial rescheduled for 12th June Merceron wasted no time in mobilising opposition to the Bill in the Commons. George Byng and William Mellish readily agreed to petition the House against it. With his local MPs so firm against his proposals, King reluctantly agreed to delay the Bill's second reading. Merceron, meanwhile, was taking great care to ensure that the public view of his activities left no room for further criticism. On 14th April, at the annual audit of his accounts, he was able to demonstrate for the first time in 25 years that the poor's rate expenditure for the year exceeded the amounts collected, resulting in another effusive vote of thanks from the vestry.[264]

But Merceron had not bargained for the possibility that King might find a lawyer equally capable of sharp practice. It was standard parliamentary procedure for local Acts of Parliament to be managed through the various stages of legislative approval by the MPs in whose constituency they arose, in this case Byng and Mellish. Somehow, on the evening of 13th April, King's solicitor John Wilks persuaded another MP to slip notice of the second reading quietly into the agenda for the next day's parliamentary business. The following day, with both Byng and Mellish unaware of the scheduled debate and absent from the House, the second reading was carried and the Committee stage of the Bill fixed for a fortnight later.[265]

Over the ensuing Easter weekend, King's party were as usual refused entry to the vestry and Merceron was unanimously re-elected to all his various positions of responsibility. King's supporters formed an unofficial committee of their own, resolving to pursue their Bill and end Merceron's abuses, which King documented and circulated throughout Bethnal Green. The allegations included Merceron's fraudulent manipulation of the poor's rates, the theft of rate money by his collectors, the excessive funds retained in Merceron's own hands and the extravagant expenses of the parish officers, all while the poor in the workhouse lacked a proper diet and were sleeping four to a bed.[266]

On 27th April, the day before the Committee stage of the Bill was due to take place, Merceron and his advisers shuttled between the City of London and the Palace of Westminster to obtain MPs' signatures to a petition against the Bill. John Wilks's conduct in sneaking the second reading through Parliament appeared to have backfired, with Byng particularly furious at the tactic. But King and Wilks had yet another trick up their sleeve. At seven o'clock that evening, after Merceron and his supporters had returned home, Wilks successfully applied to postpone the Committee stage for a further week, in order to coincide it with the visit to Westminster of a party of senior Fellows from Oxford University. The same evening, King wrote to the Principal of Brasenose College, Frodsham Hodson, asking him to use the Fellows' visit to lobby support for his Bill.[267]

News of the postponement failed to reach Merceron, and early the next morning he returned to Westminster only to discover that he had again been wrong-footed. To his intense annoyance and embarrassment, he then had to wait in the lobby of the House for several hours in order to explain to his furious parliamentary allies what had happened.[268]

The next weekend, Merceron learned from his attorney that the intervention of the Oxford Fellows was tipping support in King's favour. Suddenly there seemed a real possibility of defeat, leaving Merceron facing almost certain conviction for fraud and perjury. His attorney urged him to focus on mobilising parliamentary support and Merceron spent the day writing to more than 60 MPs, requesting an opportunity to brief them in advance of the Committee meeting the following afternoon. The next morning George Byng told Merceron he was noticeably less optimistic than before. He had met with one of the Oxford Fellows, and now 'appreciated the great influence they could bring to bear'. Byng suggested that Merceron should agree to increase King's salary in return for concessions elsewhere in the Bill.[269]

When the Committee assembled, Byng and Mellish began by abusing John Wilks for his devious tactics. When King's barrister made passing reference to the ongoing prosecutions against Merceron, he incurred a further outburst from Mellish, who robustly defended Merceron's character and cited the esteem in which he was held. After some argument it was agreed that the Bethnal Green vestry be asked to reach a compromise on the outstanding points. Two evenings later, William Platt, armed with a proposal from Merceron, met with King's representatives. The offer was simple: if King would abandon the prosecutions, Merceron would agree to double or even treble King's salary. Platt also hinted that, if King would support Merceron's activities in future, there would be no obstacle to further significant salary increases.[270]

The naive and impoverished King was unable to resist. The next day, he composed a self-justifying letter to Frodsham Hodson, the Principal at Brasenose, explaining that:

...notwithstanding the trickery of our solicitor...the business was last night at Mr. Gurney's chambers amicably arranged. Having accomplished the objects for which the prosecutions were instituted I agreed to withdraw them – and the parish has undertaken to take up the Bill in its present state...and to introduce in it a clause to increase the Rector's stipend...all things considered, I think it will be admitted that I have imposed terms on Mr Merceron sufficiently humiliating to him, and have acted by no means derogatory to my own character. While an indelible stigma will be attached to the man who has compounded felony and shrunk from legal investigation, I may indulge the pleasing hope that the public will give me credit for preferring mercy to justice – and rather than punish a delinquent, restoring peace and harmony to my parish.[271]

By agreeing to drop the prosecutions in return for his salary increase, King had ensured his own defeat. He had lost the moral high ground and Merceron knew it. If their deal were made public, King's reputation would be in tatters. Merceron now began to turn the screws. He ensured that the Committee to finalise the Bill was dominated by his own supporters. King's increased salary was pegged at £400 (nevertheless a threefold increase) but all remaining outstanding clauses were agreed in Merceron's favour. When King wrote again to Hodson on 12th May, he was still clinging to the fiction that he had won the battle. He informed Hodson that the vestry had agreed to his terms, 'fearful lest I bring in a separate Bill' to increase his salary, and added that he and Merceron had 'very amicably' sorted out the remaining differences. The reality was different. King had allowed his greed to get the better of him and had compromised himself by agreeing to drop the prosecutions in return for money. Merceron was going to make him pay.[272]

The Bethnal Green Act received Royal assent on 3rd June 1813. Two days later, King wrote to inform Hodson at Brasenose College with surprising news:

...would that [the Act] had restored harmony to the parish – but far distant, I fear, is the prospect of peace – for Merceron is determined to take his trial – and whether pronounced innocent or guilty such a feeling will be excited as cannot soon subside. Satisfied with having manifested a conciliatory disposition towards him which he has met with a contrary return, I shall now rejoice in getting what I am confident we shall have: a verdict against him.[273]

King seems genuinely to have believed that Merceron was determined to have his day in court out of sheer stubbornness, despite the strong likelihood of a guilty verdict. He spent the following week in a fog of self-congratulation. Bethnal Green was not Woodchurch, but with £400 a year and Merceron behind bars it would at least be bearable.

Merceron's trial took place the following Saturday, 12th June 1813, once again at the Court of King's Bench. In the dock, Merceron and his co-defendants faced the Lord Chief Justice, Lord Ellenborough. There was little room for the public in the court, but in any event Joshua King was not there. His solicitor, Wilks, had assured him that there was no chance of Merceron being acquitted and had advised him to stay away to avoid any appearance of gloating at his adversary's downfall.[274]

The prosecution was led by the Attorney General Sir William Garrow, a month into his second spell as the government's senior law officer. Garrow was a persuasive speaker and an aggressive and intimidating cross-examiner, although not the most refined of men. His language in court could be vulgar, one contemporary describing him as 'without education, without taste and without law'. Opening the case, Garrow explained to the jury that Merceron was 'probably well known to some of you, as having been long a magistrate, and engaged in the collection of the public rates in the neighbourhood of Bethnal Green, he himself having a large estate there'. After summarising the case and explaining the alleged alterations of the rate books, Garrow was expected to launch into a withering denunciation of Merceron's corrupt antics. But the attack never came. Instead, Garrow announced to the bewildered jury that he had looked into the case with the defence counsel, and had 'found that there is much complexity in the proof'. The defence had assured him, he continued, that they could prove that 'every shilling' drawn by Merceron 'was so drawn from no corrupt motive, but that the whole of the monies so received can be satisfactorily accounted for; and therefore...we shall decline calling evidence upon this prosecution'.[275]

The court sat in stunned silence. The jurors stared blankly at the Attorney General, at Lord Ellenborough and at Merceron, who must have found it hard to suppress a smile. What on earth was going on? As Garrow sat, Merceron's defence counsel, James Topping, stood in his place. He spoke briefly, stating that if the Reverend King had audited the rate books properly, he would have found that 'not one farthing' of the poor's rates had found its way into Merceron's pocket. Topping added that his own investigations had revealed nothing that tended to cast the slightest imputation upon the fair character or honourable conduct of his client. He concluded: 'I am convinced, that there is not a man of more peaceable temper than Mr Merceron, nor a man more disposed to promote harmony in the parish...he is a Gentleman of a most honourable mind.'

The case was over almost before it had begun. Lord Ellenborough rapidly summed up for the jury: the offence charged had proceeded from 'an irregularity, without any corrupt motives; the prosecutors don't bring the case before you in proof, and therefore it is your duty to acquit the defendants'. The jury did as they were told, and gave identical verdicts in the two other indictments. Before returning to Bethnal Green, Merceron asked his attorneys to make sure his acquittal was given prominent coverage by *The Times*. Accordingly, on the following Monday morning Merceron opened his copy of the paper to find his acquittal prominently displayed, at the foot of the paper's law report, under the heading 'advertisement'. With some satisfaction, he cut out the article, folded it neatly and filed it carefully away.[276]

Merceron's acquittal that day has never been properly explained. Joshua King was asked about it several years later under oath and responded that he believed that Wilks, seduced by Merceron, had contrived to instruct the Attorney General that King had agreed to drop the case. King always insisted, however, that he had given 'positive instructions to proceed'. His story has the ring of truth, and his failure to make any further complaint can be explained by his knowing that it would lead to the public exposure of his earlier deal with Merceron.

The most likely explanation is that some time before 5th June (when King informed Hodson that Merceron had decided to 'take his trial'), Merceron bribed Wilks to drop the case. Five years later, after a subsequent prosecution, Merceron would offer spectacular bribes in an unsuccessful attempt to stay out of prison; there is no reason to suppose he did not try the same trick with more success in 1813. There is also the intriguing possibility that Merceron personally bribed the Attorney General to drop the case: over the next few years Sir William Garrow would display a remarkable reluctance to prosecute him, despite being given every opportunity to do so.[277]

Merceron's enjoyment of his acquittal was spoiled by just one thing. His lawyers had sent in an invoice, for almost £1,000, close to £100,000 in today's terms. He paid it that July, but the idea of incurring such an enormous cost (in addition to the bribes paid to have the case dropped) was more than he could bear. Over the next few weeks, he hatched a scheme to get his money back.[278]

On 14th August, Merceron reimbursed himself for his legal fees from the Bethnal Green poor's rate funds, adding a further ten guineas to cover the cost of his return cab fares to his court appearance. The next vestry meeting was on 23rd August. The meeting was busy, with more than 100 attendees, but as it broke up Merceron instructed the Reverend Platt and eight other associates to remain behind. As soon as they were alone, they voted through a pre-prepared resolution proposing that the costs of Merceron's defence be defrayed by the parish.[279]

When the minutes of this meeting became public, there was con-sternation in Bethnal Green. At this point, no one – except the nine accomplices – was aware that Merceron had already stolen the money from the poor's rate account; it was merely assumed that he had clan-destinely sought to obtain permission to do so. King and Wrightson determined to oppose any actual reimbursement when the opportu-nity arose. Merceron played the matter down. He let it be known that his only aim in passing the resolution had been 'to obtain a public testimony that he might put in the newspapers in justification of his character'; of course, he would not accept any actual reimburse-ment. As the months went by, and Merceron made no request to the vestry for repayment, people began to believe his story. Most forgot all about it.[280]

King, however, had not forgotten. Towards the end of March 1814, a week or so before the annual audit of Merceron's accounts was due to take place, he distributed an open letter to the parish, reminding vestrymen of Merceron's resolution and urging them to attend the forthcoming audit in order to veto any attempt at reimbursement.

On the day of the audit, Merceron's loyal supporters crowded around the long vestry table. Several of his opponents, led by Robert Wrightson, forced their way near to the front in order to hear what was said. The audit proceeded in the usual way, with Platt calling out the items of Merceron's expenditure, Merceron handing over the supporting invoice and James May confirming that each had been approved by the Governors of the Poor. Wrightson and his friends listened intently, ready to shout their disapproval the moment Merceron's expenses were mentioned, but the moment never came. To Wrightson's great surprise, all seemed above board. After the audit, Platt gave the usual vote of thanks to Merceron and some three dozen vestrymen, including Wrightson, signed the ledger to signify their approval.[281]

If Wrightson had been a little wiser, he might have turned over a few pages and run his eye down some of the figures. Had he done so he would have seen, in Merceron's stylish handwriting, '14th August

1813, Dann & Crosland, £925 1s 3d'. But Wrightson failed to check and the deception was complete: the invoice was paid by the parish in accordance with a specific resolution of the vestry, and the whole transaction had apparently been formally audited and approved.

How had Merceron managed it? Quite simply, he had pre-arranged with Platt that the minister would call out the items, omitting Dann & Crosland's bill when he came to it. Unless anyone kept a running total, they would not notice that the sum of the individual payments called out did not equal the total at the foot of the page. Setting the seal on the fraud, Merceron sent word to inform Joshua King that he had decided, after all, to pay his own legal costs relating to the trial and 'would not allow the parish to pay a farthing'.[282]

A week later, on Easter Monday, Merceron was re-elected as treasurer by a massive majority. Secure in power for another year, he now sought immediate revenge on King, passing a vestry resolution that the Rector's recent letter had been a gross libel. The next day, he threw a celebratory dinner for his supporters – paid for, of course, by the parish.[283]

Affronted, King drafted his own set of resolutions condemning Merceron's behaviour and circulated them around Bethnal Green. When the vestry next met, on the evening of 4th May, it was clear that there would be trouble. Merceron had called in a few favours; hundreds of men who had been excused their rates, or had their taxes favourably assessed, had been advised that it might be in their interest to attend the vestry that evening. More than 400 arrived at St Matthew's and, with the vestry room unable to hold more than a few dozen, the meeting was adjourned to the nave of the church. Both parties were well represented and the air was heavy with intimidation. To loud jeers, Robert Wrightson opened the meeting and another King supporter, William Shevill, read out the resolutions: the Rector's supporters had heard 'with astonishment and indignation' the attack on King on Easter Monday. The imputation cast on him was 'harsh and groundless' and 'a violation of every principle of moral rectitude and civil society'. Shevill wound up by proposing that Merceron's accusations of gross libel be rescinded.[284]

Merceron responded by remarking on 'the evident improprieties' of Shevill's proposals and moved an amendment, reaffirming the accusations of libel against the Rector and adding that King had now lost all claim to the vestry's respect and confidence. This was seconded, at which Merceron leapt on a table in the aisle of the church, his hands raised above his head, and shouted 'all, all, all, the question, the question, the question!' A show of hands resulted in 324 votes in favour of the amendment; the threatening atmosphere enough to reduce King's support to just 25 men.

'A scene of disgraceful riot and tumult' followed. Scuffles broke out. Merceron strode onto the church steps and, as the mob gathered round him, removed his hat and repeatedly gave three cheers. Their passion raised, the mob turned on Shevill who was forced to run for his life to the sanctuary of the rectory, where King took him in until the crowd had dispersed.[285]

CHAPTER X

Trouble Brewing

And what control is there over the conduct of the licensing magistrate?... The difficulty of proving corruption is rendered almost insuperable... He may grant a licence to a common brothel, or he may refuse a licence to one of the most respectable inns ... let him withhold his reasons, and his conduct remains unquestionable, although the real motive... may be, that he is in the habit of using the one house, and that the landlord of the other will not suffer him to use it in the same way.

Lord Brougham[286]

It was almost a quarter of a century since the Middlesex Justices Act of 1792 had established the concept of stipendiary magistrates and local police offices under Home Office control. By passing the administration of criminal law to a new class of salaried magistrates, the Act had ended the ability of the unpaid 'county' magistrates of Middlesex to profit from 'trading in justice'. Accordingly, on becoming a county magistrate in 1795, Merceron had narrowly missed out on the opportunity – grasped so voraciously in the preceding two decades by David Wilmot – of making a fortune from selling pardons, verdicts and rewards. But there were plenty of other ways for magistrates to make money. One of the most lucrative was the granting of public house licences at the annual licensing meeting, known as 'Brewster Sessions'.[287]

The licensing process was governed by few rules. A 1753 Act of Parliament required licensed property to have an annual value of £10 or more and prohibited brewers or innkeepers from acting as justices in the licensing process. Otherwise, the licensing magistrates had absolute discretion and the courts had shown themselves unwilling to challenge magistrates' decisions.[288]

In the Tower Hamlets, Merceron was by now one of the leaders of a small group of magistrates who were responsible, each September, for granting or renewing the licences of more than 1,000 premises. These licences were extremely lucrative for the tenants, their landlords and the brewers and distillers who supplied them. Many alehouses, particularly in the areas nearest the river Thames, were fronts for brothels; dozens more operated as 'flash-houses', known haunts of thieves where crimes could be plotted and the proceeds fenced, with little or no danger of capture.[289]

The licensing sessions in the Tower Hamlets were chaired by Sir Daniel Williams and dominated by him and by Merceron. Both had forged close relationships with the big breweries, especially Sampson Hanbury's firm, Truman, Hanbury & Co. For more than 20 years, the clique of East End magistrates, brewers and property developers had enjoyed the fruits of their system – a 'commission' here, a bribe there – undisturbed by any serious challenge. Between them these men held so much power that, despite widespread anger at the impact of the corrupt licensing system, they remained seemingly unstoppable. John Liptrap's attempts to expose Merceron in 1812 had resulted in failure and bankruptcy. The following year, however, a new adversary appeared who would not be so easy to silence.

John Thomas Barber Beaumont's life, according to one obituary, was 'devoted to alleviating the insecurity of the poor, whilst crusading against those who would prey on them'. A successful and wealthy businessman, aiming to become a magistrate himself, he had embarked upon a philanthropic project to improve the lives of the East End poor. To his surprise, however, he had found his way blocked at every turn by the local magistrates who, Barber Beaumont soon realised, were abusing their power in order to enrich themselves.[290]

Barber Beaumont was a man of many talents. Aged 39 in 1813, he had tried his hand at a wide variety of careers and been spectacularly successful at all of them. A talented artist as a child, he became a student of the Royal Academy in 1791 and was soon appointed painter of miniatures to three of the sons of George III. In 1803 he turned to writing, publishing an entertaining account of a tour through Wales illustrated with a series of his own watercolours. When war broke out against France, he established England's first volunteer rifle corps, 'the Duke of Cumberland's Sharpshooters'. The marksmanship instilled by Beaumont in his men was illustrated at an exhibition in 1805 in Hyde Park, when he personally held up the target for his men while they fired at it from 150 yards away. None of them missed. Three years later, at 32, he embarked on a business career, successfully launching one of the UK's first life assurance and savings institutions, the Provident Life Office. He followed this the next year with another insurance company, the County Fire Office, which soon became one of the largest insurers in the country.[291]

Barber Beaumont had first encountered Merceron in 1812 while purchasing a plot of land in Mile End, near Bethnal Green, to develop as part of his philanthropic project. Never a man to do a thing by halves, Beaumont had come up with an ambitious design: a self-sufficient community with houses, factories, shops and pubs; everything the working classes would need. The houses were to have the most up-to-date drainage, but when Beaumont applied to the local Commission of Sewers for authority to connect his drain to the main sewer, he was met with a demand for £50 as a bribe to ensure the necessary approval was obtained. When Beaumont resisted, the clerk merely told him that 'others had given more'.[292]

For all his success in business, Beaumont seems to have been re-markably naive when it came to the corruption and nepotism that pervaded the East End's local government. He complained about the bribe to the chief local magistrate, none other than Sir Daniel Williams at the Whitechapel Police Office. Williams immediately referred him back to Merceron as chairman of the Commission of Sewers. Merceron's initial response was to suggest to Beaumont that he might perhaps have misunderstood what the clerk was saying.

Barber Beaumont

When Beaumont persisted, making a formal complaint at the next meeting of the Commission, Merceron kept him waiting outside for hours. After an increasingly frustrated Beaumont had repeatedly sent his card in to Merceron, the clerk eventually emerged from the courtroom, explaining to Beaumont that the request for £50 had not been a demand, but 'an appeal to his liberality'. Beaumont, indignant, refused to pay up; the wheels of corruption remained unoiled and permission for the drain failed to materialise. Eventually, several months later, Merceron and his fellow Commissioners rejected Beaumont's drainage plans altogether and forced him to adopt a more elaborate and significantly more expensive alternative.[293]

By the autumn of 1813 Beaumont had erected around 100 houses and two factories on his estate, and had established plans for a further 500 properties. The estate being some distance away from any existing public houses, Beaumont built one, assuming that obtaining a licence would not be problematic. He was soon put right. Brewers' and distillers' agents were soon in touch: give the beer trade to Hanbury's, they told him, and the licence would be a formality. A similar tale was told in respect of the spirits business: 'Stables & Williams' were the firm to deal with (David Stable was the nephew of Sir Daniel Williams and had been set up as an agent for Hanbury at Williams's expense). Beaumont, not wishing his house to be tied to any one brewer, declined these advances. He was warned in no uncertain terms that, unless he changed his mind, his house would not be licensed by the magistrates.

As the 1813 licensing hearing drew near, Beaumont was approached by one of Merceron's tax collectors named Smallwood, who offered to use his influence with Merceron to obtain a licence in return for Beaumont lending him £200. Beginning to realise the weight of the interests he was up against, and concerned at the impact on his project of any further delay, Beaumont reluctantly agreed to lend the money. But when the licensing day came, Beaumont's application was turned down. He went to Smallwood and angrily demanded the return of the loan.[294]

While Beaumont struggled to obtain a licence, a group of re-spectable local gentlemen were facing the opposite problem: that of trying to close down a disreputable premises that Merceron and Williams insisted remained licensed. The trustees of the watch in Shadwell, led by Joseph Fletcher – the ship owner whose complaints of corruption had been ignored by Merceron in 1809 – had long been appalled at the state of their High Street. Situated close to the docks, Shadwell was mostly occupied by seamen and was packed with alehouses, gin shops and brothels with on average one inn to every six houses. It was, as one magistrate acknowledged, a 'sink of shameless indecencies and abandoned vice'. The most notorious premises was *The Duke of York*, run by one Henekey, who had leased a row of houses in the alley behind his inn and converted the complex into an enormous brothel. The parish constables were bribed to stay away. There was such little fear of being raided that as many as 200 women – 'the lowest class of prostitutes and procuresses', ac-cording to Fletcher – roamed around half-naked, seducing the drunken sailors and leading them out of the back door of the inn to the bedrooms in the alley behind. Outside, prostitutes filled the streets night and day.[295]

Fletcher's attempts to take action against Henekey had resulted only in dark threats to mind his own business. In September 1813 he took up the matter with Williams and Merceron at the Brewster Sessions, complaining that the behaviour in *The Duke of York* was 'the most profligate and indecent it is possible to conceive'. The mag-istrates heard his complaints 'with evident reluctance', but never-theless suspended Henekey's licence for 10 days pending appeal. Over the next fortnight, Fletcher was jostled and threatened in the streets. Lewd accusations about him were posted around the parish. Merceron, meanwhile, paid an intimidating call on one of Fletcher's fellow senior vestrymen and suggested to him that the complaints against *The Duke of York* were all a mistake.[296]

When the justices reassembled for the appeal hearing, Williams and Merceron were accompanied by their usual cronies including two clergymen magistrates, Edward Robson and Thomas Thirlwall. When Fletcher was called on to give evidence, he was heckled by Merceron while Robson argued forcefully that 'sailors must have recreation': better that prostitutes ply their trade in known haunts than wander the streets. But Fletcher maintained his allegations. Despite much argument, his evidence was too strong to be denied and Henekey's licence was removed. Now his brewers, Meux & Co, appealed to the justices: 'such houses were necessary in all seaports, and were always winked at by magistrates'. The magistrates immediately gave way. Henekey was granted a new licence, at the nearby *King's Arms*, and within a month a brothel had opened there.[297]

Beaumont's and Fletcher's difficulties continued throughout 1814. That August, Fletcher discovered that Henekey was planning to apply for a new licence for *The Duke of York* and he launched a petition among the local residents to try to stop it. Beaumont, meanwhile, was approached by the tax collector Smallwood with a new offer: if he would lend £500 to Merceron and Williams, his licence would be granted. This time Beaumont rejected the offer, saying that he would soon be a magistrate and would personally seek the dismissal of any justice found trafficking in licences. He complained again to the magistrates at the Whitechapel police office.[298]

Beaumont's complaint was heard at the next magistrates' meeting and on 5th September 1814, the day of that year's licensing hearing, the justices called Smallwood before them for questioning. Unsurprisingly, Smallwood's version of events was very different to Beaumont's. According to Smallwood, it was Beaumont who had made the original approach the previous year, wanting Smallwood to under-rate his estate for tax purposes, and his alleged loan of £200 had been a bribe in this regard.[299]

Later, at the licensing meeting, Fletcher presented his petition against *The Duke of York* and was told by Williams and Merceron to come back a fortnight later for the appeal hearing. Yet within a week, word reached Fletcher that the magistrates were inspecting *The Duke of York* that very day with a view to re-licensing it. He rushed to the

Shadwell High Street to find Merceron, Williams and several other magistrates in the street outside *The Duke of York* among a crowd of sailors and prostitutes. Accosting them, Fletcher demanded to know what was going on, but was told he was too late and that the magistrates had decided to grant the licence. Fletcher tried to remonstrate but was held back, to the taunts of the crowd, while Merceron led Williams away.[300]

The following week, Fletcher tried to appeal against the magistrates' latest ruling. After being kept in a waiting room for hours, subjected to threats by Henekey and his friends, he was finally allowed into the court. But Williams refused to allow him to be heard under oath. The clergyman magistrate Robson repeated his previous argument about the necessity of brothels in a seaport: if there were no brothels, the prostitutes would walk the streets and then 'no decent woman would be safe'. Merceron and Williams insisted that they had personally inspected all the houses complained of and found them all 'quiet and peaceable'. Fletcher was shown the door and further humiliated by being manhandled by Henekey's associates on his way out. The celebrations at *The Duke of York* lasted all night.[301]

Next, the magistrates called in Barber Beaumont to hear his version of his dispute with Smallwood. Beaumont repeated his side of the story. He admitted having agreed to discount Smallwood's bill in the hope of purchasing some influence with the licensing process, but insisted that his motives were pure. Once again, Beaumont had failed completely to understand the people he was dealing with. It was clear to Merceron and Williams that Beaumont was going to be trouble. They had spent years creating a cosy world of favours and kickbacks and were prepared to fight hard to keep it. Turning the facts on their head, they took Smallwood's part and expressed disgust at what they described as an attempt by Beaumont to buy a licence. Worst of all, Williams declared that he would write urgently to the Lord Chancellor, Lord Eldon, in an attempt to block Beaumont's impending appointment as a magistrate.[302]

Lord Eldon, however, refused to act on the magistrates' complaint. Just a week after being censured by them, Beaumont was allowed to take his place at the Tower Division magistrates' sessions. He immediately requested Williams once more to address his complaint, but unsurprisingly the magistrates again censured him, describing his behaviour as 'atrocious, wicked and highly criminal'. They stated that they would 'prosecute to the utmost rigour of the law...any person... without respect to rank or station...who shall be guilty of such foul, corrupt and nefarious practices which strike at the very heart of our civil privileges'.[303]

As 1814 drew to a close, there came a sign that perhaps the corrupt magistrates' empire was less impregnable than people had thought. On 19th November, the *London Gazette* reported that the bank of Mainwaring, Son, Chatteris & Co. had failed and that the Mainwarings (father and son) had both been declared bankrupt. For the 79-year-old William Mainwaring, the announcement appeared to herald an ignominious end to his long and illustrious career. There had been signs of trouble: months earlier, Mainwaring had applied unsuccessfully to the Prime Minister Lord Liverpool for an increase in his secret government allowance, pleading the 'diligence, integrity and honour' with which his duties had been performed in more than 30 years as chief magistrate.[304]

Investigators researching the bank's failure soon discovered the extent to which the Mainwarings had taken personal control of enormous sums of public and private money over which they were in a position of trust. Despite both Mainwarings' appointment as executive officers of the County of Middlesex, they had been permitted to deposit the county's official funds in their own bank. With the help of Merceron and Sir Daniel Williams, the current accounts of the Commissions of Sewers for Westminster, Holborn & Finsbury and the Tower Hamlets had also been transferred to them, and the several private water companies of which the Mainwarings were directors had also entrusted them with hundreds of thousands of pounds of capital subscribed by investors.[305]

On 1st December, when the Middlesex magistrates met to discuss the situation, George Mainwaring insisted that the balance owing to the county would be repaid without difficulty or delay. This at least proved correct, although the vast majority of the bank's other creditors lost at least half of their money. Yet thanks to the efforts of their embarrassed fellow magistrates, the Mainwarings' ruin was largely kept out of the newspapers and failed to result in either father or son losing his position of trust within the county executive.[306]

Most astonishingly, in early January, William Mainwaring was re-elected as chairman of the Middlesex Bench, despite both his bankruptcy and the publication by an anonymous magistrate (almost certainly Barber Beaumont) of a vitriolic pamphlet exposing the corrupt system run by Mainwaring and his senior colleagues. Citing the 'undue, overwhelming influence' of the brewers and spirit dealers in the licensing process, Beaumont continued: 'Who is there, but must have boiled with indignation, when condemned to hear a recent correspondence …wherein individuals are openly charged with conniving…at a trafficking in Public House licences?' Turning his attention to the sewers commissions, Beaumont described the corrupt collaboration between Merceron, Williams and the Mainwarings as resembling a 'conjuror's shuffle at cards' and remarked on the 'extraordinary influence' and 'secret disturbing force' by which the entire funds of the three largest sewers commissions had found their way into the hands of Mainwaring, 'a mere freshman of a banker, without the least shadow of security'.[307]

Despite Beaumont's invective, Mainwaring was re-elected. Equally incredibly, his son George was allowed to remain as County Treasurer after a number of relatives and colleagues put up security for him. It was a decision that would come to haunt the magistrates a decade later when the full extent of George Mainwaring's financial knavery came to light.[308]

In Shadwell, Joseph Fletcher was making one last effort to secure justice in his campaign against the licensing magistrates. Seeking legal advice as to whether an action against the magistrates might be successful, he wrote to the barrister John Gurney and to the Attorney General, Sir William Garrow. Both Gurney and Garrow were well acquainted with Merceron from their involvement in Joshua King's failed prosecutions of 1813. Neither man's reply was helpful. On 31st December 1814, Garrow replied from his chambers in Lincoln's Inn: he accepted that in theory, an action could be brought against the magistrates, but 'the difficulty of this case, and I think it considerable, is upon the facts. If they act...not corruptly, they cannot be questioned for such exercise of judgment.' The magistrates might be unwise, Garrow continued, but he did not see them 'actuated by any corrupt or improper motive'. For a second time, the Attorney General had declined the opportunity to prosecute Merceron. A fortnight later, John Gurney's response was even clearer: '...the Court of King's Bench would not grant criminal informations against these magistrates, and that indictments against them could not be supported'. For the time being, Fletcher had exhausted his options.[309]

In February 1815 Barber Beaumont, frustrated that his complaints continued to fall on deaf ears, made a final attempt to clear his name. He presented the Tower Division magistrates with a paper justifying his conduct and asked once again that his complaint against the tax collector Smallwood be heard. But Sir Daniel Williams, encouraged by Merceron, refused even to allow Beaumont's paper to be read out. A few weeks later, a more contrite Beaumont wrote to Williams stating that he wished to end the dispute, never having intended 'to impeach the integrity' of his colleagues. His letter was intended as a private act of conciliation, but Williams joyfully shared it with his colleagues and by May Beaumont was forced to write again. 'My letter seems used as a trophy of victory', he complained. 'It was hinted at the County Sessions that my sending it was hailed as a triumph by some of the magistrates from the East, and I am now told that it was said [by Merceron] that I was eating humble pie and asking to be admitted among them'. Beaumont spent the next few months in further negotiations over the proposed licence for his inn but these proved futile and as the year closed there seemed no chance of his recouping the significant investment he had made. [310]

1815 also saw a further episode in the drawn-out Chancery case of *Merceron v. Merceron*. On 14th April, Merceron's half-sister Catherine died aged 59 at Hoxton House, a notorious private mad-house in Shoreditch. Catherine's death and the resulting disposal of her property triggered a resumption of the family battle over Merceron's theft of his siblings' share of their father's estate. Merceron, who had been paying for Catherine's keep, took on the administration of her estate and claimed it all for himself, insisting that he was her only next of kin. When his nephews (who were, after all, full-blood relatives of Catherine) disputed this, Merceron was forced to go to court to defend his action in July 1815. Among the papers he submitted was an inventory of Catherine's belongings. After deducting items to cover his own costs in administering probate, Merceron claimed that Catherine's total estate, including her property assets, was worth a little over £1,000 – about £100,000 in today's terms but nevertheless, as would be revealed years later, only about a third of its true value. Merceron's inventory of Catherine's household goods, however, reveals the relative poverty in which she had been forced to live: a chest of drawers, a tea chest, silver cup, sugar tongs, 6 teaspoons, 2 pairs of earrings, 4 gold rings, 5 silver buttons, a silk gown and a red cloak; a rather pathetic collection valued at just £25. [311]

Ironically, on 11th July 1815, the same day that Merceron submitted his evidence to the court, the House of Commons published a Select Committee report on the state of madhouses in England, revealing in detail the dreadful conditions in which Catherine had been kept. Hoxton House had become the focus of the Select Committee's attention when a naval doctor, sent there to review the condition of a large number of battle-traumatised sailors and prisoners of war, gave evidence of the horrific scenes that he witnessed. The naval inmates were mixed indiscriminately with other patients of both sexes. Some were handcuffed, others were chained to their seats; many were 'raging with inconceivable fury'. At mealtimes, patients were forced to eat with their bare hands. The stench was unbearable: many patients were incontinent and, with attendants few and far between, relieved themselves where they lay or sat, while dysenteric patients lay in bed, ignored and without medicine. Medical attention was restricted to physical ailments, while mental illness went mostly untreated. A tiny airing ground, an open and badly drained courtyard surrounded by high walls that kept out all but the midday sun, was the only source of exercise.[312]

The MP whose inquiries were chiefly responsible for publicising the conditions at Hoxton House was the Honourable Henry Grey Bennet, an unsung hero of early 19th century political history who was beginning to forge a reputation for the zealous exposure of social evils. Bennet had the credentials of the perfect gentleman: the 38-year-old son of the Earl of Tankerville, his education and career had consisted of Eton, Cambridge, the Guards and the Bar. Described by his friend the political diarist Thomas Creevey as always 'most upright and honourable' if 'occasionally most boring', he had been a Whig MP for Shrewsbury since 1806. He had become a prominent opponent of the government and a proponent of reform, with his stated aim being 'to diminish the sum of human misery'. A follower of Jeremy Bentham and close friend and protégé of the leading criminal barrister and reformist MP Sir Samuel Romilly, Bennet's zeal would soon result in him leading a detailed inquiry into the state of London's policing. It would bring Bennet into direct conflict with Merceron, and, albeit temporarily, it would bring about the Boss's downfall.[313]

CHAPTER XI

Saturnalia Revealed

Vice may be allowed to smoulder in privacy and in silence; but
it must not...aspire to the dignities of high official situation,
without encountering the consequences of public exposure.
Anonymous Middlesex magistrate (Barber Beaumont),
commenting on the corruption of Merceron
and the Mainwarings (1815)[314]

Although the Middlesex Justices Act of 1792 facilitated intelligence
gathering against potential revolutionary societies during the earlier
part of the Napoleonic Wars, its impact on everyday street crime in
London was less successful. Despite other successful innovations
in policing such as the creation in 1798 of the Thames Marine Police
and the Bow Street Horse Patrol in 1805, levels of violent crime –
especially robbery – continued to rise, especially in the areas around
the new docks.[315]

Public cynicism about the effectiveness of the police offices was
heightened in 1811 by the infamous Ratcliffe Highway murders,
when seven people were brutally killed in two separate incidents in
Shadwell. The murders caused a panic throughout London unrivalled
until the time of Jack the Ripper. The resulting inept investigation
revealed the police magistrates of the Tower Division to be, as
Richard Brinsley Sheridan put it in the House of Commons, 'totally
unfit to discharge the duties attached to them'. Dozens of men were
wrongfully arrested on the slightest grounds of suspicion and when
eventually a sailor was charged with the murders and committed to

Coldbath Fields pending trial, the supervision was so lax that he was able to hang himself in his cell.[316]

Merceron, as an unpaid county magistrate, was not personally involved in the police investigation but was nevertheless close to many of those criticised for their ineptitude, including Sir Daniel Williams. The real importance of the murders for Merceron's story, however, was that they set in train a campaign for a reform of London's policing that eventually resulted in his undoing.[317]

The Ratcliffe Highway murders led to immediate calls for improvements in the antiquated parish watch system. The *Morning Chronicle* in particular demanded a new approach, complaining that 'we never think of taking down an old, shattered ruin of incumbrance, till we find it tumbling on our heads.' In 1812, however, a fully integrated police force based on the French model was seen by many as a step too far. A future Foreign Secretary, John Ward, wrote that he would 'rather half-a-dozen people's throats be cut in Ratcliffe Highway every three or four years' than be subject to such restrictions of liberty, and even the *Chronicle* felt that such a move would be 'dexterously contrived for the purpose of tyranny'. The government seemed to concur: a Select Committee set up in the wake of the murders to enquire into the state of London's nightly watch was unimpressive in its recommendations. A draft Bill based on them was voted down in the Commons; the Whig opposition MP Henry Brougham, a future Lord Chancellor, called the Bill 'dangerous' and claimed it would give alarming powers to the police magistrates, whom he described as 'a motley collection of bankrupts, failed lawyers and poets'. But another opposition MP, Sir Samuel Romilly, was convinced of the need for change and began campaigning energetically for widespread reform of the criminal law, including the police.[318]

With the end of war against France in 1815, a crime wave boosted by hordes of unemployed sailors and soldiers led to further questions about the adequacy of London's policing. In April 1816, Romilly persuaded his friend, Henry Grey Bennet, to move in Parliament for the appointment of a Select Committee into the State of the Police in the Metropolis. Romilly's timing was perfect. Just a fortnight previously, the Chancellor of the Exchequer had been forced with great humiliation into the complete withdrawal of the income tax system (at an annual cost to the Treasury of £10 million) after Parliament received a petition from 22,000 City of London constituents against the tax. Romilly knew, therefore, that there was a good chance ministers would agree to Bennet's proposal as a way of softening Whig pressure on other issues.[319]

Bennet's selection by Romilly for the task of pursuing police reform was inspired. Armed with an impressive battery of statistics, he began his speech calling for the Select Committee with a comprehensive analysis of the causes of the recent crime wave. First was the system of 'blood money', whereby the rewards given to apprehending police officers increased in line with the severity of the related crime up to £40 for a capital offence. As a result, constables tended not to arrest petty criminals but instead encouraged them to commit increasingly greater crimes while their reward 'value' rose accordingly. This system was itself a major factor in the development of 'flash houses' – which Bennet announced numbered 'no less than 128 between Westminster Hall and Temple Bar'. These were all-night drinking dens and brothels, tolerated by constables and magistrates, where criminals could congregate without fear of arrest to plan their next heist and which cunning constables would infiltrate to gain information and line up future rewards. A further issue was the obscene severity of punishments for often relatively trivial offences, a bugbear for Romilly, who in 1808 had managed to persuade the government to cease the hanging of pickpockets. There were still, however, more than 200 different capital offences, a fact that tended to inspire juries to give compassionate acquittals and often resulted in habitual criminals being freed, only to offend again. Bennet told the House that he had visited Newgate prison the previous weekend and had found 12 men under sentence of death, a further 35 awaiting transportation and boys as young as 12 'herding with the most hardened and abandoned characters'. He astounded his fellow MPs with

Henry Grey Bennet

the claim that 9,000 children were to be found begging on the streets of London and that, in the previous year alone, 700 people had been discharged from the prison hulks and 'let loose on society, without employment and fraught with the instructions of crime.'[320]

Lord Sidmouth, the Home Secretary, was unimpressed and tried to resist Bennet's calls for an inquiry. Just days earlier, Sidmouth reported, the Middlesex magistrates had briefed him 'with the greatest satisfaction that they had never known the metropolis more tranquil than at present'. But mindful of the perilous position the government was in after the income tax defeat, Sidmouth eventually acceded to Bennet's request. It was agreed that Bennet would chair the inquiry. Romilly was delighted and agreed to take part, confiding in his diary: 'I expect very important information to be derived from this measure. Bennet's zeal and activity in promoting every thing useful to the public is well suited to such an inquiry, and I rejoice that I have prevailed upon him to undertake it.'[321]

Over the next three weeks, Bennet and Romilly set about identifying the issues they wanted the inquiry to examine and the potential witnesses to be called. These included several of the leading Middlesex magistrates, but William Mainwaring would not be one of them. On 3rd April 1816 – the very day of Bennet's speech calling for the inquiry – the octogenarian Mainwaring had formally resigned from the Middlesex Bench after 35 years as its chairman, citing 'the state of my health, my misfortunes and the inevitable infirmities of old age' and – somewhat disingenuously – bemoaning the 'unprofitable' nature of his office. Despite increasingly clear evidence of Mainwaring's corruption, 91 magistrates signed a memorial to the Prince Regent praising the 'diligence, knowledge, judgment and impartiality' with which their chief had discharged his duties and requesting a government pension for him, in light of his exposure to 'the privation of those comforts of which at such an age he must be most in need'.[322]

As news of Bennet's impending inquiry spread, one magistrate in particular jumped at the chance of a public hearing. Barber Beaumont told Bennet about the scandalous licensing of public houses in the East End, assuring him that a number of other witnesses were prepared to support such allegations. Bennet would have been well aware that the licensing process was an issue: Barber Beaumont, writing anonymously as 'A Middlesex Magistrate', had sparked a lengthy correspondence on the subject in *The Times* the previous November. Bennet, always ready to expose a scandal, readily agreed to let Beaumont appear; Beaumont in turn contacted Joshua King and Joseph Fletcher, recruiting them to the witness list.[323]

The Select Committee proceedings opened on Friday, 26th April 1816. Over the ensuing two months, Bennet – demonstrating the zeal and activity for which Romilly had chosen him – examined 54 witnesses beginning with Sir Nathaniel Conant, the chief Bow Street stipendiary magistrate and as such the man responsible for administering the existing policing of the capital. Despite being a salaried employee of the Home Office, Conant had been a staunch supporter of the Mainwarings – he had even stood as one of the sureties for George Mainwaring's continuation as County Treasurer after the collapse of the family bank – and was no stranger to corruption, as Bennet's questioning would soon reveal.[324]

According to Bennet, the most recent inquiry into London's policing, in the aftermath of the Ratcliffe Highway murders, had 'amounted to nothing at all'. By the second day of the 1816 hearing it was already clear that this one, thanks to Bennet, would be different. After Conant had outlined at length the nature of his duties and the system of rewards in operation, Bennet put it to him that several 'flash houses' openly existed within a short walk of the Bow Street police office. Conant denied it, claiming that if such places existed, he would have suppressed them immediately. But Bennet was an experienced advocate and had been well briefed. With every question, Conant – forced along a path of denial – was drawn more deeply into difficulty. Eventually Bennet put it to the flustered magistrate that his officers not only knew of the flash houses but actually frequented them, mingling with the thieves to gain information that would enable them to earn reward money. He also listed examples of brothels, which were run by notorious thieves and openly tolerated and licensed by the magistrates.

Bennet now moved on to the subject of gin-shops. The law prohibited public houses from selling spirits alone; landlords wishing to obtain a spirit licence had first to obtain one for ale, but abuses of this system were flagrant and illegal 'gin-shops' were still common in 1816. Conant made much of his efforts to suppress such places, but Bennet's reply was withering: 'You say you have done all that lay in your power to suppress houses selling gin alone; and that you have been twenty years engaged in that endeavour; are you not of opinion that gin-shops are more numerous now than at any former period?' Bennet followed up with an example of one such shop where a neighbour had counted 165 people coming and going between the hours of six-thirty and eight on a Sunday morning. Although Conant continued to insist that all such places were ruthlessly closed down, it was already clear that Bennet had unearthed the beginnings of a major scandal.[325]

It took three days of questioning before Bennet allowed the humiliated and furious Conant to stand down. The next witness was altogether more helpful. Patrick Colquhoun was Britain's leading expert on policing matters and his views (like those of Romilly and Bennet, tending towards the prevention and detection of offences rather than punishment) were based on the utilitarian principles of Jeremy Bentham. Colquhoun had been one of the first stipendiary magistrates in the early 1790s, when he succeeded David Wilmot at the Worship Street office and ran a spy network during the LCS crisis. He had followed this in 1796 with an exhaustive survey into London's policing, *A Treatise on the Police of the Metropolis*, which ran into many editions. He had also played a leading part in the establishment of the Thames Marine Police in 1798.[326]

Colquhoun's arguments were supported by a mass of detailed statistics: he had shocked Londoners in his *Treatise* with his claim that there were 50,000 prostitutes operating in the city. He now provided

Bennet with data showing a 50 percent increase in London crime between 1810 and 1815. According to Colquhoun, this crime wave was the work of more than 50,000 'floating delinquents' who had access to as many as 8,000 places known to receive stolen goods. He confirmed Bennet's assertion that the deterioration was being fed by an increase in the number of prostitutes who gained 'a considerable portion of their sustenance by the robbery of those who come into contact with them', aided and abetted by thieves who tutored them in their crimes and fenced the proceeds.[327]

On the subject of public house licensing, Colquhoun's position was similar to Conant's: that the magistrates, at least in his own district, were doing everything in their power to close down disreputable premises. But it seemed clear to Bennet that there was something in Barber Beaumont's tale of corruption in the East End. Colquhoun told Bennet that, when he had first been appointed a licensing magistrate at Worship Street in 1792, he had been shocked at the laxity of the licensing process and had suppressed 87 gin-shops in two years. It was time for Bennet to dig deeper.[328]

The following Monday, Barber Beaumont took his seat in front of the Committee. He wasted no time on pleasantries. Bennet's very first question, a gentle enquiry about Beaumont's general views on policing, drew forth a long speech on the social causes of crime, beginning with the indoctrination of children by criminal gangs and going on to attack the reward system, flash-houses, prison conditions, the treatment of discharged servicemen, receivers of stolen goods and the immoral influence of the state lottery.[329]

Among his many talents, Beaumont was a seasoned pamphleteer and had developed a knack for a well-crafted and passionate speech. His moving description of the plight of the children of the criminal classes had the ring of a sermon:

The first instructions and ideas these little creatures receive are to procure the means of life by begging and thieving. I have seen children of not more than seven or eight years of age initiated into the trade of picking of pockets, under the eye of adults, seemingly their mothers…in the next stage of their education, they are introduced to *flash-houses*, there they see thieves and thief-takers sitting and drinking together on terms of good fellowship; all they see and hear is calculated to make them believe they may rob without fear of punishment…they do not reflect that the forbearance of the officers will continue no longer than until they commit a £40 crime, when they will be sacrificed.[330]

As he itemised each vice, Beaumont articulated his own proposed remedies. It was music to Bennet's ears; the exchange between the two men gave the strong impression of having been rehearsed beforehand and was carefully planned to lead to the crux of Beaumont's arguments. He had been nursing a grudge against Joseph Merceron for more than three years and it was now time to repay it. Approaching the climax of his speech, Beaumont announced:

I am now come to a subject of universal influence on the morals of the public. It is decidedly my opinion that low public-houses, flash-houses and gin-shops, compose the foundation and hotbed of nearly all the vices and crimes which disturb the metropolis…The evil, however, is inseparable from the law, which gives to certain individuals…the power of setting up or putting down such houses, subject to no other control than that of their own private wills and unsearchable motives.[331]

Bennet took his cue. Had Beaumont ever been present when public-house licences were issued? When Beaumont answered in the affirmative, Bennet asked whether he had experienced any examples of negligence on the part of the magistrates. It was cleverly done. Mindful of the government pressure to frame his inquiry as narrowly as possible, Bennet had planned the whole exchange to enable the licensing scandal to be exposed by what both men could claim were honest answers to innocent questions. Beaumont then recounted his unsuccessful attempt to obtain a public-house licence in Mile End, although somewhat disingenuously he left out the tale of his entrapment by the tax collector Smallwood. He alleged that many of the public houses in the district were disorderly, that 'the worst practices' were allowed in them and that the magistrates had overruled objections in re-licensing such premises. He confirmed that the magistrates routinely conspired in the operation of flash houses and brothels and concluded with a full account of Joseph Fletcher's dispute with Joseph Merceron over the brothels on Shadwell High Street.

In the course of his examination, Beaumont laid bare the whole system of corruption underpinning the licensing process. He explained the pernicious influence of the brewers Truman, Hanbury & Co, and the stranglehold operated over the system by certain magistrates, naming Merceron and Sir Daniel Williams as particular culprits. He also alluded to the existence of the mysterious network of family and business relationships that pervaded the local government and business world of the East End.[332]

The next few days saw a stream of further witnesses come forward in support of Beaumont's allegations. Joseph Fletcher appeared in person and repeated the story of Merceron's persistent licensing of the Shadwell brothels. Several publicans told how Merceron had withheld their licences until they had agreed to give the trade to Hanbury's. One alleged that Merceron had personally requested a bribe of £100 in order to arrange a licence. The senior police magistrate at Worship Street, John Gifford, a well-known and respected former journalist, confirmed that he had witnessed the deliberate licensing of flash-houses and told Bennet that, impotent in the face of Merceron's great influence, he had 'in great measure absented himself' from the licensing meetings in disgust.[333]

Beaumont's allegations were sufficiently serious to warrant urgent investigation, particularly as some of the accused magistrates were Home Office employees. The Select Committee was due to suspend its proceedings for three weeks from 10th May – during which

Bennet was to be married – and so Sir Daniel Williams was hurriedly summoned to appear as the last witness before the recess. Bennet began his interrogation of Williams gently, suggesting that the Whitechapel Office, like Conant's in Bow Street, was not exactly staffed with energetic young men (Beaumont had told him that one of Williams's fellow magistrates was 76 years old and so deaf that he could not hear without the aid of an ear trumpet.) When Bennet moved the subject to the licensing process and in particular the dispute with Fletcher over *The Duke of York*, however, the increasingly irritated Williams claimed he could not remember the details. Bennet turned the conversation to the existence of brothels, whereupon Williams tied himself in knots, at first denying and then, in the very next answer, confirming the existence of such 'cock and hen' clubs.[334]

As the Committee broke up for the recess, and as Bennet prepared for his wedding, he could reflect that the first fortnight of his inquiry had been a great success, although it was unlikely that Home Secretary Lord Sidmouth would have seen it that way. Bennet's enquiries had demonstrated that the existing system of police offices was hopelessly disconnected and incapable of rooting out the causes of crime. Worse, its officers were implicated at the highest levels in a network of corruption that had dominated the East End for at least two decades.

In Bethnal Green, meanwhile, rumours had begun to spread about the unfolding scandal. The resulting passions encouraged Joshua King to launch another attack on Merceron's rule. During Sunday service on 21st April, before Bennet's Committee began its hearing, King distributed a notice protesting at the 'illegal and arbitrary proceedings' at the Easter vestry elections the previous week and criticising 'the overbearing conduct of Joseph Merceron Esquire'. In an unusual move, King ordered the parish clerk to read the notice out loud to the congregation. It announced that Merceron, in the face of potential opposition, had held the Easter elections in private, before the appointed time, ensured the success of his own candidates and then presented the results as a *fait accompli*. His confidence boosted by the knowledge that Beaumont was about to expose Merceron to the House of Commons, King's motion condemned Merceron for 'withholding money from the overseers, forcing them to use their own money or suffer the poor to go unrelieved, while the treasurer holds very large balances in his hands'. The motion went on to propose legal action to reverse the result of the elections, a detailed investigation into Merceron's accounts and a requirement for him to deposit the parish funds with the Bank of England.[335]

As usual, Merceron launched an immediate counter-attack. In the days leading up to the vestry meeting to debate King's motion, he called in some favours. A counter-resolution was issued, stating that:

> ...the vestry is fully satisfied from the clearest evidence of the upright conduct and the disinterested attention of Joseph Merceron Esq, Treasurer, to the concerns of this parish, that it cannot but express its abhorrence, reprobation and merited contempt of all the propositions and innuendoes contained in the said notice, and therefore feel a pleasure that an opportunity is given to record the high sense it has of his very valuable and truly meritorious services.

At the vestry meeting, King's support evaporated in the face of an angry crowd. Merceron's counter-resolution was passed by more than 200 votes, with just one (presumably Wrightson) daring to oppose it. To add further insult, Merceron called a vote reaffirming previous resolutions that the Rector had 'forfeited all claim to confidence and respect'.[336]

On Sunday 12th May, buoyed up by the news filtering back of the evidence presented to the Police Committee, King and Wrightson tried their hand again. In the church, King circulated a paper repeating his earlier resolutions and condemning Merceron's 'tyrannical' rule. Merceron responded by calling out a mob. Four days later, the vestry voted resoundingly that King's paper was 'libellous and defamatory' and agreed to obtain a counsel's opinion on the chances of success of a libel action against him for publishing his accusations in the church.[337]

The Police Committee resumed its inquiry on 30th May. The ensuing fortnight was mostly spent examining issues unrelated to Merceron's activities, but on Monday 10th June, Bennet called Joshua King as a witness. As with Beaumont, it seems clear that King's evidence had been well rehearsed in advance; Bennet knew just which questions to ask the Rector in order to ensure that Merceron's activities were exposed.

King began his evidence with a description of the social conditions in Merceron's Bethnal Green. The population had risen to around 40,000; mostly, as King put it, 'the lowest description of people'. The workhouse was 'overflowing with poor' with 700 people crammed into a space designed for half as many, sleeping 'as many as six or seven in a bed'. The workhouse was the only option for such people, due to the pitiful allowances provided to the outdoor poor by 'the inhumanity of the parish officers'. The moral condition of the parish was woeful, with just one church and only 120 children receiving any formal education.[338]

Asked by Bennet to elaborate, King gave an account of the Sunday bullock-hunters who would routinely disrupt his morning service. Merceron, despite his responsibilities for maintaining the peace, was a ringleader, taking no steps to prevent 'so wanton and disgraceful an outrage'. On the contrary, Merceron permitted even the parish constable, his own clerk, to join in the sport. Just two months earlier, a bullock had been chased into the churchyard. King had called in the police from Worship Street on several occasions, but they 'durst not interfere', on account of the mob being 'so numerous and so desperate'.

With the subject brought conveniently to Merceron, Bennet next asked King about the state of the local public houses. King replied that they were 'very disorderly', and that 'great blame is imputable to the acting magistrates...for not suppressing the licences'. He gave three examples of pubs in the streets around Brick Lane (either owned by Merceron or where he acted as agent for the owner) that were 'a receptacle for suspicious characters, at hours when all other public houses are closed'. *The Sun*, in Sclater Street, was particularly notorious, and hosted what King described as 'a cock and hen club'.

King, at this point somewhat economical with the truth, denied any personal difference with Merceron other than what he described as 'a disapprobation of his professional conduct'. The bitterness caused by six years of humiliation weighed heavily, however, and given his head by Bennet, the Rector launched into a powerful character assassination of his adversary:

> He is universally abhorred; but having the collection of rents to a very considerable extent...and as he can command the publicans by being a licensing magistrate, and having been a Commissioner of the Property Tax, and sitting on all appeals with respect to the assessed as well as parochial taxes, he has had an opportunity of most despotically tyrannising over the parish...he has amassed a large fortune without any ostensible means...he takes care to elect the most ignorant and the lowest characters, on whom he can depend, to fill all parish offices, and to audit his accounts...his influence is so extensive in the parish, that whoever he nominates, the vestry is sure to sanction and support...with the assistance of the dissenters, with whom he has allied himself, and the publicans who dare not withhold their support, he bears down all opposition...every officer in the parish is appointed by Mr Merceron, and all obey his mandates.

Perhaps feeling that he should support these accusations with specifics, King turned next to the £12,000 grant made by Parliament in 1800. He had brought the relevant extracts from the parish register and handed these to Bennet, claiming that he believed the money 'was not applied to the purpose for which it was intended, nor is it satisfactorily accounted for', adding that Merceron had claimed to have lost the vouchers. When Bennet asked why there had not been a full investigation into the missing funds, King, describing the events that had taken place the previous May, admitted that Merceron had been too strong for him:

> ...in order to prevent investigation, I have seen him instigate his creatures to riot and clamour, even within the walls of the church; he has taken his stand on the church steps, and proposed three times three huzzas, taking his hat off, and being the foremost in the shout; so successful was he on that occasion, that lately he has adjourned all public vestry meetings to the churchyard, where a mob has collected to support him. He instigated that mob at a late meeting, to attack a person by the name of Shevill who, had he not taken refuge in my house, would probably have fallen a sacrifice to their fury.

As King vented his frustration, Bennet listened patiently. It was a fascinating story, and would no doubt make good copy for the newspapers when the Committee's report was published, but none of it was hard evidence of illegal activity. He steered the Rector back to firmer ground. Had there not been legal steps taken to combat Merceron's behaviour? King recounted the story of his attempt to prosecute Merceron in 1813 and the mysterious manner in which Merceron had been acquitted.

Bennet realised that, despite Merceron's acquittal in a court of law, the alterations of the rate books in Merceron's own handwriting provided a golden opportunity for his exposure as a fraudster. While this was not directly relevant to the state of the police of the metropolis, and was therefore most definitely outside the narrow remit of the inquiry requested by the Home Secretary, Bennet decided that it would help his wider aim of exposing the corruption of the East End magistrates and boost his campaign for licensing reform. He immediately sent instructions for the Bethnal Green vestry clerk

James May to be called before the Committee the following day and ordered him to bring with him the parish rate books.

Returning his examination of King to public house licensing, Bennet asked about the influence of the major brewers. Having gone so far in his evidence against Merceron, King was in no mood to stop now. He replied that:

> ...a man is a fool who applies for a licence through the medium of any other person than Messrs. Hanbury; I know there is an intimacy and connection between Mr Merceron and them, for I heard Mr Merceron declare...that Hanbury was a devilish good fellow, that he was always sending him presents, that he supplied his house with beer gratis, and that the week before he had sent him half a barrel of porter.[339]

King's evidence lasted the whole afternoon. By the close, he had painted a compelling picture of Merceron's tyranny; Bennet, who had orchestrated the proceedings brilliantly, must have felt delighted. The following afternoon a very nervous James May, having lugged his heavy rate books across London, faced Bennet in what promised to be an extremely uncomfortable ordeal.

In 1816 May was 64 years old and had been the vestry clerk of Bethnal Green for 28 of them; having replaced his father in the post just a year after Merceron had first become Treasurer. Throughout all that time, no one had a more detailed understanding of Joseph Merceron's business methods. May knew that, over the next few hours, he faced the unpleasant choice either of perjuring himself or of incurring the inevitable wrath and retribution of his master. His subsequent behaviour suggests that he had not yet decided which of these options would be worst.[340]

As Bennet questioned May, it was obvious that the MP had been particularly well briefed. This was hardly surprising: the ground he was covering was that on which King's legal action of 1813 was based, and it soon became clear that Bennet had been given access to the case notes. Bennet took up the rate book for 1807 and began to turn the pages. Almost casually, he asked: 'Are the rates ever altered, after they have been approved by the magistrates?'[341]

May prevaricated. If there had been any error, he replied, he would correct the books himself. Bennet flicked through the book, presenting May with several examples of rates having been altered to double their original amount. 'Whose handwriting is this?' he asked. May tried to delay the inevitable. 'I am a very bad judge of handwriting…' he began, but after some prodding by Bennet he admitted, reluctantly, that the writing appeared to be Merceron's. Betraying the detail in which he had been briefed, Bennet asked May to locate the rate assessments for the schoolteacher Charlotte Cowdry and for Robert Wrightson. Once again, May was forced to admit that Merceron had dramatically increased these assessments. Bennet toyed with him: 'Were there a great many instances of Merceron's changes?' May could see 'six or seven'; Bennet suggested the number was nearer 80 or 90. May was unable to explain this, but had to admit that the practice was illegal. Confronted with irrefutable evidence, and realising that it would be foolish not to co-operate, he acknowledged that Merceron had altered the rates in each of the years 1805 to 1808, the years for which he had given Bennet the rate books.[342]

Bennet was armed with a convincing body of evidence against Merceron. Beaumont, Fletcher, King, May; the publicans with their stories of bribes: each had a tale to tell and, together, had painted a comprehensive and disturbing picture of the rule of law in London's East End. It was time to put the accusations to the man behind the whole crooked system. That evening, Bennet issued a general summons calling Joseph Merceron to attend before his Select Committee in three days' time.

CHAPTER XII

That Guilty, that Shuffling Magistrate...

*I must say, that it is my opinion the Lord Chancellor has
not done his duty in allowing that guilty, that shuffling
magistrate, Mr Merceron, to retain his situation.*

Henry Grey Bennet[343]

Merceron's first appearance before the Select Committee began
shortly after one o'clock on Friday June 14th 1816. Bennet began his
examination with an exchange of pleasantries in which the two men
discussed the increasing poverty among the Spitalfields weavers and
Merceron bemoaned the increase in swearing among teenage boys.
When Bennet turned the subject to bullock hunting, the questioning
remained gentle and Merceron firmly denied any involvement, claiming, on the contrary, that he was actively trying to suppress the sport.
Bennet's failure to press harder on this topic infuriated his friend,
the Radical agitator Francis Place, who had briefed him to focus
on this issue. Place later wrote that 'the enquiry was very carelessly
performed' by Bennet. In reality, Bennet had decided to concentrate
on public house licensing and was deliberately leading Merceron into
a false sense of security, the more easily to trip him up when it
mattered.[344]

When Bennet turned the conversation to the licensing process,
his questions immediately became sharper. Merceron acknowledged
that he had attended the licensing sessions for many years. Almost
immediately, he found himself on the defensive, admitting that he
owned a dozen or so public houses, with an interest in a similar
number as agent. Up until this point, his answers had been calm and

measured. But when asked if any of his own alehouses had been the subject of complaint, Merceron became flustered and began to contradict himself: 'Upon my word I cannot take upon myself to say… probably they might…I think there have been very heavy complaints against *The Sun*'.

Even Bennet could not have expected to be on such profitable ground so soon. Why then, he asked, had *The Sun*'s licence been renewed? Merceron now claimed he could not recall the complaints. He began to panic; further contradictions followed. Bennet pressed on. Should not Merceron, as a magistrate, have felt it his duty to oppose the licensing?

'Certainly', replied Merceron.
Did you so oppose it?
I do not know that there were any charges.
But you have referred to many complaints?
It was frequently shut up, and I believe there have been complaints.
Knowing it repeatedly shut up, and a bad house, did you resist the licensing?
I do not know there were complaints on the licensing day.

As the exchange continued, Bennet's questions became increasingly specific and Merceron dug himself deeper into trouble:

You were present at the last licensing and gave your sanction?
I do not know.
You said you were always present?
I think I was present, but I cannot say.
Then how do you reconcile your consent?
I do not know that I did [consent]… it was, perhaps, done as a matter of course.
Did you oppose it?
I do not know that I did.

Merceron's performance was dreadful. Similar exchanges followed in respect of *The Seven Stars* and *The Three Sugar Loaves*, two other inns owned by Merceron that Joshua King had listed as disorderly. Asked if it was possible that any of his own public houses could be 'a nightly resort of thieves, and boys and girls meeting in what are termed "cock and hen clubs" with the different varieties of low debauchery in which bad people indulge', Merceron denied any knowledge of such places. He claimed that they could not exist without being known to the police at Worship Street, and suggested that if they did exist in Bethnal Green, it was the fault of the parish constable.

Bennet now turned his attention to the re-licensing of *The Duke of York* and the other brothels of Shadwell High Street, whereupon Merceron seemed to suffer a further lapse of memory:

Did not [the parish officers of Shadwell] say it would be a great nuisance if [the brothels] were re-licensed?
They might have, but I cannot recollect.
Why were they reopened?
I cannot recollect.
Why were they reopened?
I cannot recollect, but they had suffered severely and were no worse than the others, but we were unanimous.
What is the principle you adopt [in re-licensing such premises]?
The public convenience.
Did the public convenience require the re-licensing?
I cannot say.
Did you say that the licences were taken away because these three houses were worse than others?
I did.
But you now say you re-licensed them because they were no worse?
I should presume so.
What is your real opinion?
I should suppose they might be worse.

And so it continued. As the afternoon wore on, Bennet's searching questions continued relentlessly and Merceron continued to prevaricate and contradict himself. Just before the session drew to a close and he allowed Merceron to return home, with the remainder of his examination held over until after the weekend, Bennet produced his trump card:

> This Committee has received evidence of a prosecution by the Reverend Joshua King against you for altering the parish rates... we have also examined the vestry clerk and inspected the rate books, in which are several alterations which Mr May says are your handwriting. We think it right to tell you this and ask do you have any remarks or explanations?

Merceron tried to shrug it off. The matter had been fully and satisfactorily explained in the Court of King's Bench, he said; the parish was satisfied it was all through a mistake, and all monies received had been brought to account. But there was still time for one last contradiction. As Bennet began to put away his papers for the day, the following exchange took place:

> *Do you admit you made the alterations?*
> Certainly not.
> *Do you deny making them?*
> I should wish to see them.
> *Did you ever make any alterations?*
> Certainly.[345]

That Saturday, Merceron, as was his habit, spent the morning at his office in Brick Lane. He summoned James May there to explain himself, a far more intimidating ordeal than May had endured from Bennet. Short of perjury, May had done everything he could to avoid incriminating Merceron, but it is unlikely that the latter would have seen it that way. There is plenty of evidence suggesting Merceron viewed perjury as a natural consequence of the loyalty he required from subordinates. It is easy to imagine May shaking as he talked an angry and threatening Merceron through every moment of his interview with Bennet.

On the following Monday morning, before setting off for Westminster to continue his testimony, Merceron took a folded and yellowing newspaper clipping from his desk and put it into his coat pocket. It was the advertisement he had placed in *The Times* three years earlier, announcing his acquittal for fraud and perjury in 1813. Despite his humiliation by Bennet on the previous Friday, Merceron felt confident that the clipping would be enough to silence any awkward questions. James May had also been summoned again by Bennet to answer supplementary questions. He must have spent an uncomfortable day sharing a waiting room with Merceron or passing him in the corridors as they alternated in giving evidence.

When Merceron's turn came to be examined, Bennet returned to the subject of the rate alterations. Merceron tried to stall him, pulling the *Times* clipping from his pocket and offering to read out the account of his acquittal. But Bennet stopped him, instructing him curtly to 'answer the questions as put'. In the face of persistent questioning, Merceron was forced to admit that he had altered the rates after their approval by the magistrates. Then why, asked Bennet, had he denied this the previous Friday?[346]

'Really,' replied Merceron, his face a picture of innocence, 'you must have misunderstood me.'

As Bennet began to cite specific examples of rate-tampering from the books in front of him, Merceron once again tried to read from the newspaper in his hand, quoting Lord Ellenborough's statement to the jury at his trial that the alterations had 'proceeded from irregularity, without corrupt motives'. After some argument, Bennet agreed to Merceron tabling the clipping as evidence. On reading the clipping, however, Bennet noticed that the account was not part of the usual 'Law Report' section of the newspaper, but merely an advertisement. When he queried this, Merceron admitted that it had been placed in the newspaper by his own solicitor. Bennet repeated Joshua King's assertion that the Rector's solicitor had somehow been tampered with and persuaded to drop the case, but Merceron denied this, saying: 'I believe not. I never understood it, I was ready to meet the charges…there was no compromise on my part, nor any wish to decline meeting the case; I was quite ready to have gone into it.'

Bennet now insisted upon questioning Merceron about specific instances where the rates had been altered. Forced to admit having made these alterations in the face of evidence in his own handwriting, Merceron now sought to implicate James May, stating that the vestry clerk 'must have known' of the alterations, as May had at various times commenced legal actions to recover the increased and disputed amounts. He vigorously denied the Rector's other allegations, including that of the mob's attack on William Shevill, attributing King's motives in accusing him to the 'very great personal difference' between them. Merceron admitted to a close business friendship with Sampson Hanbury – insisting that Hanbury was 'a respectable, charitable man' – but was adamant that there was no hint of corruption in their dealings. He accepted that Hanbury would give him 'every now and then a hare and a brace of pheasants' but denied any question of any favours in return.[347]

Faced with such categorical denials, Bennet saw little point in pursuing this line of questioning and allowed Merceron to go home. He had plenty of evidence about the rate alterations; the corroborating accounts of Beaumont, Fletcher and the various publicans together amounted to a compelling case when it came to the issue of public house licensing. The next day, however, Bennet made a vital breakthrough. Leafing through James May's ledgers, he noticed an unusually large entry. It was the item for £925, headed 'Dann & Crosland's bill', that Merceron had secretly posted back in August 1813 and which he had conspired to hide during the audit of his accounts the following spring. Bennet knew nothing of the transaction, but the size of the amount involved, and the fact that it was for legal expenses, aroused his curiosity. He decided to recall Merceron to the hearing.

Late the following afternoon, Merceron again took his place in the witness chair. On being asked by Bennet about the mysterious transaction, he explained that it represented the costs of defending himself against King's charges, adding that it had been 'paid by a vote of the vestry, expressly called for the purpose'. This must have seemed peculiar to Bennet but he made no further comment and allowed Merceron to leave. Bennet spent the next few days in tying up loose ends before formally closing the initial stage of his inquiry on 26th June.[348]

Bennet's first report was published in the last week of August. He had uncovered so many issues that, instead of attempting to draw conclusions at this stage, he simply published the transcripts of the evidence together with a short report in which he asked that the Committee be given more time to explore the subject at greater length. *The Times* called the report 'very important and interesting' and immediately began to serialise the transcripts. The newspaper was quick to appreciate the significance of the licensing scandal. On 29th August, it commented that 'the culpable negligence of some of the magistrates in licensing public houses and gin-shops is the source of almost all the profligacy and crime that disgrace the metropolis'.[349]

While press attention was focussed on the licensing scandal, Joshua King had been more excited by a detail almost hidden towards the end of Bennet's report. King learned that Merceron had told Bennet quite distinctly that Dann & Crosland's invoice had been paid by order of a vestry meeting expressly called for the purpose. King could recall no such meeting. He consulted with Wrightson, who insisted that there had been no mention of the invoice at the 1814 audit of Merceron's accounts. They checked the vestry notice book; as expected, there was no mention of such a meeting. They went to James May and demanded to examine the rate books for themselves. Sure enough, the entry was there, but Wrightson continued to insist that the payment of the invoice had never been disclosed at the audit.

Finally and with great reluctance, May admitted that he had long been aware of the deception. Suddenly, and almost by accident, King had unearthed hard evidence of Merceron's criminal activity.[350]

On Monday 2nd September 1816, as King and Wrightson digested the implications of their discovery, the annual public-house licensing day for the Tower Hamlets was taking place. For Isaac Rennoldson, parish constable of Bethnal Green, it was the most important day of the year. It was the constable's duty to attend the licensing hearing and inform the magistrates whether he was aware of any complaints against any of the local pubs. Rennoldson had been concerned to learn that Merceron, in his evidence to Bennet's Committee, had blamed him for not reporting disreputable houses. He determined, therefore, to prove the opposite and assembled a detailed list of complaints that he intended presenting that afternoon. At 10 o'clock, however, there came a knock at the door, and to his great surprise Rennoldson found Merceron standing outside.[351]

'Mr Rennoldson, today is our licensing day!' began Merceron, and demanded to know whether Rennoldson intended presenting any complaints that afternoon. Rennoldson showed him a list which included about a quarter of Bethnal Green's 90 or so public houses, which he intended to report for a variety of offences including keeping late hours, lewd behaviour and illegal gambling. Several of these houses were either owned by Merceron or paid their rents through him. Merceron read the list, and staring the constable firmly in the eye gave him some advice: 'Mr. Rennoldson, you must be very particular…if you present these houses before the magistrates today, you may be the means of depriving them and their families of their livelihood.' He ordered Rennoldson not to report the houses; instead, Merceron would see the publicans himself and chastise them. When Rennoldson murmured something about his report to the magistrates being under oath, Merceron told him not to worry and that such an oath was 'a mere matter of form.' The constable insisted he could not lie under oath. Merceron warned him again: 'if you must present them, be careful what you are doing…' Under pressure,

Rennoldson agreed to a compromise. The constable would present a complaint about one house only, *The Golden Key*, and would keep silent about all the others – including all those in which Merceron had a personal interest. Satisfied, Merceron took his leave, taking Rennoldson's list with him.[352]

At noon that day, Rennoldson presented himself at the White-chapel courthouse where he found Merceron and Sir Daniel Williams in attendance with two other magistrates. When Williams asked him for his report, Rennoldson did as instructed, giving only the details of *The Golden Key*. At the end of the hearing, as the magistrates signed the licences for the approved premises, Merceron himself took the lead in signing those for the ones on Rennoldson's list. *The Golden Key's* licence was held over pending the appeal hearing scheduled for September 16th.[353]

Over the next fortnight, *The Times* continued to serialise the Police Committee's report. The highlight came on 10–11th September when the newspaper printed a verbatim account of Barber Beaumont's exposure of the licensing scandal and named Merceron and Williams as the corrupt magistrates involved. Two days later came the evidence of the publicans outlining the bribes needed to obtain a licence, again alleging the involvement of Merceron and the senior management of Sampson Hanbury's brewery.[354]

Three days later, when the Tower Division magistrates reassembled for the licensing appeal hearing, Merceron and Williams were furious to find Barber Beaumont in attendance, determined to get his own pub licensed at last. For his part, Beaumont believed that having publicly exposed their corrupt system, the magistrates would not dare to refuse him again.

He underestimated them. That afternoon, it seemed to Beaumont that every decision taken by the magistrates went against the grain of morality. First, *The Golden Key* – the only Bethnal Green alehouse that Merceron had permitted Rennoldson to complain about – was relicensed. The magistrates proceeded to license 11 known brothels in the parish of Aldgate, all of which had been complained of by the local parish officers as 'the resort of most dissolute persons', committing 'indecencies of such a nature as to shock and disgust' passers-by. A constable testified that there were frequently 20 or 30 prostitutes working each of the premises but the Reverend Robson, ever the brothel-keeper's friend, proposed their re-licensing with Merceron seconding it. Beaumont found it 'a waste of breath' to protest. Yet his own alehouse, with no other pub within half a mile, was turned down 'with a sneering look' by his fellow justices, with Williams, Merceron and Robson united in their opposition.[355]

The next morning, *The Times* carried an advertisement for a book to be published that day. The book contained the evidence from Bennet's report together with more than 100 pages of caustic commentary by an anonymous 'Magistrate of the County of Middlesex' – Barber Beaumont. It was dedicated to Bennet 'as a tribute of gratitude for the zeal, assiduity and perseverance with which he has conducted an inquiry, originating with himself, and embracing objects of the highest consequence to the welfare and security of the public.' Joshua King was also congratulated: in speaking 'without fear' of Merceron's activities in Bethnal Green, he had 'unfolded such a tale as must open all eyes which are not wilfully shut'.[356]

The Times continued its serialisation of Bennet's report, printing Joseph Fletcher's account of the Shadwell High Street brothels on 19th September and Sir Daniel Williams' evidence on 18th October. But on 1st November, as the paper was due to print Joshua King's evidence (which should ordinarily have been followed by that of James May and of Merceron himself) the serialisation ended abruptly and without warning, despite the words 'to be continued' at the foot of the last extract.[357]

Why did *The Times* cease its serialisation? The obvious inference is that, yet again, Merceron intervened to prevent his exposure from becoming even more widespread. He would certainly have been willing to pay a large sum to achieve such an outcome. There is, however, another possible explanation. Political unrest among the lower orders, particularly in the East End of London, had again begun to take a disturbing turn. There were credible reports of the activities of secret gangs of revolutionaries, and the government's spy network was hard at work in keeping abreast of developments. It would be less than helpful for *The Times*, a staunch supporter of the government, to publicise accounts of wrongdoing among the governing elite of the East End. Even more importantly, aspects of Joshua King's evidence, if publicised in the national press, could compromise the government's espionage activity.

1816 had begun badly enough for the government with its humiliating defeat over the income tax. Matters thereafter had got steadily worse. The price of corn increased dramatically, triggered by fears – and then the actuality – of a poor harvest. A spate of machine breaking – vandalization of the agricultural engines that were seen as threatening labourers' livelihoods – began in May in rural East Anglia and spread towards London. By July, as economic conditions worsened, especially in the new industrial towns of the north and Midlands, there were a number of strikes. In the East End, with large numbers of unemployed sailors and soldiers on the streets, the silk weavers of Spitalfields and Bethnal Green were among the worst affected by the crisis, and the districts were included in an advertisement in *The Times* calling for subscriptions for relief of the manufacturing and labouring poor. In June, Merceron had told Bennet that there were 21,000 unemployed in the area; by November the number had more than doubled.[358]

These conditions proved inflammatory in the hands of Sir Francis Burdett, now firmly established as a Radical MP for Westminster. On 11th September, the day that Beaumont's anonymous accusations about Merceron were published by *The Times*, Burdett called for petitions for reform across the country at a huge public rally in Westminster. Word spread rapidly, and Radical societies known as 'Hampden Clubs' began to spring up almost overnight. As the downtrodden machine workers and labourers rallied to the cause, Burdett's relatively modest calls to extend the franchise to all ratepayers were soon replaced by a clamour for universal manhood suffrage.[359]

The Home Secretary, Lord Sidmouth, already annoyed at the way in which Bennet had handled the Police Committee, decided it was time to be seen to act. On 21st October he wrote to the Lord Chancellor, Lord Eldon, requesting his opinion on whether, in the light of the evidence against them, Williams, Merceron and Robson should be struck off as magistrates.[360]

Eldon replied on 4th November. Mindful of the political climate, and the effect that the government's public acknowledgement of corruption by magistrates might have, he did not see that the evidence warranted such draconian action. 'The discretion of the Crown is extremely large,' he wrote, noting that much of Bennet's report appeared 'not to have the character of evidence'. Instead, it was mere 'hearsay, without even the mention of the names of those from whom it has been heard,' and in many instances it was 'a mere matter of opinion'. Eldon realised, however, that it would be helpful if the government could state that they were considering the matter, and in that light he recommended that Sidmouth pass the evidence to the Attorney General, 'to see if he recommends any judicial proceedings against any of the gentlemen.'[361]

Sidmouth did as the Lord Chancellor suggested and wrote to Sir William Garrow accordingly. But both the Home Secretary and the Attorney General knew what the answer must be. By the time Garrow sat down to reply on New Year's Eve, the situation was such that public intervention by the government against the East End magistrates was unthinkable. By this time, the increasingly angry mood among the working classes was being skilfully exploited by a small group of ultra-Radicals, far more extreme in their views than the likes of Sir Francis Burdett. The group included the 'fanatical demagogue', Henry 'Orator' Hunt, who agreed to speak at a mass rally arranged for 15th November in Spa Fields, adjacent to Coldbath Fields prison.[362]

On the appointed day, Hunt, accompanied by friends waving a French tricolour, addressed a crowd of thousands from the windows of the *Merlin's Cave* alehouse. Pointing out the imposing walls of what he described as the 'British Bastille' across the field, he reminded the crowd of its tyrannous history in repressing their liberties less than 20 years previously. The war with France might be over, he told them, but the ruling classes were still oppressing the poor through taxation and corruption. The repeal of income tax had benefited the rich enormously, but the poor 'might go to the devil their own way' as far as the government were concerned. Only the day before, he had heard of a poor labourer in Spitalfields, who 'with a wife and three children had been heard to pray that some friendly hand would deliver him from the intolerable load of life'. The taxation system was the result of the 'immense debt contracted for a long, unnecessary and unjust war', and the lavish waste of public money on the systems of sinecures and pensions whereby Whigs and Tories alike 'fattened themselves on the spoils of the people'. Ridiculing the charitable efforts of the likes of William Wilberforce to raise money to relieve the poor, he told the crowd that such wealthy benefactors 'subscribed their mite in charity, while they drew their thousands from an oppressed people'. It was stirring stuff, and there was relief among the government and local magistrates when the meeting generated only minor disturbances and a resolution merely to petition the Prince Regent to 'redress the public wrongs'.[363]

Ironically, the next day saw an example of the middle-class philanthropic behaviour that Orator Hunt found so sickening. Conditions in Spitalfields had continued to deteriorate and were worse than any in living memory. In the weaving trade alone it was estimated that 30,000 were unemployed; when all the associated trades were taken into account the number in want was probably half as many again. Local businessmen formed a committee to organise assistance and on 16th November wrote an open address to the Lord Mayor to lobby for funds. It was impossible, they claimed, for anyone not living in the district to comprehend 'the extreme distress that prevails there'. Many of the inhabitants had been forced to sell their furniture and clothing to buy food. The workhouses in Spitalfields, Bethnal

Green and Mile End were full and the committee foresaw many dying from cold and hunger as winter approached.[364]

The letter was signed by representatives of a number of related Quaker banking families beginning to dominate the City: Barclay, Richardson, Overend, Gurney. Two other signatories were members of a wider Quaker dynasty: Sampson Hanbury, apparently living up to Merceron's description of him as 'a charitable man, doing a great deal of good' and his nephew and junior partner Thomas Fowell Buxton. Both had married into the Gurney family. Their brewery manager Thomas Aveling, who had been accused of personal involvement with Merceron in the licensing scandal, was a further signatory.[365]

As a result of the letter, a public meeting was arranged for Tuesday November 26th to discuss the Spitalfields issue. The contrast with Orator Hunt's Spa Fields rally could hardly have been greater. Given that the thousands of starving weavers under discussion were less than a mile away, the surroundings were incongruous, to say the least. The gathering took place in the splendid Egyptian Hall at the Lord Mayor's Mansion House, chaired by the Lord Mayor himself and with seats reserved for 'a considerable number of ladies'. *The Times* eulogised the noble efforts of the great and good, contrasting their efforts with those of Henry Hunt: 'the poor have many friends in this great metropolis... whose sincerity is proved, not by tedious or inflammatory harangues; but by giving food to the hungry, and clothing the naked.' Hunt, on the other hand, was simply 'an infuriated declaimer exciting the distressed to riot'.[366]

Reading the account in *The Times*, it is hard not to share Hunt's cynicism. The meeting was conducted in a spirit of pious self-congratulation. The Lord Mayor began it with a condescending list of ideas to help the poor to help themselves, which included the manufacture of cheap fuel by mixing coal with mud from the Thames. Another speaker raised a loud laugh from the audience when he suggested that the rotund former Lord Mayor Sir William Curtis would be able to vouch for the 'real goodness' of the soup being dispensed to the needy. And as he ended the meeting, the current Lord Mayor – in all seriousness – exhorted the ladies present 'to imitate his example, in prohibiting the use of puddings and pies' as a way of reducing the demand for flour and driving down the price of bread.[367]

But the highlight of the Mansion House meeting was a speech by Sampson Hanbury's nephew, Thomas Buxton. At 30 years old, Buxton was about to embark on the political career that would turn him into 'Buxton the Liberator', taking up William Wilberforce's mantle as the leader of the anti-slavery movement. It was this Egyptian Hall speech, based on his own first-hand inspections of the distress in Spitalfields, which first brought Buxton to public attention. Omitting the worst details so as to avoid offending the polite sensibilities of his audience, Buxton told them that he had witnessed 'all the varieties of human wretchedness that could arise from want, nakedness and disease.' The occupants of the workhouses were sleeping four to a bed, but they could be considered the lucky ones: the week before, a man had been found in Bethnal Green lying unconscious from hunger and cold in a field, 'the prey of the vermin'. On being rescued, his first expression had been 'to thank Heaven that he had neither wife nor children'.[368]

Despite all the piety, the appeal launched at the meeting raised £43,000 – equivalent to around £4 million at today's values – largely as a result of Buxton's powerful speech. Much of the money came from City firms but many private individuals also made large donations. The banking magnate Nathan Rothschild gave £100, the Lord Mayor £30 and the Chancellor of the Exchequer 20 guineas. Even the Lord Mayor's domestic servants, by no means the wealthiest occupants of the City, managed the impressive sum of seven pounds, ten shillings and sixpence between them. *The Times*, having supported the cause so warmly in words, gave £50, an amount matched – in what seems to have been a calculated public relations exercise – by Joseph Merceron.[369]

Such a public display of generosity by Merceron was highly unusual. What brought it about? His large donation – almost double that of the Lord Mayor – may have been triggered by a letter to *The Times* two days earlier, timed to coincide with the Egyptian Hall meeting. It was headed 'A Cure for Popular Discontent' and it was signed by 'A Middlesex Magistrate'. The letter's contents were incendiary, and its anonymous author was Barber Beaumont.[370]

Beaumont, frustrated by failure of *The Times* to print those parts of the Police Committee's report dealing with Joshua King's and Merceron's evidence, had decided to take further action himself. His letter was perfectly timed, written just as publicity over the Spitalfields distress was at its height and with government fears of public disturbances running high following the Spa Fields meeting. In it, Beaumont cleverly linked these issues; it was no wonder that the country was at risk of revolution, he argued, when the government representative in the nation's most distressed area was actively stealing from the poor, even as they starved.

Beaumont's letter began by explaining that while the nation's attention had been diverted by the war with France, 'our domestic vermin have been suffered to feed and fatten undisturbedly.' The vermin in question were those who misapplied funds intended for the poor, and those justices abusing their power 'to set up gin-shops, to protect flash-houses, to deprive men of their licences whose interest clashes with their own, and to prevent any house being licensed that may interfere with the monopoly of their brewer-chief.'[371]

In case his readers should be in any doubt as to whom he was referring, Beaumont informed them that the report of the Police Committee clearly showed:

> ...and Mr. Merceron is constrained to admit the fact, that £925 of the Poor's Fund of the parish of Bethnal Green...has been applied by him to the discharge of his lawyer's bill for defending him against certain prosecutions... Another fund, amounting to about £12,000, contributed in a period of great distress in the parish...was never satisfactorily accounted for; Mr Merceron's statement that his counting-house had been broken open, and

the vouchers stolen, the parishioners being so sceptical as to disbelieve, inasmuch as they could not imagine that any man would commit a burglary, and venture his neck, to steal a quantity of dirty receipts... Well may that parish abound with scenes of misery...when the mite extracted from the widow, and the pound bestowed by the benevolent, are alike wrested from the bank of charity in which they were deposited, to feed a vortex to which I will not trust myself to give a name...The Police Report furnishes abundant evidence of the illegal strides which are taken in raising and lowering rates [by] Justice Merceron... What reverence can be expected from the people towards their magistrates, when they are seen to pervert the power which the law gives them over their fellows to objects of personal gain or malice?

It was no surprise, argued Beaumont, that the poor were driven to the brink of revolution. He wound up his tirade with a dig at the public house licensing system, claiming that no laws had ever been 'more tyrannous in exactment, or more impotent in practice...the Spanish courts of inquisition are not more closed against the power of investigation or appeal, than the secret tribunals of public-house licensing.' The only answer to all these evils, he concluded, was to rid the corrupt bodies 'of their unworthy members...to detect and expel the morbid matter, and to restore the body to health and purity'. With that he signed off, promising that detailed proposals for reform of the licensing process would follow.[372]

Beaumont's letter was well-timed, powerfully delivered and broadcast Merceron's alleged misappropriation of public funds to a national audience. For Merceron, it was bad enough that they were published in the Police report, but to have them splashed across the pages of *The Times* was another matter. Merceron's typical response to such a move would have been an immediate libel suit against Beaumont. He had launched just such a suit against Joshua King that summer, after King had criticised him in front of the church congregation, and that case was due to come to court in just a few weeks' time. The fact that a similar suit did not result from Beaumont's letter suggests that Merceron was talked out of it by his lawyers. Perhaps they suggested that a large donation to the Spitalfields Distress Fund might be a more effective way of bolstering his public image.

In the aftermath of Beaumont's accusation that Merceron had used the Bethnal Green poor's rate fund to pay his own legal expenses, Merceron's generosity had little impact on the men running the Distress Fund. On behalf of the Bethnal Green vestry, Merceron had applied to the Fund for a payment of £50 per week to help meet the costs of running the workhouse. Having read Beaumont's letter in *The Times*, however, the committee declined the request, unsurprisingly concluding that the poor might be better off if relieved directly rather than through the hands of their corrupt treasurer.[373]

If Beaumont's letter to *The Times* had any bearing on the Attorney General's assessment of whether to prosecute Merceron, Williams and Robson, it was counterbalanced by further indications of violent unrest. Since 15th November, Henry Hunt had twice attempted to petition the Prince Regent with the resolutions from the Spa Fields rally, both times without success. Frustrated, Hunt was persuaded by colleagues to speak at a further rally at Spa Fields on 2nd December. But Hunt had been duped. John Castle, a government spy and *agent provocateur,* had infiltrated a group of ultra-Radicals and persuaded them to hijack the rally with the aim of triggering enough of an uprising to justify authoritarian counter measures and so overturn the growing reform movement. The group Castle infiltrated were dedicated revolutionaries led by a surgeon, James Watson, and Arthur Thistlewood. They had met for weeks in a number of East End alehouses, agitating among discharged servicemen and the Spitalfields weavers, spreading rumours of mutiny in the army and attacks on the Bank of England and the Tower of London.[374]

On the morning of the rally, Castle, Watson, Thistlewood and their supporters assembled in Bethnal Green, gathering a large crowd behind a French tricolour and marching them westwards down the

Bethnal Green Road. As they went, they launched a drunken rampage in which groups of men, mostly disbanded sailors, looted shops – killing a gunsmith in the process – and rioted in the streets. One small group reached the Tower of London, where they attempted to persuade the troops to mutiny. The rioters terrorised nearby streets for several hours, firing pistols as they went, until they were surrounded and captured by troops. Thanks to information passed back by Castle, however, the government was extremely well prepared. Police had been stationed prominently outside Coldbath Fields prison and, with troops placed around the key routes likely to be used by the rioters, the vast majority of demonstrators dispersed peacefully after listening to Hunt's speech.[375]

Watson, Thistlewood and several others were arrested and charged with High Treason. They were acquitted, however, when Watson's trial collapsed after Castle, the Crown's key witness, was exposed and the extent of his role as *agent provocateur* was revealed. The transcript of the trial contains a hint as to why *The Times* might have dropped its serialisation of Bennet's police report at the end of October 1816, just as it was due to report King's and Merceron's evidence. One of the public houses used by the gang to plan the riot of 2nd December was *The Sun* on Sclater Street, Bethnal Green, the very place named by King in his evidence as the worst example of a 'cock and hen club' and which Bennet had accused Merceron of corruptly licensing. According to the evidence presented at Watson's trial, the gang had met at *The Sun* in the evening of 4th November, just two days after *The Times* ceased its serialisation. It is conceivable that the Home Office was informed of the meeting by its spies and ordered the newspaper to pull its story to avoid frightening the gang underground. It also adds weight to the idea that Merceron and Williams may have been deliberately licensing the known haunts of potential revolutionaries in order to keep them above ground, where they could be spied upon.[376]

Merceron's libel hearing against Joshua King was scheduled for the week after the Spa Fields rally. Just as he had done three years previously, Merceron took his place in the Court of King's Bench under the eye of the Lord Chief Justice, Lord Ellenborough. This time the roles were reversed: Merceron, not King, was the plaintiff. Somewhat remarkably, Merceron's case was to be presented by the Attorney General, Sir William Garrow, who appeared not to have felt any conflict of interest in taking on the case, despite actively considering at that very time whether to institute criminal proceedings against his client.[377]

Garrow opened the proceedings by reading out the accusation of libel, in the form of the draft resolutions, condemning Merceron's behaviour, which King had read out in church the previous spring. There was no dispute that the resolutions had been published; the issue was whether or not they were libellous. Lord Ellenborough immediately observed that King's accusations should have been made in the relative privacy of the vestry room rather than being communicated to the congregation at large. He felt that the resolutions were defamatory, and that King had overstepped the limits of the law. Mindful, however, of the wide publicity that Merceron's activities had recently received, he put it to Garrow 'whether it can serve any useful purpose to this gentleman to pursue this prosecution further.'

Garrow conferred with Merceron, who appeared most upset at Lord Ellenborough's suggestion. Rising, Garrow replied to the judge: 'I am urged exceedingly to state, that Mr Merceron is most anxious to be allowed to show that the charges have no foundation in truth'. Ellenborough was irritated that his hint had not been taken. For a second time, he asked if Merceron would withdraw his prosecution. But Merceron remained sulkily silent, and so Ellenborough had no option but to proceed with his summing up. He told the jury that although King's motives had been honest, he was not justified in repeating his criticisms in front of the church congregation. The jury had no option but to find in Merceron's favour, but seconds later came a shock. Lord Ellenborough was not used to being ignored in his own courtroom and made it clear that any damages awarded to Merceron would be derisory. The matter was dropped.[378]

A fortnight later, on 19th December, Barber Beaumont followed up his vitriolic letter to *The Times* by publishing an open letter to the Home Secretary, Lord Sidmouth, to which he attached a draft Bill for the better regulation of public houses. This time the letter was in his own name, and in it he repeated his accusations of corruption against the East End licensing magistrates, again citing Merceron, Williams and Robson by name and stating that their practices gave them 'an absolute and uncontrollable power' over more than 1,000 public houses.[379]

Under renewed pressure to act, Sidmouth pushed the Attorney General for his views and, bizarrely, Sir William Garrow spent a second New Year's Eve composing a legal opinion on whether Merceron should be prosecuted. Exactly two years previously, he had informed Joseph Fletcher in Shadwell that he did not see the magistrates actuated by corrupt or improper motives. But since then, the full extent of Merceron's 'dirty dealings' – as Beaumont had put it in his letter to *The Times* – had been exposed both in the House of Commons and in the national press. Surely this time the Attorney General would act?

It was not to be. Garrow's opinion was unequivocal, and gave Sidmouth just the excuse he needed not to intervene:

> If these magistrates could be charged with any offence, it must be, that they have partially and corruptly exercised the discretionary power with which the law has entrusted them in granting or refusing licences...one of the accusations [is] that acting under the influence of certain brewers of the name of Hanbury & Co, they refuse licences to houses which do not belong to or deal with those brewers...we do not see there is evidence to prove any such charge.

Garrow went on to assert that it would be wrong to single out Merceron, Williams or Robson for action when all licensing decisions had been taken by 'a large majority' of those present. This showed a blatant disregard for the facts: the evidence to Bennet's Committee clearly showed that there were usually only a handful of magistrates present at the licensing sessions and several witnesses had testified that those present were in the habit of taking their lead from Merceron and Williams. The Attorney General concluded that there was therefore 'a very great, if not insuperable difficulty' in the government instituting any proceedings. If anything was to be done, it must be by 'private prosecution by those aggrieved'.[380]

Incredibly, Merceron was off the hook again. In the 28 years since *The Times* had first hinted at his corrupt activities in 1788, he had survived every challenge put forward by his opponents. Parliamentary inquiries over the Coldbath Fields prison, his temporary overthrow by the Bethnal Green vestry in 1804, John Liptrap's investigations of 1812, Joshua King's legal actions the following year; all had failed to bring him down. Now, despite all the publicity given to his activities by Bennet's Police Committee and in the press, the Attorney General had twice declined to prosecute him and the Lord Chancellor had refused to dismiss him as a magistrate.

The first weeks of 1817 saw a concerted effort by the Tower Division magistrates to salvage their reputations by attacking Barber Beaumont. In late January, Sir Daniel Williams wrote to Lord Sidmouth denying the accusations made against him by Beaumont and Fletcher. He alleged that Beaumont's evidence to the Police Committee had been riddled with untruths, enclosing papers repeating the tax collector Smallwood's allegations of bribery and usury against Beaumont in 1814.[381]

But Williams' letter was a mere squib compared with a book published a fortnight later by his fellow magistrate the Reverend Thirlwall. Entitled *A Vindication of the Magistrates acting in and for the Tower Division*, it contained 200 pages of comments on Bennet's report, including vitriolic attacks on both Beaumont and Bennet and a spirited defence of Merceron's character.[382]

In his preface, Thirlwall explained he had been stung into action by 'glaring and impudent falsehoods' in Bennet's report. His own mission, he claimed, was to allow 'The Sun of Truth to rise in his full splendour and chase away the Clouds of Falsehood.' He suggested that Bennet's Committee had exceeded its powers, likening its methods to those of Cromwell or Robespierre: 'if the body of magistrates are to be tried, I should...prefer Mr Beaumont bringing his charges before my Lord Ellenborough, rather than before a Committee of the House of Commons, with even Captain Bennet in the chair... I protest against a trial by committees, inquisitions, or star-chambers.'[383]

The most remarkable part of Thirlwall's book was a lengthy panegyric to Merceron. Thirlwall assured his readers that Merceron had been a devoted Christian throughout the 30 years of their relationship. Insisting that he was speaking as a dispassionate observer, he went on:

> ...in discharging the various important and responsible situations I have seen Mr Merceron fill, his conduct has ever been distinguished by the most correct and scrupulous impartiality. I believe him a man of unsullied honour and unshaken integrity; that no consideration on earth would, or could, prevail upon him to deviate from the path of rectitude, truth and justice.

Thirlwall continued by eulogising the domestic bliss in which Merceron dwelt, as if this somehow ensured his probity as a magistrate: 'no man, I believe, enjoys [more] the society of a pious, virtuous and amiable wife, and a dutiful, affectionate and accomplished family, nor experiences a larger portion of domestic happiness.' As Thirlwall continued, carried away in his praise, he seems to have forgotten his protested independence. Claiming that Merceron's 'friends burn with impatience for the opportunity to testify their opinion of him', he promised that 500 'honourable independent characters in the Tower Division' were ready to come forward to testify for Merceron under oath.

This was an unusual enough assertion for a supposedly independent clergyman to make. But Thirlwall's next statement showed that it was Merceron who was really behind the pamphlet:

> ...and here I have his authority to state, that he is ready at this moment, to submit his accounts, as treasurer for 30 years back, to the investigation of the two Members of the County, and the Members of the City...or to any five or seven high and honourable characters, who are indifferent and impartial, and he will abide by their decision...and further, I have his authority for declaring that, if he cannot accomplish this measure, he will lay the whole of his case before the Public, and pledges himself to produce the most satisfactory proofs of his innocence, integrity and disinterestedness.[384]

It was a typical act of bravado, designed to convince the public that Merceron must be innocent. Why else would he risk exposure in this way? Of course, Merceron knew that George Byng and his fellow local MPs had no power – let alone the will – to investigate his affairs. The only bodies that had such a power were the Middlesex magistrates, or Parliament, as a whole. And, as Merceron also knew, neither body was remotely likely to act.

The press were quick to see through Thirlwall's ranting. The *Monthly Review* announced that his character as a clergyman was degraded by the personal abuse and 'vulgar and unchristian rancour' that disgraced his book's pages. Shortly after the book's publication, Sir Samuel Romilly launched a counter-attack in the House of Commons aided by Bennet and based on further information provided by Barber Beaumont. On 21st February, Romilly presented a petition from 250 residents of Mile End, complaining of the licensing magistrates' failure to license Beaumont's public house while simultaneously keeping open many flash-houses, described by Romilly as 'the refuge of thieves and prostitutes of the lowest description.' He read out excerpts from the Police Committee report, citing examples of corruption by the magistrates, and drawing particular attention to Merceron's involvement in the licensing of his own public houses. Romilly suggested that, if Bennet's Police Committee were to be revived, the petition should be referred to and considered by that body.[385]

Responding on behalf of the government, the Chancellor of the Duchy of Lancaster agreed with Romilly's suggestion on the basis that, although an investigation had 'partially taken place', not all the parties had been fully heard. He assured the House somewhat disingenuously that the Home Secretary 'had done everything in his power to attain the ends of justice', but explained that the government had been constrained in its actions by the legal advice of Lord Eldon and Sir William Garrow. He acknowledged, however, that certain magistrates did appear to have abused the trust imposed in them.

At this, Henry Grey Bennet rose angrily to his feet. He told MPs he would move for an early resumption of his Committee, but first he must take issue with the suggestion that some of the magistrates had 'not been fully heard':

> Unfortunately for some of them, they *have* been heard. The conduct of one of them has been proved to be so improper, by me, on his being heard, that I feel inclined to blame that charity which at the time restrained me from bringing the individual in question before the House. I speak of Mr Merceron, whose evidence was such as ought to have drawn down upon him the punishment of this House.[386]

Bennet told the House that Merceron and his friends were worse than the 'trading justices' of the previous century. Despite the publicity given to their corrupt activities, they had continued in their old ways, and had re-licensed all the public houses against which complaints had been reported the previous year. Even the notorious *The Duke of York* had once again been allowed a licence, and Bennet confirmed that:

...within the last two days it has been as bad as ever. It is the resort of thieves and prostitutes, and boys are daily assembled there to be instructed in every species of debauchery and crime. If such things are suffered, it must be from the most corrupt motives. I must say, that it is my opinion the Lord Chancellor has not done his duty in allowing that guilty, that shuffling magistrate, Mr Merceron, to retain his situation.[387]

This accusation resulted in a commotion, with the Attorney General in particular leaping to Lord Eldon's defence. Several MPs attempted to defend Merceron, one suggesting that in giving evidence to the Police Committee his well-known 'irritable disposition' might have 'betrayed him into some error and intemperance' in the face of Bennet's questioning.

This was more than Bennet could stand. 'Instead of remarking any peculiar irritability in Mr Merceron's character,' he retorted, 'I heard him utter the most cool and deliberate falsehood; and although his mind appeared to be in a perpetual state of invention, so little was its consistency, that the falsehood of one minute was sure to be contradicted by the falsehood of the next.'[388]

This was enough to win the argument and it was agreed that the Police Committee would resume its work. Three weeks of feverish activity ensued during which Bennet, aided by both King and Beaumont, compiled a list of further witnesses willing to testify against Merceron. Predicting the onslaught he was likely to face, Merceron summoned his most trusted followers and ordered them to write to Bennet, asking to be called as witnesses for his character.[389]

CHAPTER XIII

Tipping the Scales

I must say his character is bad, and he is of such an overbearing
disposition that nobody has any chance against him.
    Evidence against Merceron to Police Committee[390]

On 13th March 1817, as his Select Committee on the State of the
Police in the Metropolis reassembled, Henry Grey Bennet was at the
peak of his powers. Just days after his withering attack on Merceron
in the House of Commons, he had made the speech of his life in
opposition to the government's proposed suspension of *habeas corpus*
in the aftermath of the Spa Fields riot. Claiming that previous
suspensions of individual liberty in 1794 and 1812 had proved ill-
founded and unnecessary, Bennet raised laughter by ridiculing the
government's panic in the face of 'six men in a wagon, having an old
stocking, in which there was a little [gun] powder'. Throwing the
government's Bill to the floor, he described it as 'trash' which was
'only fit to be trampled on under his feet'.[391]

Within 24 hours of the Select Committee reconvening, it became
clear that Bennet's main focus was now on exposing Merceron's corrupt licensing of East End public houses. Barber Beaumont, called
as one of the first witnesses, recounted how Merceron and Robson
had forced through the licences for a dozen brothels in Aldgate the
previous September. Beaumont's story was backed up by two other
magistrates, called up by Bennet as a precaution in order to counter
any further attempt by Merceron and his associates to damage
Beaumont's credibility.[392]

A week later it was Joshua King's turn to provide further testimony. As a result of the vestry clerk James May's defection, King now had hard evidence that Merceron had corruptly reduced rate assessments in exchange for political support. King produced data proving that this practice had been so widespread that, between 1807 and 1812, fully one-third of the assessed rates for Bethnal Green had not been collected. Furthermore, an astonishing 1,700 houses had been excluded from the rate assessment altogether.[393]

With May's help, King had obtained the rating data for 86 houses owned by Merceron himself, proving beyond doubt that Merceron was significantly under-rating his tenants and in many cases excusing them altogether. The Rector was also able to demonstrate that Merceron had more than doubled the rates on a further group of houses immediately after selling his interest in them. King outlined to the Committee how this system of corruption had kept Merceron in power for 30 years. At the annual vestry elections, Merceron would propose a list of 'low, ignorant and illiterate' men as candidates for the various parish offices. He was held in such fear that his nominees were invariably returned unopposed, but should any respectable person have the temerity to stand in opposition, Merceron would call his minions out onto the streets to intimidate vestrymen to vote for his own candidate. They would call on those whose rates had been lowered or excused, or publicans whose licences Merceron had corruptly obtained, and hint at the menaces that might result should the result go the wrong way. Sure enough, when the election came, Merceron's candidates would emerge victorious.

King concluded his evidence by explaining how those who broke the law or perjured themselves in supporting Merceron were repaid. Merceron's system required the absolute co-operation of a small army of tax and rate collectors in turning a blind eye to his bribery. In order to ensure their loyalty, Merceron would pretend not to notice if some of the collected funds went missing. According to King, one collector, who had also been Merceron's own clerk, had stolen more than £500 and been allowed to retire 'with the greater part of it, Merceron not allowing him to be sued'. Another had been rather too greedy in his thieving; Merceron – in a show of mock righteousness in front of the vestry – had forced the man to resign, but just a fortnight later had appointed him as master of the local charity school, Parmiter's. King alleged that the school, known to be significantly over-endowed, was entirely under Merceron's control 'and in the management of three or four of his creatures'. The Rector explained to the Committee his strong suspicions as to the misapplication by Merceron of the school's funds.[394]

The following day, the case against Merceron took a further dramatic turn as several witnesses – men that Beaumont and King had spent weeks persuading to testify – stepped up in support of the Rector's allegations. First to be called was Robert Wrightson, by this time 71 years old and one of only a handful of men who had experienced the entire span of Merceron's reign in Bethnal Green. Wrightson had suffered much at Merceron's hands, and over the next couple of hours his resentment poured out as he outlined for Bennet the whole story of Merceron's rise to power and subsequent ruthless domination of the parish. Wrightson supported every allegation made by Joshua King the previous day. He explained that Merceron's vast accumulation of power – as magistrate, chairman of the tax and sewer commissions, parish treasurer, trustee of the local schools – coupled with his 'overbearing disposition' and the loyalty he purchased by granting favours to his trusted associates, made him invincible throughout the East End.[395]

Wrightson gave a detailed account of Merceron's abuse of the rating system stretching back throughout the previous decade. He told of the way Merceron had incited the mob to violence from a table-top in the aisle of the church, and recounted Merceron's wholehearted encouragement of the Sunday bullock hunters, gangs of men and boys 'riotous and inebriate', whose activities were so frightening that 'no decent woman can go to a place of worship with safety'. He closed his evidence by explaining how Merceron had fraudulently obtained vestry approval for the payment of his legal fees from the 1813 court case against King.

Wrightson's evidence was backed up by several other witnesses. One, a rate collector who King had persuaded to turn against Merceron, explained that men were too scared to vote against Merceron's candidates in vestry elections, fearing he would wreak revenge by arbitrarily increasing their rates or taxes. The witness also told of the Saturday morning ritual in Merceron's Brick Lane office whereby rate reductions or exemptions were granted in return for votes. Another testified that a licensing magistrate, Thomas Windle, was used to acting 'under the immediate direction of Mr Merceron, who indemnified him for everything he did'.[396]

As the day drew on, it was clear that Bennet had finally tipped the scales against Merceron. The previous year, Merceron had been able to denounce Beaumont's and King's accusations as the rants of men seeking revenge over a local feud. The nature of those accusations – and the lack of corroborating witnesses – had made it easy for Lord Chancellor Eldon and Attorney General Garrow to justify refusing to take action. But now, the weight of independent evidence had enabled Bennet to prove corruption on a previously unimagined scale.

Bennet saved the best evidence until last: James May had finally agreed to testify against Merceron. As Bennet questioned him, it became apparent that the vestry clerk had undergone a great deal of soul-searching since his nervous and stumbling performance in front of the Committee the previous year. Gone were the timid prevarications and clumsy attempts to avoid incriminating his employer. May spoke assertively, confirming King's and Wrightson's accusations of rate tampering. He told the Committee how the people of Bethnal Green were afraid of giving the slightest offence to Merceron, who he described as 'violent and overbearing'. Most importantly, May confirmed Wrightson's charge that Merceron had stolen almost £1,000 out of the poor's rate account to pay his legal bills.[397]

Bennet now had two credible witnesses willing to testify that Merceron had stolen from the poor's rate fund. Given the government's previous refusals to act against the public-house licensing scandal, Bennet needed hard evidence of other crimes on which a private prosecution against Merceron might be based. It began to appear that the affair of Dann & Crosland's invoice might be just the thing. As Bennet closed the day's proceedings, he ordered May to produce next day the original invoice, together with any evidence that might show whether the parish had approved its payment.

The following lunchtime, as May once more took his seat opposite Bennet, he seemed less comfortable. He told Bennet that he had sent a note to Merceron the previous evening, requesting the papers that Bennet had demanded, and had received reply that Merceron himself wished to attend the Committee with them. 'And', faltered May, 'he is now attending in the lobby'.

Merceron was called into the committee room. Handing over the papers Bennet had requested, he insisted that the reimbursement of his legal fees had been entirely proper and that the vestry had resolved upon it as a mark of gratitude to him. Motioning Merceron to be silent, Bennet recalled May and asked him to corroborate the story Merceron had just told. Passing him Dann & Crosland's invoice, Bennet asked May if he recalled seeing it before. Quite steadily, May replied: 'I never saw it till this instant.'

As Bennet continued to question the two men, both stood by their version of events. Merceron insisted he had done nothing wrong, claiming that due notice had been given to the vestry of the intention to reimburse him, while May was equally insistent that the payment had never been disclosed to the vestry.[398]

Having exhausted his questions, Bennet called on four of Merceron's associates who had asked to be heard as character witnesses. One by one, these men – seemingly oblivious to the penalties for perjury or, perhaps, adequately compensated against them – launched into an almost comical defence of their master, as Bennet effortlessly trapped them into one contradiction after another.

Peter Renvoize told Bennet he had known Merceron for over 50 years, since childhood, and had always found him a 'very correct steady gentleman'. Renvoize denied all knowledge of Merceron having altered the rates but lost any credibility when Bennet pointed out that Renvoize's own four houses were assessed at only a third of their true value. Bennet also knew that Renvoize, a trustee of the Parmiter's charity school, had voted with Merceron the previous year to appoint a thief as its master. Renvoize could only limply justify this as an act of compassion for a man who 'writes a good hand'; Bennet's reply was caustic: 'you thought this was better than appointing an honest man?'[399]

The other character witnesses fared little better. Two could offer only bland claims about Merceron's honour and integrity. A third presented Bennet with a letter signed by 61 publicans claiming that Merceron was 'in every respect the reverse to despotism and tyranny.' But under cross-questioning this witness was just as unconvincing as Renvoize and undermined Merceron's own evidence about the manipulation of rate assessments.[400]

The Committee also heard from two less partisan witnesses who provided an interesting perspective on Merceron's character and on everyday life in Bethnal Green. William Hale, the parish treasurer of Spitalfields and a respected public figure through his campaigns to alleviate the poverty of the local weavers, told Bennet that Merceron had 'acquired a manner that is dictatorial, that even his best friends consider borders on rudeness'. A local Sunday school superintendent told of cockfights, gambling and a system of thieves and receiving houses remarkably similar to that depicted two decades later by Charles Dickens in *Oliver Twist*. The superintendent knew of one 12-year-old boy who, while walking in the fields near St Matthew's church, had been 'seduced by a Jew to go to the Strand, where he gave him scissors and induced him to steal watches off gentlemen'.[401]

This evidence helped Bennet portray the loose morals that were the norm in Bethnal Green, and formed a colourful backdrop to the detailed allegations against Merceron that followed. The next witness, Isaac Rennoldson, the Bethnal Green parish constable, gave a detailed account of the state of Bethnal Green's 90 public houses, a quarter of which were all-night gambling dens and the known haunts of prostitutes and criminals. Rennoldson told the Committee of his night raids on such houses: the landlord at *The King and Queen* had locked him in, with threats of such violence that Rennoldson feared for his life; at others he had been pelted with stones. The most damaging accusations came when Rennoldson and his predecessor as constable, John Perry, told Bennet that Merceron had intimidated them into maintaining silence at the licensing magistrates' hearing. Rennoldson recounted in particular Merceron's threatening visit the previous autumn and his suggestion that it would not matter if Rennoldson lied under oath to the magistrates.[402]

The evidence against Merceron continued to mount. Joseph Fletcher, the Shadwell ship-owner, accused Merceron of corruption as a tax commissioner and repeated his previous allegations about Merceron's role in licensing the Shadwell brothels. Other witnesses supported Fletcher's accusations. One of the few reputable licensing magistrates confirmed that *The Duke of York* was 'a downright gin-shop'. A local resident explained that it was 'impossible to pass the door without seeing half-a-dozen prostitutes going in or out'. In perhaps the most telling piece of evidence, a publican who had accused Merceron of bribery in the 1816 hearing returned to tell the Committee that Merceron and the Reverend Thirlwall had subsequently sought to intimidate him into retracting his evidence.[403]

The only support Merceron received was from the brewer Sampson Hanbury, anxious to defend himself against any suggestion that he had personally been involved in corruption. Hanbury read out a prepared statement in which he vehemently denied any wrongdoing, including having made any gifts to Merceron, but his credibility was undermined by Merceron's own detailed admission to having received such gifts. As the Committee broke up for the Easter recess, Bennet could once again congratulate himself. In just three weeks, he had assembled a case that made nonsense of the government's refusal to prosecute Merceron. Had the government simply been negligent? The more likely explanation is that Bennet's inquiry had disturbed a political cover-up designed to prevent a scandal amongst the East End's ruling elite, just as its unruly populace seemed to be on the verge of revolution.[404]

At the 1817 Easter vestry elections in Bethnal Green, with the neighbourhood buzzing with accounts of Bennet's Committee, Merceron's supporters pointedly celebrated the 30th anniversary of his appointment as parish treasurer. Noting the existence of an inquiry 'in which this parish appears to have no inconsiderable share', the vestry resolved that 'it would be highly improper for this vestry to express any particular opinion until the said proceedings are terminated…' Immediately ignoring its own advice, the vestry then expressed 'its deep concern, on observing the many glaring falsehoods' reported in evidence.[405]

During the break in his Committee's proceedings, Bennet provided Merceron with a courtesy copy of the evidence against him, inviting him to appear again before the Committee on 22nd April with any comments he wished to make. The transcripts left Merceron in no doubt as to just how badly things were going and he spent the next few weeks consulting his attorneys and alternately bullying, cajoling and probably bribing friends and associates into giving further evidence in his favour. At his scheduled reappearance before the Committee, Merceron read from a prepared script. In a noticeably humble departure from his previous demeanour, he began by explaining that he wished to explain the 'apparent contradictions' in his previous evidence. 'It was never my intention to deceive the Honourable Committee' he began:

> Generally, I could not help feeling a natural embarrassment in being called to reply to questions, the answers to which might create further litigation. In a long public life, I must have committed many errors, which I could not be bound to prove, and which my adversaries, from personal hostility, and disappointment of certain personal objects, have been industrious to place in the strongest light.

Merceron claimed that he was by no means the only magistrate with an ownership interest in public houses. He insisted that his conduct as a licensing magistrate had been 'wholly impartial' and that he would have withdrawn from any meeting where complaints were made against his own houses. He denied accusations that he had loaned significant sums to one of the Shadwell brothel landlords. He admitted having warned constable Rennoldson to 'be careful what he said' to the licensing magistrates, but strenuously denied any intimidation or attempting to persuade Rennoldson to lie under oath.

Merceron had an answer for every accusation made in Bennet's report. The evidence against him was a pack of lies, dreamed up by Beaumont and King out of 'personal and inveterate animosity'. As for accusations that he had appointed a known thief to be master of the local school, Merceron claimed he had acted purely out of pity: the man had stolen from the poor funds in desperation, to repay debts that his father had contracted; 'He came to me and told me the fact with tears in his eyes, that his family had ruined him.'

Having rebutted every allegation, Merceron sat back and allowed Bennet to question him again. Bennet reminded him that he had denied being aware of complaints against any Bethnal Green alehouses when licensing them. Yet Constable Perry had given evidence that he had personally informed Merceron about such complaints at the time of the 1815 licensing round. How did Merceron explain this discrepancy?

Without recourse to a pre-prepared script, Merceron's evidence once more deteriorated into a rambling stream of denials and contradictions. He suggested to Bennet that, perhaps, he *had* been told about the complaints, but 'might have forgotten them.' As Bennet persisted, Merceron's memory seemed to fail him altogether. Subsequently admitting knowledge of complaints against certain houses, Merceron claimed that his reason for nevertheless licensing them was because the complaints were merely 'trifling or slight offences'. By the end of his examination, the balance of evidence against him was stronger than it had been at the beginning.[406]

Merceron was followed by yet more of his associates who had written to Bennet during the Easter break, asking to give evidence in his favour. Several of them were co-conspirators in the fraud over Dann & Crosland's invoice and therefore equally at risk of prosecution, unless able successfully to deny what had taken place. The Reverend Platt swore that he had called out the amount of the invoice during the 1814 audit of Merceron's accounts. Several other men claimed they had heard him do so. Some insisted that Merceron had had nothing to do with the bullock hunting in the churchyard and denied that he had incited a mob to violence against William Shevill. One of Merceron's fellow charity school trustees praised his bookkeeping, telling Bennet: 'I never saw accounts more clear, regular and correct'.[407]

According to all these witnesses, Merceron was a pillar of rectitude. Bennet must have found it particularly hard to keep a straight face as he listened to the evidence of Saunderson Sturtevant, a long time vocal supporter and tenant of Merceron (although he conveniently omitted to mention the latter connection in his evidence). Sturtevant conjured up for the Committee the image of a benevolent squire, living in domestic bliss and harmony with his tenants.[408]

Bennet's work was almost done. Allowing the Rector the same courtesy as he had shown to Merceron, he permitted Joshua King to submit a written statement commenting on Merceron's final evidence. King took advantage of this opportunity to repeat many of his previous accusations, in particular ridiculing Merceron's failure to account for the £12,000 grant from the government in 1800 on the basis that the supporting invoices had been stolen from his counting house. King pointed out that Merceron had used this unlikely excuse on several other occasions, notably in the chancery cases over Mary Cheesman's estate and Merceron's dispute with his nephews.[409]

In case Bennet's Committee should be minded to give any credence to the character references given on Merceron's behalf by Platt and Sturtevant, the Rector pointed out that these men had long been

Merceron's 'confidential advisors, and the movers and supporters of the various adulatory resolutions' published regularly by the vestry. The picture they had painted of Merceron's influence in Bethnal Green could not be farther from the truth, King argued. He reminded Bennet of the ample evidence of Merceron's secret alterations of the rate assessments and claimed that 'the demoralisation of my parishioners is owing in great degree to the protection given by Mr Merceron to these nurseries of vice: low public houses'. For once, King had had the last word.

Bennet spent the next few days finalising the conclusions for his report, which was due to be completed on 2nd May. At the last moment, the report was given added weight by the receipt of a petition – instigated by Barber Beaumont and signed by 2,200 people – complaining of the abuses of power by the licensing magistrates 'from motives of partiality, personal pique and the most wanton caprice'.[410]

Before sending the report to be printed, Bennet found time for one final skirmish in his battle with the East End magistrates. He censured Merceron's apologist, the Reverend Thirlwall, for having made 'the most serious charges' against the Select Committee in his pamphlet vindicating the licensing justices. As Sir Samuel Romilly noted in his diary, Thirlwall had tried manifestly to influence the Committee's proceedings. But Thirlwall refused to apologise and used the opportunity of his appearance before the Committee to make further slurs against Barber Beaumont's character and to deny that he and Merceron had attempted to interfere with witnesses. Dismissing his outburst, a furious Bennet ordered Thirlwall to appear before the House of Commons to apologise. On 6th May, a considerably more contrite Thirlwall appeared at the Bar of the House where, to his relief, he was dismissed without further punishment after making a grovelling apology.[411]

On 6th June Bennet presented the main findings of his report to the House of Commons in support of a request to instigate a Bill to amend the licensing laws to prevent further corruption by licensing magistrates. The report praised Joshua King's role in exposing Merceron's activities and explained that a root cause of the scandal had been the incestuous relationship between brewers and magistrates:

> It is evident that the brewers and distillers…make fortunes in proportion to the sale of their respective commodities…Some of the worst conducted, as well as the most profitable houses in the Metropolis…belong to particular brewers; the closer then the connection [with] the magistrates, the less willing be the latter to injure the property of the former.[412]

It had been clear throughout Bennet's Committee's inquiries that Truman, Hanbury & Buxton were the main offending brewers in this regard. But to accuse a group of East End magistrates of corruption was one thing; to make the same accusations against men as well connected as Hanbury and Buxton was another matter altogether. First, Truman's – in the person of its chairman Sampson Hanbury – strenuously denied any impropriety. Second, Buxton – since his speech at the Lord Mayor's Mansion House the previous November and his successful charitable fundraising on behalf of the starving Spitalfields weavers – was viewed universally in Society as a man of impeccable character, almost a saint. For Bennet, there was a third and more personal difficulty. His great friend Elizabeth Fry, with whom he had been campaigning for several years for the improvement of prison conditions, happened to be Hanbury's niece and Buxton's sister-in-law.

To his credit, Bennet refused to allow these considerations to prevent him from implicating Truman's in the scandal. However, it must be admitted some punches were pulled. Bennet noted Hanbury's denials of bribery and of exerting improper influence over the licensing magistrates, making it clear that he had no evidence to prove otherwise. He concluded, however: 'by what means the firm of Hanbury and Truman have obtained that weight with the magistracy of the Tower Hamlets division, it is not possible for your Committee to determine; [but] that they possess it, they have no doubt.' The report added that the clerks both to the licensing magistrates and to the Worship Street police office, including Charles Lush, were paid agents of Hanbury whose roles were to notify the brewery immediately whenever a new licence was to be granted or any complaint was made against any licensed premises.[413]

When it came to Merceron, Bennet felt no need to pull punches. His conclusion as to who was to blame for immorality and vice in Bethnal Green was stark: Merceron stood condemned, he reported, largely as a result of his own contradictory evidence: 'for the general credit that can be given to the testimony of Mr Merceron, refer to the minutes'. For a magistrate to have a personal interest in the pubs he was responsible for licensing was bad enough, but when Merceron had prevented the constables from presenting complaints against his pubs at the licensing meeting, Bennet opined that 'a more unwarrantable exercise of magisterial discretion…cannot well be imagined'.[414]

CHAPTER XIV

On Trial at Last

It very often happens that a man who conceives ...
by his guilt and fraud, that he can screw out money
from a fund which does not belong to him, is not
sparing of it, that he takes it with a lavish hand...

James Scarlett, summing up for the
Prosecution case against Merceron

As MPs, journalists and interested members of the public pored over the Select Committee's report, Merceron and his opponents each contemplated their next move. As far as Henry Grey Bennet was concerned, the report's publication completed his role in the affair. Unlike Barber Beaumont or the Reverend King, Bennet had no personal vendetta to pursue: his desire to 'diminish the sum of human misery' drove him to follow a broader agenda and his Select Committee's focus quickly moved on to other issues. By July 1817, Bennet had written and published a second report addressing the topics of 'blood money' – the system by which police officers were remunerated based on numbers of convictions – and the increase in juvenile crime.[415]

For Beaumont and King, however, Bennet's report was just the beginning of their battle to topple Merceron from power. At last, they appeared to have enough hard evidence to support his prosecution. Would the authorities now act? Despite all the new evidence that Bennet's Committee had uncovered, however, the government showed no inclination to budge from its previously stated unwillingness to prosecute. The country, after all, was still at risk of revolution.

Habeas corpus was once again under suspension and ministers had commenced a relentless campaign of persecution against Radical publishers who – at least in the view of the ruling elite – were inciting rebellion by circulating seditious material. The two men responsible for any decision whether to prosecute Merceron – the Home Secretary Lord Sidmouth and Attorney General Sir William Garrow – would spend most of 1817 on this largely unsuccessful crusade, culminating in the humiliating acquittal of the Radical publisher William Hone that December.[416]

It became obvious to Barber Beaumont and King that their best chance of success lay with a private prosecution; over the second half of 1817, they spent many hours with their attorneys, preparing the basis for a case. The lawyers' response was encouraging: if respectable witnesses such as May and Rennoldson – Merceron's own appointees to parish office – could be persuaded to repeat their testimony in court, then a guilty verdict must surely follow.

As their case took shape, Beaumont and King were further strengthened by the recruitment to their cause of a new ally, Dr Lawrence Gwynne. Like Beaumont, Gwynne had tried his hand at a wide variety of careers. A gifted mathematician, he had started out as a teacher before becoming a lieutenant in the navy, where he wrote a book on navigation techniques. He had then tried his hand unsuccessfully in business as a corn merchant and as the owner of a clothing warehouse. During this meandering career he had also found time to take a doctorate in law and become a magistrate. Later, he would be appointed a Sheriff of the City of London. Arriving in Bethnal Green in 1817, Gwynne had allied himself to Merceron's faction, with the result that he was elected to a variety of positions of responsibility within the parish. Sensing the way things were heading, however, it occurred to Gwynne that if Merceron could be toppled, he would have as good a chance as anyone of filling the vacuum and lining his own pockets in the process. Accordingly, in November 1817 he agreed to join forces with Beaumont and King.[417]

Thus strengthened, the group worked up their case. Early in 1818, Merceron was served with two indictments in the name of the parish of Bethnal Green. The first charged him with 'fraudulently, clandestinely, deceitfully, and unlawfully inserting the sum of £925 1s 3d in his account, with intent to cheat and defraud the parishioners'; the second was 'for corruption as a magistrate in re-licensing disorderly public houses, his property.'[418]

The prosecution process was humiliating for Merceron from the start. For a private prosecution of this nature to reach court, the indictments needed first to be heard by a Grand Jury. Merceron, one of the senior magistrates of the county, with great anger and embarrassment was forced to absent himself from the court while the charges against him were heard. His greatest fury, however, came at the thought that James May, whose appointment and entire 30-year career as vestry clerk had been as a result of his own patronage, had agreed to testify against him in front of the Grand Jury. As King's lawyers had predicted, the jury found the evidence compelling and agreed that the case should proceed in the Court of King's Bench.[419]

Merceron's immediate response was to seek revenge on May for his treachery. He also needed to damage May's credibility as a witness before his trial came to court. The imminent annual vestry elections presented an opportunity to achieve both these ends. If May were dismissed from his post as vestry clerk, his evidence would have less impact in court. At a vestry meeting on 19th March, Merceron circulated a paper signed by 50 vestrymen asserting that May had 'forfeited the confidence of the parish' and making vague but nevertheless damaging insinuations about May's professional probity. An alternative candidate was proposed and, for the first time in living memory in Bethnal Green, a ballot was called for the election of the vestry clerk.[420]

When voting began on the morning of Easter Monday, it quickly became apparent that a change had come over the ordinary people of Bethnal Green. Their resentment at 30 years of Merceron's tyranny was kindled by Barber Beaumont's allegations in *The Times* and then by the revelations in Bennet's Select Committee report. The news that indictments had been presented to a Grand Jury fanned the flames; Merceron's retaliatory strike against James May caused popular feeling to explode. By lunchtime, the churchyard was packed with people anxiously discussing the progress of the ballot. When the poll closed more than 1,000 people had voted. Most of them, and many others not eligible to vote, jostled into the church to hear the result.[421]

Charles Masterman, the churchwarden, was in the chair for this unprecedented and uncomfortable gathering. A bricklayer, he had benefited from Merceron's regime as the recipient of a lucrative contract for maintaining the Tower Hamlets sewers. Years earlier Masterman had assisted Merceron, for the sake of a few shillings, to defraud the family of Mary Cheesman. His support for Merceron had been rewarded in 1817 by election as a Governor of the Poor and a trustee of the charity school, positions reserved for Merceron's most loyal supporters.[422]

Masterman announced the result: May had been re-elected by 724 votes to 283. Amid the noise, Lawrence Gwynne proposed a vote of thanks to May, commending 'his firm manly spirit and plain honest integrity' and hoping 'that his triumph this day may serve as a wholesome lesson to the enemies of truth and justice.' The cheers that ensued meant it was some time before Masterman could move on to the election of the other parish officers. When it came to the election of treasurer, Merceron was nominated as usual, but when Masterman called for those in favour only 29 hands were raised. Those against were too many to count; the vestry minutes recorded that they were 'upwards of 1,000'. Gwynne immediately offered himself as Merceron's replacement but the vestry was in no mood for another potential tyrant, resolving instead that the parish accounts be placed in the hands of the Bank of England.[423]

The parish revolution continued the following day. Merceron and his associates were dismissed from all their other positions of responsibility; Joshua King and James May were elected trustees of the charity school. Thanks were voted to Lawrence Gwynne for the part he had played in 'exposing parochial delinquency'. Merceron's demise was announced to the world at large as the vestry published its proceedings in *The Times* and other national papers.[424]

At last – or so it seemed – Merceron's rule was coming to an end. Yet the day after his expulsion he issued a stark reminder that his power was not conditional on democratic support. A baying mob more than 200 strong, brandishing wooden clubs, drove a bullock into the silk warehouse of William Racine, who had played a leading role in the weekend's events and whose family had been outspoken opponents of Merceron's rule for many years. Racine was badly beaten, seven of his workmen were wounded and the mad bullock tossed several passers-by before collapsing and dying in the street. Press reports of the episode carefully avoided any link to Merceron.[425]

Just six weeks remained before Merceron's trial. His removal from office should have meant that his opponents finally had access to parish accounts kept from view for 30 years and which contained concrete evidence to support their case. But Merceron, unsurprisingly, stalled for time. On 1st April, the vestry reluctantly agreed to give him another week; eight days later, Merceron passed over his records but the item the vestry needed most – the key Dann & Crosland invoice – was missing. Merceron claimed it was mislaid and asked for five more days to find it. It was a further month before it was handed over, 'in a mutilated state'.[426]

With the trial now just two weeks away, a vestry meeting was called to audit Merceron's final accounts as treasurer. The audit revealed a new problem for his opponents. In 1816 James May had charged Merceron £120 for personal legal advice in connection with his libel action against King. Merceron had paid May but had once again secretly recharged the amount to the parish. May claimed to know nothing of this. Merceron planned to use the transaction to smear May's character and undermine the prosecution case. If the trial went badly, his lawyers could then suggest that May – a key prosecution witness – had committed an offence in having his own fees paid from parish funds. Such a disclosure would undermine the whole case against Merceron. To prevent this, the vestry voted to disallow the payment and ordered Merceron to reimburse the money to the parish.[427]

Over the years, Merceron had used a number of legal firms, based on the principle that it was better that no single practice should know too much about his business. This time he placed his defence case, on which so much depended, in the hands of a new firm: Lush & Merceron. Its partners, epitomising the family connections linking the East End elite, were James Wilmot Lush, son of Charles Lush and grandson of David Wilmot, and Merceron's own 25-year-old son Henry.[428]

Merceron had long intended a legal career for Henry, reckoning that it would be no bad thing to have a lawyer in the family. When Henry left school, Merceron arranged for him to be articled to his old friend Major Wright, the man who had witnessed James Hadfield's attempt to assassinate the King at Drury Lane in 1800. Wright's responsibilities as clerk to various local statutory bodies meant a steady stream of interesting work for Henry and gave Merceron a means of keeping an eye on developments that affected his property empire. Wright's other clerk was James Wilmot Lush, married to Wright's daughter. The two young men hit it off and when Major Wright retired in 1816 they set up in partnership together.[429]

Shortly before nine-thirty in the morning of Saturday 18th May 1818, Merceron took his place in the dock of the Court of King's Bench. News of his trial had caused tremendous excitement 'in every class of society' and the small public gallery in the court was full. As defence counsel, Merceron had once again retained James Topping, the senior practising barrister in the court, who had been so little tested in defending him in the 1813 trials. At 62, Topping was approaching the end of a long and successful career as an advocate and it is easy to see why Merceron chose him. He was renowned for his impatience and had a ferocious temper, with one commentator describing him as 'overwhelmed in the foam of his own wrath' and picturing his face, 'never very inviting', as so distorted when angry that even 'his own witnesses are frequently terror-struck.' Topping's reputation for destroying the credibility of witnesses, in his hoarse northern brogue, led him to be nicknamed 'the castigator-general'. But his health was in decline and he was beginning to be outshone by younger rivals. Recently he had been on the losing side in two of the government's most embarrassing trial defeats for many years: the acquittal of James Watson for treason after the Spa Fields rebellion and that of the journalist William Hone for seditious libel.[430]

The prosecution counsel was James Scarlett, the most outstanding of Topping's younger rivals. Ironically, Scarlett had been Topping's junior at Merceron's 1813 trial. Since then, his Whiggish politics had held back his career during the ultra-Tory Lord Eldon's tenure as Lord Chancellor, and at the time of Merceron's trial he had only been a King's Counsel for two years. But now, at the age of 48, Scarlett was on his way to becoming the most successful advocate of the day, a future Attorney General and prominent judge. He was a prodigiously talented lawyer. As the future Lord Chancellor Henry Brougham put it:

> His sagacity, his sure tact, his circumspection, his provident care, his sudden sense of danger to his own case, his instantaneous perception of a weak point in his adversary's, all made him the most difficult person to contend against that perhaps ever appeared in Westminster Hall, when the object was to get or to prevent a verdict...no man ever was more renowned as a *verdict-getter*.[431]

Probably to Merceron's great relief, Lord Ellenborough, whose anger at Merceron's rudeness had deprived him of damages in his previous libel action against Joshua King, was not presiding in court that day. Since his humiliating failure to convict William Hone of seditious libel the previous Christmas, the elderly Lord Chief Justice had entered a rapid decline and, although it would be another three

The Court of King's Bench, Westminster Hall

James Scarlett

months before he retired, his court appearances had become rare. Ellenborough's place as judge that day was taken by Sir Charles Abbott who, while equally liable to be bad tempered with counsel, had a kinder reputation than Ellenborough in his dealings with criminal defendants. Abbott also had a reputation as a defender of authority, including in cases concerning magistrates, and this may have given Merceron some cheer as he contemplated the day ahead.[432]

Scarlett introduced Merceron to the jury as 'a gentleman, whose name you have heard, and whose name has been long known in the County of Middlesex.' Listing the many public offices that Merceron had accumulated, Scarlett told the jury that this concentration of power had led the people of Bethnal Green to be 'in a state of complete subserviency to his despotic dominion' for fear of being crushed or oppressed. Aware that Merceron might have interfered with members of the jury, Scarlett reminded them of their duty to act in accordance with the evidence they were about to hear. He proceeded to outline the long and complex saga of Dann & Crosland's invoice, detailing the Reverend King's allegations of fraud and Merceron's mysterious acquittal in 1813, Merceron's subsequent fraud on the parish and finally his attempt to cover it up.[433]

None of this was new to anyone who had followed the proceedings of Henry Grey Bennet's Select Committee, and Scarlett was aware that Merceron had a string of witnesses ready to deny under oath that the fraud had taken place. But the barrister had a surprise in store. Merceron's extreme reluctance to part with Dann & Crosland's invoice the previous month had aroused suspicions. These increased when the invoice was eventually handed over in a mutilated state. Why had Merceron been so unwilling to give it up, and why had it been damaged? Scarlett suggested an explanation:

Now little circumstances sometimes denote the character of a man's mind, and throw light upon his conduct in great affairs. One would have thought that if Mr Merceron, who is a man of fortune...had succeeded to get a sum of £914 paid by the parishioners out of the funds of the poor, that he might have spared them the expense of his own coach hire in coming to this place; but no: it very often happens that a man who conceives…by his guilt and fraud, that he can screw out money from a fund which does not belong to him, is not sparing of it, that he takes it with a lavish hand…and he thought he might as well add a little to Dann & Crosland's bill.

Dann & Crosland's invoice was in the amount of £914 11s 3d. Scarlett explained that, having fraudulently obtained a vestry resolution to pay his expenses, Merceron 'thought he might as well cover himself entirely'. Accordingly, he had scribbled on the invoice: 'My own coach hire and expenses, ten guineas', amending the total to £925 1s 3d. He had paid himself the larger amount from the poor's rate funds and entered the same figure in his account book, noted simply as 'Dann & Crosland's bill'. With the original invoice safely in Merceron's possession, no one was any the wiser.

Merceron's greed, for the sake of ten guineas, had led to his undoing. When Bennet's Committee forced Merceron to produce the bill, someone had noticed the reference to the additional amount with its giveaway reference in Merceron's own handwriting, to '*my own* coach hire'. Realising his error, Merceron had ripped off the offending page before handing the bill over to the vestry. Underneath, in an attempt to copy the original hand, he had written: "sundry expenses, witnesses' coach hire etc. JM ten guineas".

Scarlett explained that this proved that the invoice never had been produced at the vestry audit. If it had, he reasoned, the vestrymen would have noticed that the amount did not agree to Dann & Crosland's receipt. He emphasised the seriousness of the charge and reminded the jury that the victims of Merceron's greed were the starving poor of Bethnal Green. Merceron had taken almost £1,000 from 'a fund he ought to have been ashamed to touch…a fund which ought to be sacred to every person, but especially to him, who from his situation knew the wants of those who called for relief…'[434]

It was now time for the prosecution witnesses. Under Merceron's glare, James May again swore that he had never seen Dann & Crosland's invoice until Henry Grey Bennet had shown it to him, and confirmed that it had been undamaged at that time. Cross-examining, Topping sought to paint May as a disenchanted former employee. He forced the vestry clerk to admit that he had acted as Merceron's attorney, and that he had on occasion been paid for such work out of the parish funds. But thanks to the vestry's timely rejection of May's last bill, this allegation did not have the impact desired and May's evidence came across as honest and generally compelling.[435]

May was followed in the witness box by Robert Wrightson. Merceron's defence team tried hard to undermine the old man, presenting him as having long held a grudge against Merceron, and succeeded in making him flustered and confused. But Wrightson's evidence was compelling and corroborated by two other witnesses before Scarlett announced that the case for the prosecution was closed.[436]

Topping opened Merceron's defence with a long speech in support of his general character, reminding the jury that he had held high responsibility for 30 years 'without the slightest imputation upon his conduct'. Thereafter the defence case rested upon the claim that the reimbursement of Merceron's legal fees was approved and audited by the vestry at large. Topping repeated the claim that the parish had also occasionally paid fees to May himself, implying a precedent. The weakness in this argument was that in Dann & Crosland's case the funds had been paid out of the poor's rate fund, for which there was no legal justification. Topping's only hope was in the Malthusian suggestion that the poor were an intolerable tax on society. He suggested lamely that, as the poor's rates were contributed by the men of the parish, he saw no reason why the parish should not use those funds as it saw fit, provided that the transactions concerned were authorised by the vestry.[437]

Over the course of the afternoon a number of Merceron's associates testified that they had been present at the 1814 audit of his accounts, and had approved the payment of Dann & Crosland's bill. The Reverend Platt had worked up a detailed account of his part in the affair. He claimed he had written the resolutions praising Merceron's conduct and agreeing to pay his legal fees without any interference on Merceron's part, saying: 'they arose spontaneously in my own mind'. He distinctly recalled having announced Dann & Crosland's bill to the audit committee.[438]

Platt spoke with the confidence and authority of an experienced clergyman. The men following him were less impressive. Peter Renvoize told the court he had been sitting behind Platt during the audit. He claimed to have seen the bill being discussed but under cross-examination his account quickly became confused and contradictory.

James Brown Unwin, a surgeon, had 'most assuredly' heard the bill called over, and launched into a spirited defence of Merceron's character. Claiming to be a disinterested parishioner, Unwin told the court he had heard rumours that Merceron 'was a rogue and a thief' and had decided to investigate for himself. The reports were 'all false', he claimed: 'I have sifted them, I believe no man more so.' But Unwin's behaviour in front of the Police Committee had given the lie to his claims of impartiality: Scarlett revealed to the jury that Unwin had been so extreme in his support of Merceron and denunciation of King that Grey Bennet had ordered his evidence to be struck from the record and had thrown him out of the committee room. Very soon, Unwin was again sent on his way.[439]

One by one, nine further vestrymen followed Unwin into the witness box to testify for their leader. They were a sorry lot, and their testimony did Merceron more harm than good. Several were themselves implicated in the alleged fraud; others owed favours to Merceron, and it became apparent that they had been 'leaned on' to appear.[440]

With evening settling in and the last witness standing down, James Scarlett rose to make his closing speech. He began by tackling the suggestion made by the defence that Merceron's 'unblemished'

30-year career was in itself some kind of proof of his innocence. He reminded the jury that they had heard that Merceron's 'very life and death' depended on their verdict; that his rank and social standing was such that any suspicion of fraud or dishonour would be 'more fatal to him than even a sentence of death'. Scarlett disagreed. Such a conclusion, he added, would involve a gross misjudgement of Merceron's character.

Scarlett told the jury that should they find Merceron guilty, then 'the only feeling that will operate on his mind...will be a feeling of regret that [his] conduct has been discerned.' He moved on to the fraud itself, reminding the jury that they had heard from eight men who had claimed to hear Dann & Crosland's bill called out at the 1814 audit. Scarlett told the jurymen they were being asked by the defence to believe that it was pure coincidence that these eight men were the very same who Merceron had called on a year previously to secretly pass the resolutions agreeing to pay the bill. The truth was, he argued, that these men had conspired with Merceron to obtain the resolutions by fraudulent means and had then assisted him to fake the audit approval.

Scarlett concluded that this was a case of the rich, quite literally, robbing the poor. The invoice had been addressed to Merceron's personal account, and 'to make the parish pay it out of the hard-wrung earnings of seven thousand persons, many in circumstances of poverty, to put it into the possession of an affluent man, the owner of many houses' was despicable. It was therefore the jury's duty to find Merceron guilty.[441]

Sir Charles Abbott, who had been silent almost all day, began to sum up. He was balanced in relating the evidence on both sides, with his only real criticism reserved for James Unwin, whom he described as 'a very warm partisan of Mr Merceron'. But as he instructed the jury on what to base their verdict, it became clear where his sympathies lay. Put in Merceron's position, he explained, 'a prudent man would have taken...extraordinary care...It would hardly be expected that there should not be found many persons in this parish who would object to this sum constituting an item in the treasurer's accounts, in which certainly by law it ought never to have been placed'. The jury's decision was a simple one:

> If you think, as every body must, that it was the duty of any one not to charge this to the parish fund; if you think more ought to have been done to call the attention of the parish to the intention to charge this to the poor's rate, and that Mr Merceron and those others with him could not but have known that more ought to have been done than was done, then the charge of doing this in a clandestine and fraudulent manner will be made out...

In case he had not been sufficiently clear, Abbott told the jury that the only way they could find Merceron innocent was if they were satisfied 'he gave full and fair notice to the opposite party to object'. Faced with such a clear steer, the jury did not even leave the room. They consulted among themselves briefly, and as darkness began to close in outside, the foreman rose and announced the verdict – 'Guilty'.[442]

CHAPTER XV

Going Down

...the Court and country cannot but be astonished that an individual who has filled so many offices of trust, who has reached such a rank in society, and who from that rank must have acquired certain habits and modes of life, should thus have fallen from that eminence, and degraded yourself to the level of the meanest criminal.

Mr Justice Bayley, passing sentence on Merceron

Having been allowed home for the weekend, Merceron returned to the King's Bench for his second trial the following Monday, this time for corruption in public house licensing. Once again, Justice Abbott presided, with Scarlett and Topping respectively leading the prosecution and defence. The trial began with a procedural crisis when Scarlett discovered that five jurymen had also taken part in the first trial. He raised the issue with Abbott in order to avoid any accusations by the defence of prejudice. But Abbott instructed the jurors to remain, saying that Merceron had had every opportunity to complain when the juries were chosen. Merceron himself confirmed that he had 'no objection whatever' to the jurors continuing. But before Scarlett could begin proceedings the jury foreman expressed concern that the witnesses on both sides had been present in court throughout the first trial, and – again implying that intimidation was feared – asked that they be excluded this time. Further time then elapsed as the witnesses left the courtroom.[443]

When the court was finally called to order, Scarlett opened the prosecution case. This second charge against Merceron was of a 'knowing and corrupt violation of a most sacred trust'. It was the role of Justices of the Peace – the cornerstones of English liberty – to ensure that common people were not 'led into vice, dissipation and idleness' by being exposed to immoral practices in public houses. Merceron was charged with corruptly licensing public houses which were home to 'the lowest vice and debauchery', knowing them to be unfit. Crucially, some of them were his own property.[444]

The prosecution case rested mainly on the testimony of the parish constables Perry and Rennoldson, whose complaints Merceron had suppressed at the licensing hearings. Both drew on detailed notes of their nocturnal inspections of the premises in question, and Scarlett was able to present numerous examples of gambling dens, open all hours of the night and on Sundays. Importantly, both constables told the court how Merceron had intimidated them into remaining silent at the licensing hearings and lying under oath, and how he had then personally approved the renewal of the licences.[445]

Scarlett knew that Merceron's defence would focus heavily on presenting both constables as liars. To safeguard against this, six of the assistants who had accompanied Perry or Rennoldson on their inspections gave testimony corresponding exactly with those of the constables. When it came to Topping's turn to cross-examine the witnesses, he found himself struggling. The wealth of detail offered and the consistency between the various witnesses' accounts left no opportunity for him to even begin to threaten the prosecution case.

The prosecution's next witness was William Brodie Gurney, the shorthand writer for the House of Commons. Gurney confirmed that he had taken down the notes of Merceron's evidence at the Police Committee hearings in 1816 and 1817, and that Merceron had taken the opportunity to correct and confirm them before they were published. Scarlett's aim here was to convict Merceron by his own evidence. In particular, he wished to demonstrate Merceron's admission that he had known of complaints against houses at the time they were licensed, and also confirm his ownership of certain of the pubs named by Rennoldson and Perry in their evidence.[446]

But James Topping had a plan: even if the facts were against Merceron, perhaps legal procedure could still work in his favour. Before Scarlett could continue, Topping objected strongly that Merceron's evidence to the Police Committee was inadmissible in court as, in effect, it breached his right to silence. Merceron had been required to attend and answer Bennet's questions under a summons, and could have been imprisoned if he had refused. Surely, Topping appealed to the judge, answers given under such circumstances could not be used in evidence against him in a court? It was a difficult point, and for half an hour Merceron and the spectators in the gallery looked on as the lawyers became locked in a technical argument, with Gurney repeatedly recalled to the witness stand to answer detailed questions about parliamentary procedure. Eventually, Abbott decided he had had enough. He dismissed Topping's objections, stating that he was satisfied that Merceron's evidence to Bennet had been given voluntarily. If Merceron had any concerns about incriminating himself before the Select Committee, he should have requested the right to remain silent at the time. Accordingly, Scarlett was allowed to disclose to the jury Merceron's admission to owning several of the pubs referred to by Perry and Rennoldson.[447]

With the case for the prosecution over, Topping rose once more to begin his defence. Things were not going well. The case against Merceron seemed overwhelming and it now appeared that he stood convicted by his own evidence. Topping was desperate. He attempted to portray the entire case as a clash of personalities between Merceron and the Reverend King, claiming that Merceron's conduct for 20 years as a magistrate had been 'as blameless, as honourable and as fair and correct as that of any magistrate in the country', and that he had been 'put to the torture' as a result of his 'unfortunate differences' with the Rector.

As had happened in the first trial, the defence witnesses were weak and unconvincing, and if anything merely reinforced the nepotism at work within the local government of the East End. Charles Lush, the Tower Hamlets licensing clerk – and the father of Merceron's defence attorney – attempted to portray Merceron as a hard-working and honest magistrate. But Lush was soon forced by Scarlett to admit that the other magistrates simply took their lead from Merceron when it came to licensing the inns in Bethnal Green, and that none had ever been refused a licence. The parish beadle – in Merceron's pay for more than 20 years – claimed he had communicated Merceron's complaints to publicans on many occasions. The prosecution knew the real story: Merceron had sent the beadle to warn publicans of an impending visit by the constables, the beadle had had 'a glass of gin at each' and had been 'dead drunk' before he had completed his rounds. The High Constable of the Tower Hamlets claimed to have visited all the pubs listed by Rennoldson and had seen nothing worthy of complaint. But his credibility was destroyed when the prosecution reminded him that he had publicly attributed his ap-pointment to Merceron and claimed him to be his best friend. By this point, even Merceron must have been giving up hope.[448]

It was time for Scarlett to reply for the prosecution. With the case as good as won, he launched into a powerful and persuasive denun-ciation of the defence. In essence, he told the jurors, the defence rested on Merceron's word against that of Rennoldson and Perry. But if the constables were lying, surely Merceron could simply have called any of his fellow licensing magistrates as witnesses? Was it not strange that not one magistrate had come forward to support him in his hour of need? As for the claim that Rennoldson was a liar, Scarlett told the jury not to believe it for a moment: 'a more respectable witness, and a man who appears to have conducted himself in his office, with more fidelity, accuracy and discretion, I never saw.' (At this, even Justice Abbott nodded his head.) Scarlett saved his greatest ire for Merceron's attempt to persuade Rennoldson to perjure himself:

> Good God! Gentlemen, in what land do we live?...If Mr Merceron has no other crimes but that to expiate, it will require long and long before that is washed away...no honest man could have said that...Gentlemen, this is the character of Mr

Merceron's conduct: this stamps the whole...I call upon you to find him guilty of a corrupt design to poison the fountains of justice for his own private gain and advantage.[449]

In the earlier trial, Justice Abbott had remained quietly impartial throughout the day and had only allowed his sympathies to show in his final directions to the jury. This time, however, he had revealed his antipathy to Merceron when allowing Scarlett to disclose the Police Committee evidence; any slim chance of acquittal had disappeared from that point. Abbott's summing up was unequivocal and left the jury in no doubt as to what was expected of them: Merceron, he told them, had 'offered nothing that, it seems to me, meets this case'. As to the defence claims that Merceron had not gained financially from the licensing, Abbott thought them irrelevant: 'it would require much too narrow a view of this case to confine the meaning of the word corruption to pecuniary gain.' He reinforced Scarlett's comments about the sacred trust imposed in magistrates when it came to public house licensing: upon it 'depended the health and even the lives of the lower orders of society: dissipation led to crime, and crime to death'.

Abbott's directions to the jury were clear: if they could attribute Merceron's conduct to any good motive, they should acquit. If they believed his motives were bad, then such motives were corrupt and they were bound to convict him. This time the jury scarcely turned round before pronouncing Merceron guilty. The sentencing was scheduled for Monday 1st June, a fortnight later. In the meantime, Merceron was allowed to return home.[450]

For the next two weeks, Merceron's desperation reached new depths as he tried every trick to avoid justice. James Wilmot Lush and Henry Merceron were repeatedly sent to the City of London to persuade influential friends and colleagues to swear affidavits to Merceron's character. The day after his trial, Merceron wrote to the Bethnal Green parish officers offering to return the amount of Dann & Crosland's invoice to the parish funds. The next day, he personally handed over the money to the Bank of England. James Topping was critical, suggesting that the chances of leniency might be improved if Merceron – having had the money for five years – was also to refund the interest on the payment. Accordingly, on 25th May, a further £300 was handed over.[451]

Merceron had also launched an even more ambitious plan, involving a surprising ally. Less than three months earlier, Lawrence Gwynne had seemingly been at the forefront of the campaign to unseat Merceron. But the vestry's refusal to appoint Gwynne as treasurer in Merceron's place had led to a cooling of relations that Merceron was quick as ever to exploit.[452]

Days after the verdict was announced, Joshua King was surprised to be approached by Gwynne with a proposal from Merceron. He was incredulous when Gwynne told him that Merceron would pay the vestrymen £10,000 (around £1 million in today's money) plus costs if they would agree to drop the prosecutions. King was not going to be bought off, feeling that 'to arrest the arm of justice by a mercenary compromise…would be attended with eternal infamy'. He refused the offer and fed the story to the newspapers. *The Times* informed its readers that the parish were determined to make an example of Merceron, and credited King with having brought about his downfall.[453]

Having failed in his mission, Gwynne – who was after all a magistrate – tried desperately to extricate himself from accusations of bribery, but in doing so demonstrated that he was entirely under Merceron's control. On 27th May, he wrote to *The Times* claiming misleadingly to be one of Merceron's prosecutors. Gwynne insisted that the allegation of a £10,000 bribe was an 'infamous falsehood' and an attempt to prejudice the public against 'an individual about to receive the sentence of a court of justice'. He stated that he had attended the audit of Merceron's accounts, inspected the books himself and interviewed the parish officers on the subject. As a result, despite the jury's verdict, he believed firmly that Merceron had 'truly accounted for every farthing' he had received.[454]

Gwynne's letter was published on Friday 29th May. Over the weekend, with judgment day scheduled for the Monday, Merceron made a final attempt to buy off his prosecutors. A further emissary was sent to King; this time the offer was doubled to £20,000. The vestrymen again refused.[455]

The following Monday afternoon, Merceron returned to court for sentencing. Sir Charles Abbott was joined on the judge's bench by Mr Justice Bayley and the ailing Lord Ellenborough. Abbott began by reading out his report of the trials, after which James Topping submitted a large number of affidavits to Merceron's good character. Lush & Merceron had earned their fees: as Topping explained, some of the names were 'not quite unknown' to their Lordships. MP George Byng spoke to Merceron's 'zeal, regularity and ability'. William Mellish, the other Middlesex MP and former Governor of the Bank of England, swore as to the correctness of Merceron's conduct. A dozen or so magistrates from the Tower Division bore witness to Merceron's 'indefatigable industry, great ability and upright demeanour'.[456]

A keen observer, however, might have remarked upon some of the names that were missing from Topping's list. Once again, Sir Daniel Williams and the Reverends Robson and Thirlwall had clearly decided that their association with Merceron had got them into quite enough trouble and had declined to take part. Nevertheless, it was an impressive cast, and even Lord Ellenborough conceded grudgingly that it appeared there had been times when Merceron had 'conducted himself properly and meritoriously'. Topping seized on this and launched a plea for mercy: 'in awarding the penalty of the law, your Lordships will recollect there was a time when…his conduct… had the support of the most honourable gentlemen.'

Topping might sensibly have left it at that, but by this point he was quite carried away on his client's behalf, claiming that during a long period in high office Merceron had 'discharged the duties reposed in him with ability, fidelity and scrupulous conscientiousness'. Thinking that things were going Merceron's way, one of the junior defence counsel now began to suggest that the jury, perhaps biased because of what they had heard or read arising from the Police Committee, had based their verdict on unsound evidence. But Lord Ellenborough, unwell and irritable, was having none of it, telling the counsel bluntly to concentrate on matters 'better calculated to benefit Mr Merceron, and not those which injure him'.[457]

It was James Scarlett's turn to have the final word for the prosecution. He ran rapidly through the manner in which Merceron had committed the offences: the conspiracy to defraud the poor's rate, his involvement in licensing his own public houses and his attempts to suppress evidence against them. He acknowledged that Merceron had repaid the stolen funds but pointed out that he had conspicuously failed to do so for two years after the Police Committee exposed the theft. It was clear, he told the judges, that Merceron's motives had been 'base and sordid', and the punishment should be made to fit the crime.[458]

As Scarlett finished speaking, all eyes turned anxiously to Lord Ellenborough. But to everyone's surprise the elderly judge announced a further delay. The jury in another case was waiting for him: 'the court will give its judgement on Wednesday next. In the meantime the defendant must be committed.' Ellenborough left the room, and in the buzz that followed Merceron was led from the court and taken by coach to 'Ellenborough Castle', the King's Bench Prison across the river in Southwark.[459]

A standard cell in the King's Bench was nine feet square, and the whole place was filthy, infested with rats and mice and smelt terribly. But Merceron's affluence probably enabled him to avoid the worst of prison conditions and two days later he remained unbowed as he stood up in court to receive his sentence. Lord Ellenborough had succumbed to illness, and it fell to Mr Justice Bayley to administer the court's decision.[460]

Bayley began by refuting the suggestion that the jury may have convicted Merceron out of prejudice and based on unsound evidence. Having looked into this, Bayley was entirely satisfied with the propriety of the verdicts. The defence had complained that Merceron had been convicted in the second trial solely on the evidence of Perry and Rennoldson; again Bayley dismissed this, suggesting that the failure of Sir Daniel Williams to testify for his friend was a strong indication that the constables had told the truth. Bayley moved on to his justification for the punishment he was about to hand out, launching into a withering denunciation of Merceron's behaviour:

> It is obvious, from the evidence, that the first offence, the mal-appropriation of so large a sum of the money taken from those who, perhaps, could many of them very ill afford to pay, had long been in your mind; you were not actuated by a sudden and imprudent impulse, but you accomplished your fraudulent purpose by a train of the most disgraceful artifices...

Bayley was aware that Merceron had refunded the money: this 'had in a great degree redeemed him' as far as pecuniary punishment was concerned; but nevertheless, the offence was a serious one, and:

> ...the Court and country cannot but be astonished that an individual who has filled so many offices of trust, who has reached such a rank in society, and who from that rank must have acquired certain habits and modes of life, should thus have fallen from that eminence, and degraded yourself to the level of the meanest criminal.

At these words, and perhaps for the first time in the trial, Merceron was visibly shaken. But there was more to come: moving to the second offence, that of corruptly licensing public houses, Bayley described this as 'a greater crime...a crime of the highest magnitude' in light of the 'evils that might result to society'. Bayley was a deeply religious man and clearly found such depravity abhorrent. Merceron's treatment of Perry and especially of Rennoldson, claimed the judge, was compelling evidence of 'the criminality of his purpose':

...the Court cannot but wonder that a man who has hitherto borne so good a character, should so far have forgotten not only your duty as a magistrate, but all you have learned of the sanctity of religion. What can be expected of any man in future, if a magistrate is permitted to tell an individual that an oath is a mere matter of form?

As the suspense grew, Bayley approached his climax. Merceron may have been cheered briefly as the judge told him that he had taken account of the many affidavits produced on his behalf, and also 'the unavoidable degradation' he must suffer 'not merely among his friends and connexions, but in the eye of the public at large'. Perhaps he would be going home to Bethnal Green after all? Bayley's next comment jolted him back to reality, and he looked more shaken than ever as the judge told him that he would be writing to the Lord Chancellor to ask him to consider Merceron's dismissal as a magistrate and from his remaining public offices. The waiting was over. All eyes were on the accused as Bayley announced the sentence:

...for the first offence, you shall pay to the King a fine of £200, and be imprisoned in the custody of the Marshal of the Marshalsea [of the King's Bench[461]] for six calendar months; and that, for the second offence, you shall be imprisoned in the same custody for 12 calendar months, to be calculated from the expiration of the first sentence; and that you be further imprisoned until such fine is paid.

After so many escapes, Merceron was finally going down. But before he was led away, there was just a hint that his trial had not broken him, as he turned to face the Court, giving a polite bow.[462]

PART IV

Resurgence
1818–39

CHAPTER XVI

The King's Bench

Anyone can go in…but it is not everyone who can go out.
Charles Dickens, *Little Dorrit*

In contrast to the forbidding frontage of Coldbath Fields that Merceron knew so well, the entrance to the King's Bench Prison was rather more gentlemanly in its appearance. The King's Bench was not, after all, a 'house of correction' for poor felons but a prison for debtors and those sentenced by the Court of King's Bench for libel, or the sort of white-collar crimes of which Merceron was guilty. He was by no means its first illustrious inmate. The writers Daniel Defoe and Tobias Smollett had both served time there and it was where the Radical politician John Wilkes had been incarcerated after libelling the King in 1763. In more recent times the politicians John Horne Tooke and Lord Cochrane and publisher William Hone had been among those sent there as a result of their Radical opposition to the government.

The prison stood just off the Borough Road, Southwark, near the south bank of the Thames by London Bridge. Its entrance was set in a handsome courtyard containing three double-fronted Georgian townhouses. Entry to the prison was through an archway between the houses, leading to a long, four-storey cell block faced by an exercise yard, and surrounded by a 35 foot wall topped with iron spikes such that the inmates could not see beyond it, even from the uppermost windows.[463]

On his arrival, Merceron was taken by the turnkeys to the prison's coffee house to arrange his accommodation. The system for allocating rooms, known as 'chumming', was in operation in most of the London prisons of the time and involved the purchase, for anything between three shillings and a pound, of a 'chum ticket' entitling the owner to a bed, usually shared with at least one other inmate. For a rich man like Merceron, however, there were various ways in which his conditions could be improved, at corresponding prices. The cheapest was to 'buy out' another man's chum ticket. For a few shillings per week, many poorer prisoners were only too happy to clear out of their cell and find lodgings elsewhere. A more expensive alternative was to hire one of eight larger furnished 'state rooms', reserved for gentlemen prisoners, from about five guineas per week. At the top of the scale, prisoners could hire one of the three townhouses in the entrance yard, 'generally let to persons of rank and fortune' by the Marshal and the Clerk, who were willing to move out temporarily if the price was right. There is no record of which of these options Merceron took, but it seems a fair bet that he would have found a way to bargain with the Marshal or Clerk for a townhouse at preferential terms.

The chumming system meant that a small number of wealthier prisoners had at worst a comfortable cell to themselves, while elsewhere as many as six poor men could be found crammed into a space only 15 feet by 12 in area. The level of overcrowding was such that, in a prison originally built to accommodate about 220 prisoners, there were frequently more than 500. The fact that many men brought their families to live with them did not help matters. In March 1815, it was reported that there were 180 women and children lodging within the prison.

After more than 20 years as a supervising magistrate at Coldbath Fields, Merceron was fully conversant with prison conditions. Compared with Governor Aris's harsh regime the King's Bench was a relatively benign institution, but it was nevertheless an uncomfortable and deeply unpleasant place in which to live. In 1814, a parliamentary Select Committee into the state of prisons (chaired, incidentally, by Henry Grey Bennet in another of his attempts to 'diminish the sum of human misery') described it as 'ill-lighted and extremely dirty', giving special mention to the smells from the sewers, dirt heaps and barrels of urine piled up behind the buildings awaiting collection by the local scavengers.

Visitors had much greater access than those to today's prisons, and Merceron's family had ready access for visits. As a visitor to the nearby Marshalsea was told in Charles Dickens's *Little Dorrit*, 'any one can go *in*…but it is not every one who can go out'. Rowlandson's and Pugin's 1810 print of the prison compound, in Ackermann's *Microcosm of London*, depicts a scene more akin to a street market than a place of confinement. The sunlit yard is crowded with people. Top-hatted gentlemen stroll arm-in-arm with wives (or whores – Grey Bennet's Committee reported that 'women of all descriptions' were admitted 'freely and without enquiry'). Groups of men play at racquets and marbles, or stand haggling with basket-bearing trades-men. Others congregate around stalls selling meat, fish and vegeta-bles. Visitors and tradesmen could stay all day, but needed to get out quickly once the bell for 'strangers, women and children out' was rung at 9.30 p.m.. Anyone still inside the gates at ten o'clock was locked in for the night.

The cells of the King's Bench were described by the visiting mag-istrate as 'each satisfying its individual occupant' in point of cleanli-ness – meaning that, like the prisoners, some were very dirty and others tolerably clean. Each cell contained an iron range, a bed and often a small cupboard. But the better rooms like Merceron's would typically have acquired a collection of rudimentary furniture: a coat of paint and the odd print on the walls, a small table and chair, shelves, perhaps even an old carpet and curtains. Rowlandson's and Pugin's print clearly depicts a number of cells with well-stocked window-boxes. Dickens describes the room of William Dorrit in the nearby Marshalsea (based on his own experiences of visiting his father, imprisoned there for debt in 1824) as 'close and confined, poorly furnished and the fire smoked to boot, but constant pains and care had made it neat, even comfortable'; we can picture Ann

King's Bench Prison, Southwark

Merceron busying herself to make her husband's accommodation similarly habitable.

For refreshment, the yard contained several water pumps. For those seeking something stronger – and probably safer – to drink, there was a wine room and a tap room, the latter getting through as many as 40 pints of ale for each prisoner every week. There are conflicting accounts about the sale of spirits in the prison, but the ale consumption alone supports the contention in Bennet's 1814 report that drunkenness was 'most common'. As well as the coffee house, there was a bakery and a public kitchen where prisoners could get their meat roasted or boiled: free of charge before lunchtime, and for a small payment afterwards. Visitors were allowed to bring in as much food and other accompaniments as they liked. Dickens has William Dorrit enjoying dinner on a clean cloth, 'with knife, fork, and spoon, salt cellar, pepper-box, glass, and pewter ale pot' and even a 'pennyworth of pickles in a saucer' and we may picture Ann, an accomplished cook, bringing in similar feasts for Merceron.[464]

The better-off prisoner would not starve. For the poor, conditions were not so good: Bennet's 1814 report was sharply critical of the allowances for food, fuel and bedding. It was unadvisable to fall ill. There was no resident doctor, and the visiting magistrate noted that extreme suffering accompanied any outbreak of fever or disease: 'for sickness accompanied with poverty,' as he put it, 'finds here neither pity nor relief'.

For a powerful and wealthy man like Merceron, there was little that could not be bought. A contemporary writer described the King's Bench as the fountainhead of corrupt prison systems, noting wryly that 'everything moves slow…until the wheels are greased a little' and that 'a banknote, properly directed, or a dozen of wine sent, are never returned'. The Marshal was reported by Bennet's Select Committee to be making enormous profits from the rent of rooms, sale of alcohol and fees for granting permission to debtors to reside in the area immediately surrounding the prison known as 'the Rules'. Criminal prisoners like Merceron were not eligible for the latter privilege but, as Bennet had uncovered, it was the widespread practice for prisoners to bribe the turnkeys to allow them 'a run on the key': in effect, a day release pass.[465]

The resulting flexibility and ready access for visitors meant that Merceron was easily able to continue his business dealings, although certain of his former activities had been curtailed. He was dismissed as a magistrate on 24th June 1818, just weeks after his imprisonment began, and soon afterwards he resigned as chair of the Tower Hamlets Commission of Sewers. Mostly, however, things went on as before, with the centre of operations relocated from Brick Lane to the prison and Merceron's trusted lieutenants Gwynne, Renvoize and his son Henry conducting business on his behalf.[466]

In Merceron's enforced absence, the people of Bethnal Green enjoyed an unusually quiet summer. On 20th August, the vestry gathered to reflect on his defeat. A resolution was passed celebrating the 'downfall of an insupportable tyranny and despotism, and the brilliant anticipation of the future liberty, prosperity and happiness of the parish'. Buoyed up by Mr Justice Bayley's firm conclusion that there had been a wider conspiracy to defraud, the parish determined to follow up its victory by launching a further prosecution against the Reverend Platt and his co-conspirators. But even in prison, Merceron retained considerable power and support amongst the people of Bethnal Green. The resolution to pursue the prosecutions attracted 168 votes, but 77 vestrymen voted against it.[467]

Every trick imaginable was played in order to delay or prevent a prosecution. On approaching counsel to take on the case Robert Wrightson learned that Merceron, anticipating his action, had already retained every King's Bench Counsel except one, preventing them from acting against his associates. On 27th August, a legal challenge was lodged, claiming that the vestry had no power to bring a prosecution without the permission of the local watch and lamp trustees, of which the nine defendants formed a convenient majority. Eventually, though, all objections were brushed aside and on 16th

September a Middlesex Grand Jury referred the prosecution to the Court of King's Bench.[468]

With the real threat of prison now hanging over Merceron's main associates, the Rector's party had things their own way over the winter months. King took maximum advantage of this opportunity. For years, Merceron had been blocking his attempts to provide more school places in Bethnal Green. In March 1819 the vestry voted to build a National School, funded by a grant from the Bishop of London. That Easter, in scenes of great celebration, Merceron's supporters were voted out of all parochial offices, with the vestry minutes recording that the parish had been 'emancipated from gross corruption and party tyranny'. The Merceron faction's response to their dismissal was to launch a malicious prosecution, led by Gwynne, against the new parish officers for fraudulent misappropriation of poor's rate funds. But Gwynne's suit was rejected by a Grand Jury and the vestry could again celebrate victory against 'the disappointed ambition of miscalculating men'.[469]

On Friday 28th May an immense number of Bethnal Green residents made their way once more to the Court of King's Bench in Westminster Hall for the trial of Merceron's co-conspirators. The occupations of the nine defendants perfectly illustrated the breadth of Merceron's support across Bethnal Green society: Methodist minister William Platt, 'gentlemen' and Commissioners of Sewers Peter Renvoize and William Millar, surgeon James Brown Unwin, undertaker Samuel Ames, tallow chandler Saunderson Turner Sturtevant, carpenters Stephen Witherden and William Bragg and retired publican James Greenwood. Thanks to Merceron's astute interference, they were to be defended by James Scarlett – who must have found it odd to be fighting on the other side of the argument – and John Gurney, two of the most senior counsel in the King's Bench.

The prosecution had to be content with the services of Mr Sergeant Pell, widely considered a significantly less able barrister. At a final consultation with Pell on the evening before the trial, King urged Pell to adopt 'a determined perseverance' in prosecuting his cause. In doing so, he might well have expressed concerns about the solicitor for the defence. This was none other than John Wilks, who Merceron had bribed into dropping King's first attempt to prosecute him in 1813. Having once bought Wilks off, Merceron had now employed him; the prosecuting vestrymen, having suffered at Wilks's hands before, could have been forgiven for feeling uneasy.[470]

Their fears were fully justified. As had happened in 1813, the prosecution case never got off the ground. Pell, opening it, reminded the jury that the case was linked to that of Merceron, 'a name...which has very much excited the attention of the public'. He immediately launched into a speech wholly at odds with his clients' instructions, in which he lamented that the case had been brought to court and assured the jury that he 'would feel the greatest satisfaction if there was another way of returning the parish to peace and quietness'. When Scarlett, for the defence, wholeheartedly agreed, the rather bemused Lord Chief Justice Abbott interjected: 'are your clients on both sides really desirous of reconciliation?' To the astonishment of most of those present, Pell responded that 'I think I may safely say on behalf of those I represent, there is every disposition'. Scarlett seized on the opportunity to get his clients off the hook, stating that they had been innocently misled in following Merceron, thinking him 'a man of high honour and respectability'. Abbott announced that 'the thing may end without triumph if it ends now...if both parties are desirous of peace, there is a mode of obtaining that by putting an end to the prosecution'. It was only at this point that Pell consulted his furious clients. Fearing charges of contempt of court should they appear vindictive after Abbott's statements, King and Wrightson had no choice but to drop the prosecution. Abbott turned to the jury. Recalling the long list of character affidavits produced at Merceron's trial, he reflected that 'if persons of the highest consequence' could speak well of Merceron's conduct, there 'might certainly be others who might think it honourable and proper, though they might be mistaken'. He added 'I dare say you will think that what has been done on all sides is the best thing which can be'.

The foreman replied: 'perfectly so, my Lord' and the jury immediately pronounced the defendants 'not guilty'.[471]

The removal of the threat of conviction meant Merceron's associates could return to their old tricks. On 29th July, a mob led by Lawrence Gwynne hijacked a vestry meeting, overturning a ruling requiring parish officers to produce all vouchers when their books were audited. Meanwhile, in prison, Merceron fumed about the enemies that had humiliated him. With his release looming, his thoughts turned increasingly to retaliation.[472]

Between September and November 1819, as excitement grew in Bethnal Green over Merceron's imminent release, a series of political skirmishes set the tone for bigger battles to come. The two parties vied for control of the vestry and the situation became farcical as they took it in turns to hold meetings, each countermanding the resolutions made by the other. Over time, the threats and bribes of Merceron's party began to tell. In 1818, after Merceron's conviction, the poor's rate funds had been placed in the hands of a panel of five trustees in an attempt to prevent further corruption. In a cleverly manipulated and hotly disputed election, Gwynne obtained majority control of the all-important trust. He immediately brought a series of trumped-up charges against May and established a committee of investigation dominated by his own supporters. In celebratory anticipation of Merceron's homecoming, Gwynne slashed the poor's rates on the houses of Merceron and three of his acquitted co-conspirators.[473]

In typical fashion, Merceron had refused to pay his £200 fine into Court until the last possible moment. It was only on 24th November 1819, as his discharge papers were being prepared, that he finally handed over the money. Excitement over his return to Bethnal Green had reached fever pitch, with more than 300 people signing a request for a vestry meeting to coincide with his homecoming on 2nd December. The churchwardens tore up the notice and refused to call the meeting.[474]

After a week of celebrations, Merceron twice more attempted to call a vestry meeting, on 9th and 17th December. Both times, King denied him access to the church. Merceron took matters into his own hands, setting up a rival vestry in the workhouse where he formally ratified the appointments of Gwynne and his friends as trustees of the poor's rate, issued an order for the parish funds to be handed over to them and added authenticity to the proceedings by publishing the resolutions in the *Sunday Monitor*. 1819 closed with a riotous confrontation between the two parties in St Matthew's church on 29th December, involving more than 300 men and resulting in the unseemly spectacle of the Reverend King fighting with the surgeon James Brown Unwin. It ended with Merceron securing a resolution that all future vestry decisions would be made by show of hands rather than by poll, facilitating intimidation by his thugs. Less than a month after his return, the Boss was back in control of Bethnal Green.[475]

CHAPTER XVII

Supremacy Restored

*Mysterious are the ways of Providence! Oft do we see
the fairest flowers cut down and withered, whilst the
most noxious weeds are allowed to grow and flourish!*
Reverend Joshua King[476]

In 1818, the revelation of the true extent of Merceron's corruption
had led the people of Bethnal Green to vote him from office. Having
enjoyed the taste of democracy, many were reluctant to relinquish
it. Despite the rapidity with which Merceron regained initial control
of the vestry on his release from prison and the immense power he
wielded over the lives of ordinary people, it would take more than
three years of bitterly contested elections, libel actions, political skul-
duggery and good-old-fashioned violence before he could consider
the battle conclusively won.

The first three months of 1820 saw Merceron engage in a malicious campaign of retaliation against James May. An anonymous
pamphlet appeared alleging that May had rigged the 1818 election
overthrowing Merceron as treasurer. Next, an important source of
income to May, given his paltry salary and 21 children, was cut off
when Merceron persuaded the vestry to ban May from carrying out
any paid legal work on its behalf. Then, after three months' deliber-
ation, Lawrence Gwynne's committee of investigation reported to
the vestry that James May and Robert Wrightson had perpetrated
a fraud on the parish over the legal fees for Merceron's prosecution.
A minority of the committee protested that the charges were in-
vented. As usual, Merceron had arranged for the presence of enough

supporters to intimidate the vestry into submission; Gwynne's report was approved and thousands of copies circulated throughout Bethnal Green. The allegations caught hold in the mind of the public and, on 23rd March, a vote of censure was passed against May and Wrightson.[477]

With the annual vestry elections just a few days away, Merceron now put up his own candidate to stand against May as vestry clerk. Robert Brutton was an ambitious City of London attorney, about 30 years old and a tenant of the Reverend Platt in Wilmot Square. He was doubtless seduced by Merceron's financial offers, but his decision to stand was probably also influenced by the fact that Ann, Merceron's daughter, had caught his eye.

On Easter Sunday, the day before the election, Lawrence Gwynne arranged for his report against May to be republished in the *Sunday Monitor*, embellishing it with libellous observations of his own. The following day, a thousand vestrymen turned out to vote. When the result was announced, it appeared at first that Merceron's machinations had been in vain: May had scraped through by 500 votes to Brutton's 495. An argument raged over the result for several hours until, long after darkness had fallen, it was agreed that a recount would take place.[478]

The next day, Merceron posted thugs at the vestry door and polling desk for the election of the remaining parish officers. Unsurprisingly, every one of his candidates was elected by an overwhelming margin in a complete reversal of the previous year's results. Once again Merceron had absolute control over Bethnal Green's finances.[479]

The dispute over the poll result between May and Brutton continued for weeks. On 21st April, in a test of his resurgent power, Merceron announced that the surgeon James Brown Unwin – one of the eight associates acquitted of conspiracy the previous year – would act as sole scrutineer. Given that Unwin had been heard declaring 'that he would blow his brains out rather than May should continue to be vestry clerk of the parish', this announcement produced predictable outrage. Joshua King's protests were ignored and eventually, after a further fortnight, Unwin declared that following a recount Brutton was elected by 503 votes to 484.[480]

For the next eight months, the government of Bethnal Green was reduced to a farce as the Rector's party refused to accept Brutton's appointment. May refused to stand down as vestry clerk, launching libel actions against Gwynne and several other Merceron associates. In turn, Merceron moved all vestry meetings to the workhouse, which his minders could more effectively prevent opponents from entering. One vestry meeting began with the pathetic spectacle of May and Brutton each attempting to shout down the other in reading out their respective versions of the previous minutes. This situation continued throughout the summer with May being repeatedly roughed up by Merceron's associates in an attempt to bully him into conceding.[481]

Soon afterwards, Merceron's grip on power was given a significant boost by the death in Cheshire of Joshua King's father. As a result, King succeeded to his father's living of Woodchurch, meaning that he would from then on be required to spend most of his time in Cheshire, several days' journey from Bethnal Green. At long last, King's financial worries were over. His income was more than doubled, but he now had two very distant parishes to attend to. It must have been tempting to abandon Bethnal Green to a curate, as his predecessor had done, and never set foot there again. For now, however, the additional income proved the stronger attraction and King determined to split his time between his two parishes. Nevertheless, the strains of the 200-mile journey began to tell, and over the next two years King's visits to Bethnal Green became increasingly infrequent.[482]

In December 1821, James May's libel action against Lawrence Gwynne came to the Court of King's Bench before Lord Chief Justice Abbott. James Scarlett was again involved, this time opposing the Merceron interest, and tipped the balance of the case decisively in May's favour with his opening speech. In it, Scarlett gave such a compelling account of Merceron's campaign to unseat May and the events leading up to it, including Gwynne's role in offering a £10,000 bribe at the time of Merceron's sentencing, that Gwynne immediately capitulated. His only defence was to insist that the £10,000 was not a bribe, but an offer by Merceron of 'reparation to the parish for the injury it had sustained'. He insisted that his own role in the affair had been induced merely 'from pity to the distress of Mrs Merceron and her family' rather than by any pecuniary incentive. May magnanimously declined to press his advantage and agreed to accept the costs plus a payment of just £50 by Gwynne to charity, leading Abbott to remark that May had 'behaved very handsomely'. Abbott, by this time, was heartily sick of the affairs of Bethnal Green. When another of May's libel suits came to trial a year later and the Solicitor General suggested a gesture of reconciliation, Abbott remarked: 'as to the restoration of peace in the parish of Bethnal Green, I really believe it is hopeless, and therefore I shall suggest nothing.'[483]

The excitement over Gwynne's libel trial, with its public revelations of Merceron's attempts to bribe his way out of prison, was still running high in Bethnal Green the following Easter as the 1822 vestry elections approached. The previous year, May's son had stood against Brutton but had been heavily defeated thanks to Merceron's campaign of intimidation (a scribbled note from Brutton to Merceron a few days later thanked him for his 'great exertions on the day of the election, tho' it will not be wise or even politic to say so publicly'). This time, to prevent similar interference, Merceron's opponents campaigned for the right to hold a secret ballot. Shortly before the election, the tension was ratcheted up when rumours, sparked by a pamphlet circulated by an anonymous 'friend to humanity', began to spread of abuses in the workhouse. The pamphleteer alleged that certain Governors of the Poor, described as 'friends of Mr Brutton', had participated in acts of extreme cruelty to orphan children. Young boys had had their heads roughly shaved in punishment for 'imaginary offences'. Others had been beaten brutally and forced to work a tread wheel. The news caused uproar, and led to a feverish bout of canvassing by both sides in the days leading up to the election.[484]

By 9 o'clock on Easter Monday, when the vestry doors were opened, a crowd had already gathered outside St Matthew's church. Both sides had used every tactic to persuade voters to the poll, and so many had turned up that several hundred were forced to wait outside in the churchyard. Inside, a fight began over who should chair the meeting. The result was closer than in the previous year but despite the breaking scandal, Brutton was again declared the winner, by 1,363 votes to 1,034. After the election was over, however, several vestrymen moved for an inquiry into the goings-on at the workhouse. Merceron, sensing the mood, insisted that he 'entirely approved of a thorough investigation' and seconded the resolution for an inquiry, ensuring however that it was well stacked with his own supporters.[485]

As the inquiry proceeded, Merceron's representatives found it impossible to hide the clear evidence of brutality. When the committee reported back to the vestry, it became clear why Merceron had tried so hard to suppress the findings. The allegations of 'inhuman treatment' had been substantially proven. Boys had been locked all day long in tiny cupboards, flogged while sick with fever and beaten with iron spoons until they bled. Such cruelty had taken place with the express direction of the Governors of the Poor. When the committee refused to name the governors concerned, fearing reprisals, there was almost a riot. Eventually the names were released and the accused men, known associates of Merceron, were called before the vestry a few days later. But by this time Merceron's minders had persuaded a majority of vestrymen that they had better not intervene. The governors denied the charges and no further action was taken.[486]

Over the summer of 1822, Merceron's opponents made further sporadic and unsuccessful attempts to limit his power, calling several times for the introduction of secret ballots at vestry elections. A further challenge about the workhouse scandal was dropped when

Merceron insisted he had personally investigated the matter and was satisfied that there had been no wrongdoing. Then, in a move that would prove decisive in the battle to control Bethnal Green over the next decade, Merceron came up with the idea of permanently cementing his power by creating a 'select' vestry.[487]

Select vestries, where local power was vested legally by the people in a controlling oligarchy of larger landowners, were not new. In the shifting sands of political representation after the Glorious Revolution of 1688, as England's ruling classes began to accept the necessity of some widening of the franchise for both local and national government, the select vestry was a fairly obvious way of limiting that widening at the local level. After the Napoleonic wars, with Poor Law costs spiralling out of control (the national cost of the poor's rate rose by 45 percent in the three years to 1818) it was argued that select vestries would counter this trend by placing the administration of the Poor Law squarely in the hands of those who were paying for it. This argument had been given support by the economic preaching of Thomas Robert Malthus in his *Essay on the Principle of Population*, first published in 1798 and updated in several subsequent editions. Malthus had argued consistently that the old Poor Laws ran counter to economic theory, claiming that they increased food prices, undermined the independence of the lower classes, encouraged improvident marriages, raised the birth rate and so created more of the paupers they were designed to maintain. The alarming increase in Poor Law costs after the war seemed to support Malthus's arguments and provided the government with an imperative to take action.[488]

In 1817, a parliamentary Select Committee chaired by William Sturges-Bourne MP recommended significant changes to the existing laws, proposing that parishes be permitted to give more power to their principal landowners and occupiers by means of select vestries. These proposals were enabled over the following two years by the passing of the 'Sturges-Bourne Acts'. For 'open' vestries that had enjoyed a wide ratepayer franchise for centuries, it was a profoundly undemocratic step. The government's aim was simply to prevent swathes of lower class ratepayers from voting ever-increasing payments to the poor.

For Merceron, the Sturges-Bourne Acts provided a golden opportunity to lock in his control over Bethnal Green in a perfectly legal way, with the full backing of the government and supported by the leading economists of the day. Instead of having annually to win over – or coerce – an electorate of more than 2,000 people into voting him and his associates into office, a select vestry would make many of them permanent officers by dint of their property qualification.[489]

A plan took shape. Robert Brutton was despatched to Westminster to research the process and appoint advisers. In late September, he gave formal notice of an intention to apply to Parliament to amend the local Acts by which Bethnal Green was governed. To avoid suspicion the scheme was portrayed simply as an attempt to clarify and codify the existing qualifications of vestrymen, and the term 'select vestry' was deliberately excluded from the notice. Nothing was announced locally, and most vestrymen knew nothing about it until early October, when James May saw the notice in the papers. When challenged, Merceron insisted that the scheme included nothing for vestrymen to worry about: 'I shall watch very narrowly, and with great jealousy, the privileges of the vestrymen, endeavouring at the same time to protect the interest and welfare of the parishioners generally, by every means in my power'.[490]

Despite his distractions in Cheshire, Joshua King's suspicions had been aroused. Writing to his superiors at Brasenose College, he accused Merceron of duplicity: 'Their ostensible object is to make the vestry more select by raising the qualification of vestrymen, but as they invariably profess one thing and practise another…they will most probably attempt to introduce some obnoxious clauses injurious to [my] interests…' Grieving after the death of his youngest brother and faced with the serious illness of one of his sisters, King then allowed a rather unchristian resentment of Merceron to escape his pen: 'Mysterious are the ways of Providence! Oft do we see the fairest flowers cut down and withered, whilst the most noxious weeds are allowed to grow and flourish!'[491]

The Rector's suspicions were well founded. Despite their protestations of innocence, Merceron and Brutton pressed ahead with their plans in secret and it was not until the end of January 1823 that a summary of the proposals was put to the vestry. Merceron again avoided all mention of a select vestry and insisted that the Bill was simply to clarify the qualifications of vestrymen. As darkness descended, and amid much shouting, a show of hands was called. King's party claimed victory but Merceron insisted it had been too dark to count properly and demanded a poll for the following day. The minders went to work as usual, with the result that at the poll only four vestrymen dared to vote against the motion, with 268 in favour.[492]

When King called a further meeting in the church, hundreds of vestrymen from both sides began the meeting with yet another fight over who should take the chair. A riot ensued. According to Brutton's account:

> The greatest tumult and disorder now began to be manifested in opposition to Dr. Gwynne. The uproar and confusion continued without intermission for more than an hour when a scene of riot prevailed...The great pressure and suffocating heat added to the vociferation and menacing attitude of various parties caused the greatest terror and alarm in the vestry room. The cry of 'Murder' was heard and the lives of several vestrymen appearing to be in serious danger...[493]

Gwynne, still a magistrate, read the Riot Act and the meeting was ordered to disperse. But more than 500 remained in the church, where the Rector's party conducted a protest meeting and won a vote against the select vestry proposals. The crowd was eventually dispersed but only after, according to Brutton, 'several persons had been materially bruised and otherwise seriously injured'. He neglected to mention his own, less than heroic, part in the struggle: apparently he had fainted in the heat and had to be carried out to safety.[494]

If Joshua King had a weakness, it was money. Greed had got the better of him in 1813, and so it proved again. With the Committee stage of the select vestry Bill imminent, and sensing that his chances of stopping it were negligible, King's thoughts once again turned to his salary. The 1813 Bethnal Green Act had fixed it at £400 a year, but a new Act meant the opportunity for a further increase, and King now determined to seek such a raise in return for dropping his opposition to the Bill. With this in mind, he requested the Principal of Brasenose College to use his influence with MPs to support his salary increase.[495]

The Commons Committee to debate the Bill met on 11th March. King had persuaded Henry Grey Bennet to lead the parliamentary opposition to it. The opportunity to challenge Merceron again was irresistible to Bennet and, 'zealous in the cause', he agreed to personally champion the clause increasing King's salary, although he warned that King might have to commit to spending more time in the parish in order to get it.[496]

To drum up the support of MPs, King penned a detailed account of the history of his relationship with Merceron in an exercise book. Written in the third person, it stated that 'Mr Merceron and his Partizans...have ever shewn the most vindictive feeling towards the present Rector Dr. King, in consequence of his manly and independent conduct, by exposing Mr Merceron's delinquency and bringing him to justice and merited punishment'. Anticipating accusations of being an absentee clergyman seeking payment for doing nothing, King claimed that he had always done his duty in Bethnal Green, and had only ever been away because the deaths of his father and brother had forced him to spend more time in Cheshire than intended, despite having been 'harassed, opposed, traduced and persecuted' by Merceron and his 'low Methodist' friends.[497]

When the draft Bill was published, it finally became apparent to the Bethnal Green vestry that a select vestry was in the offing, although Merceron continued to deny it. Over the next few weeks every vestry meeting ended with a riot, with accusations that Merceron had 'prostituted' the vestry for his own purposes and King launching an attempt to unseat Brutton. On Easter Monday, the usual intimidation resulted in Merceron's supporters all being reappointed and Brutton elected vestry clerk by 1,556 votes to just 3 against. The following day both parties met separately and elected rival boards of Governors of the Poor.[498]

Afterwards a frustrated King sought legal advice whether to indict Merceron once again for conspiracy. But he had been worsted too many times to contemplate taking on yet another private prosecution. He was beginning to feel that he would never fully defeat Merceron; more than ever, the relative peace and harmony of Woodchurch must have seemed a compelling alternative to Bethnal Green. From this point on, it is clear from King's frequent letters to his superiors in Oxford that his only remaining object was to maximise his salary without having to commit to spend any more time in Bethnal Green. Over the following weeks, as it became more and more apparent that he would not be able to achieve both goals, the tone of King's letters became increasingly desperate. On 21st April, the Commons Committee agreed several clauses of the Bill in Merceron's favour, and King complained to Brasenose College the next day that none of his supporters in Parliament had turned up as promised, so that Merceron's party 'had all their own way'. 'The general tendency,' he wrote, 'will be to re-establish Mr. Merceron's power and influence in the parish'.[499]

As the Committee finalised its deliberations, King wrote almost daily to Brasenose College with news. On 24th April, the MPs representing King proposed a compromise, offering 6 months' residence in Bethnal Green per year in return for an additional £200 salary per annum. From the point of view of his Bethnal Green parishioners, when compared with the terms of the 1813 Act, King was requesting a 50 percent salary increase in return for an equal *reduction* in his duties. Unsurprisingly, therefore, the suggestion was unpopular with

MPs and was withdrawn. King's perceived impudence was punished the following day when, in front of the whole Committee, he was subjected by George Byng to 'a most violent philippick' for almost an hour.[500]

By 5th May the Bill still remained unsigned but King, by this time having accepted defeat, had calmed down somewhat and accepted that 'should it be the means of preventing the parishioners from continuing to be the victims of factions and unprincipled demagogues, most desirable change will be effected'. A week later, the Act was finally passed. It provided that the select vestry would comprise the Rector and a small number of parish officials, all owners of property worth £80 per annum and a further 30 elected by and from parishioners rated at over £15 per annum, of whom ten would retire and be replaced annually. This last group of parishioners was about 2,000 strong, all of whom had been vestrymen under the old system, and whose participation in the vestry would now be limited to the annual election of ten representatives.[501]

In passing the Act, the Commons Committee – sick to the gills of the politics of Bethnal Green – had told the warring factions that the new law 'should be considered by all parties as an act of conciliation, and that no cause of triumph shall be given to either'. But when the election of the first estate governors took place just nine days later on 21st May, Merceron wasted no time in letting the people of Bethnal Green know how the select vestry was really going to work. When the poll began at 11 o'clock, the usual thugs were posted at the doors of the workhouse and the Rector's supporters were threatened against entering. Only King, Robert Wrightson and three other men dared to enter, whereupon they found themselves outnumbered by more than 80 of Merceron's supporters.

The new Act, however, had prescribed that King as the Rector should take the Chair at the election. King refused to do so unless all those entitled to vote were allowed in. He reminded those present of Parliament's call for conciliation and suggested that, in such a spirit, 15 governors be elected to represent each party. At this Merceron and

Gwynne laughed out loud, and King was 'assailed on every side with the vilest calumny and abuse, with hissing, hollowing, shouting and the most violent exclamations'. 'They wanted none of my speeches,' King wrote later, '[and said] that I had no right as chairman to dictate to them – that I ought to be ashamed of myself – that they were not going to give up the advantages they had gained by the Act'.

The arguments went on for three hours before, eventually, Gwynne and Wrightson each put forward a list of candidates. But Merceron still refused to hold an open election and, calling an immediate show of hands, pronounced the men named on Gwynne's list elected before adjourning the meeting till the next day and walking out. His supporters locked King and Wrightson in the committee room, bolting the door and placing benches against it to prevent their rescue, all the time assailing them 'with the vilest abuse and insult' and threatening them with violence. Late in the evening they were eventually allowed to leave, whereupon they led their supporters to the church, drafted a petition complaining at their treatment and conducted their own elections.[502]

The following day, King and Wrightson returned to the work-house with their petition. Again, they were allowed to enter, but their supporters were forced to remain outside. There followed the remarkable spectacle of a fight between the Rector and the resident magistrate, Gwynne. All hell broke loose. King's supporters rushed the door. The Riot Act was called for and King's party were forced back outside. As they left the room, 'the most discordant yells were set up' and King, according to his own account, 'was literally hunted like a wild beast amidst the vilest exclamations'. In the Rector's absence, Merceron locked the doors, reconvened the meeting and, having 'lavished the most copious abuse' on King, proceeded to appoint his own list of governors. The list included all the old names: Merceron himself, his son Henry, Gwynne, Renvoize, Platt, Unwin, Green-wood, Millar; most of them the associates who had been acquitted of conspiracy in 1819. Appreciating that possession would be nine tenths of the law, Merceron immediately drafted a report to the local magistrates to get the appointments confirmed, before anyone should have chance to protest.[503]

A few days later, King reported to Brasenose College that his forebodings had been 'fearfully realised'. He claimed that he was un-deterred by the violence, even though 'my life may fall a sacrifice to vindictive rage', but the constant abuse had:

> ...a direct tendency to make me a most obnoxious individual with all the unprincipled and undiscerning part of my parish, so that unless some remedy can speedily be applied, I shall be driven for ever from the parish, as my predecessor was, and I will venture to predict that, should such an event take place, no incumbent will be permitted to reside in the parish. After the enormous sums I have already expended...and witnessing so little gain therefrom...I should not feel disposed again to seek a remedy at my own cost.[504]

King also wrote to the Bishop of London and to Henry Grey Bennet, seeking their advice as to whether he should lay his case before the Home Secretary or the Attorney General. But it seems either that the advice was unpromising or that King decided that he could not risk a further confrontation with Merceron in the courts. At some point over the summer of 1823, King packed his bags, moved out of Bethnal Green for good and headed back to a quiet life in Cheshire.[505]

A new curate, James Mayne, was soon recruited. The pittance that King allowed him made Mayne an easy target for Merceron's bribery. That August, the vestry voted a 75 percent increase in his fees for copying the parish registers, an amount that they had steadfastly refused to increase throughout King's tenure. Before long, Mayne was adding a veneer of respectability to Merceron's select vestry by chairing its meetings. He proved so flexible that he would stay on as curate for a further 20 years, eventually presiding over Merceron's funeral.[506]

CHAPTER XVIII

In Distress

'Twas August and the fierce sun overhead
Smote on the squalid streets of Bethnal Green
And the pale weaver, through his windows seen
In Spitalfields, looked thrice dispirited.

Matthew Arnold[507]

With Joshua King's departure, Merceron once more ruled unchallenged in Bethnal Green; for the next decade or so, things were much as they had been in the years before King's arrival in 1809. From the point of view of the ruling clique, as Robert Brutton would later put it to a parliamentary Select Committee, 'anarchy and confusion' were replaced with 'perfect tranquillity'.

Brutton, however, was hardly an impartial observer. In September 1824, he had gained the ultimate reward for his services: the hand in marriage of Merceron's daughter Ann and a wedding in ultra-fashionable Brighton. By the time he made the above remarks, he was an established member of the Merceron clan, taking an increasingly dominant role in parish affairs and living in considerable comfort just three doors from his father-in-law on the village green. Brutton's was therefore a peculiarly skewed viewpoint, one that the vast majority of Bethnal Green's 60,000 inhabitants would have found laughable. For them, the decade from 1823 was spent in conditions of the vilest poverty: an endless struggle for food, clothing and shelter. 'Perfect tranquillity' was something that they achieved only in death.[508]

The event primarily responsible for triggering this period of distress was the 1824 repeal of the Spitalfields Acts, which had regulated the wages of the local silk weavers for half a century. A parliamentary campaign to repeal the Acts had begun a year earlier, just as Merceron and King were locking horns over the select vestry Bill. The fact that the campaign went unnoticed by the Bethnal Green vestry for some time sums up the local politics of Merceron's era, with egotism and personal gain invariably trumping matters of fundamental economic importance.

The Spitalfields Acts had originated in 1773 in response to a murderous campaign of violence and destruction plaguing Spitalfields for a decade. By giving local magistrates the power to fix wages and thereby artificially hold up prices, it was widely agreed that the Acts had prevented economic disaster and the total collapse of the rule of law. Supporters were also quick to point out that, by maintaining local employment levels, the Acts had kept the poor's rates at a significantly lower level than in many other parts of the country. Yet many people saw the continuation of the Spitalfields Acts as hypocrisy in a government supposedly wedded to free trade. They argued that the silk industry was hardly in need of protection, having grown enormously in the 50 years since the Acts were passed (the annual value of silk imports had risen by a factor of 20, from £100,000 to more than £2 million). Moreover, the Acts applied only to Spitalfields. It was an anachronism that one area should be protected while other silk weaving centres, such as Manchester and Coventry, were not. In addition, the free-traders argued that price controls merely postponed the inevitable. In the face of increasing mechanisation, they contended, Spitalfields was becoming decreasingly viable for anything other than the most fancy work, and the relief provided by the Acts was merely stifling any incentive to innovate.[509]

For these reasons, the Spitalfields Acts became a target for a rising star of the Tory government. William Huskisson, President of the Board of Trade, an avid free-trader and a key influence on government economic policy, was engaged in a wider campaign to repeal protectionist legislation. In the spring of 1823, Huskisson was approached by a group of master weavers, frustrated at their inability to match the prices of provincial competitors. In May, with his encouragement, the weavers presented a petition to Parliament to repeal the Spitalfields Acts. Huskisson spoke warmly in the Commons in favour of the petition to general acclaim, with not a single MP arguing against him. Even the Brick Lane brewer Thomas Fowell Buxton – who knew more about conditions in Spitalfields than anyone else in the House – promised his support.[510]

But Buxton had completely underestimated the depth of feeling of the people of Spitalfields and Bethnal Green. News of the proposed repeal caused consternation. Within a fortnight, petitions were presented against Huskisson's Bill by the residents of the City of London, Mile End and – as Merceron and his friends finally woke up to what was happening – Bethnal Green. Local MPs were forced to retract their support. The Lord Mayor spoke out against the Bill. George Byng, presenting the Bethnal Green petition, denounced the repeal campaign as the work of an unrepresentative group of dominant master weavers and claimed that it was opposed by most of the smaller masters and all of the journeymen. The most embarrassing U-turn came from Buxton, forced upon him by a petition from Spitalfields that produced 11,000 signatures against repeal in just three days. When it was suggested in Parliament that the people of Spitalfields were too simple to understand the necessities of political economy, Buxton raised laughter by ridiculing economics as a pseudo-science whose principles appeared to change every couple of years. By the end of the debate, the mood of the Commons had shifted. MPs who had welcomed Huskisson's proposals only a fortnight earlier suddenly became nervous of a public reaction. While a clear majority of members privately agreed that repeal was economically appropriate, there was equally wide agreement of the need to devote more time in persuading the local population of the need for change.[511]

The second reading of Huskisson's Bill took place on 9th June. An army of weavers and their families trudged across London from the East End to the Houses of Parliament, filling the public gallery and crowding the pavements outside. Buxton made another effective speech against repeal. It was difficult, he argued, to tell poor people that they must go without food because of principles of political economy. He reminded colleagues that the poor's rates in Coventry, a city one hundred miles to the north, were more than three times those prevailing in Spitalfields, and that a Spitalfields weaver's average wage was three times that of his fellow in Coventry. Responding, William Huskisson acknowledged these facts but insisted that the principles of free trade must be sacrosanct, even if people had to suffer as a result. Huskisson's argument was enough to give the government a tiny majority on the ensuing vote.[512]

Two days later, an even bigger crowd gathered for the Bill's third and final reading. Several MPs, including the Lord Mayor, Buxton and Byng, pressed for a further inquiry to assess the Bill's impact on the local people, but they attracted insufficient support and the Bill was passed by 53 votes to 40. The Bill then passed to the House of Lords, where it met greater opposition. On 25th June, Robert Brutton was one of several East End officials interviewed by the Lords' Committee and who argued against the measure. Their Lordships were sympathetic to the weavers' pleas, and on 18th July the Bill was sent back to the Commons with so many amendments that Huskisson gave it up in disgust.[513]

A year later, Huskisson tried again to repeal the Spitalfields Acts. By this time, economic conditions had improved significantly. The 11,000 petitioners against the unsuccessful 1823 Bill were mostly back in full employment and unwilling to jeopardise their wages by protests. The opposition to Huskisson's Bill, so implacable the previous year, had evaporated. On 22nd May 1824, the Spitalfields Acts were repealed by a narrow margin.[514]

While the arguments over repeal raged and Merceron once more enjoyed an untroubled reign in Bethnal Green, the Mainwaring family's dominance over the Middlesex magistracy, dating back almost 40 years to the Gordon Riots, had come to an inglorious end. After his retirement in 1816 at the age of 81, William Mainwaring lived off his generous government pension for a further five years before dying in 1821. In doing so, he narrowly avoided the shame of seeing his son George exposed beyond all doubt as a fraudster: in 1822, a committee of magistrates uncovered serious discrepancies in the Middlesex County Fund and began to investigate George Mainwaring's accounts.[515]

Mainwaring at first refused to hand over his records but was eventually forced to do so by threat of legal action. The investigating magistrates soon discovered that he had been defrauding the County of Middlesex for more than a decade. It was estimated that £18,000 was missing. The discovery that the fraud had been ongoing at the time of the collapse of the Mainwarings' bank in 1814, and just as the magistrates had voted to retain George Mainwaring as County Treasurer, could not have been more embarrassing. A few weeks later, on 26th March 1822, Mainwaring resigned in disgrace and was struck off as a magistrate, promising to give 'a full account of those transactions which have finally involved me in my present melancholy situation'.[516]

Mainwaring's contrition, however, seems to have been entirely faked. His 'full account' never materialised, and the magistrates were left to try to piece together what had happened from his financial records, which they found to be in the utmost disorder. They soon discovered that the fraud had gone on for far longer than previously thought, dating back almost to Mainwaring's appointment as County Treasurer in 1804. The investigators also began to suspect that their work was being mysteriously hampered. The records for 1805 to 1807 (the first three years of Mainwaring's tenure as Treasurer), together with various other important papers, had disappeared. In December 1825, after more than three years of 'a long and laborious enquiry', the committee was forced to admit defeat. They had uncovered significant corruption, bribery and interference in court proceedings and were able to demonstrate that officials had been bribed by extraordinary increases – as much as 500 per cent – in salaries and allowances. They were confident that evidence had been hidden or destroyed by persons with 'sinister motives' in order to obstruct the inquiry. Despite all this, however, no case was ever brought against George Mainwaring. He disappeared abroad and was apparently never heard of again.[517]

Was Merceron involved in Mainwaring's fraud on the County Funds? The close links between Merceron and the Mainwarings, including Merceron's connivance in placing the funds of the Tower Hamlets and Holborn & Finsbury Commissions of Sewers with the Mainwarings' bank, strongly suggest collusion between them. Merceron was a prominent member of the magistrates' committee auditing Mainwaring's accounts each year. In addition, after his reappointment as Bethnal Green's treasurer in 1805, Merceron persuaded the Bethnal Green vestry that the significant payments he made regularly to Mainwaring's County Fund were exempt from any kind of vestry review or approval, a circumstance that was remarked upon at Merceron's 1818 trial, years before Mainwaring's fraud was uncovered.[518]

As the inquiry into George Mainwaring's fraud drew to a close, an economic crisis was developing in the City of London with dire consequences for the poor weavers of Spitalfields. 1824 was a boom year in the City; many fortunes were made by speculators raising capital for mines in the new South American republics of Columbia and Peru. The boom spread, and 1825 saw a host of exotic but implausible schemes – with names such as 'Westminster Fish' and 'Economic Funeral' – gobble up the funds of gullible investors. By March 1825, the Duke of Wellington as privately predicting 'the greatest national calamities' as the result of a rash of 'bubble' companies set up to defraud the public. The Duke was right: markets collapsed in the latter half of the year, and in December came arguably London's most severe financial crisis of the 19th century, with no fewer than 66 banks suspending payments in the course of a single week.[519]

The crisis continued into 1826 and soon spread to the manufacturing sector. To the east of the City of London, the Spitalfields masters – no longer hampered by protectionist legislation – responded to falling demand for silks by slashing wages and jobs. The impact, as many had predicted, was immediate and drastic: the streets were soon filled with desperate men with no work and with large families to feed. The distress, however, did not keep Merceron and his associates from feasting at the parish expense. At a vestry event that May, after paying for beer, musicians and a dinner for 50 people, Merceron recharged the bill to the parish, noting – without a hint of irony – that 'the dinner at *The Green Man* was too costly.'[520]

The prospect of starvation drove men to increasingly desperate lengths. *The Times* reported the return of 'the Cutters', as master weavers received anonymous letters threatening 'very swift destruction' unless their men's wages were increased. The vestry recorded the reappearance of 'resurrection men', with increasingly gruesome incidences of grave robbery leading to a general alarm when a woman's head and a child's body were stolen from St Matthew's churchyard. The bullock-hunters were back, too: by September, unemployed weavers swelled the ranks of a 'lawless set of ruffians of formidable character' (as Robert Brutton put it), terrorising the local population with a series of brazen and violent robberies. Three times a week, on market days, a gang of 500 men would surge onto the Bethnal Green Road, steal a beast from the cattle drovers and hide it on the local marshes until nightfall. They would then drive it into the streets, looting food, robbing anyone in their path, before taking the spoils – one witness saw a gang member produce 'half a hat-full of watches' – back to the brickfields and cook the food on the kilns.[521]

Just a few years earlier, the bullock-hunters had been firmly under Merceron's control, one of the principal tools he used to settle scores and keep his enemies in check. Now, the level of desperation had reached a point where even he could not bring them to heel. This was hardly surprising, given that Merceron's usual methods of coercion involved pecuniary punishment: increased rates or taxes, eviction or denial of poor relief. The new bullock-hunters had already lost everything. They had no jobs, no houses and no food. Numbering in the hundreds, they were defiantly beyond the reach of the local watchmen. One source reported that more than 50 people had been robbed and cruelly beaten by the gang within a fortnight. Five victims were in hospital, without hopes of recovery. A local butcher lost an arm after being attacked by about 20 men armed with hatchets, hammers and sticks. Merceron despatched Robert Brutton to beg for assistance from the Home Secretary, Robert Peel. Peel reacted decisively, sensing an opportunity to push for government control of local policing. 40 mounted police – former soldiers with cutlasses, pistols and blunderbusses – were stationed in Bethnal Green day and night, at Home Office expense.[522]

As the winter of 1826–7 approached, the parish authorities of Bethnal Green and Spitalfields admitted that the crisis was beyond their control. The population of the Bethnal Green workhouse had risen from 588 to 842 during the year, but this was nothing compared with the threefold rise in the number of outdoor poor – those living at home but unemployed and requiring support from the parish – with almost 1,000 receiving relief by the end of 1826. In October, Merceron again sent Brutton to Robert Peel, this time bearing a letter to the King explaining the extent of the crisis. Peel received Brutton, apparently 'with much kindness', but little of substance came of the visit and in December 1826 the Bethnal Green vestry again petitioned Parliament to take action.[523]

With parish funds running ominously low, in the latter part of 1826 the vestry expressed strong opposition to an unusually proactive proposal by the Tower Hamlets Commission of Sewers to upgrade the local sewers. Citing the 'alarming' expense that would be incurred, the vestry resolved to oppose it by every legitimate means. It was a decision that would appear terribly short-sighted just five years later, as cholera brought death to the East End. The vestry's protests appear plainly negligent in light of its agreement, just a few months later, to levy almost £2,000 on the ratepayers for fitting out the new church of St John being erected on Bethnal Green.[524]

With the parish population at around 60,000, it was argued that the provision of a new church would cut local poverty and crime by curbing the spiritual destitution that many saw as the root of all evils. St John's was built by the eminent architect Sir John Soane but budgetary constraints led to his grand design for a steeple being aborted, replaced with a stunted tower of particularly phallic design that rapidly became a source of bawdy amusement throughout the neighbourhood. Merceron was outraged. Announcing that the design had 'mortified and disappointed the expectations of almost every individual', he ordered Brutton to write on his behalf to the Principal of Brasenose College, Oxford – who had commissioned the design – to complain. The task put Brutton in an acutely awkward position: how to explain to a leading churchman the exact nature of the problem? The vestry clerk's literary skills were tested to the limit as he described the tower's 'abrupt termination in point of altitude' that made it 'an object of low wit and vulgar abuse', in a letter that must have left the Principal at a loss as to quite what had been built.[525]

In January 1827, against a background of economic disaster and general financial incompetence, and with more than 800 people starving in the parish workhouse, Bethnal Green's coffers finally ran empty. Merceron recommended that the parish borrow on bonds in order to meet its debts and took the lead on a committee charged with identifying cost savings. The committee came up with few practical ideas – the workhouse was already run on a shoestring – and in April, the vestry was again forced to petition Parliament for help.[526]

As the crisis deepened, the Merceron family continued to grow. In 1826 Merceron became a grandfather on the birth of the Bruttons' daughter, Ann-Eliza. In February the following year, Elizabeth Merceron married William Adair Bruce, the son of a Bath clergyman. The successful marriage of both her daughters must have been a relief to Ann Merceron. The scandal attached to Merceron's trial and imprisonment, not to mention his fearsome reputation as a tyrant, must have made Ann fearful of a lack of suitors, notwithstanding the ever-growing family riches. As with most wives of public

Spire of St John on Bethnal Green

men of the time, we know almost nothing of Ann. The few scraps of evidence suggest a patient, homely and stabilising influence: the recipe book, the family breakfasts, the documenting and careful filing of family keepsakes. As her daughters grew up and with Merceron tied to business in London, it seems Ann frequently took them away to Bath and to Brighton, where the young women could escape the summer heat and dirt of the East End, acting the part of Jane Austen heroines among an entirely different class of people.[527]

A few weeks after Elizabeth's wedding, the painfully slow machine that was the Court of Chancery finally released the report of its investigation into Merceron's handling of his half-sister Catherine's estate. After an investigation lasting eight years, the judge announced that he had valued Catherine's estate at more than £3,000 (about £300,000 today), three times the amount that Merceron had stated as its value in 1815. Even this valuation appears to have been conservative. In calculating it, the judge had deducted over £1,000 in expenses that Merceron claimed to have incurred in maintaining the various properties. As a result of the findings, in June Merceron was ordered to pay a substantial sum into court for the benefit of his nephews and great-nephews. It had taken more than 40 years since John Merceron's death for his heirs to get justice, but even now there was little cause for celebration. In a bitter twist one of the plaintiffs, John's grandson Frederick, died a week before the court order was issued. As things turned out, it would have made little difference had he lived, as Merceron continued to dispute the judgment and refused to hand over the money.[528]

The properties at the centre of the family feud, including the old pawnshop at 77 Brick Lane, continued to be administered by the court pending final resolution of their ownership. James Francis Merceron, Merceron's eldest nephew and main adversary in the dispute, was still living at number 77 and insisting that the buildings belonged to him. That autumn, it appeared that Providence finally had her fill of the family wrangling. In the early morning of 11th October 1827 a violent gale ('one of the most destructive tempests

witnessed in the vicinity of the metropolis for many years') blew
through the East End 'with all the impetuosity of a tropical deluge',
accompanied by a shower of hailstones of extraordinary size. The
storm tore down trees, destroyed acres of orchard and smashed the
greenhouses of the local gardeners. One building, however, seemed
to be singled out for especially violent treatment. At the height of
the storm, lightning struck the old Merceron pawnshop. Every window in the house was smashed. The thunderbolt 'tore and split the
wainscot of the second and third floor, and broke a quantity of stone
coping in several parts'. Amazingly, nobody was hurt, but both sides
of the family feud must have pondered the divine significance of
the event.[529]

As the gap grew ever wider between Bethnal Green's rich and poor,
early in 1827 allegations once again began to emerge of vestry extravagance and corruption, ignited when a scandal broke in Spitalfields. It was alleged that the controlling members of the Spitalfields
select vestry lent £7,000 to the parish at interest and then spent it on
repairs to the church. The contracts were awarded corruptly and the
funds then reclaimed from the parishioners at large by an increase
in the rates. It transpired that some householders were assessed 'up
to the hilt' whilst Sampson Hanbury's brewery, supposedly worth
about £250,000, was valued for rating purposes at only £1,000. The
story was widely reported and led to similar allegations being levelled
in Bethnal Green the following year, with Merceron's house prominent among those accused of being under-rated. Backed by Robert
Brutton, he refused repeatedly to allow the complainants access to
vestry records in order to substantiate their accusations.[530]

The distress continued to worsen. The Bethnal Green workhouse,
with beds enough for 300 people, had nevertheless accommodated
between 800 and 950 since 1826. It had always been assumed that
the occupants could be put to some sort of weaving duties to earn
their keep, but by the end of 1828 there was simply no work to do.
That December, in desperation, the vestry purchased several tons of
granite and set the paupers (described by Brutton as 'a great number

of lazy and abandoned characters') to break it, with the resulting stone sold on to the engineer John McAdam for his famous road-building programme.[531]

With no prospect of employment, the number of outdoor poor spiralled from just over 300 in 1825 to 1,300 in 1828 and 2,500 in early 1829. The parish finances, already precariously in the red, were further dented when a tax collector absconded with almost £700. In January 1829, the parish treasurer announced that he could no longer meet debts as they fell due. The vestry again refused to increase the rates, arguing that it was already impossible to collect them, and decided instead to borrow a further £1,500 on bonds. There is no hint that Merceron, by far the richest man in the neighbourhood, considered for a moment that this might be an attractive investment of his own funds. Instead, he sent Robert Brutton once more to request help from Robert Peel and the City of London. Throwing himself into the project, Brutton established a distress fund and persuaded the Lord Mayor to help promote it. Pleas for subscriptions appeared prominently in the newspapers, asserting that 'the privations and misery which upwards of 50,000 human beings now endure can hardly be imagined'. Once again, the great and good trumpeted their generosity in *The Times*: Nathan Rothschild – probably the richest man in the country – gave 50 guineas; Truman, Hanbury & Buxton contributed 30 guineas; George Byng gave £20. In Bethnal Green, the Natt family put in £50 and even Merceron, for once with no obvious ulterior motive, donated £25. Among other fundraising activities, Brutton organised a grand performance of Handel's *Messiah* at the Guildhall, under the patronage of four dukes and the archbishops of Canterbury and York. The appeal eventually raised £10,000.[532]

Despite the crisis, no one opposed Merceron in that year's vestry elections. On his reappointment, Merceron returned thanks, engaging to discharge his duties 'without favour or affection, prejudice or malice'. A few weeks earlier, despite the damning evidence all around him to the contrary, he had given a speech celebrating the success of Bethnal Green's urban democracy, which extended 'the right of voting for representatives in the vestry' to all ratepayers. No-one dared remind him that, before his interference in 1823, all the ratepayers had automatically *been* vestrymen.[533]

For all his influence over the people of Bethnal Green, Merceron could do nothing to improve their conditions. By May 1829, the number receiving outdoor relief had doubled to above 5,000. It was costing the vestry £750 a week to relieve them, swallowing up the entire amount collected from the rates and leaving all suppliers' bills unpaid. The parish debt was £6,000 and rising. At a crisis meeting, the vestry agreed to borrow a further £2,000 immediately and to crack down on fraud among the claimants of relief. Identity cards were issued to the starving paupers and inspectors were appointed to check their entitlements. Meanwhile the desperate weavers were again taking to the streets in force. When master weavers refused to accede to demands to raise wages, cutters destroyed the silk in their looms. A crowd 500-strong threw bricks and stones at two foremen trying to carry their master's silk to safety, seriously wounding a policeman.[534]

In July 1829, with its existing borrowings falling due for repayment, the vestry was obliged to refinance its debt at 8 per cent interest. The stress was beginning to tell: by this time 1,100 people were crammed into a workhouse that had been described as overflowing when it had housed 600. Again, the vestry refused to countenance a rate increase, claiming 'that every species of economy, and if possible retrenchment in the [work] house, should be the order of the day'. One such method of 'retrenchment' was the farming out of babies and infants to nurseries in villages outside London. Another was the apprenticing of pauper children and orphans to masters outside the parish – who would thereby gain cheap labour – and in doing so absolve the parish of the costs of their keep, as illustrated so well by Charles Dickens in *Oliver Twist*. Mechanisation, and the resulting growth of the northern textile industry, had given rise to a huge increase in demand for child labour; the officers of Bethnal Green, like

their counterparts in many other London parishes, found the temptation irresistible to send children northwards, literally by the cart-
load. The practice had been going on for several years and dozens of
children were got rid of in this way, often against the wishes of their
parents, but even this tactic could not hold back the tide of increasing
poverty: by the end of 1829, the number in the Bethnal Green workhouse had increased still further to 1,200.[535]

Soon afterwards, the tactics adopted by Merceron's vestry threatened to backfire when complaints were made to the local magistrates
about the treatment of several pauper children sent from Bethnal
Green to work at the Cressbrook Mill in Derbyshire. Despite the
1819 Factory Act, which had imposed a minimum working age and
limited the working hours of children, conditions were still appalling
in the cotton mills. Merceron, fearing prosecution, sent the Bethnal
Green overseers to Derbyshire to investigate but on their return they
reported their 'entire approval of what they had seen, as to the excellent arrangements, general treatment and healthy appearance of the
children in that part of the country'. Such covering up of the true
conditions in the cotton mills was routine. Many years later, one
'Orphan John' told how he had been 'sold' to a Derbyshire mill-
owner by Merceron's vestry in 1820, when he was six years old, and
how he had suffered serious beatings, including a smashed elbow.
His attempt to complain to the Bethnal Green parish officers backfired when his letter was intercepted, resulting in a further beating.
Perhaps the overseers were telling it as they saw it. After all, compared with being crammed with over a thousand others into the
Bethnal Green workhouse, life in a Derbyshire sweatshop might
have seemed almost idyllic.[536]

With rates being swallowed up faster than they could be collected,
the last thing Bethnal Green needed was a further increase in expenditure. But Robert Peel's new Metropolitan Police Force, established
in 1829, provided just that: parishes were expected to pay their share
of the costs and at £1,300 per annum Bethnal Green's share represented another fourpence on the rates. It was just three years since a

desperate Brutton had virtually begged Peel to send a mounted patrol to Bethnal Green to keep the bullock-hunters off the streets, but that was forgotten as the vestry resolved that the new police force was 'wholly unconstitutional in its origin, highly objectionable in its system and very defective in its operation'. The vestry petitioned Parliament for permission to police itself once more. With no money to pay the government's invoice, Brutton made several begging visits to the Home Secretary over the course of 1830 until, eventually, Peel agreed to let him pay by instalments.[537]

The ordinary ratepayers of Bethnal Green were by no means alone in suffering at the hands of a select vestry. In the aftermath of the Sturges-Bourne Acts, other London parishes had elected to replace the turbulent and unpredictable democracy of their previously open vestries only to find themselves at the mercy of a corrupt and unaccountable oligarchy that it could no longer vote out. Hackney, St James's Piccadilly, St Pancras, St Martin-in-the-Fields and Marylebone were five parishes with such vestries: all suffered conspicuously similar fates to that of Bethnal Green. Across London, realisation began to dawn that the Sturges-Bourne Acts, instead of putting the control of Poor Law costs in the hands of a scrupulous and interested class of local officials, had instead introduced a new source of jobbery and inept management. Devastated by the unemployment resulting from the economic crisis, London's select vestries haemorrhaged money into the hands of corrupt officials and contractors, while the intended recipients went without.

Widespread and determined agitation against such abuses, however, driven by well-known figures like Sir Francis Burdett and James Scarlett, led eventually to a movement for the total abolition of select vestries. *The Times* threw itself behind the protestors, pointing out that the select vestry possessed what even 'the House of Commons does not, unbounded control over the fortunes of the public,' and describing it as a 'modern excrescence upon the constitution of the country'. Eventually, in the spring of 1829, Burdett's fellow Radical MP for Westminster John Cam Hobhouse was appointed chairman of a Select Committee to inquire into vestry administration.[538]

As the Committee commenced its work, Merceron could have been forgiven for fearing a repeat of his 1816 humiliation by Henry Grey Bennet's Police Committee. Hobhouse heard evidence concerning 26 urban vestries, mostly situated in London. In shades of 1816, two disgruntled Bethnal Green ratepayers came forward with strong hints of Merceron's absolute rule, his partiality in rate assessments and his refusal to allow any inspection of the vestry accounts. Hobhouse, however, did not share Grey Bennet's terrier-like ability as an advocate. This time, Merceron was not called to defend the accusations. Instead, Robert Brutton attended the Committee and made light of them, successfully distancing himself from the events surrounding Merceron's prosecution and imprisonment, playing down any suggestion of wrongdoing and claiming that Bethnal Green had been 'in a state of perfect tranquillity' since 1823. Francis Place, a Radical agitator who had been instrumental in establishing the Committee, was furious, confiding in his diary that Hobhouse 'did not push his examination of witnesses to the extent he ought to have done'.[539]

Hobhouse nevertheless reported that 'great discontent' had arisen in many parishes and promised to put forward a Bill in favour of elective vestries. In formulating his proposals, however, Hobhouse found it impossible to find a compromise that would satisfy the myriad of vestry models around the country and in the end managed to turn almost everyone against him. His original draft Bill required the repeal of all relevant Local Acts of Parliament that were inconsistent with its provisions. This included Bethnal Green, and in February 1831 Brutton was one of many vestry clerks who travelled to Westminster clutching a petition against the Bill. Despite all Francis Place's agitation, Hobhouse failed to maintain Parliament's interest in his Bill, and eventually the issue was eclipsed by the great debate raging over parliamentary reform. Hobhouse persevered but was forced to water down the Bill, dropping the proposal to repeal

Local Acts, and by Easter 1831 Brutton was able to predict confidently – and accurately – that Hobhouse's Vestry Act would not affect Merceron's rule in Bethnal Green.[540]

CHAPTER XIX

Unsanitary and Insolvent

...deep in debt, if not absolutely bankrupt; houses deserted in consequence of the pressure of the rates... rents declining, and ruin impending.
Evidence to Poor Law Commission of 1834
about conditions in Bethnal Green[541]

London in 1831 was a sanitary time bomb. Only five years earlier, one commentator had claimed that the metropolis was 'one of the most healthy on earth'. The reality was starkly different. In three decades, London's population had soared by two-thirds, from just under one million in 1801 to 1.7 million in 1831. It was now the biggest city in the world, and no government had ever managed an urban infrastructure on this scale. The capital was still governed by a disparate collection of autonomous parish vestries, trusts and sewers commissions, whose responsibilities were increasingly cut across by private commercial enterprises such as the water companies. Bled by corruption, this administrative tangle combined in the worst areas with dirt, unemployment and hunger to create appalling social conditions.[542]

Few areas were as bad as Merceron's Bethnal Green. By June 1831, the parish was almost £12,000 in debt. Its population had reached 61,000, an increase of 35 percent in a decade and four times as many inhabitants as when it was established in 1743. The poverty resulting from the repeal of the Spitalfields Acts and the economic crash of the mid 1820s was compounded by a serious outbreak of fever, probably typhus, which spread from the workhouse throughout the

Monster Soup, commonly called Thames Water

parish. The streets, full of refuse, were in the 'most disgraceful neglect, and characteristic of the most primitive barbarism'. In April 1831 Merceron was challenged in the vestry over the awarding of contracts for street cleaning but as usual shrugged this off without difficulty, despite the fact that the job of cleaning 33 miles of paved streets and almost 100 miles of unpaved byways lay with 'thirteen decrepit old men, nine horses, and five carts'.[543]

A vivid description of life in Bethnal Green around this time is given in an anonymous letter to the *Crisis*, a journal edited by the northern manufacturer and social reformer Robert Owen. Responding to claims that the repeal of the Spitalfields Acts had been a positive result of the triumph of free trade, the writer says:

> I should like to take a person, who says that the silk trade has improved, into Hare Street, Bethnal Green; I would take him into a house falling down almost for want of repair…I would let him into a room, and I would show him the sash covered with paper where once was glass…the chairs without bottoms, some without backs, one or two perhaps with only three legs… and placed on the table some potatoes, called chats, which in general are given to pigs, and which are to form the next meal for the miserable inmates of this dwelling. I would show him, in another corner, a human being, with thin cheeks, trembling limbs, dim eyes…an appearance too plainly speaking the poverty which this silk slave in free England undergoes. I would point out his miserable partner, sinking daily for want of nourishment, with a baby in her arms, crying for food, which she has not got to give it. I will take him into the street, and show him the offspring of this wretched couple, uneducated, ill-trained – infants in years, men in crime. If he asks me, where is the furniture of this wretched couple, I will point to the splendid house with the three golden balls over the door. The next step which their children will take, is to Brixton, or the hulks; and the parents will shortly enter that large house opposite Bethnal Green

church [the workhouse], where hundreds crowd the door every day to receive a miserable pittance, while the inmates of this crowded house sleep by turns, day and night.[544]

The outlook was poor, but by the end of the 1830s, and despite all the previous failed attempts at vestry reform, English local government as it had operated since Tudor times would be no more. A number of factors combined to bring about change. First, the accession to power of the Whigs in 1830 meant that the followers of Jeremy Bentham's utilitarianism, in general believers in the efficiency of central government, finally found a voice. Second, the increasingly wide acceptance of free trade theory, when interpreted by the likes of Thomas Robert Malthus, attributed the spiralling costs of maintaining the poor to an inherently economically unsound system of outdoor relief and allowances. Third, the outbreak of cholera in 1832 supplied further evidence that public sanitation in urban areas was woefully inadequate and that the corruption and inefficiency in its management needed to be weeded out.

The origins of London's first cholera outbreak lay in an alarming deterioration in the capital's water supply. Until 1815, householders were forbidden to discharge human waste into the common sewers, which were designed purely for rainfall run-off. Instead, it was poured into thousands of cesspits. After the invention of the flushing water closet, however, the law was changed to permit the discharge of waste directly into the sewers, and thence into the Thames. Compounded by the failings of the Commissions of Sewers and private water companies, and the inadequacy of building regulations, this led over the next two decades to a slow poisoning of the river from which almost all London's drinking water was drawn.[545]

There had been ominous signs for years. The numbers of salmon caught in the Thames had fallen dramatically. In 1827, a pamphleteer accused the Grand Junction Waterworks Company (whose directors had included Merceron's allies George Boulton Mainwaring and Daniel Hinley) of supplying the householders of Westminster with

'a dilute solution of animal and vegetable substances in a state of pu-
trefaction – alike offensive to the sight, disgusting to the imagination
and destructive to the health'. Partly as a result of this publicity,
in 1828 the tireless Sir Francis Burdett managed to secure a Royal
Commission into the state of London's water supply. The Commission heard plenty of compelling evidence. The pollution was so bad
that it had almost destroyed the livelihood of fishermen from Putney
to Greenwich, and the larger brewers had altogether ceased to use
the river as a source. Despite the wilful obstinacy of the management
of the water companies (one officer of the Grand Junction Company
insisted that the Thames water was as pure as almost any spring
water in the country), the Commission concluded that new, cleaner
sources of drinking water were needed.[546]

It would be years, however, before significant improvements were
made. As the writer and clergyman Sydney Smith wrote in 1834: 'He
who drinks a tumbler of London Water has literally in his stomach
more animated beings than there are Men, Women and Children on
the face of the Globe'. In the meantime, the East London Water
Works continued to pipe drinking water 'thrice weekly, and for two
hours at a time, and at low pressure' to standpipes in the streets or
courts, from which the people of Bethnal Green and the neighbouring districts would take it in jugs or buckets to their homes. The water
was described as 'highly coloured' and containing 'much sediment';
hardly surprising, since until at least 1829 it was drawn directly from
a source on the River Lea, fed at high tide by a backwash from the
Thames carrying the effluent from the entire metropolis.[547]

With the East End a perfect breeding ground for germs of all
kinds, it was only a matter of time before a virulent disease arrived to
take advantage of the conditions. As cholera began to spread through
India and Russia in late 1830, the risks to the British population
from infected ships became obvious and led the Privy Council to put
all ships from Russia under quarantine in January 1831. Six months
later, as the cholera reached the German port of Hamburg, the
British government set up a Central Board of Health that met daily

to advise parish vestries on preventative measures. In October 1831, the disease finally reached the UK at the north-eastern port of Sunderland and ships from there to London were quarantined. For the Mercerons, the scare came at the worst possible time: Henry's wife Matilda was pregnant, with the baby due at the end of November.[548]

On 20th October, the Central Board ordered parish vestries to set up local Boards of Health. The fundamental lack of understanding about the nature of cholera meant that the local Boards were in no position to come up with sensible advice. At the time, it was almost universally agreed that infectious diseases such as cholera were transmitted through some kind of 'miasma' or 'bad air'. It would take a further 20 years, and 25,000 London cholera deaths, before scientists began finally to understand the role of impure drinking water in the transmission process. As the public showed signs of panic, local officials were at best confused (and at worst dangerously misled) by a flood of articles and strident advice in the press. The City of London Board of Health, writing in *The Times*, advised residents to shut windows to 'avoid currents of night air'; to wear 'flannel next the skin, more especially round the bowels'; to 'protect the feet and legs by woollen stockings' and above all to 'preserve a cheerfulness of disposition'. In their diet, people were solemnly instructed to stick to plain meats, bread and well-boiled vegetables and to reject salads, raw fruits and any such items 'found by experience to create flatulence'. Perhaps unsurprisingly, such advice did little to calm public fears.[549]

In any event the local Boards – impotent in the face of parish vestries that made all the important decisions and controlled the purse strings – could do little of substance to protect their neighbourhoods. The Bethnal Green Board of Health was established by mid-November 1831, but was powerless to prevent Merceron's vestry from setting a rate of one shilling in the pound, despite the overseers' protests that half as much again would be insufficient. The overseers were also overruled over their proposals to expand the workhouse on grounds of public safety, despite overwhelming evidence in support of their claims. In one ward there were 99 boys sharing 14 beds and a further 16 sleeping on the floor. Measles and whooping cough were rampant; food and other waste piled up in the yard, a source of infection.[550]

Eventually accepting that such conditions presented an unacceptable risk to the neighbourhood, the Bethnal Green vestry decided to 'farm out' a significant number of paupers. An advertisement for proposals to accommodate up to 300 inhabitants of the workhouse led to a businessman in the north London suburb of Islington offering to take one hundred paupers at four shillings and ninepence per head per week. The vestry, however (no doubt horrified by the man's offer to provide the paupers with roast pork on Easter Sunday, roast beef and plum pudding at Christmas and mackerel 'once in plentiful seasons') rejected the proposal as exorbitant. But when a vestry committee, led by Merceron, came up with the idea of spending £100 on heating for the new church on the Green, there were no such qualms. Heating the church, argued Merceron, would encourage the poor to attend, improving their moral conduct and thereby reducing parochial expenditure, 'it being universally proved that a neglect of public worship on the Lord's Day, leads to indolence, extravagance and all those vices by which pauperism is produced and misery engendered'.[551]

To add to their fear of cholera, the inhabitants of Bethnal Green found themselves at the centre of an even more macabre source of panic as the winter of 1831 arrived. November had seen the arrest of the 'London Burkers', a gang of 'resurrection men' who had lured unsuspecting victims back to their Bethnal Green cottage before murdering them and selling their corpses for dissection. The crimes – reminiscent of the notorious Edinburgh killings by Burke and Hare three years earlier – and the subsequent trial and execution of two of the murderers in December competed with the cholera panic for newspaper column inches for several weeks. For the Mercerons, though, there was some good news amid the scares. Henry and Matilda's baby – named Ann after her grandmother – was born safely on 1st December and christened at St Matthew's three days after Christmas.[552]

It was February before the cholera finally reached London, by which time the death toll nationwide – mostly centred around the north-eastern ports of Sunderland and Newcastle – had risen to more than 1,000. The first London cases were reported near the docks in Limehouse and by 14th February seven deaths had occurred. The rapidity with which the disease took its victims was startling. Panic now set in across the capital, with the East End becoming a no-go area for those living elsewhere. Alarmed more by the potential impact on trade than by a few deaths amongst the East End poor, *The Times* was scathing and belittled the authorities in a series of editorials. As late as 21st February, despite the rising death toll, *The Times* continued to express doubt whether any really infectious disease existed, and two days later claimed that the idea of an epidemic had become the subject of ridicule in the City.[553]

Thankfully, the House of Commons was taking the matter more seriously. When Parliament debated the outbreak in mid-February, with the aim of taking steps to prevent the spread of the epidemic, Bethnal Green was identified as an area of primary concern. The House was told that there were 6,000 outdoor poor there and a further 1,100 in the workhouse, sharing only 370 beds. 'Orator' Henry Hunt, the veteran of Spa Fields and by this time a respectable MP, added that the population of Bethnal Green was in the most miserable condition, and trusted something would be done for them. Finding an unlikely supporter in Robert Peel, Hunt pushed for the cost to be met out of government funds, arguing that to levy a further rate on the inhabitants was impossible.[554]

A week later, the prominent Whig MP Joseph Hume reported to Parliament that every exertion had been made by the overseers of Bethnal Green to relieve the poor, 'but that their humane efforts have been crippled from the want of sufficient funds'. As a champion of the repeal of the Spitalfields Acts in 1824, however, Hume could not accept that repeal had contributed to the distress. To Hume, an avid free trader, the solution was simple: repeal the Corn Laws and put the food supply on a free-trade basis and all would be well. But the

Commons eventually agreed that something must be done for Bethnal Green. With the vestry's decision not to 'farm out' some of the workhouse occupants looking increasingly ill-advised, Parliament voted £2,000 towards the cost of evacuating 500 paupers until the epidemic subsided.[555]

The London death toll continued to mount. By 2nd March it was 96; four days later it had risen to 142. *The Times,* still in denial, printed the daily statistics of new cases and deaths alongside editorials leavened with a mixture of disbelief and sarcasm. Acting as the mouthpiece for a City of London-led campaign to avoid a catastrophic trade collapse, the paper repeatedly accused the authorities of exaggerating the impact of the disease, and portrayed local coroners as a bunch of incompetent doomsayers who fed the panic by reporting every suspicious local death as cholera. But the deaths continued and by 12th March had reached 260 in London and over 1,800 in the country as a whole.[556]

With claims among evangelicals that the epidemic was 'proof of the judgment of God among us', a national day of fasting and prayer was announced for 21st March 1832. Organisations representing the poor were outraged, pointing out that the people most exposed to cholera had already been fasting for months, through no choice of their own. On the appointed day, a protest meeting in Finsbury Square just outside the City attracted a crowd of 25,000 who battled with police for hours, pelting officers with stones and seriously wounding many of them. A contingent of 1,000 from Bethnal Green and Spitalfields never reached Finsbury Square, being turned back by the police en route. After engaging in running battles through the City, the mob returned to Bethnal Green, where after empty threats to tear down the workhouse they were eventually persuaded to go home.[557]

As panic continued to paralyse the East End, Merceron found himself under attack on a number of different fronts. This time, some of his opponents were his own relatives. His nephews, James and Daniel Merceron, had continued their battle in the Court of Chancery for an equitable settlement of the disputed family estates.

Merceron continued to ignore an 1829 court order to hand over to his nephews a significant sum of money arising from his sister Catherine's estate. Eventually, in February 1832, after repeated complaints by James and Daniel, the Court ordered Merceron to sell the properties bequeathed to Catherine by her father. Because of the cholera, however, the auction was delayed until April and it was June before the proceeds were handed over.[558]

Merceron also faced heavy criticism from a number of Bethnal Green men angered by his policy of cutting poor relief just when local conditions were at their most desperate. A committee dominated by Merceron had proposed in January 1832 to cancel weekly payments to supplement wages falling below a certain level. In doing so, Merceron was merely acting in accordance with the widely accepted economic and political view that the allowance system was depressing labouring wage rates. The timing of the move, however, was felt by many to be cruel. In March, with the cholera epidemic worsening, a group of vestrymen including the 86-year-old Robert Wrightson, Michael Atkins and William Shevill decided to force a more humanitarian approach. Circumventing the vestry authorities, they founded the Bethnal Green Benevolent Association and persuaded the brewer and MP Thomas Buxton to act as President. In turn Buxton recruited several members of the Royal family as patrons and the association announced itself to the world in *The Times* of 31st March, with its aim the relief of the unemployed and distressed of Bethnal Green 'by supplying bread, coals, potatoes, flannel and bedding, at reduced prices'. With the exception of Robert Brutton, the Mercerons and their associates were notable for their absence from the published list of supporters. In a dig at Merceron, the Association assured potential donors that it was 'quite distinct from the parochial authorities' and intended 'to distribute the funds more particularly among those unfortunate persons who do not receive parochial aid'.[559]

Despite the publicity and aristocratic support given to the Benevolent Association, its activities had little effect on the policies adopted by the vestry. In April 1832, with cholera still raging and conditions critical, Merceron and Brutton purchased 20 tons of stone and set the poor to breaking it, rather than pay £20 a week to young paupers 'for literally doing nothing'. But their activities were increasingly coming under criticism. In September, after opponents demanded to inspect Merceron's accounts, a mob forced the vestry to adjourn to the body of the church. A week later, a review of the poor's rate books revealed more evidence of systematic fraud by Merceron's rate collectors.

The cholera epidemic reached its height in July 1832 and lasted until November, although it broke out again briefly the following summer. In the country as a whole, there were 71,600 cases reported, with 16,437 deaths. 14,144 Londoners had been infected and 6,729 of them had died, more than 1,000 of them in the East End. An analysis of the data by parish suggested that despite the government's fears, Bethnal Green had suffered relatively lightly compared with its neighbours. Given the state of Bethnal Green's sanitation and overcrowded workhouse, however, not to mention its corrupt and inept government, it seems more likely that many cases were simply ignored or unreported.[560]

With the Whig reformers securely in power, the increasingly long arm of central government now began to wrest control of the Poor Law away from parish vestries. In establishing a Poor Law Commission in 1832, the government's main aim was to eliminate the allowance system that Merceron had already taken steps to dismantle in Bethnal Green. The use of a Royal Commission rather than a parliamentary Select Committee for such a purpose was an unusual step, entrusting the conduct of the review largely to a mix of academics and clergymen. Through the interests of its chairman, the Bishop of London, Charles Blomfield, the Commission's enquiries grew increasingly wide and soon reached Bethnal Green. On Boxing Day 1832 Robert Brutton informed the Bethnal Green vestry that the Poor Law Commissioners had 'commenced their duties…regarding this parish…by a series of examinations'.[561]

Bethnal Green was unsurprisingly high on the list of parishes for detailed examination by the Commission and there was no shortage of men willing to testify to corruption and negligence. Charles Masterman, a builder and for many years the recipient of lucrative development contracts from Merceron, told the Commissioners of 'favouritism' in Merceron's allocation of poor relief to his own tenants:

Many of the landlords of the smaller tenements have always mustered their friends on the days of election, to get them appointed governors or guardians of the poor. When parties came to be relieved, who were tenants of the governors who sat at the Board, the governors have given testimony to their meritorious characters, and urged that they might have relief.[562]

Masterman added that he had witnessed instances of awards to paupers being doubled at the suggestion of 'their landlord' (Merceron). He also explained that the payment of poor relief 'affords very great opportunities for fraud on the parts of the overseers, as well as the paupers... [I] have seen a person's condition greatly improved after having served the office of overseer...having, in short, no ostensible reason except that he has been in office'. Knowing he was treading on dangerous ground, Masterman insisted that he was personally unaware of any examples of such fraud, and took care never to mention Merceron specifically by name.

Another local tradesman, a Mr Hooker, outlined the perilous nature of Bethnal Green's finances: 'deep in debt, if not absolutely bankrupt; houses deserted in consequence of the pressure of the rates...rents declining, and ruin impending'. Asked what action the parish officers were planning, Hooker did not know, adding 'we must depend on Providence; I do not see what is to save us from ruin, if Government does not do something for us'.[563]

Yet again, witnesses to a government-sponsored inquiry had given abundant evidence of Merceron's nefarious activities. But again nothing was done. The Commission's priorities were elsewhere and this time not even Brutton was called to give evidence. When the Commission's report was eventually published in 1834, Merceron's name was not even mentioned, although the evidence of Masterman, Hooker and others was quoted at length.

The next few years saw Merceron and his associates clinging desperately to power while local rivals, sensing his decline, tested their strength. The challenges were increasingly led by William Shevill, an auctioneer whose father had been chased from the church by Merceron's mob a generation before. In March 1833, with the parish debt standing at £16,000, Shevill was elected a Governor of the Poor on a tide of popular support. In May, Michael Atkins was elected to the Lighting and Cleansing Trust, hitherto the sole preserve of Merceron, and the two men began to mount a sustained campaign against corruption.[564]

A slip of paper hidden among the leaves of one of Merceron's account books, still in his family's possession, gives a rare glimpse of Merceron's own version of these events. Bethnal Green's new-fangled street lights were powered by gas from the Imperial Gas Company, paid for by Merceron out of rates collected for the purpose. In October 1833, Michael Atkins discovered that Merceron – at his old tricks again – was holding on to more than £1,000 he had collected in lighting rates, yet had delayed payment of the parish gas account, resulting in a higher price being charged by the gas company. When this situation was revealed during a meeting with the directors of the gas company, Atkins turned on Merceron in a great rage. The heading of Merceron's note, marked ominously 'Merceron v Atkins', hints at what happened next. The threat of legal action clearly worked. A fortnight later, Merceron added to his note: '13th Nov: Mr A. asked pardon'.[565]

Merceron's time was increasingly taken up by legal battles against the relentless tide of reform, as the government (supported and encouraged by Radical MPs such as Sir Francis Burdett) continued to chip away at vestry responsibilities. 1834 saw the publication of the Poor Law Amendment Act, bringing cries of outrage from many

London parishes determined to resist government interference in their management of the poor. Bethnal Green was at the forefront as usual, with Merceron leading a committee formed to 'protect the parish interests' and drawing up a petition of protest to Parliament. In common with several other London parishes, Bethnal Green mounted a spirited resistance to the implementation of the Act. The vestry defied the Poor Law Commission for almost three years, refusing to establish a Board of Guardians until it was eventually ordered by the government to do so in March 1837. However, the Board of Guardians simply carried on where the vestry had left off, and the Poor Law Commission was soon castigating the Bethnal Green workhouse as 'the most inconvenient, crowded and in all respects the worst' of any premises under its remit, threatening the Board of Guardians with amalgamation with its neighbours if things did not improve.[566]

Around the same time as the new Poor Law was enacted, a Commons Select Committee, in another result of Sir Francis Burdett's constant agitation, began an inquiry into the state of London's sewers. The Committee unearthed evidence of large-scale corruption and wasting of public money by the various Commissions of Sewers, with both the Tower Hamlets and Holborn & Finsbury Commissions particularly criticised for their lavish entertaining. Between 1814 and 1833, the Holborn & Finsbury Commission had incurred £70,000 in management expenses (a significant proportion of it on dinners for the Commissioners) whilst spending only £144,000 on works. The overwhelming influence of Merceron and his old friend Sir Daniel Williams is obvious. Merceron chaired the Tower Hamlets Commission until his imprisonment in 1818. He thereafter ceased to be a Commissioner but his son Henry, together with Brutton, Renvoize, Charles Lush, James Wilmot Lush and other associates are listed as members of one or both Commissions during the period covered by the Commission's report. Sir Daniel Williams took over the chair of the Tower Hamlets Commission from Merceron, and chaired the Holborn & Finsbury Commission throughout the period covered by the Committee's report until his death in 1831.[567]

In yet another attack by the reformers, a new Highways Act in August 1835 took responsibility for road maintenance away from the vestry and local magistrates, placing it instead in the hands of a new local Highway Board. Merceron resisted once again, obtaining legal advice to the effect that the vestry, rather than the individual rate-payers, was entitled to elect the Highway Board. Despite William Shevill's repeated protests, Merceron proceeded to rig the election such that all the members of the old vestry Paving Committee, including himself as chairman, were appointed to the new Board. He was going to fight to the last.[568]

CHAPTER XX

Old Men Fighting

The aged man that coffers up his gold
Is plagu'd with cramps, and gouts and painful fits...
        William Shakespeare, *The Rape of Lucrece*

Merceron turned 70 in the winter of 1833–4. His extended family was growing: a long-awaited grandson, named Joseph after him, was born to Henry and Matilda in April 1833 and three further grand-children would follow by early 1838. Conscious of the Mercerons' Huguenot heritage, Ann assiduously added the details of each new arrival to her family tree.

As his family grew, old friends disappeared. Sir Daniel Williams passed away, aged 78, in 1831. In August 1835, 'after lingering eigh-teen months', Merceron's great friend the brewer Sampson Hanbury died aged 66. Hanbury had been in charge of the Truman brewery since the age of 20 and had seen it grow into the second largest in the world; half a century of collaboration with Merceron had contributed materially to both men's wealth. Enemies, too, were falling victim to old age. Robert Wrightson was a remarkable 91 years old when he died in May 1837. Others showed no sign of decline: James May, well into his 80s, was still channelling his bitterness into support for William Shevill's battles against Merceron.[569]

Merceron himself was subject to increasingly severe bouts of a vague illness. His doctors diagnosed 'suppressed gout' – as Roy Porter has put it: a convenience 'for covering medical ignorance with a diagnostic figleaf while conferring upon the patient a prestigious diagnosis'. Gout, the fashionable gentleman's illness, was poorly understood and it became common for confused doctors to attribute an ever-increasing litany of symptoms to it. According to medical theory of the time, gout was unable to manifest itself in the usual way in the foot or joints of some patients. Instead, it would 'force its way through an unnatural channel' via a 'sort of poisoning of the blood'. Such a diagnosis could be applied to almost any baffling set of symptoms: as late as 1873, a monograph on the illness contained chapters on headaches, sciatica, anxiety, bronchitis, dyspepsia, stomach cramps, bladder infections and even insanity. The idea caught on and a number of famous people were diagnosed with the condition. In 1848 Charles Darwin, too ill to attend his father's funeral, was told by his doctor that his symptoms, not fitting any known pattern, were 'not quite' dyspepsia and 'nearer to suppressed gout'. Darwin, suffering 'extreme spasmodic and nightly flatulence' and severe bouts of vomiting, continued to receive this diagnosis until his friend Joseph Hooker wrote to him in 1865: 'What the devil is this "suppressed gout" upon which doctors fasten every ill they cannot name? If it is suppressed how do they know it is gout? If it is apparent, why the devil do they call it suppressed? I hate the use of cant terms to cloak ignorance'.[570]

Unfortunately, the diagnosis of 'suppressed gout' was so widely and vaguely applied that it is impossible to ascertain Merceron's real condition and symptoms with any accuracy. For the time being, however, his illness did not stop him from transacting business. His presence was regularly recorded at meetings and in a constant stream of communications with his lawyers, including a final act in the drawn-out drama of *Merceron v. Merceron*. In late 1835, the Court ordered Merceron to pay a further £385 to his nephew James, who by this time was ill and 'in a state of paralysis'. The court's decision sparked the usual cycle of fury, plotting and revenge, culminating the following January when Merceron had James arrested for non-payment of a debt of £150. Despite his paralysis, poor James spent the next 10 months in a debtors prison. His appeal was eventually heard in November 1836 before Lord Denman, the Lord Chief Justice, who refused to release him despite acknowledging James's perilous health and the fact that Merceron's suit was time-barred under the statute of limitations.[571]

Sweet as it was, revenge for Merceron generally came second to money-making and the latter part of the 1830s provided him with several opportunities for speculative property development. First, the demand for improved transport links between London and its growing suburbs, combined with technological advances, had given rise to the railways and to a boom in road building. Second, the 1832 cholera epidemic and subsequent repeated outbreaks of typhus had exposed the public health risks of the East End slums and led to calls for their wholesale demolition and replacement. Lastly, the burgeoning population in Bethnal Green and its perceived spiritual destitution led to demands for new churches. Perfectly placed to take advantage, Merceron threw himself into all these projects with vigour despite his advancing years and deteriorating health.

After an inauspicious start when the MP William Huskisson was run down and killed by Stephenson's *Rocket* at the opening of the Liverpool to Manchester railway in 1830, train travel had quickly become popular and London's first line, from Greenwich to London Bridge, opened in December 1836. A number of companies were planning new lines, among them the Eastern Counties Railway that was building a line from Romford in Essex to a terminus at Bishopsgate in the City. A key factor in positioning the new railways was to find a route avoiding expensive property whose owners would require significant compensation. The Eastern Counties Company therefore planned to save money by driving its line through the Bethnal Green slums without inconveniencing anyone but the poor. From early 1836, ostensibly acting on behalf of the Bethnal Green vestry, Merceron and Brutton entered into negotiations with the railway company. Their proposed route cut through the poorest and least developed part of the parish, through the sites of the workhouse and the Parmiter's Charity School. It was June 1838 before Merceron's plans were revealed to the vestry, by which time they were well advanced, and three months later the railway company offered £4,200 in compensation for the workhouse site. In January 1839, Brutton told the vestry that he had signed the contract with the company, informing them that the railway viaduct would be driven through the existing hospital ward for the lunatic poor, who would simply be moved elsewhere.[572]

As chairman of the Highways Board Merceron also represented Bethnal Green's interests in discussions over the government's proposed Metropolitan Improvements Bill. A parliamentary Select Committee of 1836 to 1838 had concluded that, by forcing great thoroughfares through the poorest and most degraded districts of the metropolis, transport improvements could be achieved at low cost while obliterating some of London's worst slums. The Committee's second report in 1838 coincided with a particularly serious typhus outbreak in the East End, with Bethnal Green suffering more than 2,000 fever cases among a population of 62,000. The resulting concern for public health led the Poor Law Commissioners to appoint an independent medical expert, Thomas Southwood Smith, to investigate and report on local conditions.[573]

Southwood Smith conducted a personal inspection of the streets of Bethnal Green, entering the houses and examining the state of the sick. His report, a street-by-street catalogue of appalling sanitary conditions, made shocking reading. As well as listing the problems, Southwood Smith's report attempted to prescribe solutions. Key among them was to improve ventilation, the report noting the possibility that opening up the streets, and clearance of some of the most confined courts and alleys, could only improve the sanitary condition of the district.[574]

Merceron galvanised the vestry into action. Support grew for a plan to extend the proposed improvements eastwards, and following a vestry meeting on 4th April Brutton drew up a memorial to Parliament containing detailed proposals for three new roads linking the London Docks with existing trunk roads to the north, east and west of the City. The plan shrewdly drew attention to the link between the proposed new roads and the need for sanitary improvements.

It also highlighted the benefits to trade, and did not forget to stress the 'comparatively inconsiderable expense'.[575]

Perhaps with an eye on the rapidly approaching hereafter, Merceron also took a leading part in the Bishop of London's campaign to build new churches in Bethnal Green. In 1836, Bishop Blomfield chaired a committee to investigate where new churches were most needed in the metropolis and to raise the finance to build and endow them. The result was the Metropolitan Churches Fund, with its ambitious aim of establishing 50 new churches across London. Blomfield's enthusiasm was not matched by public generosity, however, and when contributions to his fund began to tail off a new plan was hatched of splitting it into smaller funds for specific localities in order to stimulate local donations. At the suggestion of William Cotton, the Governor of the Bank of England and a strong supporter of the Bishop's scheme, Bethnal Green was chosen as the first location in early 1839 and a fundraising target of £75,000 was set to build 10 churches in the parish.[576]

A committee was formed to direct operations. Several of the greatest names in the City were recruited to it, including the founding fathers of several famous financial institutions, Thomas Baring, Philip Cazenove and Samuel Hoare, together with a future Prime Minister, the young William Gladstone MP. Perhaps wisely, the organisers realised that they would make little progress on a matter involving property in Bethnal Green unless Merceron was involved, and he was invited onto the committee. He accepted, but in view of his failing health requested that his son Henry also be appointed to represent him. Joshua King, still officially the local Rector, was also a member, and managed to secure the role of secretary for his young nephew Bryan King, who had recently been appointed Minister at St John's, Bethnal Green. Subscription cards were circulated, bearing the inscription 'The God of Heaven; He will prosper us; therefore we his servants will arise and build'. The *Church of England Magazine*, in an article entitled 'Spiritual Destitution of the Parish of Bethnal Green', contrasted its 'poverty, destitution and misery' with 'the wealth, magnificence and luxury of other districts of the metropolis' and explained that 'a great effort is now commenced to rescue this parish from its present unhappy state'.[577]

The Bethnal Green fund was an immediate success. Subscriptions poured in: £2,000 from George Byng; £1,000 from the Archbishop of Canterbury and from Truman, Hanbury & Buxton; £500 from both Brasenose College and the Bank of England. Gladstone contributed £50. The Mercerons gave generously: Joseph £100, Henry £31 and Brutton 10 guineas. In total, £13,000 was raised in the first year.[578]

Merceron clearly intended being an active participant on the new churches committee and on 27th March 1839 he was appointed to a small working group charged with selecting and procuring sites for the churches. But he was not well, and the strain was beginning to tell. Later the same day, he attended the Bethnal Green vestry but was too ill to give a report on his participation at 'a great public meeting' in the City of London on the Metropolitan Improvements Bill. Robert Brutton gave the report on his behalf and proposed, in light of his father-in-law's health, that others be nominated to represent the vestry in future. It was to be Merceron's last vestry meeting. A week later he was too ill to attend the annual Easter elections, the first time he had missed them for over 60 years apart from in 1819 while in prison.[579]

With Merceron's health in an uncertain and precarious state, James May – himself a frail old man of 87 – chose this moment for a last attempt at revenge. After more than half a century of bullying, May's early resentment had grown into the deepest hatred as Merceron, returning to power, had forced him out of his lucrative job as vestry clerk. May now realised that time was running out, and he launched a legal action against Merceron and Peter Renvoize for misappropriation of the local charity school funds.

Earlier that year, William Shevill and Michael Atkins had learned that Merceron and Peter Renvoize, as the sole trustees of the charity, had secretly obtained an agreement to sell the Parmiter's charity school site to the Eastern Counties railway company for £1,200 and were planning to spend the funds on 'an extravagant and unnecessary' new building to replace the existing school and almshouses. Their demands for an explanation had been ignored repeatedly by Merceron. Now, on 6th July, with Merceron confined to bed and sinking fast, he was served with a 145-page writ by the Attorney General on behalf of May and Atkins. The writ pointed out ('in no very measured language', as Robert Brutton later commented) that, despite Thomas Parmiter's clear intent that his bequest be used for the benefit of the local poor, Merceron and Renvoize had never made any attempt to use the 'very large' income and property of the charity for the relief of Bethnal Green's many starving families. May alleged that, instead, for more than a decade they had appropriated considerable amounts of the charity's funds for their own use.[580]

The writ came too late. Merceron battled through that week from his bed, and on 13th July he summoned the energy to bring his account books up to date. The next day, 14th July 1839, with the ever-faithful Brutton at his bedside, he died. It was the 50th anniversary of the fall of the Paris Bastille: a nicely ironic day for a tyranny to end.[581]

In death, Merceron had defeated James May yet again. Under the constitution of Parmiter's charity, once only a single trustee remained, elections were required to bring the number back up to the original ten. The vestry was extremely hostile to any criticism of Merceron so soon after his death. Under the circumstances, Michael Atkins dissociated himself with May's suit, 'the death of Mr Merceron… obviating the need for further proceedings', and claimed lamely that May had used his name without permission in filing 'a personally vindictive attack'. A week later, the vestry room was packed full for the election of new trustees. 37 men put their names forward. The nine successful candidates were all ardent Merceronites, with Henry Merceron topping the poll. Peter Renvoize made a touching speech, claiming that he 'was only desirous of still passing the short period he had to live, without the slightest imputation or stain on

Peter Renvoize

his character', which the vestry agreed to have been 'unimpeachable'. May, however, stubbornly refused to drop his action. Brutton took on Renvoize's defence, stating that he would never desert his father-in-law's great friend. With Brutton's help, Renvoize continued to deny all the charges. He insisted that he and Merceron had brought about great improvements in the management and economy of the charity, pointing out that the Charity Commissioners had twice reviewed Parmiter's and found nothing amiss. Eventually the case simply petered out, the accusations forgotten. When Renvoize died three years later, aged 86, he left £500 to Parmiter's in his will. The grateful school, now relocated to Hertfordshire and perhaps unaware of Renvoize's murky career, named one of its houses after him.[582]

Probate was granted on Merceron's will on 28th September 1839. There was plenty of money for everyone. When the funeral took place, the press had speculated that Merceron was worth £300,000, although they pointed out that 'he always appeared to be in poor circumstances'. According to the Inland Revenue records, the estate – excluding Merceron' extensive portfolio of freehold property – was worth approximately £180,000 – equivalent to many millions today. About £140,000 of it was in government stocks. Ann got £33,333 (an income of £1,000 a year) plus all the household goods, and the use of the family home for life. Merceron's two daughters also got £1,000 a year for life, plus the sum of £20,000 each to do with what they pleased. His sons-in-law Robert Brutton and William Adair Bruce, both extremely wealthy through the legacies to their wives, got an additional £500 each. There was £200 each for the Parmiter's school and its associated 'bread fund charity'.[583]

A further enormous sum, perhaps £120,000 in freehold property plus £27,000 in cash, went to Henry who soon afterwards erected a tablet to his father's memory in St Matthew's church. It stated simply that he was 'born in this parish, descended from pious parents whose ancestors took refuge in this Kingdom on the revocation of the Edict of Nantes, A.D. 1685', and that he 'lived to an honoured old age'.[584]

Victorian street poverty, Harrow Alley, Aldgate

EPILOGUE

Street Abomination

Will you come with me now to Bethnal Green,
Where the saddest sights are the oftenest seen...
Where the deadly, poisonous vapours meet
The labouring lungs in every street.

Edith Pym[585]

What legacy did Joseph Merceron leave behind in Bethnal Green? There is no shortage of contemporary accounts. In *Oliver Twist*, published in monthly parts between February 1837 and April 1839, Charles Dickens describes the early morning bustle as the murderer Bill Sikes takes Oliver along the Bethnal Green Road towards Shoreditch:

> ...a few country wagons were slowly toiling on...now and then, a stage-coach, covered with mud, rattled briskly by...The public-houses, with gas-lights burning inside, were already open ...straggling groups of labourers going to their work; then, men and women with fish-baskets on their heads; donkey-carts laden with vegetables; chaise-carts filled with live-stock or whole carcasses of meat; milk-women with pails; un unbroken concourse of people, trudging out with various supplies to the eastern suburbs of the town.[586]

This seems mild enough: Dickens could just as easily have been writing of any of the main approach roads into the metropolis. But there was a reason why he chose Bethnal Green in particular as the

337

home of one of his most obnoxious characters. In the nearby courts, alleys and back streets, there were sights that even Dickens baulked at sharing with his readers. By the time of Merceron's death, Bethnal Green's population had soared to around 74,000. Of these, around 14,000 were children between the ages of five and fourteen, and fewer than 2,000 were receiving any form of education. Unsafe, cramped housing, insufficient food and clothing and woefully inadequate sanitation were breeding dreadful diseases and a race of diminutive and often deformed creatures whose average life expectancy at birth was only 16 years.[587]

Merceron's death coincided with a number of reports on local sanitary conditions by the early Victorian reformers, whose commentaries paint a clear and consistent picture of appalling social deprivation, the source of much of which can be traced to Merceron's corrupt and inept local government of the previous half-century. The shocking descriptions set out in Thomas Southwood Smith's report to the Poor Law Commissioners, compiled in the spring of 1838 a year before Merceron's death and just as *Oliver Twist* was appearing, make it abundantly clear why the 'mean and dirty streets' of Bethnal Green were an obvious choice for Sikes's lair:

'In many parts...fever of a malignant and fatal character is always more or less prevalent. In some streets it has recently prevailed in almost every house...Cases are recorded in which every member of a family has been attacked in succession... some whole families have been swept away. Instances are detailed in which there have been found, in one small room, six persons lying ill of fever together: I have myself seen this – four in one bed, and two in another...A large portion of Bethnal Green is a swamp...in rainy weather some entire streets are under water, and large collections of stagnant water cover, winter and summer, considerable spaces of ground in every part of the district.'[588]

Southwood Smith went on to list the conditions that he encountered on his tour, cataloguing street after street filled with 'uncovered sewers, stagnant ditches and ponds, gutters always full of putrefying matter, night men's yards, and privies, the oil of which lies openly exposed, and is seldom or never removed.' The people he met were in 'a very wretched condition', with 'enfeebled constitutions'. In St John Street – near many of Merceron's own properties; and the site of the workhouse and Parmiter's school, both of which would shortly be demolished to make way for the railway – he found 'a close and densely populated street, in which malignant fever has been remarkably prevalent, and has stalked from house to house. In one room... eight feet by ten, and nine feet high, six people live by day and sleep at night; the closeness and smell almost intolerable.'[589]

Initially, the recipients of Southwood Smith's report were incredulous that such conditions could really exist in London. The Home Secretary, the Marquis of Normanby, so doubted the report's veracity that he accompanied Dr Southwood Smith on his next visit to Bethnal Green. He was soon convinced, however, announcing afterwards that, if anything, the doctor had understated the extent of the poverty existing there.[590]

A further report by the Poor Law Commissioners in 1842 noted the impact that a starvation diet and cramped conditions was having on the local people and described the young men of Bethnal Green as 'conspicuous for a deficiency of bodily strength'. Two years later Friedrich Engels, in *The Condition of the Working Class in England*, described 'such a mass of helplessness and misery that a nation like ours must blush that these things can be possible'. But in a catalogue of damning accounts of Merceron's legacy, perhaps the most shocking of all is Dr Hector Gavin's 1848 *Sanitary Ramblings*, a harrowing, street-by-street description by the surgeon to the Bethnal Green workhouse. Gavin's account is important, partly because it spells out the local conditions in mind-numbing detail, partly because it makes clear that those conditions existed long before Merceron's death. Furthermore, it pulls no punches in ascribing blame to the parish officers, the Commissioners of Sewers, the officials of the water company and, not least, the builders of slum houses – all categories in which Merceron's name must be squarely included.[591]

According to Gavin, Bethnal Green had 'long possessed an unenviable notoriety on account of its neglected state and defective sanitary condition.' In 1842, the members of an inquiry had been astonished to hear the clerk to the local Commission of Sewers insist he was unaware that typhus was endemic in large parts of his neighbourhood. Yet almost a decade after Southwood Smith had first drawn attention to the squalor, Gavin was still able to complain of the 'profound indifference' of the parish authorities – of whom Henry Merceron and Robert Brutton were among the most influential – to the issues. Even worse, he accused them of throwing 'very considerable difficulties' in the way of his attempts to procure information.[592]

On reading Gavin's detailed report of street conditions, one begins to understand why the local authorities might not have wanted the publicity that another report would bring. One street, the ironically named Pleasant Place, is described as 'the *ne plus ultra* of street abomination…nothing more or less than an elongated lake or canal; only, in place of water, we have a black, slimy, muddy compost of clay and putrescent animal and vegetable remains.' Another area, Lamb's Fields, was 'a stagnant lake of thickened putrefying matter; in this Pandora's box dead cats and dogs were profusely scattered, exhibiting every stage of disgusting decomposition.' (As Gavin wrote this account, a row of 22 new houses was being built just 10 feet away from the mire.) Even the Bethnal Green Road, the district's main street, was wholly without a sewer.[593]

Gavin's report is pertinent in providing a detailed account of conditions in streets, such as those on the Busby estate, where Merceron had personally been the landlord or agent. These streets were described variously as 'very filthy', 'beastly' and 'perfectly dirty', with deaths from fever routinely reported. Swan Street, where many of the houses had been built by James Merceron and owned and let by his son for decades, was 'an abomination, its condition utterly disgraceful'. The parish medical officer told Gavin that he was called there to attend the sick more frequently than to any other street. Situated around the northern end of Brick Lane, the houses in this district were packed with weavers and labourers, with six to nine people (and sometimes as many as 14) sleeping in one room. Street cleaning was utterly neglected and there was a complete lack of drainage and sewers, with the water supply conducted on the principle of 'utter indifference to the welfare and comfort of the miserable tenants'.[594]

Not all of Bethnal Green was like this. Just a mile to the east, where Merceron's large house stood on the Green with its stables, coach house and large garden, Southwood Smith found a very different set of conditions. '... There is an excellent under-ground common sewer completely covered in. Here the inhabitants are healthy; no case of fever is known to have occurred in the neighbourhood.' Here, Ann Merceron continued to live after her husband's death, with the Bruttons close at hand three doors away, until she died in 1852. By that time, however, the Green had clearly lost some of its attraction; immediately after his mother's death Henry leased the house to the Tower Hamlets Militia as a storehouse for arms and equipment.[595]

Despite the proximity of poverty and disease, and his now enormous wealth, Henry Merceron stayed in Bethnal Green, never moving away from his house off the Hackney Road. Together with his partner, James Wilmot Lush and Daniel Williams's nephew David Stable, he continued as clerk to the Tower Hamlets magistrates until at least 1852, and by 1861 was himself a magistrate. Lush was appointed Chief Bailiff of the Tower of London; their firm seems to have prospered nicely. Henry eventually died in 1864 and was buried in his father's grave under the wall of St Matthew's church.[596]

What became of the men who fought so hard and yet failed to remove Merceron from power? Joshua King remained Rector of Woodchurch in Cheshire, where he continued to campaign against the behaviour of 'selfish and vindictive' magistrates until his death in

1861. His nephew, Bryan King, became briefly famous in 1859 as Rector of St George-in-the-East, Shadwell, another East End parish, when his introduction of High-Church liturgical practices led to fierce rioting in the church.[597]

After his part in Merceron's brief downfall in 1818, Henry Grey Bennet enjoyed a short period of parliamentary success in his campaign 'to diminish the sum of human misery', notably in the abolition of 'blood money' rewards. He was also the hero of a sustained attempt to prevent the abuse of 'climbing boys' by chimney sweeps. After so much early promise, however, Bennet's career was destroyed by a series of tragedies. Devastated by the deaths of two of his children and troubled by his own sexuality, he was threatened with criminal prosecution for propositioning a young male servant in Belgium in 1825. Forced to resign as an MP, Bennet spent the rest of his life in exile and died in Florence in 1836.[598]

John Barber Beaumont, who perhaps did more than anyone to trigger Merceron's temporary downfall, continued his successful business career while finding the time to champion a diverse range of political and social causes. In 1823, however, his life almost came to an untimely end when one of his insurance policyholders, John Thurtell, resolved to murder him. Beaumont had refused to pay a fire insurance claim, accusing Thurtell of arson, but Thurtell (who was deranged) was prevented from carrying out his plan when he was apprehended for another murder and hanged. Beaumont eventually died in 1841 leaving an extensive fortune which he bequeathed to found a philosophical institution on the site of his Mile End estate for 'the mental and moral improvement' of the local people, in an environment free (as his obituary put it) 'from the baneful excitement of intoxicating liquors'. The institution was a lasting success; it became known as 'the People's Palace' and is today Queen Mary College, part of the University of London.[599]

As for Joseph Merceron, lying buried in the shadow of the vestry room he dominated for half a century, there is one last strange episode to recount. In the afternoon sunshine of Saturday 7th September,

1940, as millions of Londoners sat down to their tea, the 'Blitz' began. 300 German planes, their main target the London docks, dropped hundreds of tons of bombs on the East End with devastating results. Many residential areas were hit and almost 500 Londoners killed. Bethnal Green suffered terribly, and in the carnage St Matthew's church took a direct hit from an incendiary bomb. Next morning it was a roofless, burnt out shell.[600]

The graveyard had been cleared in 1897 and turned into a public garden, but two gravestones survived the bombing intact. They are still there today, in strange isolation in the otherwise empty church-yard. The first, outside the main entrance to the church, is that of Merceron's old friend Peter Renvoize, still maintained and visited for a special annual service by the staff and children of Parmiter's School. About twenty paces away, a large pink granite slab, surrounded by a low iron rail in the shelter of the south wall of the church, is the grave of Joseph Merceron and his family. He spent a lifetime cheating the law; somehow it is fitting that he should have cheated the Luftwaffe too.[601]

Merceron family grave

Renvoize family grave

ACKNOWLEDGEMENTS

This book has taken 11 years to complete, and I have many people to thank. I am deeply grateful to the late Susan Kendall and Claude Merceron and to their nephew Daniel Merceron for providing access to private papers, without which it would have been impossible to untangle the threads of their ancestor's background. David Beaumont generously gave me a copy of his biography of Barber Beaumont, and Xanthe Pitt sent me her late father Colin Pitt's unpublished dissertation on Merceron's trials.

My research was aided by staff at the Tower Hamlets Local History Library & Archives (especially Malcolm Barr-Hamilton), London Metropolitan Archives, Brasenose College Archives, British Library and The National Archives. Stefan Dickers at the Bishopsgate Library generously sourced maps and images.

Mark Gristock was relentlessly enthusiastic, a constructively critical reviewer and a reliable nag when I needed it most. Sarah Reavley, Jeremy Gavron, Aruna Vasudevan and Jolyon Goddard commented on early drafts; all helped improve it. Luckily my research coincided with that of Professor Arthur Burns at King's College London, who reviewed the text and provided encouragement that I was on the right tracks.

Thanks to the wonderful team at Spitalfields Life Books for a publishing experience combining superb professionalism with a personal touch. It has been a privilege to learn from my editor Walter Donohue and to have David Pearson design my book. Grateful thanks are also due to Joe McLaren, Janet Andrew, Vicky Stewart, Sydney Diack and So-Shan Au. Above all I appreciate the support, ideas and enthusiasm of The Gentle Author, who also generously took many of the photographs accompanying the text (any residual errors in which are mine alone).

Most importantly, I could not have written the book without the love, encouragement and support of my family Sarah and Edith Reavley and George Woodford, who have allowed Joseph Merceron into our family life for much longer than they bargained for.

Merceron Houses, erected in 1901 by the East End Dwellings Company
on land formerly part of Joseph Merceron's garden in Bethnal Green

BIBLIOGRAPHY

I. MANUSCRIPT AND ARCHIVAL SOURCES

BL: British Library

Add. MSS: Additional manuscripts.

BNC: Brasenose College Archives, University of Oxford

Bethnal Green papers (D/148).
Bethnal Green papers (Hurst, Bethnal Green 3).

LMA: London Metropolitan Archives

Burial registers of St Matthew's, Bethnal Green (X025/020).
Holborn & Finsbury Commission of Sewers (HFCS).
London Land Tax Records 1692–1932.
Middlesex Sessions of the Peace (MR).
Middlesex Sessions Records: County Day Minutes (MJ/OC/011–021).
Middlesex Sessions: Minutes of Prisons Committee (MA/G/GEN).
Tower Hamlets Commission of Sewers (THCS).

Merceron family archives

Private papers in the possession of the Merceron and Kendall families.

PRO: National Archives (Public Record Office, Kew)

Census Returns (HO 107, RG 9).
Chancery records (C 12, C 13, C 101, C 111, C 112, C 127).
Court of King's Bench (KB 1, KB 33).
High Court of Delegates (DEL 2).
Home Office correspondence (HO 42).
Inland Revenue, death duty records (IR 26).
King's Bench Prison, Commitment and Discharge books (PRIS 4, PRIS 7).

Privy Council (PC 1).
Probate Records (PROB 11, PROB 31, PROB 37).
Treasury Solicitor (TS 11).

SOC. GEN: Society of Genealogists Library

Faculty Office marriage allegations.
Pallot's Marriage Index.

THLHA: Tower Hamlets Local History Archives

Deeds (various).
VM: Vestry Minutes of St Matthew's, Bethnal Green, 1747–1840 (BG 273–281).

II. PUBLISHED SOURCES
(PUBLISHED IN LONDON UNLESS OTHERWISE STATED)

Primary Sources

Newspapers, magazines and periodicals

Analectic Magazine
Annual Register
Church of England Magazine
Civil Engineer and Architects' Journal
Daily Universal Register
Eclectic Review
Gentleman's Magazine
London Gazette
London Magazine, or Gentleman's Monthly Intelligencer
Monthly Review, or Literary Journal
Morning Chronicle
Royal Military Panorama
The Times
Universal Magazine

Parliamentary papers, etc.

Debrett, J., *Parliamentary Register.*
Hansard, T.C., *Parliamentary Debates.*

Metropolitan Sanitary Commission, *First Report of the Commissioners appointed to inquire whether any and what special means may be requisite for the Improvement of the Health of the Metropolis*, 1848.

Middlesex Poll Book, 1802.

PP *1814 (Prisons)*: *Report from the Committee of the House of Commons on the King's Bench, Fleet, and Marshalsea Prisons, etc*, 1814, (reprinted in *The Pamphleteer, Vol. VI*, 1815).

PP *1816 (Education)*: *Report from the Select Committee of the House of Commons appointed to inquire into the Education of the Lower Orders in the Metropolis, etc*, 1816.

PP *1816 (Police)*: *Evidence of the Select Committee of the House of Commons into the State of the Police in the Metropolis*, 1816.

PP *1817 (Police)*: *First Report and Evidence of the Select Committee of the House of Commons into the State of the Police in the Metropolis*, 1817.

PP *1830 (Select Vestries)*: *Report from the Select Committee appointed to inquire into the general operation and effect of the laws and usages under which Select Vestries are constituted in England and Wales*, 1830.

PP *1832 (Silk Trade)*: *Minutes of Evidence taken before the Select Committee of the House of Commons into the Silk Trade, 1832*.

PP *1834 (Sewers)*: *Report from the Select Committee on Metropolis Sewers; with minutes of evidence, etc.*, 1834.

Poor Law Commissioners' Report of 1834.

Fourth Annual Report of the Poor Law Commissioners for England and Wales, 1838.

Poor Law Commissioners, *Report of an Inquiry into the Sanitary Condition of the Labouring Population of Great Britain*, 1842.

Books

Ackermann, Rudolph, *The Microcosm of London – or London in miniature* (3 volumes). Methuen & Co, 1904.

Anon. ('Amicus Curiae'), *Criticisms on the Bar, including Strictures on the Principal Counsel, etc.* Simpkin & Marshall, 1819.

Arnold, Matthew, *The Poems of Matthew Arnold, 1840 to 1867.* OUP, 1909.

Bentham, Jeremy, *The Correspondence of Jeremy Bentham.* OUP, 1984.

Brayley, Edward Wedlake, etc, A *Topographical and Historical Description of London and Middlesex ... By Messrs Brayley, Brewer, and Nightingale ... Illustrated with One Hundred and Fifty Views, Etc.* (5 volumes). Sherwood, Neely & Jones; George Cowie & Co, 1820.

Brougham, Lord Henry, *Historical Sketches of Statesmen who Flourished in the Time of George III.* Richard Griffin & Co., 1856.

Brougham, Lord Henry, *Opinions of Lord Brougham, etc.* Paris, 1841.

Buckingham and Chandos, Duke of, *Memoirs of the Court and Cabinets of George III, etc* (4 volumes). Hurst & Blackett, 1855.

Burn, Richard, *The Justice of the Peace, and Parish Officer* (5 volumes). 23rd edition, 1820.

Chesterton, George L., *Revelations of Prison Life, etc.* Second edition, Hurst and Blackett, 1856.

Colquhoun, Patrick, *A Treatise on the Police of the Metropolis.* Sixth edition, Joseph Mawman, 1800.

Defoe, Daniel, *A Tour through the Whole Island of Great Britain.* 1724–27.

Dickens Charles, *Sketches by Boz,* 1836.

Dickens, Charles, *Oliver Twist,* 1838.

Dickens, Charles, *Barnaby Rudge,* 1841.

Dickens, Charles, *Little Dorrit,* 1857.

Dickinson, James, *Suppressed Gout: its dangers, varieties and treatment, etc.* Baillière, Tindall & Cox, 1873.

English Historical Documents, Vol. XI, (1783–1832). Routledge, 1995.

Gavin, Hector, *Sanitary Ramblings: Being Sketches and illustrations of Bethnal Green, a Type of the Condition of the Metropolis and Other Large Towns.* John Churchill, 1848.

Grosley, Pierre Jean, *A Tour to London (trans. Nugent, T.),* 1772.

Gurney, William Brodie, *Merceron's Trials for Fraud and Corruption, etc.* W. Wright, 1819.

Harrison, S. B., and Wollaston, F. L., *Reports of cases argued and determined in the Court of King's Bench, etc., Vol. II (1836).* Butterworth, 1837.

Hawkins, Laetitia Matilda, *Memoirs, Anecdotes, Facts & Opinions, Vol. I.* Longman, 1824.

Holland, Lady, *A Memoir of the Reverend Sydney Smith, etc.* New York: Harper & Brothers, 1855.

Howell, Thomas Jones, *A Complete Collection of State Trials, etc.* Longman, 1820.

Huguenot Society of London, *Quarto Series,* Vol. XI, *Registers of "La Patente" Huguenot chapel, Spitalfields 1689–1785.*

Huskisson, William, *The Speeches of the Rt. Hon. William Huskisson: with a biographical memoir, Vol. II.* John Murray, 1831.

Johnson, Samuel, & Murphy, Arthur, *The Works of Samuel Johnson, etc.* New York: Alexander V. Blake, 1846.

Nield, James, *State of the Prisons in England, Scotland, and Wales, etc.,* 1812.

Owen, Robert, & Owen, Robert Dale, *The Crisis, or the Change from Error and Misery, to Truth and Happiness.* J. Eamonson, 1833.

Pearce, James, *A Treatise on the Abuses of the Laws, etc.* Sherwood, Neely & Jones, 1814.

Pym, Edith E., *Tales for my Grandchildren.* Hamilton, Adams & Co., 1861.

Robinson, Charles, *A Register of the Scholars admitted into Merchant Taylors' School.* Farncombe & Co, 1883.

Romilly, Sir Samuel, *Memoirs of the life of Sir Samuel Romilly, etc.* John Murray, 1840.

Scarlett, Hon. Peter Campbell, *A Memoir of the Rt. Hon. James, first Lord Abinger, etc.,* 1877.

Southey, Robert (writing as Espriella, Alvarez), *Letters from England,* (3 volumes). Second edition, Longman, 1808.

Southey, Robert, *Poems*. 1799.

Southey, Robert, *Poetical Works: Joan of Arc; Ballads, Lyrics and Minor Poems.* Routledge, 1894.

Thale, Mary (Ed.), *Francis Place: Autobiography.* Cambridge: CUP, 1972.

The Spirit of the Public Journals for 1804, etc. James Ridgway, 1805.

Thistlewood's Trial: Anon: The Trials at large of Arthur Thistlewood, etc., for High Treason, in the Court of King's Bench, Westminster, on Monday June 9, 1817. W. Lewis, 1817.

Wade, John, *A Treatise on the Police and Crimes of the Metropolis, etc.* Longman, 1829.

Pamphlets

Anon., *An Address to the Magistracy of the County of Middlesex...on the motives that should influence their votes in the election of a Chairman of the Quarter Sessions, in the place of William Mainwaring, Esq., vacated,* 1815.

Anon., *An Impartial Statement of the Inhuman Cruelties Discovered in the Coldbath Fields Prison, reported in the House of Commons on Friday the 11th of June, 1800.* J. S. Jordan, 1800.

Anon., *Considerations on Select Vestries, etc.* Effingham Wilson, 1828.

Anon., *Considerations on the late elections for Westminster and Middlesex together with some facts relating to the House of Correction in Cold Bath Fields.* Hatchard, 1802.

Anon., *Minutes of Evidence taken [26 April – 26 June 1816] before a Select Committee ... to inquire into the State of the Police in the Metropolis...with observations, and a preface by a Magistrate of the County of Middlesex.* Sherwood, Neely & Jones, 1816.

Anon., *The Abuse of Prisons; or, an...account of the House of Correction in Cold-Bath-Fields, and the treatment of Mr. Gale Jones.* 1811.

Anon., *The only edition that contains a Full Account of the Proceedings at the Middlesex Election (1804), including the Speeches, etc.* M. C. Springsguth, 1804.

Anon., *The Poor Man's Friend, or the Frauds of the Pawnbrokers Exposed.* H. Chance, c. 1835.

Anon., *The Revelations, in six chapters (An account, partly in Biblical Phraseology, of the election for Middlesex between Sir F. Burdett and Mr Mainwaring),* 1805.

Anon., *The Scum Uppermost – when the Middlesex Porridge Pot Boils Over!! – an heroic election ballad, with explanatory notes,* 1802.

Anon. (Glasse, Rev. Dr Samuel), *The Secrets of the English Bastille Disclosed, by a Middlesex Magistrate.* F. & C. Rivington, 1799.

Anon., *The whole proceedings and resolutions of the Freeholders of the county of Middlesex...at Hackney, October 29th 1800,* 1800.

Beaumont, John Thomas Barber, *A Letter to the Right Honourable Lord Sidmouth, etc.,* 1817.

Bowles, John, *Thoughts on the late General Election by John Bowles, as demonstrative of the progress of Jacobinism.* F. & C. Rivington, 1802.

Defoe, Daniel (writing as Andrew Moreton), *Parochial Tyranny, etc.*, J. Roberts, 1727.

Hale, William, *A Letter to Samuel Whitbread, Esq., MP, etc.*, 1816.

Henekey, George, *A Full and Complete Refutation of the evidence of...Joseph Fletcher before the Committee appointed by the...House of Commons, for the purpose of investigating the Police of the Metropolis, etc.*, 1816.

Kirby, R. S., *Kirby's Wonderful and Eccentric Museum, or Magazine, etc*, Volume V., R. S. Kirby, 1820.

Phipps, Joseph, *The Vestry Laid Open, etc.*, J. Millan; F. Noble, 1739.

Stone, William, *Evidence of William Stone and other witnesses, etc., extracted from a Report by E. Chadwick*, reprinted 1837.

Thirlwall, Thomas, *A Vindication of the Magistrates acting in and for the Tower Division, etc.*, 1817.

Wright, John, *The Dolphin; or, Grand Junction Nuisance, etc.*, 1827.

Secondary Sources

Books

Ashton, John, *A History of English Lotteries.* Leadenhall Press, 1893.

Barnes, Gordon, *Stepney Churches – an Historical Account.* The Ecclesiological Society, 1967.

Beaumont, David Anthony, *Barber Beaumont.* Witherby, 1999.

Biber, George Edward, *Bishop Blomfield and his Times.* Harrison, 1857.

Briggs, Asa, *The Age of Improvement, 1783–1867* (second edition). Longman, 1979.

Broodbank, Sir Joseph G., *History of the Port of London* (2 vols). Daniel O'Connor, 1921.

Brundage, Anthony, *The English Poor Laws, 1700–1930.* Basingstoke: Palgrave, 2002.

Burns, Arthur (ed.), '*My unfortunate parish: Anglican urban ministry in Bethnal Green, 1809–c.1850*', *From the Reformation to the Permissive Society*, Church of England Record Society Volume 18. Boydell, 2010.

Cox, Margaret, *Life and Death in Spitalfields, 1700–1850.* York: Council for British Archaeology, 1996.

De Castro, J. Paul, *The Gordon Riots.* Oxford: OUP, 1926.

Donohue, Joseph (ed.), *The Cambridge History of British Theatre, Vol. 2 1660–1895.* Cambridge: Cambridge University Press, 2004.

Draper, F. W. M., *Four Centuries of Merchant Taylors' School (1561–1961).* Oxford: OUP, 1962.

Engels, Friedrich, *The Condition of the Working Class in England*, 1845 (paperback edition). Penguin, 1987.

Foster, *Alumni Oxiensis 1715–1886.*

Gavron, Jeremy, *An Acre of Barren Ground* (paperback edition). Scribner, 2006.

George, M. Dorothy, *Catalogue of Political & Personal Satires, etc.* British Museum, 1978.

George, M. Dorothy, *London Life in the Eighteenth Century.* Chicago: Academy Chicago Publishers, reprinted 1984.

Gilbert, Martin, *Second World War.* Fontana, 1990.

Glinert, Ed, *East End Chronicles.* Allen Lane, 2005; paperback edition Penguin, 2006.

Graham-Leigh, John, *London's Water Wars.* Francis Boutle Publishers, 2000.

Gwynn, Robin D., *The Huguenots of London.* Brighton: The Alpha Press, 1998.

Hague, William, *William Pitt the Younger.* HarperCollins, 2004.

Halévy, Elie, *England in 1815.* Ernest Benn, paperback edition 1961.

Halévy, Elie, *The Liberal Awakening, 1815–1830.* Ernest Benn, paperback edition 1961.

Halliday, Stephen, *The Great Stink of London: Sir Joseph Bazalgette and the Cleansing of the Victorian Capital.* Stroud: Sutton, 1999 (paperback edition, 2001).

Hammond, J. L., & Hammond, Barbara, *The Village Labourer, 1760–1832.* Longman, 1911.

Hammond, J. L., & Hammond, Barbara, *The Town Labourer, 1760–1832* (second edition). Longman, 1925.

Hammond, J. L., & Hammond, Barbara, *The Skilled Labourer, 1760–1832.* Longman, 1919, republished Stroud: Sutton, 1995.

Holdsworth, Sir William, *A History of English Law,* Vol. X. Methuen, 1938.

Hone, J. Ann, *For the Cause of Truth: Radicalism in London 1796–1821.* Oxford: OUP, 1982.

Horne, R. H. (ed.), *A New Spirit of the Age.* New York: Harper & Brothers, 1844.

Hudson, Kenneth, *Pawnbroking: an Aspect of British Social History.* The Bodley Head, 1982.

Hughson, David, *London: being an accurate history and description of the British Metropolis and its Neighbourhood.* J. Stratford, 1805.

Huish, Robert, *Memoirs of Caroline, Queen of Great Britain.* (2 volumes). T. Kelly, 1821.

Huish, Robert, *Memoirs of George the Fourth, etc.* T. Kelly, 1830.

Inwood, Stephen, *A History of London.* Macmillan, 1998.

James, P. D., and Critchley, T. A., *The Maul and the Pear Tree: the Ratcliffe Highway Murders 1811.* Constable & Company, 1971 (paperback edition, Sphere Books, 1987).

Jay, Mike, *The Unfortunate Colonel Despard.* Bantam, 2005.

Keir, David L., *The Constitutional History of Modern Britain since 1485* (eighth edition). A. & C. Black, 1966.

Kershen, Anne J., *Strangers, Aliens And Asians: Huguenots, Jews and Bangladeshis in Spitalfields, 1666–2000.* Routledge, 2005.

Kynaston, David, *The City of London, Volume I: A World of Its Own, 1815–1890.* Chatto & Windus, 1994.

Langford, Paul, *A Polite and Commercial People: England 1727–1783.* Oxford: OUP, 1989.

Linebaugh, Peter, *The London Hanged: Crime and Civil Society in the Eighteenth Century* (second edition). London: Verso, 2006.

Linnane, Fergus, *London's Underworld.* Robson Books, 2004.

Low, Donald A., *The Regency Underworld*. Stroud: Sutton, 2005.

Manwaring, G. E., & Dobrée, Bonamy, *The Floating Republic – an account of the Mutinies at Spithead and The Nore in 1797*. Pelican Books, 1935, reprinted Barnsley: Pen & Sword Military Classics, 2004.

Matthews, William, *Hydraulia; an historical and descriptive account of the Water Works of London, etc.* Simpkin, Marshall & Co, 1835.

May, Allyson N., *The Bar and The Old Bailey, 1750–1850*. The University of Carolina Press, 2003.

May, J. C. C. (ed.), *The Collected Works of Samuel Taylor Coleridge*. Princeton, N. J.: Princeton University Press, 2001.

Mayhew, Henry, & Binny, John, *Criminal Prisons of London*. Frank Cass & Co., 1862.

McCalman, Iain, *Radical Underworld – Prophets, Revolutionaries and Pornographers in London, 1795–1840*. Cambridge: Cambridge University Press, 1988, reprinted Oxford: OUP, 1993.

Merchant Taylors' School Archaeological Society, *Merchant Taylors' School: its Origin, History and Present Surroundings*. Oxford: Blackwell, 1929.

Morris, Arthur D., *The Hoxton Madhouses*. Goodwin Bros., 1958.

Patterson, M. W., *Sir Francis Burdett & his Times (1770–1844)*. Macmillan, 1931.

Pevsner, Nikolaus, *The Buildings of England: London, Vol. 2* (1952 edition). Penguin, 1952.

Picard, Liza, *Dr. Johnson's London*. Weidenfeld & Nicolson, 2000.

Porter, Roy, *English Society in the Eighteenth Century* (paperback edition). Penguin, 1982.

Porter, Roy, *London: A Social History*. Hamish Hamilton, 1994 (paperback edition). Penguin, 2000.

Porter, Roy, and Rousseau, G. S., *Gout: the Patrician Malady*. Yale University Press, 1998.

Price, Richard, *British Society 1680–1880: dynamism, containment and change*. Cambridge: Cambridge University Press, 1999.

Radzinowicz, Leon, *A History of English Criminal Law and its Administration from 1750* (4 Vols.). Stevens & Sons, 1956.

Robinson, A. J., & Chesshyre, D. H. B., *The Green*. London Borough of Tower Hamlets, 1986.

Rudé, George, *Hanoverian London*. Martin, Secker & Warburg, 1971. Paperback edition, Stroud: Sutton, 2003.

Rudé, George, *Wilkes and Liberty* (second edition). Lawrence & Wishart, 1983.

Sheppard, Francis H. W., *London – A History*. Oxford: OUP, 1998.

Steinberg, Marc W., *Fighting Words: working class formation, collective action, and discourse in early nineteenth century England*. Cornell University Press, 1999.

Survey of London: London County Council, Survey of London, Vol. XXVII, *Christ Church and All Saints, Spitalfields*, 1957.

Taylor, Rosemary, *Walks Through History: Exploring the East End*. Derby: Breedon Books, 2001.

Taylor, William, *This Bright Field*. Methuen, 2000.

Thompson, Edward P., *The Making of the English Working Class* (third edition). Penguin, 1980.

Thorne, R. G., *The History of Parliament: The House of Commons, 1790–1820*. Secker & Warburg, 1986.

Toone, W., *The Chronological Historian, etc.* Longman, 1836.

Truman, Hanbury, Buxton and Company, *Truman's: the Brewers*. Newman Neame, 1966.

Uglow, Jenny, *Hogarth*. Faber & Faber (paperback edition 2002).

Vale, George F., *Old Bethnal Green*. The Blythenhale Press, 1934.

VCH: Victoria County History, *A History of the County of Middlesex: Volume XI: Stepney, Bethnal Green: 1998*.

Waller, John, *The Real Oliver Twist*. Cambridge: Icon Books, 2006 (paperback edition).

Watson, J. Steven, *The Reign of George III, 1760–1815*. Oxford: OUP, 1960.

Webb, Sidney and Webb, Beatrice, *The History of Liquor Licensing in England, principally from 1700 to 1830*. Longman, 1903.

Webb, Sidney and Webb, Beatrice, *English Local Government. Vol. I: The Parish and the County*. London: Longman, 1906.

Webb, Sidney and Webb, Beatrice, *English Local Government. Vol. IV: Statutory Authorities for Special Purposes*. Longman, 1922.

Webb, Sidney and Webb, Beatrice, *English Prisons under Local Government*. Longman, 1922.

Weinreb, Ben, and Hibbert, Christopher (Eds.), *The London Encyclopædia*. Macmillan, 1983 (paperback edition 1987).

White, Jerry, *London in the Nineteenth Century*. Jonathan Cape, 2007.

Wilson, Ben, *The Laughter of Triumph – William Hone and the Fight for the Free Press*. Faber & Faber, 2005 (paperback edition).

Wise, Sarah, *The Italian Boy – Murder and Grave-Robbery in 1830s London*. Pimlico, 2005.

Woodward, Sir Llewellyn, *The Age of Reform, 1815–1870 (second edition)*. Oxford: OUP, 1962.

Wright, T. H., *The Works of James Gillray*. Reprinted Amsterdam: S. Emmering, 1970.

Wright, Thomas, *England under the House of Hanover*, (Vol. II). Richard Bentley, 1848.

Articles

Baker, Jean N., *The Proclamation Society, William Mainwaring and the Theatrical Representations Act of 1788*, Historical Research 76 (193), August 2003, pp. 347–63.

Emsley, Clive, *The Home Office and its Sources of Information and Investigation, 1791–1801*, English Historical Review 94, July 1979, pp. 532–61.

Higgins, Robert McR., *The 1832 Cholera Epidemic in East London*, East London Record, no. 2, 1979 (published online at www.mernick.org.uk/thhol/1832chol.html, accessed 10 July 2016)

McCalman, Iain, *Ultra-Radicalism and Convivial Debating Clubs in London, 1795–1838*, English Historical Review 102, April 1987, pp. 309–33.

Murphy, Elaine, *The New Poor Law Guardians and the Administration of Insanity in East London, 1834–1844,* Bulletin of the History of Medicine 77, 2003, pp.45–74.
Notes on the Parish of Woodchurch, Cheshire, Trans. Hist. Soc. of Lancashire and Cheshire, N.S. xvii, pp.153–5.
Sheppard, Francis H.W., *The Huguenots in Spitalfields and Soho,* Proc. Huguenot Soc. London, Vol. XXI, 1965–1970.
Sparrow, Elizabeth, *Secret Service under Pitt's Administrations, 1792–1806,* History 83 (270), 1998, pp.280–94.
Webb, Sidney and Webb, Beatrice, *What Happened to the English Parish,* Political Science Quarterly Vol. XVII No.2, June 1902, pp.223–46.
Wickstead, Thomas, *Observations on the Past and Present Supply of Water to the Metropolis, read before the Society of Arts, May 24th, 1835,* Reprinted in The Civil Engineer and Architect's Journal, etc. Vol. III, 1840.

Unpublished University thesis

Paley, Ruth, *The Middlesex Justices Act of 1792: its Origins and Effects.* University of Reading, 1983.

III. ONLINE SOURCES

Online versions of key primary source documents

Merceron's Trials
http://bit.ly/2cb2QND
PP 1816 (Police): Evidence of the Select Committee of the House of Commons into the State of the Police in the Metropolis, 1816:
http://bit.ly/2chAioi
PP 1817 (Police): First Report and Evidence of the Select Committee of the House of Commons into the State of the Police in the Metropolis, 1817:
http://bit.ly/2c25Oqd

Websites

www.motco.com/map (Rocque and Horwood maps of London).
www.oldbaileyonline.org (Old Bailey Proceedings Online).
www.oxforddnb.com (Oxford Dictionary of National Biography, OUP, 2004; online edition, May 2006).
www.mernick.org.uk/thhol (Tower Hamlets History Online).
www.st-matthews.co.uk/history (St Matthew's, Bethnal Green)
www.spitalfieldslife.com (East End culture and history)

ENDNOTES

INTRODUCTION

1. Inwood, *A History of London*, p.860. See also Kershen, *Strangers, Aliens and Asians*; Taylor, *This Bright Field*. Both these books provide an excellent overview of the historical development of Spitalfields as a succession of migrant communities.
2. Kershen, *Strangers, Aliens and Asians*, p.1; Gwynn, *The Huguenots of London*, p.18.
3. Porter, *London: A Social History*, p.182.
4. George, *London Life in the Eighteenth Century*, p.295; Linnane, *London's Underworld*, pp.77–9; Webb & Webb, *What Happened to the English Parish*, pp.223–46; Webb & Webb, *The Parish and the County*, pp.80–90; Webb & Webb, *Statutory Authorities for Special Purposes*, pp.68–103; Laski's review in *Economica*, No. 8 (June 1923), pp.148–50.
5. Gavron, *An Acre of Barren Ground: 'Two Brewers'*.

PROLOGUE
THE BOSS OF BETHNAL GREEN

6. Southey, *Poetical Works*, p.252, *'The Alderman's Funeral'*.
7. *The Gentleman's Magazine:* August 1839, p.211, March 1847, p.307; *The Times*, 2 June 1818.
8. Webb & Webb, *The Parish and the County*, pp.79–90; LMA: *Xo25/o22, Burial registers of St Matthew's, Bethnal Green*, 24 July 1839.
9. LMA: *Xo25/o22, Burial registers of St Matthew's, Bethnal Green*, 24 July 1839; Gavin, *Sanitary Ramblings*; Dickens, *Oliver Twist*, chapter XIX. For a detailed account of the 'London Burkers', see Wise, *The Italian Boy*.

CHAPTER I
BLUE APRON MEN

10. Hansard, *Parliamentary History of England*, Vol. XXI (1780–1781), p.592.
11. Thomas, Peter D.G., *Wilkes, John, Oxford DNB*, (www.oxforddnb.com/view/article/29410, accessed 3 August 2006).
12. *The Gentleman's Magazine*, February 1764, pp.44, 88, 94.
13. *The Annual Register*, 1763 p.105; Toone, *The Chronological Historian*, Vol. II, p.158; Linebaugh, *The London Hanged*, p.271.

14. Huguenot Society of London, *Quarto Series*, Vol. XI, p.150; *Survey of London*, Vol. XXVII, p.190; Romilly, *Memoirs*, p.14.
15. Gwynn, *The Huguenots of London*, p.10; Sheppard, *The Huguenots in Spitalfields and Soho*, p.355.
16. Kershen, *Strangers, Aliens and Asians*, p.1; George, *London Life in the Eighteenth Century*, p.106; see also Rocque's map of 1746.
17. Barnes, *Stepney Churches*.
18. Many of the Spitalfields streets, for example Fournier, Wilkes and Hanbury Streets, still contain these Georgian townhouses, now beautifully restored and much in demand. For conditions to the east of Brick Lane see Linebaugh, *The London Hanged*, p.256.
19. *Survey of London*, Vol. XXVII, p.190; Huguenot Society of London, *Quarto Series*, Vol. XI, pp.137, 142, 148. The church of *La Patente* is clearly marked on Brown's Lane on Rocque's map of 1746 as 'Fr. Ch' (www.motco.com/map/). The chapel building still stands (although the courtyard is built over) and is now Hanbury Hall, in Hanbury Street. For the placing of 77 Brick Lane and the *Black Eagle* Brewery, see also Horwood's map of 1799. Truman, Hanbury Buxton & Co: *Truman's: the Brewers; Survey of London*, Vol. XXVII, p.124. For street conditions see Picard, *Dr. Johnson's London*, pp.26–30; Grosley, *A Tour to London*, p.33.
20. The portrait of Germanus Merceron is still in the possession of the Merceron family.
21. Merceron family archives; Grandet, *Les Saints Prêtres Français du XVIIeme Siécle* (1897), pp.80–81; Gwynn, *The Huguenots of London*, postscript.
22. James's other children were named Anne, Lidie and Josue, born in 1753, 1756 and 1758 respectively, see Huguenot Society of London, *Quarto Series*, Vol. XI, pp.97, 138, 139, 143, 144. Apprenticeship records are in the private possession of the Merceron family. Burial information: LMA: *X025/020, Burial registers of St Matthew's, Bethnal Green.*
23. For James's second marriage, see Soc. Gen: *Faculty Office Marriage Allegations, (James Merceron, 14th June 1760).*
24. THLHA: *VM:* 12 April 1762 *et seq.*
25. VCH: *Middlesex: Volume 11: Stepney, Bethnal Green*, pp.114–117; 155–168; THLHA: *Deeds 2906, 2893, 2891.*
26. Sheppard, *London – A History*, p.182.
27. George, *London Life in the Eighteenth Century*, p.90; Grosley, *A Tour to London*, p.77.
28. George, *London Life in the Eighteenth Century*, p.90; *Fourth Annual Report of the Poor Law Commissioners*, 1838, App. A, no.1, p.140.
29. Price, *British Society, 1680–1880*, pp.155–166; Keir, *The Constitutional History of Modern Britain since 1485*, pp.312–314; Webb & Webb, *What Happened to the English Parish*, pp.236–237.
30. George, *London Life in the Eighteenth Century*, pp.179, 187, 332–333, 410.
31. The various powers for Bethnal Green were set up under the following acts: 23 Geo. II, c.30; 11 Geo. II, c.29; 24 Geo. II, c.26; 3 Geo. III, c.40.

32. VCH: *Middlesex: Volume 11: Stepney, Bethnal Green*, pp.190–202; Webb & Webb, *The Parish and the County*, p.80; Webb & Webb, *What Happened to the English Parish*, p.237.
33. THLHA: *VM:* 24 April 1764, 8 April 1765; Defoe, *Parochial Tyranny*, pp.16–17.
34. Linebaugh, *The London Hanged*, p.272; Rudé, *Wilkes & Liberty*, p.100.
35. THLHA: *VM:* 8 July 1768, 2 September 1768; Grosley, *A Tour to London*, pp.48–49.
36. Rudé, *Wilkes & Liberty*, p.100.
37. Webb & Webb, *The Parish and the County*, p.324. For Wilmot's appointment see Paley, *The Middlesex Justices Act*, p.214. Wilmot's reputation became such that *The Times* included him in a list of the worst trading magistrates, despite the fact that he had been dead for three years. See *The Times*, 9 April 1792.
38. *The Times*, 30 September 1788, p.1.
39. George, *London Life in the Eighteenth Century*, pp.180–181, 186, 189.

CHAPTER II
THE TYRANT IN THE BOY

40. This verse accompanied the publication of Hogarth's print 'The First Stage of Cruelty' (1751).
41. Linebaugh, *The London Hanged*, pp.280–281; *Annual Register*, 1769, p.159.
42. Linebaugh, *The London Hanged*, p.279; Rudé, *Wilkes & Liberty*, pp.101–2; *Annual Register*, 22 August 1769.
43. Linebaugh, *The London Hanged*, p.279.
44. *The Annual Register*, 1769 p.138.
45. *Old Bailey Proceedings Online:* www.oldbaileyonline.org/browse.jsp?ref=t17691018-22 , accessed 10 July, 2016), October 1769, trial of John D'oyle, John Valline (t17691018-22); Rudé, *Wilkes & Liberty*, p.102. An account of the dispute over the location of the execution is given in Hughson, *London, etc.* pp.588–593.
46. *Annual Register*, 6 December, 1769; Rudé, *Wilkes & Liberty*, p.103; Linebaugh, *The London Hanged*, p.281.
47. *Old Bailey Proceedings Online:* www.oldbaileyonline.org/browse.jsp?ref=t17691206-31 , accessed 10 July 2016), December 1769, trial of William Eastman (t17691206-31).
48. THLHA: *VM:* 17 April 1770, 1st April 1771, 2 April 1771.
49. VCH: *Middlesex: Volume 11: Stepney, Bethnal Green*, pp.155–168.
50. *Old Bailey Proceedings Online:* www.oldbaileyonline.org/browse.jsp?ref=t17710703-59, accessed 10 July 2016), July 1771, trial of Henry Stroud, Robert Cambell & Anstis Horsford (t17710703-59).
51. The *Gentleman's Magazine*, April 1771, p.189.
52. The *Gentleman's Magazine*, July 1771, p.231; Linebaugh, *The London Hanged*, p.283.
53. Thale, *Francis Place: Autobiography*, pp.40, 54; Romilly, *Memoirs, etc*, Vol. I, p.15.

54. Hudson, *Pawnbroking*, p.33; Radzinowicz, *A History of English Criminal Law*, *Vol. 3*, p.69; *The Times*, 16 June, 1788.
55. George, *London Life in the Eighteenth Century*, p.54; Dickens, *Sketches by Boz*.
56. Anon., *The Poor Man's Friend*; PRO: *J 90/434*, an inventory of the pawnshop of a Mr Godier of Fleet Street, Bethnal Green, close to Brick Lane, taken in 1793.
57. Anon., *The Poor Man's Friend*.
58. LMA: *MR/B/C/1776/192, MR/B/C/1781/112, MR/B/C/1781/113, MR/B/C/1781/108*.
59. IGI; PRO: *PROB 11/1147*, Will of James Merceron.
60. IGI: (Huguenot Society of London – registers of French Church, Threadneedle Street); THLHA: *VM:* 6 April 1776, 31 March 1777; Langford, *A Polite and Commercial People*, p.456; Vale, *Old Bethnal Green*, p.29; Robinson, *A Register of... Merchant Taylors' School*, Vol. I, p.142.
61. Merchant Taylor's School Archaeological Society, *Merchant Taylors' School, etc.*, pp.34, 55, 58; Robinson, *A Register of...Merchant Taylors' School*, Vol. I, xiii; Draper, *Four Centuries of Merchant Taylors' School*, p.107.
62. Draper, *Four Centuries of Merchant Taylors' School*, pp.102–107; Robinson, *A Register of...Merchant Taylors' School*, Vol. I, ix–xi; Merchant Taylor's School Archaeological Society, *Merchant Taylors' School, etc.*, p.56.
63. *PP 1816 (Police)*, p.79 (evidence of Robert Wrightson).
64. Langford, *A Polite and Commercial People*, p.572; *PP 1816 (Police)*, p.67 (evidence of J.T.B.Beaumont).
65. Ashton, *A History of English Lotteries*, p.293; Colquhoun, *A Treatise on the Police of the Metropolis*, pp.142, 152.
66. George, *London Life in the Eighteenth Century*, p.306; Thale, *Francis Place: Autobiography*, p.98; Ashton, *A History of English Lotteries*, p.293.
67. *PP 1816 (Police)* (Evidence of Joshua King); Thale, *Francis Place: Autobiography*, p.68.
68. THLHA: *VM:* 6 April 1779; Merceron Family Archive; PRO: *PROB 11/1064*, will of James Merceron.

CHAPTER III

DOING DAVY

69. Brecht, *The Resistible Rise of Arturio Ui*, p.32.
70. Langford, *A Polite and Commercial People*, p.551; Rudé, *Hanoverian London*, pp.220–224; Johnson, *The Works of Samuel Johnson*, Vol. I, p.521.
71. *Old Bailey Proceedings Online:* www.oldbaileyonline.org/browse.jsp?ref=t17800628-22, accessed 10 July 2016), June 1780, trial of John Gamble (t17800628-22); de Castro, *The Gordon Riots*, p.123.
72. Dickens, *Barnaby Rudge*, chapter 68.
73. *Old Bailey Proceedings Online:* www.oldbaileyonline.org/browse.jsp?ref=t17800628-9, accessed 10 July 2016), June 1780, trial of William Bolton (t17800628-9);

www.oldbaileyonline.org/browse.jsp?ref=t17800628-22; trial of John Gamble (t17800628-22).

74. Merceron Family Archives: family trees; IGI.

75. Merceron Family Archives: exercise book marked *Wills. Joseph Merceron, 1780'*.

76. Merceron's exercise book contains a copy of Grant's will, in which Grant left Merceron a legacy of £20: see Merceron Family Archives: exercise book marked *'Wills. Joseph Merceron, 1780'*.

77. THLHA: *Deed 7973*. Merceron signed as a witness to this deed in August 1784 as agent to Busby. For his appointment as Natt's agent, see Merceron Family Archives: exercise book marked *'Wills. Joseph Merceron, 1780';* also PRO: *PROB 37/148, (deposition by Joseph Merceron 22 January 1802);* The *Red Cow* estate contained 295 houses in 1751 and 467 houses by 1809: see VCH: *Middlesex: Volume 11: Stepney, Bethnal Green,* pp.103–109.

78. Merceron Family Archives. See also White, *London in the Nineteenth Century,* p.80, where this practice by property developers is described in detail.

79. Merceron Family Archives: exercise book marked *'Wills. Joseph Merceron, 1780';* THLHA: *Deed 7973*.

80. LMA: *London Land Tax Records, Tower Hamlets, St Mary, Straford-le-Bow, 1786, f.48;* The wills of James and John Merceron and Peter Paumier are all copied in Merceron's exercise book.

81. Merceron Family Archives; IGI; PRO: *PROB 11/1141, Will of John Merceron;* John Merceron was buried on 13 April 1786: see LMA: *X025/020. Burial registers of St Matthew's, Bethnal Green.*

82. PRO: *PROB 37/148; C 13/70/17; DEL 2/57.*

83. PRO: *PROB 11/1147, will of Ann Merceron;* Merceron Family Archives; Ann Merceron was buried on 2 November, 1786: see LMA: *X025/020, Burial registers of St Matthew's, Bethnal Green.*

84. Catherine's incarceration at Hoxton House at the time of her death in 1815 is recorded in *The London Gazette,* 2 March 1822, p.372; Morris, *The Hoxton Madhouses.*

85. PRO: *PROB 31/955, f.507* (inventory of John Merceron's estate).

86. THLHA: *VM:* 18 September 1786, 23 March 1787.

87. THLHA: *VM:* 18 April 1786, 9 March 1787, 9 April 1787, 10 April 1787, 18 April 1787.

88. THLHA: *VM:* 18 June, 21 June, 25 June, 2 July 1787. It is probably this committee that Robert Wrightson was thinking of when he told a House of Commons Select Committee in 1816 (a statement disputed by Merceron) that Merceron had been an assistant poor-rate collector to Bampton. See *Report from Committee on the State of Police in the Metropolis (1816),* p.79 (evidence of Robert Wrightson).

89. THLHA: *VM:* 19 July 1787.

90. THLHA: *VM:* 26 July 1787.

91. THLHA: *VM:* 25 March 1788.

CHAPTER IV

CERBERUS

92. Anon., *The Vestry Dinner*, included in the Bodleian Library's collection of ballads, cited at www.ballads.bodleian.ox.ac.uk/view/edition/17288 , accessed 10 July 2016).

93. Defoe, *Parochial Tyranny, etc.*, pp.8,10; Phipps, *The Vestry Laid Open, etc.*, p.34; THLHA: *VM*: 31 July 1788.

94. For example, in November 1790, a meeting chaired by Merceron voted unanimously to excuse the poor's rate collector from all parochial taxes during his period in office. A similar resolution was made in respect of James May, the vestry clerk. See: THLHA: *VM*: 12 November 1790, 12 May 1791.

95. Anon, *Minutes of Evidence taken…into the State of the Police in the Metropolis, etc.*, p.281 (evidence of Joshua King). For Witherden, see *Merceron's trials, First trial*, p.127 (evidence of Stephen Witherden). For Masterman's role in the Mary Cheesman affair, see later in this chapter.

96. *The Times*, 18 September 1788, p.1; THLHA: *VM*: 6 June 1788, 12 May 1791, 9 April 1792.

97. THLHA: *Deed 2898*; PRO: *PROB 11/1213, (will of Henry Busby);* THLHA: *VM*: 17 April 1788.

98. The *Gentleman's Magazine*, Vol. XIV, December 1744, p.654.

99. THLHA: *VM*: 25 March 1788, 31 July 1788, 8 October 1788; *PP 1817 (Police)*, pp.80, 109 (evidence of John Betts, William Hale).

100. *The Times*, 29th May 1788, p.3.

101. *The Times*, 29th May 1788, p.3; Barker, Hannah, *Walter, John (1739?–1812)*, *Oxford DNB*, (www.oxforddnb.com/view/article/28636, accessed 19 April 2006).

102. *The Times*, 16 June 1788, p.3, 12 September 1788, p.2.

103. *The Times*, 13 September 1788, p.2; 18 September 1788, p.1.

104. *The Times*, 27 September 1788, p.3.

105. To give a sop to Cerberus: to give a bribe, to quiet a troublesome customer. In legend, Cerberus is Pluto's three-headed dog, stationed at the gates of the infernal regions. The ancient Greeks and Romans would place a small cake in the hands of their dead as a sop to Cerberus to allow them to pass without molestation.

106. *The Times*, 2 October 1788, p.1, Barker, Hannah, *Walter, John (1739?–1812)*, *Oxford DNB*, (www.oxforddnb.com/view/article/28636, accessed 19 April 2006).

107. *The Gentleman's Magazine*, 1789, p.671; Copy of James Grant's will in Merceron Family Archives.

108. For Sampson Hanbury's family tree see: Truman, Hanbury & Buxton & Co, *Truman's: the brewers*, pp.19–22; Gavron, *An Acre of Barren Ground*, p.244.

109. THLHA: *VM*: 5 April 1790, 6 April 1790, 22 April 1790, 13 May 1790, 1 June 1790, 5 June 1790, 4 July 1790.

110. THLHA: *VM*: 24 September 1788, 4 March 1789, 18 February 1790, 26 April 1791.

111. PRO: *PROB 37/148, C 13/70/17, DEL 2/57.*

112. Merceron Family Archives; Soc. Gen: *Faculty Office Marriage Allegations; Pallot's Marriage Index.*

113. Merceron Family Archives: undated and unidentified newspaper clipping found among Merceron's private papers.

114. For Henry's birth, see: IGI; Merceron Family Archives: a handwritten note bearing the imprint of a coin and the inscription 'This crown being the first piece of money belonging to Henry was given to him by his Father in the month of June 1792, a few days after his birth. Ann Merceron.'

115. THLHA: *VM*: 25 April 1791, 6 June 1791, 1 August 1791; *The Times*, 27 March 1794; George, *London Life in the Eighteenth Century*, pp.67, 108.

116. THLHA: *VM*: 20 March 1788, 9 April 1789, 1 April 1790, 18 April 1791, 4 April 1792, 22 August, 1792, 12 February 1793, 28 March 1793, 14 May 1793. For Busby's death, see THLHA: *Deed 2906.*

117. Webb, *The Parish and the County*, p.82; PRO: *C/202/183/4.*

CHAPTER V

THE ENGLISH BASTILLE

118. Coleridge, *The Devil's Thoughts*, 1799. The poem is sometimes attributed jointly to Coleridge and Robert Southey. It was first published (including the extract quoted) under Coleridge's name in the *Morning Post* of 6 September 1799 and was expanded by Southey in 1827.

119. Mayhew & Binny, *Criminal Prisons of London*, p.279.

120. T. H. Shepherd, *Coldbath Fields Prison*, August 1814, in BM (*Crace* 32.36); Mayhew & Binny, *Criminal Prisons of London*, p.285; Chesterton, *Revelations of Prison Life*, Vol. I, pp.16–17.

121. Paley, *The Middlesex Justices Act of 1792.* pp.66, 69; Porter, *English Society in the Eighteenth Century*, pp.306–7; Chesterton, *Revelations of Prison Life*, p.16.

122. Paley, *The Middlesex Justices Act of 1792.*

123. Paley, *The Middlesex Justices Act of 1792*, pp.227–261; Radzinowicz. *A History of English Criminal Law, Vol. 3*, pp.108–148; Low, *The Regency Underworld*, pp.7–11; Wright. J. (Ed), *The Speeches of the Right Honourable Charles James Fox in the House of Commons*, Vol. IV, p.430 (London: Longman, 1815).

124. Briggs, *The Age of Improvement*, p.132; Thompson, *The Making of the English Working Class*, pp.19, 116; Sparrow, *Secret Service under Pitt's Administrations.*

125. Emsley, *The Home Office and its Sources of Information and Investigation*, pp.550, 561.

126. Thompson, *The Making of the English Working Class*, pp.156–157; Hammond & Hammond, *The Village Labourer 1760–1832*, p.121.

127. LMA: *MJ/OC/012*, p.534, County Day Minutes, 26 October, 1795; Rowlandson & Pugin, *Session House, Clerkenwell: in The Microcosm of London*, 1809; see also Ackermann, *The Microcosm of London, Vol. 3*, p.42. The Sessions House still stands and is today occupied by a Masonic centre.

128. Baker, *The Proclamation Society;* Thorne. *History of Parliament: the House of Commons 1790–1820, Members G–P,* p.524; Webb & Webb. *The Parish & The County,* p.562.

129. Thorne, *History of Parliament: the House of Commons 1790–1820, Members G–P,* p.524; *Constituencies,* p.258; Webb & Webb, *The Parish & The County,* p.562; Baker, *The Proclamation Society;* Emsley, *The Home Office and its Sources of Information and Investigation,* p.561; James & Critchley, *The Maul and the Pear Tree,* pp.20–22.

130. Watson, *The Reign of George III,* p.360; Thompson, *The Making of the English Working Class,* p.157.

131. Thompson, *The Making of the English Working Class,* pp.158–159; Wright. *The Works of James Gillray,* pp.199–200.

132. LMA: *MJ/OC/013,* County Day Minutes, 14 January 1796.

133. LMA: *MJ/OC/013,* County Day Minutes, June 1796, September 1796.

134. Hammond & Hammond, *The Town Labourer,* p.106; *The Times,* 6 March, 1797; Watson, *The Reign of George III,* pp.372–3.

135. Watson, *The Reign of George III,* pp.372–3; Manwaring & Dobrée, *The Floating Republic,* pp.237, 250.

136. Manwaring & Dobrée, *The Floating Republic,* p.238; LMA: *MA/G/GEN/2,* Minutes of Prison Committee, 13 September 1797.

137. LMA: *MA/G/GEN/2,* Minutes of Prison Committee, 12 June 1797.

138. LMA: *MA/G/GEN/2,* Minutes of Prison Committee, 22 May 1797, 12 June 1797.

139. Watson, *The Reign of George III,* pp.392–397; Thompson, *The Making of the English Working Class,* pp.183–188.

140. PRO: *PC 1/44/161;* McCalman, *Ultra-radicalism and Convivial Debating Clubs in London,* p.318; Emsley. *The Home Office and its Sources of Information and Investigation,* p.554; McCalman, *Radical Underworld,* p.22; Hone, *For the Cause of Truth,* p.63; Paley, *The Middlesex Justices Act of 1792,* p.312; Gurney, *Merceron's Trials,* Second Trial, p.96.

141. Jay, *The Unfortunate Colonel Despard,* pp.278–279; Thompson, *The Making of the English Working Class,* p.188.

142. LMA: *MJ/OC/013,* County Day Minutes, 23 April, 1798; *Considerations on the late Elections for Westminster & Middlesex, etc.* pp.21, 24.

143. LMA: *MA/G/GEN/2,* Minutes of Prison Committee, 11 April 1798; *MJ/OC/013,* County Day Minutes, 24 May 1798.

144. Jay, *The Unfortunate Colonel Despard,* pp.282–284.

145. Jay, *The Unfortunate Colonel Despard,* p.285; Thorne, *History of Parliament: the House of Commons 1790–1820, Members A–F,* p.510.

146. Baer, Marc, *Burdett, Sir Francis (1770–1844), Oxford DNB,* (www.oxforddnb.com/view/article/3962, accessed 4 May 2006); Patterson, *Sir Francis Burdett and his Times,* frontispiece, p.67; Thompson, *The Making of the English Working Class,* p.493; LMA: *MA/G/GEN/2,* Minutes of Prison Committee, 26 November 1798; *MJ/OC/013,* County Day Minutes, 14 January 1799.

147. *The Times*, 22 December 1798; *Annual Register*, 1799, p.197.
148. *The Times*, 22 December 1798; George, *Catalogue of Political & Personal Satires, etc, Vol. 8*. No. 9341: Gillray, *Citizens Visiting the Bastille*.
149. *Annual Register*, 1799, p.199; *The Times*, 22 December 1798.
150. Thompson, *The Making of the English Working Class*, p.160; *The Times*, 22 December 1798.

CHAPTER VI

INFAMY, OPPRESSION, CRUELTY AND EXTORTION

151. Southey, *Letters from England*, Vol. II, p.252.
152. *The Times*, 27 December 1798, 7 January 1799.
153. *The Times*, 7 January 1799.
154. *The Times*, 7 January 1799; Patterson, *Sir Francis Burdett and his Times*, p.71.
155. LMA: *MJ/OC/013*, County Day Minutes, 10 January 1799.
156. LMA: *MJ/OC/013*, County Day Minutes, 14 January 1799.
157. LMA: *MJ/OC/013*, County Day Minutes, 14 January 1799.
158. *The Times*, 7 January 1799; LMA: *MJ/OC/013*, County Day Minutes, 15 January 1799.
159. *The Times*, 21 February 1799, p.2.
160. *The Times*, 26 February 1799, p.2.
161. *The Times*, 7 March 1799, p.2.
162. Bowles, *Thoughts on the late General Election*, p.96; LMA: *MA/G/GEN/2*, Minutes of Prison Committee, 6 May 1799.
163. Patterson, *Sir Francis Burdett and his Times*, p.73; *The Times*, 22 May 1799.
164. LMA: *MA/G/GEN/2*, Minutes of Prison Committee, 28 May 1799; PRO: *PC 1/44/161* (Ford to Mrs Despard, 31 August 1799); Jay, *The Unfortunate Colonel Despard*, p.290. Jay's book gives an account of Despard's subsequent career: released in April 1801, he was rearrested in November 1802, tried and convicted of High Treason and executed in a blaze of publicity in February 1803.
165. *The Times*, 16 May 1800, p.2.
166. *The Times*, 16 May 1800, p.2; *Trial of James Hadfield*, p.1296; PRO: *TS 11/223*, deposition of Major Wright.
167. PRO: *TS 11/223*, interrogation of James Hadfield; Buckingham, *Memoirs of the Court and Cabinets of George III, etc*, Vol. III, p.70 (Grenville to Buckingham, 16 May 1800).
168. PRO: *PC 1/3490*, deposition of Bannister Truelock; Buckingham, *Memoirs of the Court and Cabinets of George III, etc*, Vol. III, p.70 (Grenville to Buckingham, 16 May 1800); *The Times*, 17 May 1800, p.3.
169. PRO: *PC 1/3490*, depositions relating to Hadfield case.
170. Eigen, Joel Peter, *Hadfield, James (1771/2–1841)*, *Oxford DNB*, (www.oxforddnb.com/view/article/41013, accessed 30 January 2007); PRO: *PC 1/3490*, depositions relating to Hadfield case; PRO: *TS 11/223*.

171. PRO: *PC 1/3490, depositions relating to Hadfield case;* PRO: *TS 11/223; PP 1817 (Police),* p.82 (evidence of John Willson), p.182 (evidence of Joseph Fletcher).

172. Howell, *State Trials,* Vol. XXVII (1798–1800), pp.1281–1356; *The Times,* 27 June 1800, p.2; Eigen, Joel Peter, *Hadfield, James (1771/2–1841), Oxford DNB,* (www.oxforddnb.com/view/article/41013, accessed 30 January 2007).

173. PRO: *TS 11/223, deposition of Major Wright;* Howell, *State Trials,* Vol. XXVII (1798–1800), p.1296, *evidence of Major Wright;* PRO: *PROB 11/1600, will of Major Wright;* Merceron Family Archives.

174. Debrett, *Parliamentary Register,* Vol. XII (1800), p.352.

175. LMA: *MA/G/GEN/2,* Minutes of Prison Committee, June 1800.

176. LMA: *MA/G/GEN/2,* Minutes of Prison Committee, June 1800; *MJ/OC/013,* County Day Minutes, 10 July 1800.

177. *An Impartial Statement of the Inhuman Cruelties Discovered in the Coldbath Fields Prison.*

178. *The Times,* 12 July 1800, Debrett, *Parliamentary Register,* Vol. XII (1800), p.352.

179. *An Impartial Statement of the Inhuman Cruelties Discovered in the Coldbath Fields Prison;* Webb & Webb, *English Prisons under Local Government,* p.52.

180. *The Times,* 12 July 1800.

181. LMA: *MA/G/GEN/2,* Minutes of Prison Committee, 18 July 1800.

182. *The Times,* 22 July 1800, Hague, *William Pitt the Younger,* p.458.

183. *The Times,* 23 July 1800. Pitt's comments have been translated into a first person narrative from the reported speech in which they were printed.

184. Thorne, *History of Parliament: the House of Commons 1790–1820, Members Q–Y,* p.147; *The Correspondence of Jeremy Bentham: Vol. 6 (1798–1801),* p.335. Bentham, the philosopher and a proponent of prison reform, saw the Coldbath Fields scandal as vindicating his proposals for a radical new design of prison building known as 'Panopticon', whereby a small number of supervisors, housed at the hub of a wheel, could monitor and control the activity of a far greater number of prisoners housed along the rim. His letter (to Henry Addington, the Speaker and future Prime Minister) states that the Panopticon would render 'all such abuses physically impossible'.

185. LMA: *MA/G/GEN/2,* Minutes of Prison Committee, 26 September 1800.

186. *The Times,* 13 February 1801; 16 May 1801.

187. Burke, *The Knightage of Great Britain and Ireland,* p.213 (London: Edward Churton, 1841); *The Criminal Recorder, etc.,* Vol. II, p.197 (Nottingham: R. Dawson, 1815).

CHAPTER VII

DEMOCRACY IN ACTION

188. *The Scum Uppermost, etc.* p.12.

189. LMA: *MA/G/GEN/2,* Minutes of Prison Committee, 1796–1807.

190. Pevsner, *The Buildings of England: London Vol. 2,* p.66 et seq; Weinreb & Hibbert,

The London Encyclopædia. p.61; Robinson & Chesshyre, *The Green;* Brayley, *London & Middlesex,* Vol. V, p.279; LMA: *MA/DC/008; The Times,* 7 April 1801.

191. *English Historical Documents,* Vol. XI (1783–1832), (Hale to Colquhoun, 21 October 1800); Hale, *A Letter to Samuel Whitbread, etc.,* pp.5–8.

192. *The Eclectic Review,* Jul–Dec 1818, p.210.

193. *English Historical Documents,* Vol. XI (1783–1832), (Hale to Colquhoun, 21st October 1800); Hale, *A Letter to Samuel Whitbread, etc.,* pp.15 *et seq.; The Times,* 20 December 1800, pp.1–2.

194. THLHA: *VM:* 9 April 1798; 15 April 1800; 6 April 1801.

195. THLHA: *VM:* 19 May 1801.

196. THLHA: *VM:* 15 April 1802; 19 April 1802.

197. PRO: *C 13/70/17; PROB 11/1366 (will of Anthony Natt).*

198. *The Times,* 2 July 1802.

199. *The Times,* 13 July 1802.

200. *The Times,* 14 July 1802.

201. *The Times,* 14 July 1802, *Morning Chronicle,* 14 July 1802 (cited in Anon., *The Abuses of Prisons, etc.,* p.31.)

202. *The Times,* 15 July 1802; Bowles, *Thoughts on the late General Election,* pp.54–55.

203. Thorne, *History of Parliament: the House of Commons 1790–1820, Members A–F,* p.353; *Middlesex Poll Book 1802.*

204. *The Times,* 16–30 July 1802, especially 16–17 July, 19 July, 21 July, 23 July.

205. *The Times,* 31 July 1802; *Morning Chronicle,* 30 July 1802 (cited in Anon., *The Abuse of Prisons, etc.,* p.31); Thorne, *History of Parliament: the House of Commons 1790–1820, Constituencies,* p.258; Thompson, *The Making of the English Working Class,* p.494; Patterson, *Sir Francis Burdett and his Times.* p.140.

206. THLHA: *VM:* 19 April 1802, 11 April 1803.

207. *Report from Committee on the State of Police in the Metropolis (1816)* (evidence of Joshua King); *The Times,* 26 November 1816.

208. THLHA: *VM:* 31 March 1804.

209. THLHA: *VM:* 2 April 1804, 3 April 1804, 12 April 1804.

210. THLHA: *VM:* 12 April 1804, 17 April 1804, 27 April 1804, 22 May 1804.

211. THLHA: *VM:* 15 April 1805, 16 April 1805.

212. LMA: *MJ/OC/014,* County Day Minutes, 13 January 1803, 12 April 1804.

213. *The Times,* 14 July 1804, p.2.

214. Anon., *Full Account of the Proceedings at the Middlesex Election (1804),* p.13.

215. Thorne, *History of Parliament: the House of Commons 1790–1820, Members G–P,* p.523; Anon., *Full Account of the Proceedings at the Middlesex Election (1804),* pp.4,12,18; *The Spirit of the Public Journals for 1804,* Vol. VIII, p.367.

216. Anon., *Full Account of the Proceedings at the Middlesex Election (1804),* pp.21–30.

217. Anon., *Full Account of the Proceedings at the Middlesex Election (1804);* George, *Catalogue of Political & Personal Satires, etc, Vol. 8.* No. 10,264.

218. Patterson, *Sir Francis Burdett and his Times.* p.151; Thorne. *History of Parliament: the House of Commons 1790–1820, Members G–P,* p.523.

CHAPTER VIII
ABSOLUTE POWER CORRUPTS ABSOLUTELY

219. *The Universal Magazine*, August 1807, p.100.

220. THLHA: *VM*: 1805–1809; *London Gazette*, 1 November 1808, p.1493, 7 November 1809, p.1784, 3 November 1810, p.1751; PRO: *C 13/70/17*.

221. Webb & Webb, *Statutory Authorities for Special Purposes*, pp.80–91.

222. Webb & Webb, *The Parish and the County*, pp.513, 564–566; LMA: *MJ/OC/ 19–21, County Day Minutes, 1822–1825*; LMA: *HFCS 19, Minutes* 26 August 1800; *The Times*, 23 January 1792, p.1, 20 June 1794, p.1, 24 June 1794, p.1, 14 July 1804, p.2; THLHA: *VM*: 30 March 1807.

223. Inwood, *A History of London*, p.323; Broodbank, *History of the Port of London*, Vol. I, pp.92–121; *The Times*, 5 August 1806, p.3.

224. Inwood, *A History of London*, p.323; PRO: *KB 1/41/1, affidavit of William Venning*.

225. Graham-Leigh, *London's Water Wars*, pp.85–87.

226. *London Gazette:* 18 October 1808, p.1429; 15 May 1810, p.716; PRO: *KB 1/41/1, affidavit of John Ord & Thomas Barnes; The Times*, 28 October 1809, p.3, 4 July 1811, p.10, 31 October 1818, p.2; Wright, *The Dolphin*, pp.38, 68; The Law Journal for the Year 1825, Vol. III, p.241 (London: J.W.Paget, 1825).

227. *The Civil Engineer and Architect's Journal*, January 1850, pp.29; Matthews, *Hydraulia*, pp.112–113; *The Times*, 28 October 1809, p.3; Graham-Leigh, *London's Water Wars*, p.35.

228. Matthews, *Hydraulia*, pp.112–113; Inwood, *A History of London*, pp.434–435; Wright, *The Dolphin*, pp.38, 68; *The Times*, 31 October 1818, p.2, 28 November 1818, p.3.

229. *London Gazette*, 21 February 1797, p.181; *The Royal Military Panorama*, Vol. IV (1814), p.553.

230. Watson, *The Reign of George III*, pp.365, 376, 415.

231. George Mainwaring was paid £425 per annum from 1811 for his 'extraordinary trouble' in administering the relief payments for militia families. See LMA: *MJ/OC/016*, County Day Minutes, 31 October 1811; *MJ/OC/016*, 29 October 1812; see also LMA: *MF/L*, introduction.

232. A comprehensive account of the corrupt system in place, in which both Williams and Stable are clearly implicated, is described in the court-martial of Colonel Mark Beaufoy in 1813. See *The Royal Military Panorama*, Vol. IV (1814), pp.30–50, 117–132, 261–264, 362–369, 479–488, 543–578.

233. *LMA: MJ/OC/16, County Day Minutes*, 2 June 1808.

234. *LMA: MJ/OC/16, County Day Minutes*, 27 April 1809.

235. LMA: *MA/G/CBF/005; MJ/OC/16, County Day Minutes*, 18 May 1809, 20 September 1810; Anon., *The Abuse of Prisons, etc.*

236. Anon., *The Abuse of Prisons, etc.*

237. *PP 1817 (Police)*, p.180 (evidence of Joseph Fletcher).

238. *PP 1817 (Police)*, p.181–2 (evidence of Joseph Fletcher).

239. *Minutes of evidence before a Select Committee, etc (Police, 1816)*, pp.305–310, (evidence of James May); PP 1817 (Police), p.69 (evidence of Joshua King); THLHA: *VM:* 3 April 1809.

240. *PP 1817 (Police)*, p.76 (evidence of Robert Wrightson). Wrightson's petition is at LMA: *MJ/SP/1810/01/041*.

241. *PP 1817 (Police)*, p.84 (evidence of James Weston).

242. *Minutes of evidence before a Select Committee, etc (Police, 1816)*, pp.305–310, (evidence of James May); PP 1817 (Police), p.204 (evidence of Joseph Merceron).

243. Foster, *Alumni Oxiensis 1715–1886, Ser. 2, 1–2*.

CHAPTER IX
THE REVEREND KING

244. The description of King comes from a private memoir by his niece, later the wife of the Bishop of Carlisle, quoted in *Notes on the parish of Woodchurch*, p.154.

245. *Notes on the parish of Woodchurch*, pp.153–155.

246. IGI; *Notes on the parish of Woodchurch*, pp.153–155.

247. Burns, *My Unfortunate Parish*, p.272; THLHA: *VM:* 23 August 1813 (Report of sub-committee on Bethnal Green Bill, 4 May 1813); VCH *Middlesex*, Volume 11, *Stepney, Bethnal Green*, pp.212–217.

248. THLHA: *VM:* 24 April 1810, 6 May 1806, 19 May 1801; BNC: *D/148, Liptrap to inhabitants of Bethnal Green*, 25 March 1812; VCH *Middlesex, Vol. 2: General*, pp.112–120, *Table of population 1801–1901* (www.british-history.ac.uk/report.asp?compid=22159), accessed 10 July 2016.

249. Anon, *Minutes of evidence before a Select Committee, etc. (Police, 1816)*, p.278, (evidence of Joshua King).

250. Anon, *Minutes of evidence before a Select Committee, etc. (Police, 1816)*, p.278, (evidence of Joshua King).

251. BNC: *D/148, King to inhabitants of Bethnal Green*, 14 February 1812.

252. BNC: *D/148, Liptrap to inhabitants of Bethnal Green*, 28 February 1812; THLHA: *VM:* 27 February 1812.

253. Huish, *Memoirs of George the Fourth*, pp.138–139.

254. Huish, *Memoirs of George the Fourth*, pp.138–139.

255. BNC: *D/148, Liptrap to inhabitants of Bethnal Green*, 28 February 1812, 17 March 1812.

256. BNC: *D/148, Liptrap to inhabitants of Bethnal Green*, 17 March 1812.

257. BNC: *D/148, Merceron to inhabitants of Bethnal Green*, 21 March 1812.

258. THLHA: *VM:* 25 March 1812; 30 March 1812; 31 March 1812.

259. Anon, *Minutes of evidence before a Select Committee, etc. (Police, 1816)*, p.283, (evidence of Joshua King).

260. THLHA: *VM:* 15 December 1812; Anon, *Minutes of evidence before a Select Committee, etc. (Police, 1816)*, p.283 (evidence of Joshua King).

261. *The Times*, 30 May 1804, 14 July 1813, 2 September 1813, 30 August 1814, 15 December 1815; *London Gazette*, no.16705, 20 February 1813, p.391. Despite the failure of his business, Liptrap's name lives on in Cape Liptrap, on the coast of Victoria, Australia. It was named after Liptrap by its discover, James Grant in 1802. See *The Logbooks of The Lady Nelson*, by Ida Lee and Alice J.Christie, (paperback edition) Kessinger Publishing, 2004. p.22.

262. THLHA: *VM:* 28 January 1813; IGI (Batch M046985, W.F.Platt to Mary Elizabeth Wilkinson, 8 January 1806; Batch M046984, Mary Elizabeth Wilmet (sic) to David Wilkinson, 28 May 1789; Batch C046982, Mary Elizabeth Wilmot born, daughter of John Wilmot, 7 April 1770); PP 1817 (Police), p.268 (*evidence of W.F. Platt*); Merceron's Trials, first trial, p.42 (*evidence of James May*).

263. THLHA: *VM:* 28 January 1813; *The Times*, 24 February 1813, p.4 col. C.

264. THLHA: *VM:* 14 April 1813, 23 August 1813 (Report of sub-committee on Bethnal Green Bill).

265. THLHA: *VM:* 23 August 1813 (Report of sub-committee on Bethnal Green Bill).

266. THLHA: *VM:* 19 April 1813; 20 April 1813; BNC: *D/148, Resolutions of the Committee for obtaining a New Act, etc.*, 19 April 1813.

267. THLHA: *VM:* 23 August 1813 (Report of sub-committee on Bethnal Green Bill, 27 April 1813); BNC: *D/148, King to Hodson*, 27 April 1813.

268. THLHA: *VM:* 23 August 1813 (Report of sub-committee on Bethnal Green Bill, 4 May 1813).

269. THLHA: *VM:* 23 August 1813 (Report of sub-committee on Bethnal Green Bill, 4 May 1813).

270. THLHA: *VM:* 10 May 1813, 23 August 1813 (Report of sub-committee on Bethnal Green Bill, 4 May 1813, 7 May 1813); BNC: *Hurst, Bethnal Green 3, King to Heber*, undated (1823).

271. BNC: *D/148, King to Hodson*, 7 May 1813.

272. THLHA: *VM:* 23 August 1813 (Report of sub-committee on Bethnal Green Bill, 11 May 1813, 17 May 1813); BNC: *D/148, King to Hodson*, 12 May 1813.

273. BNC: D/148, King to Hodson, 5 June 1813.

274. *The Times*, 14 June 1813, p.2 col. E; Anon, *Minutes of evidence before a Select Committee, etc. (Police, 1816)*, p.283 (evidence of Joshua King).

275. Beattie, J.M., *Garrow, Sir William (1760–1840),Oxford DNB*, (www.oxforddnb.com/view/article/10410, accessed 8 September 2006; Scarlett, *A Memoir, etc*, p.87; Anon, *The Law Student*, published in *The Analectic Magazine, etc.*, April 1811, pp.326–39; *The Times*, 14 June 1813, p.2 col. E.

276. *PP 1816 (Police)* p.201–3 (evidence of Joseph Merceron); *The Times*, 14 June 1813, p.2 col. E.

277. Anon, *Minutes of evidence before a Select Committee, etc (Police, 1816)*, p.283, (evidence of Joshua King); Davenport-Hines, Richard, *Wilks, John (1776?–1854)*, *Oxford DNB*, (www.oxforddnb.com/view/article/29432, accessed 25 July 2007).

278. Gurney, *Merceron's Trials*, first trial, pp.3,7,11.

279. Gurney, *Merceron's Trials*, first trial, pp.8,9.

280. Gurney, *Merceron's Trials,* first trial, pp.10,11.

281. Gurney, *Merceron's Trials,* first trial, pp.45, 51; THLHA: *VM:* 6 April 1814, 11 April 1814.

282. Gurney, *Merceron's Trials,* first trial, p.13; *PP 1817 (Police),* p.72 (evidence of Joshua King).

283. *VM:* 11 April 1814, 12 April 1814, 4 May 1814.

284. *VM:* 4 May 1814.

285. *VM:* 4 May 1814; *PP 1817 (Police),* p.83 (evidence of John Willson); p.76 (evidence of Robert Wrightson); p.273 (evidence of Saunderson Sturtevant); *PP 1816 (Police),* (evidence of Joshua King).

CHAPTER X

TROUBLE BREWING

286. Brougham, *Opinions of Lord Brougham, etc,* p.222.

287. Webb & Webb. *History of Liquor Licensing,* p.76; Holdsworth, *A History of English Law,* Vol. X, p185.

288. Holdsworth, *A History of English Law,* Vol. X, p185; Burn, *The Justice of the Peace, and Parish Officer,* Vol. I, p.33.

289. *PP 1816 (Police),* p.45 (evidence of Patrick Colquhoun); PP 1817 (Police), p.37 (evidence of J.T.B.Beaumont); for 'flash-houses', see Low, *The Regency Underworld,* p.70.

290. PRO: *HO 42/155* p.123. See also Thirlwall, *A Vindication, etc.,* p.285. Quote on Beaumont from: Beaumont, *Barber Beaumont,* p.viii.

291. Pearson, Robin, *Beaumont, John Thomas Barber (1774–1841),Oxford DNB,* (www.oxforddnb.com/view/article/1877, accessed 4 January 2006; also Beaumont, *Barber Beaumont.*

292. *PP 1816 (Police)* pp.68, 241 (evidence of J.T.B.Beaumont); Thirlwall, *A Vindication, etc,* p.297. The clerk to the Sewers Commission was John Wright Unwin, another of those men whose name seems to crop up whenever contracts are awarded. Wright Unwin was both a lawyer and a surgeon, and combined his duties for the Sewers Commission with another lucrative post as a County Coroner, in which role he acted in the case of the Ratcliff Highway murders. See LMA: *THCS 36,* 25 October 1811, *MJ/OC/016,* 19 July 1810; James & Critchley, *The Maul and the Pear Tree.*

293. *PP 1816 (Police)* p.241 (evidence of J. T. B. Beaumont); Thirlwall, *A Vindication, etc,* pp.339–341.

294. *PP 1816 (Police)* pp.68–69, 242 (evidence of J. T. B. Beaumont); PRO: *HO 42/155,* p.123.

295. *PP 1816 (Police)* (evidence of Joseph Fletcher) (also reported in *The Times,* 19 September 1816, p.2); *PP 1817 (Police)* pp.130–148 (evidence of Joseph Fletcher); Henekey, *A Full and Complete Refutation, etc;* Thirlwall, *A Vindication of the Magistrates, etc,* p.252.

296. *PP 1817 (Police)* pp.130–148 (evidence of Joseph Fletcher).
297. *PP 1817 (Police)* pp.130–148 (evidence of Joseph Fletcher).
298. *PP 1816 (Police)* p.242 (evidence of J.T.B.Beaumont).
299. *PP 1816 (Police)* p.242 (evidence of J.T.B.Beaumont); PRO: *HO 42/155*, p.123.
300. Henekey, *A Full and Complete Refutation, etc*, p.16; *The Times*, 19 September 1816, p.2.
301. *PP 1817 (Police)* pp.130–148 (evidence of Joseph Fletcher).
302. PRO: *HO 42/155*, p.123; Thirlwall, *A Vindication, etc*, p.297.
303. *PP 1816 (Police)* p.242 (evidence of J.T.B.Beaumont); PRO: *HO 42/155*, p.123.
304. *London Gazette*, 19 November 1814, p.2301; Thorne, *History of Parliament: the House of Commons 1790–1820, Members G–P*, p.524.
305. LMA: *MJ/OC/017, County Day Minutes*, 1 December 1814; Webb & Webb, *Statutory Authorities for Special Purposes*, pp.80–91; *London Gazette:* 18 October 1808, p.1429; 15 May 1810, p.716; *The Times*, 4 July 1811, p.10.
306. LMA: *MJ/OC/017, County Day Minutes*, 1 December 1814; *THCS 36*, 13 January 1815; Anon., *An Address to the Magistracy of the County of Middlesex, etc.*
307. Anon., *An Address to the Magistracy of the County of Middlesex, etc.*
308. LMA: *MJ/OC/017, County Day Minutes*, 1 December 1814, 12 January 1815, 6 April 1815.
309. *PP 1817 (Police)* p.145 (evidence of Joseph Fletcher).
310. PRO: *HO 42/155*, p.123.
311. *London Gazette*, 2 March 1822, p.372; LMA: *DL/C/575/100/2*.
312. *The Times*, 25 August 1814, p.2.
313. Thorne, *History of Parliament, Vol. III*, p.178; Thorne, Roland, *Bennet, Henry Grey (1776–1836, Oxford DNB*, (www.oxforddnb.com/view/article/37179, accessed 12 October 2006).

CHAPTER XI

SATURNALIA REVEALED

314. Anon., *An Address to the Magistracy of the County of Middlesex, etc*, p.4.
315. Low, *The Regency Underworld*, pp.21–24.
316. Low, *The Regency Underworld*, pp.25–27; LMA: *MJ/OC/017, County Day Minutes*, 20 February 1812; James & Critchley, *The Maul and the Pear Tree*.
317. *Kirby's Wonderful and Scientific Museum, etc*, pp.114–148; James & Critchley, *The Maul and the Pear Tree*.
318. Low, *The Regency Underworld*, p.29; Halévy, *England in 1815*, p.44.
319. Radzinowicz, *A History of English Criminal Law, Vol. 3*, p.354; *The Times*, 4 April 1816, p.2. For the government's defeat on income tax, see Halévy, *The Liberal Awakening*, pp.6–8.
320. *The Times*, 4 April 1816, p.2; Low, *The Regency Underworld*, p.35.
321. *The Times*, 4 April 1816, p.2; Hansard, *Parliamentary Debates*, Vol. XXXIII,

pp.888–892; Radzinowicz, *A History of English Criminal Law, Vol. 3*, p.354; Romilly, *Memoirs*, Vol. III, p.239.

322. LMA: *MJ/OC/o18, County Day Minutes:* April 1816, 30 May 1816.

323. *The Times*, 17 November 1815, 24 November 1815. Beaumont's letters to *The Times* were subsequently published in pamphlet form on 9 January 1816: Beaumont, *Letters on Public House Licensing, etc.*

324. *PP 1816 (Police)* pp.1–31(evidence of Sir N.Conant); *The Times*, 28 August 1816; LMA: *MJ/OC/o17, County Day Minutes:* 1 December 1814.

325. *PP 1816 (Police)* pp.1–31(evidence of Sir N.Conant); *The Times*, 30 August 1816.

326. Paley, Ruth, *Colquhoun, Patrick (1745–1820), Oxford DNB*, (www.oxforddnb.com/view/article/5992, accessed 4 January 2006).

327. Low, *The Regency Underworld*, p.17; *PP 1816 (Police)* pp.32, 45–51 (evidence of P.Colquhoun); *The Times*, 2 September 1816.

328. *PP 1816 (Police)* p.50 (evidence of P.Colquhoun).

329. *PP 1816 (Police)* pp.65–70 (evidence of J.T.B.Beaumont); also reported in *The Times*, 10–11September 1816.

330. *The Times*, 10 September 1816, p.2.

331. *The Times*, 10 September 1816, p.2.

332. *PP 1816 (Police)* pp.68–71 (evidence of J.T.B.Beaumont).

333. *PP 1816 (Police)* (evidence of Wm. Stocker, J.Huxen, John Gifford, Joseph Fletcher). Also reported in *The Times*, 13 September 1816, 19 September 1816.

334. *The Times*, 2 October 1816, 11 October 1816. For Rice Davies, see *PP 1817 (Police)* p.46 (evidence of Rice Davies).

335. THLHA: *VM:* 24 April 1816; *The Times*, 7 December 1816.

336. THLHA: *VM:* 24 April 1816.

337. THLHA: *VM:* 16 May 1816; *The Times*, 7 December 1816.

338. *PP 1816 (Police)* (evidence of Joshua King).

339. *PP 1816 (Police)* (evidence of Joshua King).

340. May became Bethnal Green's vestry clerk in June 1788. See *VM:* 6 June 1788.

341. *PP 1816 (Police)* (evidence of James May).

342. *PP 1816 (Police)* (evidence of James May).

CHAPTER XII

THAT GUILTY, THAT SHUFFLING MAGISTRATE...

343. Hansard, *Parliamentary Debates*, Vol. XXXV, pp.499–500.

344. *PP 1816 (Police)* (evidence of Joseph Merceron); Thale, *Francis Place: Autobiography*, p.70.

345. *PP 1816 (Police)* (evidence of Joseph Merceron).

346. *PP 1816 (Police)*, p.200 (evidence of Joseph Merceron).

347. *PP 1816 (Police)*, p.200 (evidence of Joseph Merceron).

348. *PP 1816 (Police)*, p.241 (evidence of J.T. B. Beaumont).

349. *PP 1816 (Police); The Times,* 28 August, 29 August, 30 August, 31 August, 2 September 1816.

350. *PP 1816 (Police),* p.223 (evidence of Joseph Merceron), *PP 1817 (Police),* p.72 (evidence of Joshua King).

351. *The Times,* 2 September 1816; *PP 1817 (Police),* p.114 (evidence of Isaac Rennoldson).

352. *PP 1817 (Police),* p.114 (evidence of Isaac Rennoldson); Gurney, *Merceron's Trials, 2nd Trial,* pp.35–54.

353. Gurney, *Merceron's Trials, 2nd Trial,* pp.35–54.

354. *The Times,* 10, 11, 13 September 1816.

355. *PP 1817 (Police),* p.37 (evidence of J.T.B.Beaumont); Gurney, *Merceron's Trials, 2nd Trial,* p.41.

356. *The Times,* 17 September 1816; Anon, *Minutes of evidence before a Select Committee, etc (Police, 1816),* frontispiece, p.283, etc, (evidence of Joshua King).

357. *The Times,* 19 September, 18 October, 1 November 1816.

358. Halévy, *The Liberal Awakening,* pp.12–14; Thompson, *The Making of the English Working Class,* pp.693–694; Anon, *Minutes of evidence before a Select Committee, etc (Police, 1816),* p.349 (evidence of Joseph Merceron).

359. See Halévy, *The Liberal Awakening,* pp.12–14; *The Times,* 29 August 1816.

360. PRO: *HO 42/155,* p.111, Eldon to Sidmouth, 4 November 1816.

361. PRO: *HO 42/155,* p.111, Eldon to Sidmouth, 4 November 1816.

362. Halévy, *The Liberal Awakening,* p.16.

363. *The Times,* 16 November 1816.

364. *The Times,* 23 November 1816.

365. *The Times,* 23 November 1816.

366. *The Times,* 26 November 1816.

367. *The Times,* 26 November 1816.

368. Blouet, Olwyn Mary, *Buxton, Sir Thomas Fowell (1786–1845), Oxford DNB,* (www.oxforddnb.com/view/article/4247, accessed 30 October 2006); *The Times,* 26 November 1816.

369. *The Times,* 28 November 1816.

370. *The Times,* 26 November 1816.

371. *The Times,* 26 November 1816.

372. *The Times,* 26 November 1816.

373. *PP 1817 (Police),* p.104 (evidence of James Greenwood).

374. Thompson, *The Making of the English Working Class,* p.694; Halévy, *The Liberal Awakening,* p.17.

375. *Thistlewood's Trial,* pp.99–103; Thompson, *The Making of the English Working Class,* p.695; Halévy, *The Liberal Awakening,* pp.17–18.

376. *Thistlewood's Trial,* pp.242–243.

377. *The Times,* 7 December 1816.

378. *The Times,* 7 December 1816.

379. Beaumont, *A Letter to the Right Honourable Lord Sidmouth, etc,* pp.441, 452.

380. PRO: *HO 42/155,* p.113, Garrow to Sidmouth, 31 December 1816.

381. PRO: *HO 42/155*, p.117, Williams to Sidmouth, 28 January 1817.
382. Thirlwall, *A Vindication, etc.*
383. Thirlwall, *A Vindication, etc*, preface; *The Times*, 7 May 1817, p.6.
384. Thirlwall, *A Vindication, etc*, pp.223–226.
385. *The Monthly Review*, April 1817, p.419; Hansard. *Parliamentary Debates*, Vol. XXXV, pp.495–498; *The Times*, 22 February 1817, p.2.
386. Hansard. *Parliamentary Debates*, Vol. XXXV, p.499.
387. Hansard. *Parliamentary Debates*, Vol. XXXV, pp.499–500; *The Times*, 22 February 1817, p.2. NB. The two accounts of this debate differ slightly and are in reported speech: I have drawn Bennet's words from both accounts and written them in the first person.
388. *The Times*, 22 February 1817, p.2.
389. *PP 1817 (Police)*, p.98 (evidence of Peter Renvoize).

CHAPTER XIII
TIPPING THE SCALES

390. *PP 1817 (Police)*, pp.76–79 (evidence of Robert Wrightson).
391. Hansard, *Parliamentary Debates*, Vol. XXXV (Jan–Apr 1817), p.714; see also Thompson, *The Making of the English Working Class*, p.530.
392. *PP 1817 (Police)*, pp.37, 46, 47 (evidence of J. T. B. Beaumont, Rice Davies, Casten Rohde).
393. *PP 1817 (Police)*, pp.69–73 (evidence of Joshua King).
394. *PP 1817 (Police)*, pp.73–74 (evidence of Joshua King).
395. *PP 1817 (Police)*, pp.76–79 (evidence of Robert Wrightson).
396. *PP 1817 (Police)*, pp.82–85 (evidence of John Betts, John Willson, James Weston, John Blundell).
397. *PP 1817 (Police)*, pp.86–90 (evidence of James May).
398. *PP 1817 (Police)*, pp.89–94 (evidence of James May, Joseph Merceron).
399. *PP 1817 (Police)*, pp.98–103 (evidence of Peter Renvoize).
400. *PP 1817 (Police)*, pp.103–105 (evidence of James Greenwood).
401. *PP 1817 (Police)*, pp.108–109 (evidence of Edward Wentworth, William Hale).
402. *PP 1817 (Police)*, pp.114–119 (evidence of Isaac Rennoldson, John Perry).
403. *PP 1817 (Police)*, p.243 (evidence of Sampson Hanbury).
404. *PP 1817 (Police)*, pp.128–148 (evidence of Edward Markland, Joseph Fletcher, John Williams, William Stocker).
405. THLHA: *VM:* 7 April 1817.
406. *PP 1817 (Police)*, pp.257–267 (evidence of Joseph Merceron).
407. *PP 1817 (Police)*, pp.267–275 (evidence of W. F. Platt, Samuel Ames, Alexander Forbes, George Seaman Inman, Saunderson Sturtevant, John Desormeaux).
408. *PP 1817 (Police)*, p.273 (evidence of Saunderson Sturtevant).
409. *PP 1817 (Police)*, pp.278–279 (evidence of Joshua King).
410. *PP 1817 (Police)*, p.294 (licensed victuallers petition).

411. *PP 1817 (Police)*, pp.280–292 (evidence of Thomas Thirlwall); *The Times*, 3 May 1817, 7 May 1817; Romilly, *Memoirs*, Vol. III, p.291.

412. *The Times*, 4 June 1817, 7 June 1817; *The Gentleman's Magazine*, 1817 p.69; *PP 1817 (Police)*, pp.1–21.

413. *PP 1817 (Police)*, pp.15–16.

414. *PP 1817 (Police)*, pp.17–18.

CHAPTER XIV

ON TRIAL AT LAST

415. *The Gentleman's Magazine*, 1817 pp.257–258.

416. For a detailed account of the government's campaign, and of Hone's trials, see Wilson, *The Laughter of Triumph*.

417. *The Times*, 13 December 1821, p.3; THLHA: *VM:* 18 February 1820.

418. *The Times*, 28 March 1818; Gurney, *Merceron's Trials*.

419. *The Times*, 28 March 1818.

420. THLHA: *VM:* 19 March 1818; *The Times*, 28 March 1818.

421. THLHA: *VM:* 23 March 1818; *The Times*, 28 March 1818.

422. LMA: *THCS 36*, p.126; THLHA: *VM:* 8 April 1817.

423. THLHA: *VM:* 23 March 1818; *The Times*, 28 March 1818, 13 December 1821.

424. THLHA: *VM:* 24 March 1818; *The Times*, 28 March 1818.

425. *Annual Register*, 1818, pp.266–267. Several members of the Racine family are listed among Merceron's opponents in: BNC: *D/148, Resolutions of the committee for obtaining a new act, etc*, 19 April 1813.

426. THLHA: *VM:* 1 April 1818, 15 April 1818, 29 April 1818, 20 August 1818.

427. THLHA: *VM:* 29 April 1818.

428. Gurney, *Merceron's Trials*.

429. PRO: *PROB 11/1600;* IGI (James Wilmot Lush, b. 30 July 1783, son of Charles Lush and Elizabeth Mary Lush, nee Wilmot); LMA: *THCS 36*, p.354.

430. Anon., *Criticisms on the Bar, etc.*, pp.109–121; The Analectic Magazine, etc, *Vol. IV (July 1814)*, p.335; *The Trial of James Watson*, London: Butterworth & Co, 1817; *The Trials of William Hone*, London: William Hone, 1817.

431. Barker, G. F. R., *Scarlett, James, first Baron Abinger (1769–1844)*, rev. Cawthon, Elizabeth A., *Oxford DNB*, (www.oxforddnb.com/view/article/24783, accessed 10 March 2006); Brougham, *Historical Sketches of Statesmen, etc.* Vol. II, pp.277–295. Another, anonymous, commentator was less kind to both Scarlett and Topping:
'Scarlett neighs like a stallion, and Marryat
Barks out his short words like a dog;
Gurney looks like and talks like a parrot;
Topping croaks between raven and frog.'
(Anon., *Criticisms on the Bar, etc.*, p.116.)

432. Barker, G. F. R., *Scarlett, James, first Baron Abinger (1769–1844)*, rev. Cawthon, Elizabeth A., *Oxford DNB*, (www.oxforddnb.com/view/article/24783, accessed

10 March 2006); Lobhan, Michael, *Law, Edward, first Baron Ellenborough
(1750–1818), Oxford DNB,* (www.oxforddnb.com/view/article/16142, accessed
10 March 2006); Lobhan, Michael, *Abbott, Charles, first baron Tenterden
(1762–1832), Oxford DNB,* (www.oxforddnb.com/view/article/12, accessed
10 March 2006).

433. Gurney, *Merceron's Trials,* First Trial, pp.1–16; *Annual Register,* 1818 p.277–283.
434. Gurney, *Merceron's Trials,* First Trial, pp.14–16.
435. Gurney, *Merceron's Trials,* First Trial, pp.22–49.
436. Gurney, *Merceron's Trials,* First Trial, pp.50–66.
437. Gurney, *Merceron's Trials,* First Trial, pp.67–83.
438. Gurney, *Merceron's Trials,* First Trial, pp.88–97.
439. Gurney, *Merceron's Trials,* First Trial, pp.98–109.
440. Gurney, *Merceron's Trials,* First Trial, pp.110–129.
441. Gurney, *Merceron's Trials,* First Trial, pp.132–150.
442. Gurney, *Merceron's Trials,* First Trial, pp.151–187.

CHAPTER XV

GOING DOWN

443. Gurney, *Merceron's Trials,* Second Trial, pp.1–3. The trial was also reported in
The Times, 19 May 1818, p.3.
444. Gurney, *Merceron's Trials,* Second Trial, pp.4–11.
445. Gurney, *Merceron's Trials,* Second Trial, pp.12–51.
446. Gurney, *Merceron's Trials,* Second Trial, pp.55–70.
447. Gurney, *Merceron's Trials,* Second Trial, pp.55–70. Abbott's decision in Merceron's
case established an important legal precedent that the testimony of a witness could
still be admitted in court despite great pressure, if not legal compulsion, having been
applied in securing it: see Helmholz, R.M., *The Privilege Against Self Incrimination*
(University of Chicago Press, 1997), p.271.
448. Gurney, *Merceron's Trials,* Second Trial, pp.71–99.
449. Gurney, *Merceron's Trials,* Second Trial, pp.100–106.
450. Gurney, *Merceron's Trials,* Second Trial, pp.107–115.
451. *The Times,* 25 May 1818, 2 June 1818, 13 December 1821.
452. *The Times,* 13 December 1821.
453. *The Times,* 25 May 1818, 13 December 1821; BNC: Hurst, Bethnal Green 3,
King to Gilbert, 12 March 1823; THLHA: *VM:* 20 August 1818.
454. *The Times,* 29 May 1818.
455. BNC: Hurst, Bethnal Green 3, King to Gilbert, 12 March 1823.
456. Gurney, *Merceron's Trials,* Second Trial, p.118; *The Times,* 2 June 1818.
457. Gurney, *Merceron's Trials,* Second Trial, p.130.
458. Gurney, *Merceron's Trials,* Second Trial, pp.130–147; *The Times,* 2 June 1818.
459. Gurney, *Merceron's Trials,* Second Trial, pp.130–147; *The Times,* 2 June 1818.
460. Gurney, *Merceron's Trials,* Second Trial, pp.148–151; *The Times,* 4 June 1818.

461. The reports of the trial confusingly refer to Merceron being committed to the custody of 'the Marshal of the Marshalsea'. This did not mean the Marshalsea Prison, which was strictly a debtors' prison, but rather the 'Marshalsea of the King's Bench', the full title of the King's Bench prison. The records of the latter prison make it clear that Merceron served his sentence there (see PRO: *PRIS 4/30*, p.243).

462. Gurney, *Merceron's Trials*, Second Trial, pp.148–151; *The Times*, 4 June 1818; PRO: *PRIS 4/30*, p.243.

CHAPTER XVI

THE KING'S BENCH

463. The descriptions of prison life in this chapter are drawn from the following sources: Nield, *State of the Prisons, etc*, p.304; Ackermann, *The Microcosm of London: King's Bench Prison*; Hansard, Vol. XXX, p.39, 7 March 1815; *PP 1814 (Prisons)*, p.492; Wade, *A Treatise on the Police and Crimes of the Metropolis, pp.260–266*; Pearce, *A Treatise on the Abuses of the Laws*, pp.88–108; Dickens, *Little Dorrit*, chapter VIII. For 'chumming' see *PP 1814 (Prisons)*, p.506, which describes the practice as it operated at the Marshalsea prison.

464. Ann Merceron's recipe book, a rare Georgian example, survived until recently in the possession of the Merceron family and contained a variety of recipes for main dishes, cakes and preserves: see Cox, *Life and Death in Spitalfields*, p.41.

465. *PP 1814 (Prisons)*, pp.475, 481; Pearce, *A Treatise on the Abuses of the Laws*, pp.102–105.

466. Webb & Webb, *The Parish and The County*, p.82; LMA: *THCS 36*, p.398.

467. THLHA: *VM:* 20 August 1818; Gurney, *Merceron's Trials*, Third Trial, preface.

468. Gurney, *Merceron's Trials*, Third Trial, preface; THLHA: *VM:* 27 August 1818; *The Times*, 17 September 1818, p.2.

469. THLHA: *VM:* 18 March 1819, 13 April 1819, 6 May 1819. For the previous attempts to improve schooling, see King's evidence to the 1816 Commons Select Committee on Education: *PP 1816 (Education)*, pp.410–15.

470. Gurney, *Merceron's Trials*, Third Trial, preface.

471. Gurney, *Merceron's Trials*, Third Trial, pp.1–5.

472. THLHA: *VM:* 29 July 1819; *The Times*, 13 December 1821, p.3 (Law Report, *May v. Gwynne*).

473. THLHA: *VM:* 19 August 1819 to 26 November 1819.

474. PRO: *PRIS 7/38*; THLHA: *VM:* 9 December 1819.

475. THLHA: *VM:* 9 December 1819, 17 December 1819, 29 December 1819.

CHAPTER XVII

SUPREMACY RESTORED

476. BNC: Hurst, Bethnal Green 3, *King to Gilbert*, 2 December 1822.
477. THLHA: *VM:* 28 January 1820, 18 February 1820, 23 March 1820,
29 March 1820.
478. THLHA: *VM:* 3 April 1820.
479. THLHA: *VM:* 4 April 1820.
480. THLHA: *VM:* 21 April 1820, 28 April 1820, 3 May 1820; *The Times*,
19 December 1822.
481. THLHA: *VM:* 3 May 1820, 15 June 1820, 28 June 1820, 24 April 1821.
For May's lawsuits, see: *The Times*, 13 December 1821, p.3 (Law Report, *May v.
Gwynne*), 19 December 1822, *(May v. Unwin)*, 10 November 1823 *(May v. Brown)*.
482. THLHA: *VM (BG 276):* 16 August 1821; Bryan King died on 17 September
1820: see *Notes on the parish of Woodchurch*, p.153, footnote 8; BNC: Hurst, Bethnal
Green 3, *King to Heber* (undated, 1823).
483. *The Times*, 13 December 1821, p.3 (Law Report, *May v. Gwynne*); 19 December
1822 (Law Report, *May v. Unwin*).
484. THLHA: *VM (BG 276):* 23 April 1821, 24 April 1821, 13 March 1822,
27 March 1822, 9 April 1822, 21 June 1822; Merceron family archives: *Brutton
to Merceron*, 2 May 1821.
485. THLHA: *VM:* 8 April 1822, 9 April 1822.
486. THLHA: *VM:* 21 June 1822, 26 June 1822.
487. THLHA: *VM:* 24 July 1822, 22 August 1822, 23 September 1822,
2 October 1822.
488. Halévy, *The Liberal Awakening*, pp.40–43; Brundage, *The English Poor Laws,
1700–1930*, pp.44–52; Pullen, J.M., *Malthus, (Thomas) Robert (1766–1834), Oxford
DNB*, (www.oxforddnb.com/view/article/17902, accessed 4 September 2007).
489. Halévy, *The Liberal Awakening*, pp.40–43; Brundage, *The English Poor Laws,
1700–1930*, pp.44–52.
490. THLHA: *VM:* 2 October 1822.
491. BNC: Hurst, Bethnal Green 3, *King to Gilbert*, 2 December 1822; Nockles,
Peter B., *Gilbert, Ashurst Turner (1786–1870), Oxford DNB*,
(www.oxforddnb.com/view/article/10682, accessed 4 September 2007).
492. THLHA: *VM:* 30 January 1823.
493. THLHA: *VM:* 6 February 1823.
494. THLHA: *VM:* 6 February 1823, 27 February 1823.
495. BNC: Hurst, Bethnal Green 3, *King to Gilbert*, 7 March 1823, 12 March 1823.
496. BNC: Hurst, Bethnal Green 3, *King to Gilbert*, 18 March 1823, 29 March 1823,
4 April 1823.
497. Sherbo, Arthur, *Heber, Richard (1774–1833),Oxford DNB*,
(www.oxforddnb.com/view/article/12854, accessed 4 September 2007); BNC:
Hurst, Bethnal Green 3, *King to Heber* (undated, 1823).

498. THLHA: *VM:* 13 March 1823, 26 March 1823, 31 March 1823, 1 April 1823, BNC: Hurst, Bethnal Green 3, *King to Gilbert*, 6 April 1823.

499. BNC: Hurst, Bethnal Green 3, *King to Gilbert*, 9 April 1823, 10 April 1823, 22 April 1823.

500. BNC: Hurst, Bethnal Green 3, *King to Gilbert*, 25 April 1823, 26 April 1823.

501. BNC: Hurst, Bethnal Green 3, *King to Gilbert*, 27 May 1823; THLHA: *VM:* 30 January 1823.

502. BNC: Hurst, Bethnal Green 3, *King to Gilbert*, 27 May 1823; THLHA: *VM:* 21 May 1823.

503. BNC: Hurst, Bethnal Green 3, *King to Gilbert*, 27 May 1823; THLHA: *VM:* 22 May 1823, 25 May 1823.

504. BNC: Hurst, Bethnal Green 3, *King to Gilbert*, 27 May 1823.

505. BNC: Hurst, Bethnal Green 3, *King to Gilbert*, 27 May 1823.

506. THLHA: *VM:* 15 August 1823, 19 April 1824, 29 December 1824, 18 February 1825; LMA: *X025/022*, p.107, *Burial registers of St Matthew's, Bethnal Green,* 24 July 1839.

CHAPTER XVIII

IN DISTRESS

507. Arnold, *The Poems of Matthew Arnold, 1840 to 1867,* p.395.

508. For Brutton's comments, see *PP 1830 (Select Vestries),* p.107.

509. For a robust defence of the Spitalfields Acts, see William Hale's evidence to the 1817 Select Committee on the Poor Laws, cited (with accompanying commentary) in the *Eclectic Review, Jul–Dec 1818,* pp.210–214. For the contemporary economic arguments, see *The Times,* 10 May 1823, p.2; 22 May 1823, p.2; also Hammond & Hammond, *The Skilled Labourer,* pp.216–219.

510. For a general background to the free-trade campaign, see Halévy, *The Liberal Awakening,* pp.187–210. For the petition and its reception in the Commons, see *The Times,* 10 May 1823, p.2.

511. *The Times,* 22 May 1823, p.2.

512. *The Times,* 10 June 1823, p.2.

513. *The Times,* 12 June 1823, pp.2, 3.

514. THLHA: *VM:* 25 June, 1823; Huskisson, *Speeches,* p.211; *The Times,* 22 May 1824, p.5; Hammond & Hammond, *The Skilled Labourer,* p.218.

515. Thorne, *History of Parliament: the House of Commons 1790–1820, Vol. IV (Members G–P),* pp.523–4.

516. LMA: *MJ/OC/019,* pp.427, 446, *County Day Minutes,* February – March 1822; Thorne, *History of Parliament: the House of Commons 1790–1820, Vol. IV (Members G–P),* p.523; Webb & Webb, *The Parish and the County,* p.565.

517. LMA: *MJ/OC/020,* p.407; *MJ/OC/021,* pp.116, 259, 263, 385, *County Day Minutes,* April 1824 to December 1825; *The Law Journal for the Year 1825,* Vol. III, p.241 (London: J.W. Paget, 1825).

518. THLHA: *VM:* 30 March 1807.

519. Kynaston, *A World of Its Own*, pp.63–72; Halévy, *The Liberal Awakening*, p.227.

520. Kynaston, *A World of Its Own*, p.73; Stone, *Evidence of W. Stone, etc.*, pp.22–23; Merceron Family Archives: Note by Joseph Merceron, *Expenses paid by Mr Wood Churchwarden, perambulating the parish 4 May 1826*.

521. *The Times*, 31 July 1826, p.2; THLHA: *VM:* 7 September 1826, 26 October 1826; THHOL: *Riots and Outrages in Bethnal Green* (unattributed news cutting in THLHA), 24 September 1826, (www.mernick.org.uk/thhol/riots.html, accessed 10 July 2016).

522. *Annual Register*, 1826, p.140; *Old Bailey Proceedings Online:* (www.oldbaileyonline.org/browse.jsp?ref=t18260914-61, accessed 10 July 2016), September 1826, trial of George Houghton and others (t18260914-61).

523. *PP 1832 (Silk Trade)*, p.478; Steinberg, *Fighting Words*, p.106; *The Times*, 21 October 1826, p.2; THLHA: *VM:* 22 December 1826.

524. THLHA: *VM:* 21 August 1826, 10 November 1826.

525. THLHA: *VM:* 11 July 1828; BNC: *D/148, Brutton to Gilbert, 30 July 1827;* English Heritage, *Conservation Bulletin, 46 (Autumn 2004)*, p.24.

526. THLHA: *VM:* 31 January 1827, (undated) April 1827.

527. Merceron family archives: *Merceron family tree.*

528. PRO: *C 13/2246 (papers in Merceron v. Merceron, 1831).*

529. PRO: *C 101/753 (receiver's accounts in Merceron v. Merceron, 1819–1833);* *Annual Register, 1827*, p.172.

530. Webb & Webb, *The Parish and the County*, p.265; Anon., *Considerations on Select Vestries*, p.49; THLHA: *VM:* 26 March 1828, 11 August 1830, 1 September 1830; *PP 1830 (Select Vestries)*, pp.105–106.

531. *PP 1832 (Silk Trade)*, p.478; THLHA: *VM:* 4 December 1828.

532. *The Times*, 16 February 1829, p.4, 30 April 1829, p.3; VCH, *Middlesex: Volume 11: Stepney, Bethnal Green*, pp.190–202.

533. THLHA: *VM:* 3 March 1829, 20 April 1829, 21 April 1829.

534. THLHA: *VM:* 1 May 1829, 22 May 1829; *Annual Register, 1829* ('Chronicle'), p.99.

535. THLHA: *VM:* 1 July 1829, 30 September 1829, 30 December 1829, 5 April 1831.

536. THLHA: *VM:* 13 May 1830, 25 June 1830. The 'exporting' of children from Bethnal Green to the cotton mills had taken place as early as 1811: see the account of 'Orphan John' in Waller, *The Real Oliver Twist*, p.136. Orphan John's tale was told in an interview in *The Ashton Chronicle* on 19 May 1849.

537. THLHA: *VM:* 8 January 1830, 31 March 1830, 27 October 1830.

538. Webb & Webb, *The Parish and the County*, pp.264–270.

539. *PP 1830 (Select Vestries)*, pp.105–110; Webb & Webb, *The Parish and the County*, p.270.

540. THLHA: *VM:* 25 February 1831, 4 March 1831, 4 April 1831; Webb & Webb, *The Parish and the County*, pp.271–275.

CHAPTER XIX
UNSANITARY AND INSOLVENT

541. *Poor Law Commissioners' Report of 1834*, II.3.37 (evidence of Hooker).

542. John Britton, *The Original Picture of London, etc* (London, 1826), cited in Halliday, *The Great Stink of London*, p.18.

543. THLHA: *VM:* 5 April 1831, 22 June 1831, 29 June 1831; Gavin, *Sanitary Ramblings.*

544. Owen & Owen (Eds.), The *Crisis, etc.,* p.203.

545. Halliday, *The Great Stink of London*, p.29.

546. Halliday, *The Great Stink of London*, pp.21–9. For G.B.Mainwaring's involvement with the Grand Junction Waterworks, see *The Times*, 4 July 1811, p.10.

547. Holland, *A Memoir of the Reverend Sydney Smith*, Vol. II, p.335 (*Smith to Countess Grey*, 19 November 1834); Gavin, *Sanitary Ramblings;* Wickstead, *Observations on water supply to the Metropolis.*

548. Higgins, *The 1832 Cholera Epidemic in East London.*

549. White, *London in the Nineteenth Century,*p.50; *The Times*, 12 November 1831; Higgins, *The 1832 Cholera Epidemic in East London.*

550. Higgins, *The 1832 Cholera Epidemic in East London;* THLHA: *VM:* 4 November 1831, 16 November 1831.

551. THLHA: *VM:* 16 November 1831, 21 December 1831.

552. For a detailed account of the 1831 Bethnal Green murders, see Wise, *The Italian Boy.* IGI; *Merceron Family Archives.*

553. *The Times*, 6 February 1832, p.3; 15 February 1832, p.3; 16 February 1832, p.4; 20 February 1832, p.6; 21 February 1832, p.4; 23 February 1832, p.3.

554. *Hansard (3rd Series)*, Vol. X, pp.270, 339–340, 13–14 February 1832.

555. *Hansard (3rd Series)*, Vol. X, pp.582–5, 21 February 1832; Higgins, *The 1832 Cholera Epidemic in East London; The Times*, 1 March 1832, 15 March 1832, 31 March 1832.

556. See the daily official reports, and the editorial and letters pages of *The Times* for the months of February and March 1832, for example: 21 February (p.4), 23 February (p.3), 2 March (p.1), 6 March (p.1), 8 March (p.2), 12 March (p.5) and 29 March. See also Higgins, *The 1832 Cholera Epidemic in East London;* Gavin, *Sanitary Ramblings.*

557. *The Times*, 22 March 1832, p.3; Higgins, *The 1832 Cholera Epidemic in East London.*

558. PRO: C 13/2246; *The Times*, 21 March 1832; *London Gazette*, 7 February 1832, 16 March 1832; *Merceron Family Archives.*

559. *The Times*, 31 March 1832, p.3.

560. *Annual Register*, 1850, p.425; parish data from Metropolitan Sanitary Commission, *First Report*, pp.24, 26.

561. THLHA: *VM:* 18 April 1832, 28 September 1832, 26 December 1832.

562. Brundage, *The English Poor Laws, 1700–1930*, pp.62–6; Woodward, *The Age of Reform*, p.450; Burns, Arthur, *Blomfield, Charles James (1786–1857),Oxford DNB*, (www.oxforddnb.com/view/article/2668, accessed 4 September 2007).

563. *Poor Law Commissioners' Report of 1834*, I.1.79; II.3.113 (evidence of Masterman); II.3.37 (evidence of Hooker).

564. THLHA: *VM:* 5 March 1833, 27 March 1833.

565. Loose note by Merceron within *St Matthew Bethnal Green Watch & Lamp Trust Treasurer Account* (Merceron Family Archives); THLHA: *VM:* 25 October 1833.

566. Brundage, *The English Poor Laws, 1700–1930*, pp.73–4; THLHA: *VM:* 1 April 1834, 14 May 1834, 23 March 1837, 27 March 1837; Murphy, *The New Poor Law Guardians, etc.*, p.59.

567. *PP 1834 (Sewers)*, pp.72–7, appendix pp.61–62.

568. THLHA: *VM:* 4 May 1836, 27 March 1837.

CHAPTER XX

OLD MEN FIGHTING

569. *The Royal Lady's Magazine*, Vol. I (1831) p.201; LMA: *B/THB/J/001/1;* The *Gentleman's Magazine*, July 1837, p.98; PRO: *C 13/399/14.*

570. Porter and Rousseau, *Gout: the Patrician Malady*, pp.43, 162–3; Dickinson, *Suppressed Gout, etc.*

571. *The Times*, 8 July 1844, p.7; Harrison & Wollaston, *Reports of Cases argued and determined in the Court of King's Bench, etc*, Vol. II (1836), pp.380–1.

572. Howe, A.C., *Huskisson, William (1770–1830)*, *Oxford DNB*, (www.oxforddnb.com/view/article/14264, accessed 16 May 2007); White, *London in the Nineteenth Century*, p.37; THLHA: *VM:* 24 February 1836, 5 April 1836, 25 May 1838, 27 June 1838, 21 November 1838, 25 January 1839.

573. White, *London in the Nineteenth Century*, pp.30,33,35; THLHA: *VM:* 5 April 1838, 27 March 1839.

574. *Fourth Annual Report of the Poor Law Commissioners*, 1838, App. A, No.1, pp.129–144.

575. *The Times*, 15 March 1839, p.7; *Fourth Annual Report of the Poor Law Commissioners*, 1838, App. A, No.1, pp.152–153. The three roads were all eventually built. The first led southwards from Shoreditch to the London Docks (today's Commercial Road), the second from Haggerston to the docks at Wapping (today's Vallance Road), and the third extended the City Road eastwards linking Old Street to the Bethnal Green Road, thereby connecting the latter with the main trunk road around the north of the city (today's Great Eastern Street).

576. Barnes, *Stepney Churches*, pp.35–37; Biber, *Bishop Blomfield and his Times*, pp.187–8; *Church of England Magazine*, Vol. VIII, 1839, p.9.

577. BNC: *D/148: Spiritual Destitution of the Parish of Bethnal Green, London; Church of England Magazine*, Vol. VIII, 1839, p.9.

578. BNC: *D/148: Third Report of Metropolitan Churches Fund, June 19 1839; Spiritual Destitution of the Parish of Bethnal Green, London.*

579. BNC: *D/148: notes of meeting 27 March 1839;* THLHA: *VM:* 27 March 1839, 1 April 1839, 2 April 1839.

580. PRO: *C 13/399/14;* THLHA: *VM:* 31 July 1839.

581. Merceron Family Archives: *St Matthew Bethnal Green Watch & Lamp Trust Treasurer Account*, 13 July 1839; Death Certificate, Joseph Merceron 14 July 1839.

582. THLHA: *VM:* 31 July 1839, 7 August 1839, 13 September 1839, 19 February 1840; PRO: *C13/399/14;* www.parmiters.herts.sch.uk/school-life/houses/ (accessed 10 July 2016).

583. The *Gentleman's Magazine*, August 1839, p.211; PRO: *IR 26/1524 f.672;* PRO: *PROB 11/1916,* Will of Joseph Merceron.

584. Vale, *Old Bethnal Green*, p.34.

EPILOGUE

STREET ABOMINATION

585. Pym, *Tales for my Grandchildren*, p.10.

586. Dickens, *Oliver Twist*, chapter 21.

587. *Annual Register,*1838, p.233; Gavin, *Sanitary Ramblings*, p.106.

588. *Fourth Annual Report of the Poor Law Commissioners*, 1838, App. A, No.1, pp.139–144.

589. *Fourth Annual Report of the Poor Law Commissioners*, 1838, App. A, No.1, pp.139–144.

590. Horne, *A New Spirit of the Age*, p.74.

591. Poor Law Commissioners, *Report on the Sanitary Condition of the Labouring Population, etc.*, pp.186, 202; Engels, *The Condition of the Working Class in England*, pp.72–3; Gavin, *Sanitary Ramblings*.

592. Gavin, *Sanitary Ramblings*, pp.4–5; Poor Law Commissioners, *Report on the Sanitary Condition of the Labouring Population, etc.*, p.313.

593. Gavin, *Sanitary Ramblings*.

594. Gavin, *Sanitary Ramblings*.

595. *Fourth Annual Report of the Poor Law Commissioners*, 1838, App. A, No.1, pp.139–144; Poor Law Commissioners, *Inquiry into the Sanitary Condition of the Labouring Population of Great Britain*, p.166; LMA: *ACC/295/1.*

596. Census Returns: PRO: HO 107/693/8; HO 107/1539; RG 9/152; *Post Office London Directory 1852.*

597. Foster, *Alumni Oxiensis;* Cheshire and Chester Archives, *DHL/56/2, DHL/56/7;* Morris, Jeremy, *King, Bryan (1811–1895), Oxford DNB,* (www.oxforddnb.com/view/article/56293, accessed 17 May 2007)

598. Thorne, Roland, *Bennet, Henry Grey (1777–1836),Oxford DNB,* (www.oxforddnb.com/view/article/37179, accessed 17 May 2007); Hammond & Hammond, *The Town Labourer,*pp.78, 187–91.

599. Beaumont, *Barber Beaumont*, pp.103–109; Pearson, Robin, *Beaumont, John Thomas Barber (1774–1841),Oxford DNB*, (www.oxforddnb.com/view/article/1877, accessed 21 May 2007); obituary in *The Times*, 22 June 1841, p.3.

600. Gilbert, *Second World War*, p.123; THLHA: *Bethnal Green during the war 1939–45:* Photographs Vol. I.

601. Taylor, *Exploring the East End*, p.167.

Author photo by George Woodford

JULIAN WOODFORD was born in Burton-upon-Trent in 1963. Since graduating from the University of York he has combined a City career with a passion for London's history. *The Boss of Bethnal Green* is his first book. Follow him @HistoryLondon.